Critical Essays on the Western American Novel

Critical Essays on the Western American Novel

William T. Pilkington

G. K. Hall & Co. • Boston, Massachusetts

Library of Congress Cataloging in Publication Data
Main entry under title:

Critical essays on the western American novel.

(Critical essays on American literature)
Includes index.
1. Western stories—History and criticism—Addresses, essays, lectures. 2. American fiction—The West—History and criticism—Addresses, essays, lectures. I. Pilkington, William T. II. Series.
PS374.W4C7 813'.0874'09 80-18223
ISBN 0-8161-8351-1

CRITICAL ESSAYS ON AMERICAN LITERATURE

This series seeks to publish the most important reprinted criticism on writers and topics in American literature along with, in appropriate volumes, original essays, interviews, bibliographies, letters, manuscript sections, and other materials brought to public attention for the first time. William T. Pilkington's volume on the Western American novel is indicative of this series' attempt to cover important genres and topics in American letters in addition to volumes on individual works and writers. This book contains essays on such early Western writers as Emerson Hough, Owen Wister, and Vardis Fisher. It ranges from authors like A. B. Guthrie and Walter Van Tilburg Clark, to such modern figures as William Eastlake and Larry McMurtry. Among the scholars included in the volume are John Cawelti, Max Westbrook, John R. Milton, and Don D. Walker. Of particular interest are Lawrence J. Evers on N. Scott Momaday and Daniel Testa on Rudolfo Anaya. We are confident that this collection will make a permanent contribution to American literary scholarship.

JAMES NAGEL, GENERAL EDITOR

Northeastern University

CONTENTS

INTRODUCTION ix

GENERAL CRITICISM

Overview of the Western Novel

John R. Milton, "The Novel in the American West" 3

Early Critical Statements

Andy Adams, "Western Interpreters" 21

W. H. Hutchinson, " 'Virgins, Villains and Varmints' " 24

Max Westbrook, "The Themes of Western Fiction" 34

History and Theory of the Popular Western Novel

Mody C. Boatright, "The Beginnings of Cowboy Fiction" 41

Richard W. Etulain, "Origins of the Western" 56

John G. Cawelti, "Prolegomena to the Western" 61

Theories of the Literary Western Novel

Max Westbrook, "The Western Esthetic" 73

Richard W. Etulain, "Frontier and Region in Western Literature" 86

Don D. Walker, "Can the Western Tell What Happens?" 93

CRITICAL ESSAYS ON INDIVIDUAL WESTERN NOVELISTS

Early Western Novelists

Delbert E. Wylder, "Emerson Hough and the Popular Novel" 111

Donald E. Houghton, "Two Heroes in One: Reflections on the Popularity of [Owen Wister's] *The Virginian*" 118

The Classic Generation of Western Novelists

John R. Milton, "The Primitive World of Vardis Fisher: The Idaho Novels" 125

Donald C. Stewart, "A. B. Guthrie's Vanishing Paradise: An Essay on Historical Fiction" 136

John D. Nesbitt, "Change of Purpose in the Novels of Louis L'Amour" 150

L. L. Lee, "Walter Van Tilburg Clark's Ambiguous American Dream" 164

Russell Roth, "The Inception of a Saga: Frederick Manfred's 'Buckskin Man' " 172

William T. Pilkington, "[On Jean Stafford's *The Mountain Lion*]" 182

Don Graham, "Tragedy and Western American Literature: The Example of Michael Straight's *A Very Small Remnant*" 187

Contemporary Western Novelists
Delbert E. Wylder, "The Novels of William Eastlake" 197
William T. Pilkington, "Edward Abbey: Western Philosopher" 210
Kerry Ahearn, "More D'Urban: The Texas Novels of Larry McMurtry" 223
The Rise of Minority Western Fiction
Lawrence J. Evers, "Words and Place: A Reading of [N. Scott Momaday's] *House Made of Dawn*" 243
Daniel Testa, "Extensive/Intensive Dimensionality in [Rudolfo] Anaya's *Bless Me, Ultima*" 262

INDEX 271

INTRODUCTION

For most American readers, no doubt, the term "Western novel" connotes cowboys and Indians, gunfights at the O. K. Corral, "shoot-'em-up" Westerns on the paperback racks of drugstores and supermarkets. Without question the formula Western novel—beginning with dime novels in the late nineteenth century—is largely responsible for promulgating the mythic West that continues to inhabit the imaginations of the American people, and it has proven to be the most durable and profitable form of Western fiction. Moreover, with the recent rise of scholarly interest in popular culture, the formula-story Western is increasingly the subject of serious study. The American West, however, has produced a sizable body of more "respectable" fiction that fewer readers seem to be familiar with, even though the fiction has for some time engaged the interest of a growing band of literary critics and scholars. Criticism of the Western novel—both the popular and the literary novel—has proliferated impressively over the past few decades. This collection of essays is intended as a sampling of some of the best of that criticism.

To be sure, close critical scrutiny of Western American fiction is a relatively recent phenomenon.[1] During the early years of the twentieth century most critics of American literature apparently took their cue from Professor Barrett Wendell of Harvard University. Writing in 1900, ten years after (as Frederick Jackson Turner was the first to note) the official closing of the Western frontier, Professor Wendell declared that life in the West had "not yet ripened into an experience which can possibly find lasting expression."[2] Considering the fact that, as Wendell was writing, several important Western authors—Bret Harte, Mark Twain, and Hamlin Garland for example—had already appeared on the scene, and that others—such as Frank Norris and Jack London—were rapidly achieving popularity and a measure of literary celebrity, this judgment seems today astonishingly provincial and short-sighted.

It was, however, a view perpetuated by subsequent commentators on American literature. Some interpreters, of course, protested the view. In 1928 Norman Foerster ruefully acknowledged that, in American literary criticism, the "influence of the frontier has been strangely neglected."[3] He did little to correct the oversight except to include in his *Reinterpretation of American Literature* a vague chapter on "The Frontier" by Jay B. Hubbell. A few scattered literary scholars in the 1920s—in particular Ralph Leslie Rusk and Lucy Lockwood Hazard—saw Western writing as significant enough to warrent full-scale critical studies. Rusk's two-volume work, *The Literature of the Middle Western Frontier*

(1925),[4] is of little use today since most of the commentary in it is outdated description and summary rather than critical analysis. The book was, however, important as a pioneer effort in Western literary criticism. Hazard's *The Frontier in American Literature* (1927),[5] on the other hand, remains a generally sensitive and convincing examination of the role that frontier individualism played in the social and political excesses of late nineteenth- and early twentieth-century American life, and clarifies how both the individualism and the excesses had been portrayed in our literature.

Andy Adams's "Western Interpreters," reprinted below, represents much of this early criticism of Western literature. No sophisticated literary critic, Adams was himself a cowboy who helped drive cattle up the trail from Texas. Upon turning to writing, he produced one of the classics of early Western fiction—the superbly realistic *Log of a Cowboy* (1903). Adams's attempts at rudimentary critical commentary, while not very illuminating, at least began to bring to public attention the subject of serious Western writing—and, in Adams's judgment, the poverty of Western fiction-writing.

In the 1930s and 1940s the slow pace of scholarship in Western literature continued. Most of the work that did appear during those decades was literary history with only the lightest flavor of critical comment. For instance, the *Literary History of the United States*, a widely used reference work first published in 1948, contained several helpful chapters that summarized literary activity in the West in the late nineteenth century, but it offered only random comments on the works of important contemporary Western writers.[6]

Perhaps the most accomplished and knowledgeable literary historian the region has yet produced is Franklin Walker, whose best work appeared during this period. Focusing on the ninetenth-century literature of California, Walker has published such studies as *San Francisco's Literary Frontier* (1939) and *A Literary History of Southern California* (1950). Generally traditional in format, these books are fully researched, thoroughly reliable, and eminently readable. However, they cover only a fraction—albeit an important fraction—of the literary West.

The 1950s marked the coming of age of Western literary criticism. In the early 1950s Bernard DeVoto, a native of the West and a respected novelist and historian, offered a number of much-discussed opinions on Western fiction. Most of those opinions were incorporated into DeVoto's "Easy Chair" columns in *Harper's* magazine, thus reaching an educated and book-buying public. At about the same time W. H. Hutchinson initiated a sprightly campaign to reassess the reputations of several early-twentieth-century Western fiction writers—especially Eugene Manlove Rhodes. Unquestionably, however, the most important event of the early 1950s (though its immense significance was not perceived at the time) was the publication of Henry Nash Smith's provocative study, *Virgin Land:*

The American West as Symbol and Myth (1950).[8] *Virgin Land* has been both praised and damned. Although the ultimate validity of Smith's method and wide-ranging thesis is still questioned, no one can doubt the book's enormous influence. From the standpoint of literary criticism, in particular, *Virgin Land* provided younger scholars with an excellent model for the use of formula Western fiction in deducing popular attitudes and beliefs.[9]

The seeds planted by these pioneer critics of Western writing—DeVoto, Hutchinson, Smith—produced a remarkable fruition of Western literary scholarship in the 1960s. In 1965 the Western Literature Association was formed by a determined group of teacher-scholars that included John R. Milton, Don D. Walker, C. L. Sonnichsen, Delbert E. Wylder, J. Golden Taylor, and Max Westbrook. These are the critics that have made the greatest contributions to the study of Western literature to date, and as a group they still ride tall in the saddle.[10] Upon its founding, the Association's first collective action was to sponsor a journal, *Western American Literature*, currently edited by Thomas J. Lyon. In the pages of *Western American Literature* have appeared scores of worthwhile critical articles on many well-known and little-known Western books and authors. At present the Association is promoting an ambitious project that will result, it is hoped, in a definitive *Literary History of the American West*, a volume scheduled for publication in the mid-1980s. Presumably the *Literary History* will satisfy at least two major desiderata in Western scholarship: for a reliable reference tool that projects a consistent view of the development of Western writing, and a thorough bibliography of available primary and secondary materials. In sum, it seems clear that the respectability and attractiveness of Western literary studies have been enhanced significantly by the Western Literature Association and by the scholarly activity that it has stimulated.

Since 1965, then, the body of Western literary criticism has grown steadily and impressively. From even a cursory survey of that criticism one fact emerges plainly: the richest and most vital genre in Western writing always has been, and still is, the novel. Certainly the West has produced a respectable number of good poets and even a few decent playwrights. It has spawned a great many talented writers of nonfiction prose, particularly a batch of so-called nature writers (examples range from John Muir to Joseph Wood Krutch to Edward Abbey). Moreover, its ongoing folk-tradition has inspired the work of many creative and industrious folklorists—J. Frank Dobie, from the Southwest, being a leading example. But it is from Western fiction that the West's biggest literary names have emerged. Not surprisingly the preponderance of recent Western scholarship, since it inevitably reflects trends in the creative work that is its subject, has been focused on the region's fiction writers.

For most casual observers of American literature, the phrase "American novel" probably suggests a fairly well-defined tradition that flows in a unified stream from a pantheon of acknowledged masters of the fictional art. It connotes, in short, high artistic and moral seriousness. The phrase "Western novel" carries no such lofty suggestion. It is a phrase that, instead, conjures up a double vision, a confusing dichotomy that resists unification. The dichotomy, alluded to at the beginning of this introductory essay, strictly separates the popular Western novel from what may be called the literary Western novel; and on balance it is the popular Western novel that remains foremost in the public mind. "Formula" Western fiction and "serious" Western fiction are, at any rate, widely thought to be mutually exclusive terms. One is "trash"; the other comprises works of genuine literary merit. One is written for entertainment and money; the other, for artistic expression and fulfillment. These are distinctions that, however bogus, seem inevitable and enduring; they will not disappear as long as critics and readers continue to insist on the differences between "highbrow" and "lowbrow" culture. Indeed one commentator, C. L. Sonnichsen, speaks of the "high road Western" and the "low road Western."[11] "High road" Western novels are written by such serious literary artists as Walter Van Tilburg Clark, Frank Waters, A. B. Guthrie, Frederick Manfred, and Larry McMurtry. "Low road" Western novels are cranked out by such prolific wordsmiths as Emerson Hough, Zane Grey, Ernest Haycox, Max Brand, Luke Short, Will Henry, and (most notable and astonishing of all) the ubiquitous Louis L'Amour.

Criticism of Western fiction, like the fiction itself, usually divides rather sharply along "high road" versus "low road" lines. Until recent decades all popular Western fiction—from nineteenth-century dime novels to the paperback originals of the twentieth century—was consigned by critics to the cellar of the subliterary, where it rested in nearly total obscurity. No self-respecting "literary" critic would admit to reading such fiction, much less using it as the subject of serious analysis. As late as 1954 Bernard DeVoto complained that "a literary critic can discuss detective stories without being called before the board of governors, but the even more popular form of packaged fiction called the Western appears to be off limits."[12] This statement came, of course, four years after Henry Nash Smith, in *Virgin Land*, had employed a wide knowledge of dime novels to draw conclusions concerning nineteenth-century popular attitudes about the West. The impetus provided by Smith and several other critics in the 1950s grew slowly, then accelerated and expanded into a general scholarly interest in the entire subject of popular culture. In the 1960s the Popular Culture Association was founded, and with it an important new journal, *The Journal of Popular Culture*, was born. From the beginning *The Journal of Popular Culture* has been receptive to essays dealing with all aspects of the popular Western novel, and many of the seminal analyses of that genre have appeared in its pages. As an introduction to such analyses, *The Popular Western: Essays Toward a Definition*

(1974),[13] edited by Richard W. Etulain and Michael T. Marsden, is a highly useful collection of theoretical articles that were first published in *The Journal of Popular Culture*.

Of the several recent scholars who have advanced comprehensive theories of popular Western fiction, the most significant achievement is probably John G. Cawelti's. Initially in a series of journal articles, and then in *The Six-Gun Mystique* (1971) and *Adventure, Mystery, and Romance* (1976),[14] Cawelti developed a provocative explanation of the plot and character formulas often associated with the popular Western. These formulas seem, to a great extent, a literary byproduct of Frederick Jackson Turner's historical thesis. Especially relevant to Cawelti's theory is Turner's conception of the frontier as a moving line, the outer edge of a "wave—the meeting point between savagery and civilization."[15] This is precisely the mythological terrain in which, in Cawelti's view, the formulas work most predictably. Since Western movies, like popular Western novels, are normally set in a mythic rather than a realistic West, Cawelti—as well as numerous other scholars working in this area—travels easily between print and film, an approach that seems not only justified but necessary.[16] "Prolegomena to the Western," reprinted below, is an excellent introduction to some of Cawelti's basic ideas.

A rather bizarre complement to Cawelti's Turnerian hypothesis is offered by Leslie Fiedler in *The Return of the Vanishing American* (1968). Fiedler sees the relationship between white European and Indian—the uneasy meeting of the civilized and the savage—as being *the* overriding theme of Western fiction. "It is the presence of the Indian," he writes, "which defines the mythological West."[17] Fiedler, as always, provokes thought and occasionally assists insight. Unfortunately his definition of the "New Western"—a definition that embraces many works not set in the West—is so eccentric as to border on the useless. Moreover, his belief that the typical novel about the contemporary West chronicles a journey into madness can be maintained only by ignoring a sizable shelf of recent Western fiction.

C. L. Sonnichsen's *From Hopalong to Hud: Thoughts on Western Fiction* (1978) is a work that imaginatively and convincingly follows the example of *Virgin Land*. At the start Sonnichsen proclaims himself to be a "social historian" who reads Western novels "not for what they tell him about the subject matter, but for what they tell him about the reader."[18] Using a vast array of "horse operas, shoot-'em-ups, hayburners . . . oaters"[19] as evidence, the author clearly demonstrates how Westerns work as a barometer of evolving popular attitudes—attitudes toward sex and violence; toward Indians and Mexican-Americans; toward, indeed, almost any topic of general public concern. Despite Sonnichsen's tendency to shoot from the hip—to make snap judgments that are scarcely as self-evidently valid as he apparently assumes they are—*From Hopalong to Hud* is an exceptionally helpful and illuminating study of popular Western fiction as a reflection of widely held social values; it is, in sum, a worthy continuation of the scholarly method begun by Smith.

While one group of critics and scholars, then, burrows its way ever deeper into the mass of formula stories, stereotyped characters, and stock situations and symbols commonly associated with the popular Western, another group—most of whose members identify themselves with the Western Literature Association—concerns itself almost exclusively with the region's "serious" fiction writers and with the select list of classics and near-classics that those writers have turned out. Several worthwhile books that deal with "high road" Western novels have been published since the founding of the Western Literature Association in the mid-1960s. James K. Folsom's *The American Western Novel* (1966),[20] for instance, is perhaps the best general introduction to the topic. Novelist Wallace Stegner had some interesting things to say in the late 1960s about his fellow Western writers, and many of his comments on Western fiction, though difficult to distill into a consistent theory, have been collected in *The Sound of Mountain Water*(1969).[21] The subtitle of William T. Pilkington's *My Blood's Country: Studies in Southwestern Literature* (1973)[22] might well read "Studies in Southwestern Fiction," since most of the essays in the book are critical examinations of important Southwestern novelists—such as Harvey Fergusson, Paul Horgan, Frank Waters, and Edwin Corle. Jay Gurian's *Western American Writing: Tradition and Promise* (1975)[23] is also a series of essays that explore works by Western fiction writers. Gurian in particular is concerned with analyzing some of the characteristic themes and styles of classic Western novels (Clark's *The Ox-Bow Incident* and Thomas Berger's *Little Big Man*, for instance).

The two critics, however, whose views on the literary Western novel have been most influential are John R. Milton and Max Westbrook. Milton, editor of the *South Dakota Review* and professor of English at the University of South Dakota, began to publish critical articles on Western fiction in the late 1950s. In those articles he advanced a consistent thesis: a Jungian perspective on Western fiction is more productive and helpful than a Freudian one. "The Western novel," Milton has written, "is extensive, constantly engaged in an opening-out, from character to action to landscape to a concern with racial consciousness (rather than individual) which is Jungian and which allows significant acceptance of the myths and rituals of the American Indian."[24] Milton's ideas, previously scattered in journals, have now been richly amplified and elaborated in *The Novel of the American West* (1980).[25] First published in 1964, his essay "The Novel in the American West," reprinted below, provides a useful overview of the Western novel as well as a good introduction to Milton's approach. In *The Novel of the American West* the critic's assessment of the Western novel has remained much the same although he has altered his opinion slightly on the "Westernness" and the relative importance to the West of a few writers, notably Paul Horgan.

Max Westbrook, who teaches at the University of Texas at Austin and is a former president of the Western Literature Association, is responsible for what is to date the most provocative and most often-cited critical theory concerning Western writing. Picking up where Milton left off and drawing insights from Mircea Eliade as well as from Jung, in the late 1960s Westbrook developed the argument that most Western literature may be seen as part of a tradition that he calls "sacrality." Sacrality begins, Westbrook writes, with the recognition that modern people "have lost contact with the source, with sex, God, land." In particular, he says, the modern mind fails to acknowledge the ultimate source of energy: "the dark caverns of the unconscious where the artificial 'bifurcations' of twentieth-century perception—good and evil, the rational and the irrational, the practical and the spiritual—are united."[26] According to Westbrook, Western writers—perhaps because of their closeness to the land, perhaps because of their intimate contacts with American Indian life and philosophy—have instinctively recognized this failure and have, in effect, preached a restoration to modern life of the sense of sacrality. Most of Westbrook's examples are taken from the region's fiction. He finds the works of such writers as Walter Clark, Frederick Manfred, Vardis Fisher, Wallace Stegner, Frank Waters, and John Steinbeck especially good illustrations of his contentions. Many of the more salient points of Westbrook's theory are raised and discussed in "The Western Esthetic," reprinted below.

Recently there have been complaints in some quarters that the Milton-Westbrook views on Western fiction are, on the one hand, too vague in outline and terminology and, on the other, too narrow to encompass the whole of the region's writing. No doubt both complaints are justified to some extent. And no doubt, as scholarly interest in Western literature expands and deepens, new theories will surface to supplement, to challenge, and perhaps to supplant the current critical orthodoxy. Until such new theories appear, however, there can be no question that Milton and Westbrook have supplied their readers and fellow scholars with the most suggestive and helpful framework yet constructed for studying and understanding the Western novel.

The essays that follow have been included in part because they are worthwhile analyses of various aspects of Western fiction; in part because they provide a cross section of some of the more fruitful critical approaches to that fiction. As the title of the collection indicates, the subject of the essays is limited generically to the novel. That limitation automatically excludes from consideration a writer such as Katherine Anne Porter. Porter is in some sense a Westerner (though she is, of course, more often thought of as a Southerner), and several of her most highly-acclaimed short stories are set in the American Southwest; her only novel, though, can in no way be called a Western novel. As the title further indicates, the subject of the pieces is the "Western American novel." The term "Western" is meant to designate that vast American region west of the Mississippi River—the trans-Mississippi West. This definition, then, would exclude as a subject an author such as James Fenimore Cooper, who is a novelist of the American frontier but (with the exception of *The Prairie*) is scarcely a novelist of the American West. In the determination of whether or not a writer is Western, the chronological setting of his or her works is not as important as their geographical setting. A. B. Guthrie writes fiction mainly about the nineteenth-century West; Larry McMurtry writes fiction about the contemporary West. Both, however, are Western writers because they employ Western settings and see people and events from a recognizably Western vantage point (though McMurtry's perspective, admittedly, currently seems in the process of change).

The essays are divided into two main groupings: those that deal with the general aspects of the Western novel and those that focus on specific Western novelists. The general pieces explore both the popular Western and the literary Western. The novelists who are the subjects of the essays in the second section of the book are all, in one way or another, important Western writers, though most of them are not generally well known outside the region. Essays on Western novelists such as Mark Twain, Hamlin Garland, Frank Norris, Jack London, Willa Cather, and John Steinbeck have not been included, since these are writers whose works have been widely heralded and whose achievements seem significant enough to merit separate and individual collections of criticism. In terms of historical development the writers treated range from turn-of-the-century novelists—Emerson Hough and Owen Wister—to representatives of that generation of Western novelists whose best work was done in the period from the 1930s to the 1950s—for example, Vardis Fisher, A. B. Guthrie, Walter Clark, and Frederick Manfred—to contemporary novelists who are still in the process of building reputations—William Eastlake, Edward Abbey, and Larry McMurtry. A notable recent development in Western literature is the emergence of a number of talented writers from the region's minority ethnic groups. The final two essays in the present volume examine contemporary novels by an American Indian (N. Scott Momaday's *House Made of Dawn*) and a Mexican-American (Rudolfo Anaya's *Bless Me, Ultima*) that are already generally recognized as landmarks in Western literary history. Unfortunately, because of limitations of space, critical essays on such excellent Western novelists as Harvey Fergusson, H. L. Davis, Frank Waters, and Jack Schaefer are not included; these omissions are in no way meant to imply a judgment on these writers' importance.

Like the novelists whose works they explore, the authors of these essays also represent a succession of generations. Andy Adams and W. H.

Hutchinson are certainly among the pioneers of Western literary criticism. John R. Milton, Max Westbrook, John G. Cawelti, Don D. Walker, and Delbert E. Wylder constitute an impressive delegation from the generation that brought Western criticism to its maturity. Several younger critics whose work is anthologized here—Richard W. Etulain, Don Graham, and Kerry Ahearn, for example—are at the start of promising careers as scholars and students of Western writing.

This volume of essays offers a collection of valuable insights into the dynamics of the Western novel; it is also intended to illustrate the progress, both quantitative and qualitative, that criticism of Western American literature has achieved over the past quarter-century. As has already been mentioned, not all of the criticism that ought to have been included *has* been. The canon of Western literary criticism is now rich and bountiful enough to make the job of selection a very difficult one indeed. As Etulain has written, "first-rate scholars" are now turning their attention "to the literary West and producing provocative books and essays about the subject. Western literary studies are no longer in their adolescent stage. . . ."[27] The essays brought together here testify eloquently to the accuracy of that assessment.

Notes

1. A helpful survey of the criticism of Western writing is Richard W. Etulain's "The American Literary West and Its Interpreters: The Rise of a New Historiography," *Pacific Historical Review*, 45 (1976), 311–47.

2. Barrett Wendell, *A Literary History of America* (New York: Charles Scribner's Sons, 1900), p. 513.

3. Norman Foerster, ed., *The Reinterpretation of American Literature: Some Contributions Toward the Understanding of Its Historical Development* (New York: Harcourt, Brace, 1928), p. 28. Jay B. Hubbell's "The Frontier" may be found on pp. 39–61 of this volume.

4. Ralph Leslie Rusk, *The Literature of the Middle Western Frontier*, 2 vols. (New York: Columbia Univ. Press, 1925).

5. Lucy Lockwood Hazard, *The Frontier in American Literature* (New York: Thomas Y. Crowell, 1927).

6. Robert E. Spiller, Willard Thorp, et al., eds., *Literary History of the United States* (New York: The Macmillan Co., 1948) offers such useful chapters on nineteenth-century Western literature as "Literary Culture on the Frontier," "Western Chroniclers and Literary Pioneers," and "Western Record and Romance."

7. Franklin Walker, *San Francisco's Literary Frontier* (New York: Alfred A. Knopf, 1939) and *A Literary History of Southern California* (Berkeley: Univ. of California Press, 1950). An important recent work that derives in large measure from Walker's influence is Kevin Starr, *Americans and the California Dream: 1850–1915* (New York: Oxford Univ. Press, 1973).

8. Henry Nash Smith, *Virgin Land: The American West as Symbol and Myth* (Cambridge: Harvard Univ. Press, 1950).

9. Some examples of studies that, in one way or another, reflect Smith's method are Kent L. Steckmesser, *The Western Hero in History and Legend* (Norman: Univ. of Oklahoma Press, 1965); Edwin Fussell, *Frontier: American Literature and the American West*

(Princeton: Princeton Univ. Press, 1965); Joseph G. Rosa, *The Gunfighter: Man or Myth?* (Norman: Univ. of Oklahoma Press, 1969); and C. L. Sonnichsen, *From Hopalong to Hud: Thoughts on Western Fiction* (College Station: Texas A & M Univ. Press, 1978).

10. For an excellent collection that contains essays by several of these founding scholars of the Western Literature Association, see Daniel Alkofer, Richard W. Etulain, William A. Gibson, and Cornelius A. Hofman, eds., *Interpretive Approaches to Western American Literature* (Pocatello: Idaho State Univ. Press, 1972).

11. C. L. Sonnichsen, "The New Style Western," *SDR*, 4, no. 2 (1966), 23.

12. Bernard DeVoto, "Phaethon on Gunsmoke Trail," *Harper's*, Dec. 1954, p. 10.

13. Richard W. Etulain and Michael T. Marsden, eds., *The Popular Western: Essays Toward a Definition* (Bowling Green: Popular Press, 1974).

14. John G. Cawelti, *The Six-Gun Mystique* (Bowling Green: Popular Press, 1971) and *Adventure, Mystery, and Romance: Formula Stories as Art and Popular Culture* (Chicago: Univ. of Chicago Press, 1976).

15. Frederick Jackson Turner, *The Significance of the Frontier in American History*, ed. Harold P. Simonson (New York: Frederick Ungar, 1976), p. 28.

16. For summaries and illustrations of some of the more common theoretical approaches to Western films (and, by extension, to much popular western fiction), see William T. Pilkington and Don Graham, eds., *Western Movies* (Albuquerque: Univ. of New Mexico Press, 1979).

17. Leslie Fiedler, *The Return of the Vanishing American* (New York: Stein and Day, 1968), p. 21.

18. Sonnichsen, *From Hopalong to Hud*, p. 65.

19. Sonnichsen, *From Hopalong to Hud*, p. 6.

20. James K. Folsom, *The American Western Novel* (New Haven: College and Univ. Press, 1966).

21. Wallace Stegner, *The Sound of Mountain Water* (Garden City: Doubleday, 1969).

22. William T. Pilkington, *My Blood's Country: Studies in Southwestern Literature* (Fort Worth: Texas Christian Univ. Press, 1973).

23. Jay Gurian, *Western American Writing: Tradition and Promise* (DeLand: Everett/Edwards, 1975).

24. John R. Milton, "The Western Novel: Whence and What?" in *Interpretive Approaches to Western American Literature*, p. 19.

25. John R. Milton, *The Novel of the American West* (Lincoln: Univ. of Nebraska Press, 1980).

26. Max Westbrook, "Conservative, Liberal, and Western: Three Modes of American Realism," *SDR*, 4, no. 2 (1966), 13–15. See also "The Practical Spirit: Sacrality and the American West," *WAL*, 3 (1968), 267–84, and *Walter Van Tilburg Clark* (New York: Twayne, 1969).

27. Etulain, "The American Literary West," p. 347.

GENERAL CRITICISM

Overview of the Western Novel

The Novel in the American West

John R. Milton*

In some respects it should be easier to talk about the Western novel to historians than to professors of literature. The former will at least react sympathetically to the subject matter of many Western novels: the cowboy, the mountain man, the military scout or cavalry man, the Indian, and the historical events in which these people played a part. The literature professor wants to know whether the western novel is literary. More than that, perhaps, he has already decided that the western novel is not literary, and to prove it he sets Zane Grey beside William Faulkner, forgetting that Faulkner too was a kind of westerner in some of his concerns. In any case, we need not labor to make the point that the western novel is, and has been, in critical disrepute. Partly for this reason, some western novelists do not want to be called western: Harvey Fergusson quotes the Virginian—"When you call me that, *smile!*" And Paul Horgan feels much the same way. It is true that these men have written novels whose subject matter was non-western. But it is equally true that their best writing has been done with western materials. They are simply reluctant to be wholly identified with a region which in turn has been wholly identified with what we loosely call "the western."

We all know that in the terminology of the professor of literature there are no such labels as "easterns" or "southerns" to match "westerns." We do, however, speak of an eastern novel or a southern novel; that is, we recognize regional distinctions but we are less inclined to pay attention to the eastern-ness or the southern-ness of a novel than we are to its western-ness. The same is true of television. A story which portrays the man in the grey flannel suit on Madison Avenue is not called an eastern or a New Yorker; but a story which centers on a man from Laramie is inevitably a western. There are several reasons for this distinction. The West as a region is, of course, newer than the East or South in terms of established literary and European-cultural traditions. A novel written by a native

**SDR*, 2, no. 1 (1964), 56–76. © 1964 by *South Dakota Review*. Reprinted by permission of *South Dakota Review*. This essay was first presented as a paper read at the 1964 meeting of the Western History Association.

westerner is still viewed with some curiosity and perhaps mild condescension by the New York critics, as though it had been created by a talented cow much like the chimpanzees which have been painting pictures recently. But more important than this is the stigma attached to the formula novel—the Wild West romance, the cowboy saga, or the cavalry-Indian adventure. We are all too familiar with this story as we have seen it on television. We know, too, of the curious development of the "adult Western," and the sporadic attempts to debunk the myths of the Old West. Some of these myths need debunking, and some do not. The degree to which each western novelist gives serious thought to this matter of myth determines in part his place in the hierarchy of the literary West.

At the risk of over-simplifying a complex matter, let us put western novelists in three groups. At the very least this will give us a point of departure. All western writers maintain some kind of defensive attitude toward eastern publishers, but this collective concern is not enough to make them brothers. Beneath the surface, if we dig, we can see a caste system operating in the West. The so-called upper-crust consists more or less of Walter Van Tilburg Clark, Vardis Fisher, Harvey Fergusson, Frank Waters, Frederick Manfred, and Paul Horgan. Even here we run into difficulties, because Fergusson and Horgan have written eastern novels, and Manfred began his career as a midlander. The group is not a mutual admiration society, although Clark and Fisher are generally ceded the top positions. The second group is a complex one, including major writers who are not convincingly western, good writers who have not produced a large body of work, writers who have moved around just enough to escape some of the regional emphases, and competent novelists who have on occasion nodded in friendly fashion toward popular success. In this last point we see one of the functions of the caste system: it is understood by those "in the know" that a good and honest western writer must be something of a mountain man himself, independent in thought and action, shunning the easy success which his talent could bring him if he bowed slightly to the wishes of the eastern publishers. For this reason, even such a fine writer as Paul Horgan is suspect, although I insist on his position in the first group.

The second group, however, would include at least the following: Wallace Stegner, A. B. Guthrie, Jr., Wright Morris, Tom Lea, Willa Cather, Edward Loomis, Jack Schaefer, Forrester Blake, Conrad Richter, Oliver La Farge, William Eastlake, John Steinbeck, Frank Norris, William Goyen, and Mary Austin—strange bed-fellows. Stegner's novel, *The Big Rock Candy Mountain*, has been rated by Frederick Manfred as one of the twenty best American novels, western or not. I will agree, as long as I do not have to name the other nineteen. *Wolf Willow*, Stegner's most recent book, is a masterful evocation of the northern plains, certainly one of the finest books ever written by an American. Because it is neither a novel nor strictly speaking an exposition or an autobiography, reviewers have not always known what to do with it, and this should please the mavericks. Yet, Stegner publishes often in the slick magazines as an authority on the West, and so displeases his brethren. Guthrie's three novels—*The Big Sky, The Way West,* and *These Thousand Hills*—are highly competent re-creations of the West as it once was. They contain some of the most sensitive and perceptive descriptions of the land in western literature. But they lack originality in many respects, and, with their subsequent movie versions, they proved tremendously popular, as though Guthrie had written them toward that end. Wright Morris flits in and out of Nebraska and is difficult to classify, although his *Ceremony in Lone Tree* must be given serious consideration. Tom Lea *(The Wonderful Country)* is not a big producer, nor is Forrester Blake, else these men would move up in the hierarchy. Blake wrote two excellent novels of the mountain man some years ago—*Johnny Christmas* and *Wilderness Passage*—then retreated to the classroom until his recent book, *The Franciscan.* Willa Cather has achieved a national reputation, and is remembered for two Nebraska novels and *Death Comes for the Archbishop.* But one asks whether her farm novels are not midwestern rather than western, and whether, as Mary Austin has suggested, Miss Cather really knew enough about New Mexico to be considered a westerner. Edward Loomis shows great promise, especially in *Heroic Love* and *The Hunter Deep in Summer,* but he has not yet produced the major work which will make assessment more meaningful. Jack Schaefer stops short of greatness, but not by much. His *Shane* stands as the classic treatment of one of the formula stories—the mysterious stranger riding into a town beset with evil, ridding it of its evil, and riding off into the sunset. Schaefer's most recent novel, *Monte Walsh,* will also become a classic in time. It strips the myth and the mist from the cowboy and shows him plausibly, authentically, and excitingly, with much understanding, insight, and humor. Conrad Richter is, I think, a major and neglected American novelist who has suffered critically because his work is associated with the frontier and yet does not seem bound to it. *The Sea of Grass,* although a slight novel, portrayed the pioneer rancher in opposition to the encroaching farmer so well that it seems silly for anyone else to attempt the same theme. More recently, *The Lady* also uses western materials, but Richter remains best-known for his Ohio trilogy. La Farge upsets me because I respect his knowledge of the Southwest and I want to admire his books, but I prefer the short fiction to the novels. His *Laughing Boy* seems to be highly respected, and yet it is so full of flaws that it is highly susceptible to parody. La Farge's intentions were honest and worthwhile, but he did not succeed completely in fulfilling them. William Eastlake also writes of the Southwest in *The Bronc People* and *Portrait of an Artist with Twenty-Six Horses.* These novels are imaginative and strong, treating the Indian with a compassion desentimentalized through humor. However, Eastlake's imaginative powers often lead him into fantasy which, when not properly handled, is distracting. William Goyen, of Texas, has quietly gathered a small group of admirers and will soon have to be recognized critically. Steinbeck, too, must be considered seriously even though the critic-professors seem to have resented his Nobel Prize. At the very least, *The Grapes of Wrath* must be read in relation to the westward movement, and *East of Eden* will one day be seen as a major western novel. Frank Norris, usually associated with the naturalists, was deeply interested in the course of empire and in the forces of the land as well as the encroachment of the city. *The Octopus* is a kind of compendium of western problems, both social and literary. Mary Austin, considered by some to be the queen of western writers, is indeed a writer of major importance; but, her best book is *The Land of Little Rain*, not a novel.

The third group, containing many levels of competence and literary worth, has perhaps 100 writers who have turned out thousands of novels, largely in paperback. These are the writers who have made considerable use of the romance, adventure, excitement, nostalgia, and exoticism of the Old West and who usually follow the established formulas closely with particular attention to the cowboy. Some of these are hack-writers, with no further pretensions; others occasionally rise above mediocrity and give us something worth reading. All, however, are part of the phenomenon known as the "western" and must be recognized for what they are. Some of the names are fairly well known: Zane Grey, Luke Short, Eugene Manlove Rhodes, Ernest Haycox, Wayne Overholser, Clay Fisher, Frank Gruber, William McLeod Raine, Frank Bonham, Louis L'Amour, Frank O'Rourke, Max Brand, and the man who is said to have started it all, Owen Wister. The sad thing is that most of the novelists in this group are capable of better writing than they have usually exhibited. In part, of course, this is simply proof that talent will often submit to commercialism. Rhodes, Wister, and Haycox all have admirers who will defend them on literary grounds as well as historical; but most of the others are old pros who have glutted the market, some of them writing under several names as though in admission of the guilt of overindulgence. Frederick Faust wrote as Max Brand, Evan Evans, and Peter Dawson—at least. Henry Allen does one kind of novel as Clay Fisher and another as Will Henry. Louis L'Amour, in addition to "his own" novels, carries on the Hopalong Cassidy series under the name of Tex Burns. Harry Sinclair Drago uses his own name in addition to Will Ermine, Bliss Lomax, and Joseph Wayne, giving him the dubious pleasure of being four men rather than one. Only in the formula "western" does one find pseudonymity carried to such length, and if it is not just a method of confounding the tax collector it must surely reveal the commercial attitude which controls this kind of novel.

The three groupings I have made are not entirely defensible, nor are the categories I wish to suggest as a temporary method of breaking down the term "western novel." What the reading public refers to as the "western" is only the formula novel, usually with the cowboy as subject. The formula has also been applied to other materials: the mountain man, the Indian, the cavalry trooper, the settler, the Mormon, the railroad builder, the scout, and so on. If, however, the western novelist takes his work seriously, both in research and composition, and avoids the easy formulas, he is doing for the American West what any good historical novelist has done elsewhere in the United States or in Europe. And so I would like to establish a special place for the historical novel. Finally, we have novels which are semi-historical, in which the author has a pertinent theme going beyond the mere historical facts; we have novels with a contemporary setting in the West, in which the region receives various degrees of emphasis; and we have marginal novels, such as Manfred's *Morning Red,* whose action takes place on the fringes of the Great Plains and Rocky Mountain area, but whose spirit is western. These I call, simply, the western regional novel, for lack of a better term. Again, I think, we have seen the difficulties of laboring under the single term, western novel, for the fiction which is produced in, by, or about the American West. As in any other region, we are confronted with good writing and bad, and with such a variety of intentions, approaches, and subjects that it is unfair to apply a single label indicating little more than an area designation. It just happens that the popularity of one kind of western novel set a pattern from which we are still trying to break away. I am not sure of the precise origins of this pattern, but I am willing to hazard some guesses.

The exploitation of western material for the benefit of naive and awe-struck eastern readers may have begun by accident in James Fenimore Cooper, but it reached a professional level in Bret Harte. Cooper used the image of Daniel Boone, a kind of national frontier hero, to point up the dilemma arising from the confrontation between civilization and the wilderness. To Cooper's credit, he remained stuck with his dilemma, not providing easy answers to sticky questions. Harte, on the other hand, seemed to show that the evils of society could be cured with a breath of fresh and pure western air. We may well believe him, those of us who live in the West, but we must still deplore the artificiality and the ease with which he presented the problem, and the appeal to the exotic qualities of the West with little reference to complicating factors.

Pure adventure and escapism, with emphasis upon thrills and great deeds, became a staple in the dime novels, given considerable impetus by the fame of William Cody in his role as Buffalo Bill. The Daniel Boone image moved a little farther west. At the turn of the century the frontier had closed, but yet another image—that of Teddy Roosevelt—inspired he-man fiction, and the best-sellers of Kipling were easily made over into American novels with the cowboy replacing the British Colonial soldier. The major era of the cowboy had just ended around 1900, and it was no trick to take him off his horse and put him into books; he was there, unemployed and available, and he became a hero. At first, however, he was not the hard-riding, straight-shooting superman which he grew up to be. As the Virginian he talked himself out of trouble, rather than shooting his opponent, until he finally ran out of arguments near the end of the novel and was forced to kill Trampas. He spent a great deal of his time pursuing a young lady, whereas we all know that the young lady ought to pursue the hero. And, as many readers have pointed out, there are no cows in the life of this cowboy—at least none are visible in the novel. What makes the novel entertaining and interesting is not really the formula which many students of the western novel have attributed to Wister, but the sly fun, the anecdotes, and the pranks which are reminiscent of Mark Twain. In any case, *The Virginian* was a best seller in 1902, and Roosevelt wrote to its author: "I really think you have done for the plainsmen and mountainmen, the soldiers, frontiersmen and Indians, what nobody else but Bret Harte or Kipling could have done"—and this was intended as a compliment. Henry James, perhaps better able to evaluate Wister's novel, spoke of the "subject itself, so clearly and finely felt," the "personal and moral complexion" of the hero, the "admirable objectivity," and concluded that the novel was a "rare and remarkable feat." What James objected to was the happy ending, and he begged Wister not to revive the Virginian.

In trying to determine who really lit the fire under the cowboy novel, we note that Zane Grey's *The Spirit of the Border* was the national best seller in 1906, and that his *Riders of the Purple Sage* made the same dubious distinction in 1912. Obviously, people wanted to read about the hero of the western plains, this embodiment of southern chivalry, of strength and skill, of romance in the isolation of the wilds. Perhaps the approaching war turned American readers toward this peculiarly American hero who represented Good and always found some way to conquer or stave off Evil. At such times of national crisis it is comforting to discover a national hero with whom the reader may share success vicariously and at the same time escape from his own real-world problems. There was another hero at this time also, one who curiously represented our allies in Great Britain. Lord Greystoke, better known as Tarzan, appeared in the African jungle the same year that Lassiter rode through Deception Pass. Edgar Rice Burroughs, the creator of Tarzan, had served a stretch in the famous Seventh Cavalry and had herded cows in the West before he turned to writing. And so in 1912 the American subliterary scene was blessed with a pair of heroes from whom it has not yet recovered: the ape-man swinging through the trees, and the cowman galloping over the plains. For a time, at least, the jungles of Africa and the plains of Western America were equally exotic.

The flood was on, even though the next western novel to become a national best seller—Max Brand's *Singing Guns*—was not published until

1938, only two years before Clark's *Ox-Bow Incident* disturbed the formula and indicated new possibilities for the cowboy novel. The years before and after 1940 saw hundreds of conventional "western" novels, most of them fun to read (I have read over 400), some very badly written, and a few possessing qualities which might be called literary. Their very titles are revealing of the kinds of thing which these novels deal with—and I take some of the better ones as examples: *Blood Brother* by Elliot Arnold, *The Apache* by James Warner Bellah, *The Dice of God* by Hoffman Birney, *Montana Road* by Harry Sinclair Drago, *Red Blizzard, Yellowstone Kelly, Return of the Tall Man,* and *The Big Pasture* all by Clay Fisher, *The Bad Lands Beyond* by Norman Fox, *Desert Guns* by Steve Frazee, *Broken Lance* and *The Big Land* by Frank Gruber, *Bugles in the Afternoon* and *The Earthbreakers* by Ernest Haycox, *No Survivors* by Will Henry, *Law Man* by Lee Leighton, *Roads from the Fort* by Arvid Shulenberger, *Mr. Big* by Robert Walsh, *Hondo* by Louis L'Amour, *The Chieftain* by Robert Payne, *The Searchers* by Alan Le May, *Valley of the Shadow* and *Only the Valiant* by Charles Marquis Warren, *Winter of the Sioux* by Robert Steelman, *Broncho Apache* by Paul Wellman, *The Violent Land* by Wayne Overholser, and *The Hostiles* by Richard Ferber. Here are cowboys, Indians, cavalrymen, settlers, army scouts, and celebrated figures such as Lt. Col. George Custer. Each of these novels, although it has some historical or literary merit, is at least similar to several hundred other novels in that it appeals to the reader who is satisfied with stereotyped characters and well-rehearsed events. There are hero and villain, good and evil, chase and capture, sun-scorched desert and snow-blown plain, the renegade white man and the noble red savage, the Christian and the Pagan, and, of course, the gun, the horse, revenge, violence, death, and an aura of moral satisfaction floating over it all.

Is it myth, or neurosis? Warren Barker, M.D., writing in *The Psychoanalytic Quarterly*, says that the western novel's reliance on stereotype has produced an indistinct authorship, and reminds us that "anonymity of authorship is a characteristic of ancient myths." The western hero, too, is anonymous, according to this theory. "Where did you come from, baby dear?" "Out of the everywhere into here." Like the nursery rhyme, suggests Dr. Barker, the western novel is a re-enacting of the basic mysteries of life, laced liberally with the usual fantasies, regressions, oedipal complexes, fears, transferences, and ego problems. Riding his phallic horse, and with his phallic pistol pointed unerringly, the cowboy avenges his father, replaces his mother, and engages villains in threats and counterthreats of castration. The end of all this is the ride into the sunset, or the wishful return to the womb. Stated in this fashion, however, the problem is no less complex: whereas the psychiatrist may see the habitual reader of "western" novels as an immature and maladjusted ego, the literary historian or the anthropologist may regard the western novel as an extension or repetition in regional terms of ancient and basic mysteries, drives, desires, and tensions. And this is myth, neither good nor bad, neither true nor false, but simply necessary. When, on occasion, the many ingredients of the western novel are brought together in a deliberate and stylized attempt to formulate or re-state the myth, we have a novel like Jack Schaefer's *Shane*, or Oakley Hall's *Warlock*, or (one that failed) Harry Brown's *The Stars in Their Courses*. Here we see direct relationships between the western novel and the morality play or the quest narrative from Malory's *Arthur*.

What is wrong with the conventional western novel is not the myth itself but the fact that it is taken for granted and exploited with a nonliterary ease, so that the western landscape becomes only an accidental stage on which the medieval players may re-enact their old truth. The serious novelist, whether he writes the historical novel, the autobiographical novel, the objective novel, or the contemporary novel, is concerned with the traditions of his region, with the physical aspects of the region, and with the ways in which the region affects those people living within it. This, I take it, is what every reputable novelist does. If, in so doing, he is able to delineate characters who can speak beyond the region, or if he can locate values which transcend the immediate area in which they originate, then his work has simply done what it ought to do. It must be a cliché by now that good literature is first regional and then universal. In the American novel, do we need to mention *The Scarlet Letter*, *Moby Dick*, *Washington Square*, *Huckleberry Finn*, and *The Grapes of Wrath* to prove the point? The fact that the western novelist has not always gone far enough beyond the things of his region may serve to illustrate one of his major problems: because the West is relatively new, in terms of culture and social organization, the novelist must in a sense create or locate the traditions he wishes to use, and he must do so at the very same time that he uses them. Frequently, then, the collection of facts or things, toward the making of a tradition, takes precedence over the evaluation, judgment, or use of them.

A. B. Guthrie, Jr., is the prime example of the novelist who rebuilds the Old West without, in a sense, coming to terms with it. In his well-known trilogy, *The Big Sky* covers the years 1830 to 1843, *The Way West* concentrates on the year 1845, and *These Thousand Hills* takes place from 1880 to 1887. Thus, Guthrie's three novels span most of the nineteenth century, from the mountain man to the builders of town and society. The broad panorama is vivid with details, many of which come from Garrard, Ruxton, and Parkman, plus other journals. Other details, especially those of the land itself, come from Guthrie's personal experience with the West and his sensitive perceptions of the landscape. As panorama the novels work; as individual books they do not. Guthrie, like many other western writers, has a keen eye for natural details, a sharp ear for speech sounds, and a tendency toward formlessness or looseness of construction. He is less concerned with art, or form, than he is with the facts of his material.

The Big Sky is nevertheless one of the best mountain man novels, along with Fergusson's *Wolf Song*, Blake's *Johnny Christmas*, and Manfred's *Lord Grizzly*. It nicely chronicles the westward movements of a boy who has not been able to get along in the social structure of his town on the eastern side of the Mississippi. Boone Caudill flees to St. Louis, beset along the way by the villains of "civilization." Eventually he joins up with Dick Summers, a veteran mountain man, and is cut off from organized society. His life from that point on may be regarded more or less as the "typical" life of the mountain man, and Guthrie's descriptions of the land and of this life are memorable:

> The mountains fell away behind them, reaching high and jagged into the sky and the blue of distance settling on them. Gophers heavy with the young ones they carried piped at the horses and dived underground, their tails whisking, as the horses came close. A badger, surprised, while he chewed on a dead bird, lumbered off to one side and halted on the mound of earth he had scratched up digging a hole and watched them with a slow blaze in his eyes.
>
> The feel of the country settled into Jim, the great emptiness and age of it, the feel of westward mountains old as time and plains wide as forever and the blue sky flung across. The country didn't give a damn about a man or any animal. . . . What did it care about a man . . . ? There would be other men after him and others after them, all wondering and all wishful and after a while all dead.

In *The Big Sky*, Guthrie seems to have a tight grasp on the little things, but he cannot get them into an order or pattern which might raise them to a higher level of significance. The novel is episodic and plotless; it is an impressionistic sweep of the mountain man West, a travelogue, a source book. But the author's imagination plays only upon the details, not on the concept. *The Way West* has the same faults and is not saved by the ready-made form of the journey. Like the preceding novel it provides us with a catalogue of materials, this time concerning the trail and the wagon train, but it also simply "trails off" at the end with no real theme or sense of fate to cover the sentimentalism of the last page. The closest that Guthrie comes to saying anything is a brief statement to the effect that all men are kin through their common "hurtful, anxious, hoping look . . . the bone-deep look of man." Again, the chief value of the novel is its authentic dialogue and its precise descriptions. However, if we consider the trilogy as a unit rather than as separate volumes, we can defend these first two books as preparation for the third. *These Thousand Hills* has long been considered the least successful of the three; but it is the culmination of the earlier experiences, it suggests a theme, and it is therefore the key to the trilogy. From Boone Caudill to Lat Evans a refinement of the American character is taking place, although even Lat falls short of this kind of fulfillment. Lat, however, is the tragic person, because he is on the line between the old and the new, between two ways of life which were both necessary in their own times. Lat is caught in the change from frontier to civilization, and Guthrie allows us to see some of the potential of this cultural and historical position.

The idea of refinement was not new to Guthrie. In 1943, thirteen years before Guthrie's trilogy was completed, Wallace Stegner said much the same thing in *The Big Rock Candy Mountain.* In point of time, Stegner's narrative is later than Guthrie's and might be read as the conclusion of the idea that the American westerner carries his dead unquietly within him. We are close to our past; we are made up of the roughness of Boone Caudill, the crudeness of Lije Evans, the recklessness and dreaming-foolishness of Bo Mason. To understand ourselves we must turn to our recent past and find at least a part of our identity in the scoundrels and heroes of the nineteenth-century West. The process of recovering a usable tradition is not always an easy one, and Guthrie's lack of form may perhaps be excused with the argument that he is laying the base on which other novelists will build. We would like to think, at least, that the hardness, the discipline, the fire which shapes the vision will come later.

There has been a tendency toward very long novels in the West, and often toward trilogies or even longer groupings. It is as though the western novelist is content to take his "given" forms—the travel narrative, the quest, the sense of space—and to concentrate upon his wealth of materials rather than upon the formal organization of them. Perhaps, as has been suggested, he succumbs to the irrationalities of his land of extremes, losing sight of the rational attitudes and esthetic distance which might give him better control over his subjects. In any case, we are inclined to read a western novel for its information, its evocation of the land, its historical vision, rather than for its artistic control or its meaningful form. I should like to point out, however, that a very elementary sense of form is indeed present in the western novel, and that its simplicity need not be considered detrimental.

Walter Clark, in *The Ox-Bow Incident* and *The Track of the Cat*, has used the three-part organization of the biblical passion story. In each case the resurrection is only hinted at, but the elements of the myth are there. Art Croft in *Ox-Bow* is a kind of Everyman, average in intelligence and courage, swayed by emotions even though he can occasionally see himself objectively. With the lynch mob he partakes of two days of passion and guilt, with a certain measure of punishment, and only senses that the dawn of the third day might bring a new and better life. Three days of evil in *Track of the Cat* are climaxed by the killing of the cat, but we are led to understand that salvation is not something to be achieved only once—each man and each generation must undergo the same ordeal and arrive at a personal solution. Yet, the western landscape seems particularly well-suited to the handling of this universal theme, and so space and time—both nonlogical methods of organization—become the basic elements of form. The men of Ox-Bow and Bridger's Wells fluctuate in their intentions as they move into the wind and cold of the mountains. Temporarily discouraged, and tempted to give up the search for rustlers, they are then made irritable by the same winds and are driven recklessly onward, their emotional control shattered by the elements of nature. In the shadow of the tall mountains they feel small and insignificant, so that they can regain their stature only through violence enacted upon creatures of their own kind. Granted, nature is not the only force in this drama; the mob is also stirred by the commanding personality of Tetley, whose military bluster is more effective than the pleading compassion of Davies. The question of justice achieves special importance because the question is raised slightly outside the pale of established law and regulated order. Furthermore, the novel has special distinction in light of the kind of western story which had preceded it, because no strong or courageous man steps in to halt the injustice, and no gun is raised toward Tetley when an act of determined rebellion would have stopped the lynching. The situation is complicated by the degrees of guilt found in the otherwise innocent victims: one man has a questionable past, the second is irresponsible in senility, and the third has not taken the proper business precautions in the buying of cattle. These elements of the story are all plausible, in fact they are frighteningly realistic, thereby contributing to the emotional impact of the novel. Yet, we return to the myth, because there are three men killed by an unreasonable mob in the same way that Christ was killed in the company of two thieves.

The Track of the Cat, with its extensive use of the symbol, is a more complex novel than *Ox-Bow* and a larger effort to come to terms with the concept of evil. Here again the frame of the narrative is a three-day period and our attention is focused on three men. The cat seems to represent Evil, so that on one level Clark is dealing with an ancient and universal theme. But, like Moby Dick, the black cat is also an object against which men may try themselves—a testing-board. Arthur Bridges is a mystic of sorts who thinks of the land in dream-like terms which are conducive to peace and to a limited understanding of life. He is killed by the cat. Curt is earthy, practical, and completely self-confident until his mind finally betrays him during a snowstorm and he too is killed by the cat. These two men are reminiscent of frontier types, one the dreamer who had visions on the land but could not cope with everyday necessities, the other a self-reliant destroyer of the wilderness who could not think in terms of the long view or the values which go beyond the minimum necessities. When Hal, the youngest brother, is successful in killing the cat, Clark is obviously suggesting that the ideal western man must be a combination of visionary and exploiter, of new-culture white and old-culture Indian, of thinker and doer. At the moment he is a rather innocent and ignorant young man, historically, who is yet to evolve into something more spiritual and less animalistic than he is now, and who must turn to his past for help. In a passage which also illustrates the vivid images found throughout Clark's novels, Hal sees the Indian Joe Sam's print in the snow:

> Harold stopped too, to stare down. It made him uneasy to see the print of a naked human foot in snow. It wasn't right there. The split-heart print of a deer, the dots and dashes of rabbits, the fine tail line and tiny forget-me-nots of woods mice, or even the big, broken flower of a panther or a bobcat, these were all as right in snow as black letters on paper. But this complicated, unique print, not even a little like any of them, was all wrong. There was too much time forgotten between.

The evolution of man in Western America, whether it be short term or long, is of prime concern to western novelists. Harvey Fergusson's province is the nineteenth-century Southwest, beginning with the mountain man in *Wolf Song*, published in 1927, and continuing through four equally superb novels: *The Blood of the Conquerors*, 1921, *In Those Days*, 1929, *Grant of Kingdom*, 1950, and *The Conquest of Don Pedro*, 1954. Frank Waters has sensitively recorded the cultural evolution in the Southwest, as Indian, Spaniard, and White American come into contact with each other. *People of the Valley*, 1941, shows the isolated Spanish-speaking people of the Sangre de Cristo mountains approaching a time of change; *The Man Who Killed the Deer*, 1942, is about Taos Indian justice confronting the new white man's justice; and *The Yogi of Cockroach Court*, 1947, is a melting-pot of Mexicans, Indians, Chinese, and whites, with the conglomerate breeding which results. Forrester Blake's first novel, *Johnny Christmas*, 1948, is set in the Southwest in the early nineteenth century; his second, *Wilderness Passage*, 1953, moves forward to the Oregon Trail and the advent of the Mormons in Utah; and his most recent novel, *The Franciscan*, 1963, jumps back to the seventeenth century. Paul Horgan, after writing three novels of contemporary New Mexico—*Main Line West* in 1936, *Far From Cibola* in 1936, and *The Common Heart* in 1942—went back to the years following the Civil War in *A Distant Trumpet*, 1960. And here—although there are more examples to follow—we run into an interesting problem in western fiction. Horgan's *Distant Trumpet* was well-received and made into a movie, although it is not even close to *The Common Heart* in quality of style, seriousness of intention, or significance of theme. The reading public wants the strangeness and the nostalgia of the past, and at times it is very difficult to determine whether a western novelist is returning to the past for the serious reasons I suggested earlier or whether he is going back to meet his reading public. I shall not mention those cases in which I suspect the latter reason, but shall instead offer two examples of the former, even though these men also have achieved popular success with their "historical" novels and not with their contemporary ones.

Frederick Manfred, after publishing seven novels of the American Midlands under the name Feike Feikema, has looked farther to the west for people and events which will help him explain the contemporary characters of the region he calls Siouxland. He has conceived of a five-novel series which will be called *The Buckskin Man*. Like Cooper's

Leatherstocking Tales, Manfred's novels are being written in an order different from the chronological order of the subject matter. The first to appear was *Lord Grizzly*, 1954, based on the exploits of Hugh Glass. The second, *Riders of Judgment*, 1957, presented the Johnson County Cattle War from the perspective of Nate Champion. *Conquering Horse*, 1959, then went back to an earlier all-Indian era. The fourth, *Scarlet Plume*, will be published next month; it has a captivity theme coming out of the Sioux uprising in Minnesota. The last to be written—now in progress—will be a novel of darkness and fate, beginning in Sioux City and culminating in the Black Hills. Of these novels, *Conquering Horse* must certainly rank with Waters' *The Man Who Killed the Deer* and, reluctantly, La Farge's *Laughing Boy* as the best of the novels about the western Indian. (In my less critical moments, I am also inclined to put in this select group *Blood Brother*, by Elliot Arnold, a novel which is guilty of numerous literary sins but which, like the prodigal son, I still love.) At this point, incidentally, you will recall that I have as yet made no attempt to name the best, or classic, cowboy novels. Frankly, I am afraid to do so, not wanting to get into lengthy arguments with devotees of Owen Wister, Andy Adams, Eugene Manlove Rhodes and others of whom I am equally suspicious for one reason or another. However, if such a list were to be drawn up, I would probably put at or near the top three recent novels which hardly resemble each other: Manfred's *Riders of Judgment*, Jack Schaefer's *Monte Walsh*, and Max Evans' *The Rounders*. Had Wister done what I think he was capable of doing, had Adams written novels, and had Rhodes been a writer, they would undoubtedly have to be added to the list.

Manfred's *Lord Grizzly* is his only novel to become a best seller. Although it takes advantage of one of the supreme western adventures, which would assure a certain amount of popularity, it is also the book in which Manfred most deliberately attacks the problem of form. In fact, it almost suffers from too much form. Happily, however, this condition affords us the opportunity of looking at some structural possibilities with western material. What I shall propose, briefly, is that form in the western novel seems to be based upon the rhythms of the land. Mary Austin, in *The American Rhythm*, identifies a two-beat pattern in Indian poetry and relates it to man's two-handedness—to up and down, to light and dark, to back and forth movements which are elemental. If one extends this basic beat very slightly, so that from a beginning position we count 1 and then the up and down or back and forth become 2 and 3, we have merely re-stated Aristotle's famous insistence on beginning, middle, and end. This basic rhythm permeates *Lord Grizzly*. During a fight with Indians, mountain men as they die look inward, then outward at nature and their companions, and then inward again. Hugh Glass is established in the first third of the novel as a companyero, a member of the brotherhood; in the second part he wanders off by himself, is mauled by the grizzly, and survives miraculously as an individual; in the final third he becomes uneasy in his aloneness and rejoins the group. The point of view of the novel has three stages: one is in Hugh's mind, a second is at his eyes, and the third is at a slight distance from him. Even in style, Manfred has adhered to patterns of three:

> He slept. The wind soughed up from the south and tossed the heavy cattail cobs back and forth.
>
> He slept. The November sun shone gently and revived the green grass in the low sloughs.
>
> He slept. The wind soothed softly and rustled the ocher leaves in the rushes.

When Hugh Glass feels that he is special because of his survival, three of his former companions walk in from the plains, one at a time, having survived similar ordeals. Also, there are—if you will pardon an unavoidable allusion—three bears: Hugh himself is a grizzly among men; he is mauled by a grizzly; while traveling through the Badlands he is followed by what seems to be a phantom bear, perhaps a psychological force in Hugh's mind associated with revenge and guilt. And, to return to the question of man's evolution, we note that Hugh crawls on his belly during the first stage of survival, crawls on all fours during the second stage, and walks upright during the third. That is, he resembles the three main stages of the evolutionary development of man—reptile, four-footed animal, and two-footed upright man. The basic issues in the novel are those of the individual as related to the group and revenge as opposed to forgiveness. Because Hugh Glass is able to forego his revenge, but does so without understanding his actions, he has risen to the level of the group-human, with some insight into the necessity of the brotherhood, but he has not yet achieved a status which might be called spiritual. At this point stands mankind, Manfred seems to say, and in this way a western historical novel takes on universal significance and an almost epic quality. In spite of its avowed faults, *Lord Grizzly* is one of the outstanding novels of our time. At the very least, it stands with Hemingway's *The Old Man and the Sea* and Faulkner's *A Fable*, all three of these novels published in 1954 and having the same general celebration of the endurance of man.

The dean of western writers is Vardis Fisher, a man of extremes and of continuous production. Fisher has published about twenty-five novels, falling rather easily into three groups: the Idaho novels, the historical novels, and the Testament of Man series. For authenticity and seriousness, Fisher's historical novels rank with the best. *Children of God*, a thorough and exciting tale of the Mormons, is authoritative as well as literary. *Tale of Valor*, based closely on the Lewis and Clark expedition, proposes two of Fisher's main themes—fear and hunger. These are illustrated in the historical novels through the obvious devices associated with survival on the western frontier. In the Idaho novels it is largely the isolation and the somewhat brutal behavior of his fellow men which frighten Vridar Hunter (a slight alteration of Vardis Fisher) and warp his "natural" personality. Vridar is shaped by the cruelties of the frontier, and later in life he attempts to locate the sources of man's inhumanity. Vridar's story was first told in a tetralogy: *In Tragic Life*, 1932, *Passions Spin the Plot*, 1934, *We Are Betrayed*, 1935, and *No Villain Need Be*, 1936. He also appeared in *Dark Bridwell*, 1931, as a neighbor of the Bridwells. Reprinted in paperback as *The Wild Ones*, *Bridwell* has gone through several editions but has not yet caught the attention of many literary historians. *Bridwell* is a dark and mythic novel, splashed here and there with the beauties of nature and the exuberance of natural man. Charley Bridwell is an American Lear with his sense of satisfaction in life and his tragic amazement at its destruction by the hands of his wife and son. Here are some of the most beautiful passages in American fiction as well as some of the most violent and challenging. *Bridwell* is a supremely irrational novel, although it is under careful control. Its rhythms are those of the land—mountains, forests, rushing streams, placid but destructive solitude—and its frame is the three-fold narration by Charley, his son Jed, and his wife Lela—these very repetitions setting up another rhythm.

In spite of the frequent presence of the irrational in Fisher's novels, he is a rationalist who has spent his life locating the sources of man's irrationality and superstitiousness. When he failed to come to terms with the problem in his early tetralogy, he embarked on the amazing project which appeared in twelve volumes between 1943 and 1960 under the general title, *The Testament of Man*. Beginning with the origins of man, Fisher traced his intellectual and social progress meticulously through the thirteenth century and concluded it with a rewritten and expanded version of the Vridar Hunter tetralogy—*Orphans in Gethsemane*. The series is a work of scholarship turned into fiction. Much could be said about it, but for our purposes it is enough to note that Fisher's project was designed to explain the fears, hungers, and lack of love suffered by a boy on the early twentieth-century Idaho frontier. Thus, the history of the western world (in the broad sense) is linked as tradition to the American frontier, and it is no longer possible to say that the western novel is divorced from the realities of the world-at-large. It is true, however, that the western novel has little patience (and little contact) with the whims and fashions of metropolitan society. It is a novel of the land, of primary passions, of conquest and search. Vardis Fisher, as clearly as any writer, epitomizes four major aspects of the Western American novel:

1. Reliance on nature, on the land, for functional rhythms which become one kind of form;
2. Desire to explore the past in order to illuminate and explain the present, and to provide a workable tradition for literature;
3. Susceptibility to irrationality, because of the extreme characteristics of the land in the Great Plains-Rocky Mountains region;
4. Attempts to bring the materials of the West under rational scrutiny and control.

This last matter is proving difficult, but the Western American novel is yet young, with a bright future ahead of it. It has grown tremendously in the past several decades, and I am sorely tempted at this point to introduce thirty or forty novels which surely ought to be mentioned. Instead, let us suggest some generalizations which may lead to a profitable discussion at a later time. As the novel stands now, there are differences between the one written in the eastern or metropolitan area and the one written in the semi-arid lands of the western half of the United States. These differences will not apply to every pair of novels from the two regions, but they indicate some means of making a comparison. The eastern novel is concerned with a psychological, social or economic ordeal, with current affairs, and with a relationship of characters in time rather than space because of the confinement of space in the East. The western novel is more often concerned with physical and anthropological matters, with characters related in space. This novel is essentially timeless, except for certain historical events, and uses or attempts to create myth through archetypal characters. The eastern novel comes from the formal traditions of the eighteenth and nineteenth century British social novel. The western novel is rooted in medieval romance, in Malory, in the morality plays, and in the journals and travel narratives of the nineteenth century West. The eastern novel is based on sophistication and disillusionment; the metropolitan person rebels, or pulls in, compromising eventually with society while seeking identity within his immediate group and environment. The eastern character is shaped directly by society. In the western novel characters are relatively independent and have a good deal to say about their destinies except as they are shaped by the land. The surrender is not to society but to the conditions of the land, and the western character seeks identity within the entire natural scheme of things. The eastern novel has been heavily influenced by Freud, while the western novel tends to absorb the theories of Jung. The eastern novel is *in*tensive, probing into the centers of problems which are often small and temporary. The western novel is *ex*tensive, opening outward from the character into action, racial consciousness, and the almost unlimited landscape. The eastern novel is dramatic; the western novel is epic, romantic, mythic, and lyrical. The eastern novel is a people-novel, while in the western novel Nature becomes an additional character or force. The eastern novel has a pattern of people coming to terms with hell, compromising with it, remaining lost in it, or explaining it away in Freudian analyses. The western novel features the ancient pattern of destruction, the experience of hell, and ultimate rebirth. Eastern characters have conditioned fears; western characters have primitive fears. All of which proves very little, perhaps, except that the continent on which we live is large enough to permit totally different landscapes and environments, and that the literature from the various areas will of course reflect that variety. When the professional critics, most of whom live in the East, recognize this simple fact, they may be able to strip away the long-imposed stereotyped notions and come to grips with western fiction. And when the learned professors follow suit, we may find more colleges and universities offering courses in Western American literature. In the meantime, quite apart from the critics and the Britain-oriented professors, the American West is growing and maturing and producing a literature which is worthy of our serious attention.

Early Critical Statements

Western Interpreters

Andy Adams*

A protest has recently arisen in Texas to the effect that its oil fields have no chronicler who speaks with authority. The same might be said of other Western occupations. Bret Harte gave us, it is true, the red shirt days of California, the discovery of gold, placer mining, in an imperishable fiction, and Jack London did a similar service for Alaska; but these are the exceptions. The lode mine has had no spokesman. Cripple Creek and Goldfield poured the yellow metal into the coffers of the nation unnoticed. And so why should the oil industry, still in its swaddling clothes, complain? Before its advent, the Ranger Service of the Lone Star State redeemed that commonwealth from crime and lawlessness, without a historian worthy of mention. As subjects for a heroic literature, the Texas Rangers met the final test in that they were willing to lay down their lives, if necessary, for the good of others.

The cattle industry was a primal factor in winning the West and has proved to be an inviting field for pen and pencil. Yet when reduced to a last analysis, when subjected to an acid test or a fire assay, as transcripts of life, the books about it reveal few values. The primal, high notes have been overlooked, and its mole hills have been magnified into mountains. The West was not brought under subjection by Alkali Ikes and Rattlesnake Petes. Current standards, however, have been established and are accepted without question.

The Virginian, a readable book, will serve to illustrate the point. Originally a series of short stories, it was finally unified with a love thread; and a number of incidents, delightful in their way, complete the picture. Still, the story might have been more convincing to some readers if the author had given one glimpse of his hero in connection with his occupation. Had he been shown in the thick of a roundup, cutting out a trainload of beeves for his employer, his identification would have been complete. A cowboy without cattle is comparable to a lord without lands or a master without slaves. The omission of the cattle, however, is preferable to their inclusion, if the author lacks a mastery of his material.

* *SWR*, 10 (1924), 70–74.

In the field of Western romances by writers who do not have any apparent knowledge of the cowboy's life or insight into his character, the harvest is plenteous and the laborers are not lacking. The movie lends its aid and the publishing mills grind out a constant grist. Admittedly a man's occupation, women write about it acceptably. A naval officer wrote a story in which his hero was pitted in a roping contest. At the proper moment, the cast was made—"*as a sailor heaves a line*"—and the loop perfectly encircled the horns of the animal. The fact that a cowboy and a sailor cast a rope differently, to different ends, had evidently not occurred to the writer. The noose obligingly opened, without wand or magic, without a heavy or light side to the loop, and settled true, amid the huzzahs of an admiring throng. Quite fittingly, the story was awarded a cash prize.

About twenty years ago, Mr. Hamlin Garland, the novelist, was a frequent visitor in Colorado. He spent several summers in the mountains, gathering material for Western books. An established writer, a pleasant gentleman to meet, he was a welcome guest in many homes. At that time he was ambitious to establish himself as our foremost writer of Western realism. He has a number of books to his credit, and his many friends furthered his every wish in the way of securing material.

He even invited friendly criticism of his work. After his return home one summer, a number of his intimate friends were discussing his Western stories. "If it ever falls to Mr. Garland to write 'the great American novel'," said an old newspaper writer present, "I will risk the opinion that the scene of it will be laid in a country in which he will be the master of his material. If material governs, and it does, he should return to a field in which he could speak with authority. The West cannot be written from mere observation."

After writing some half dozen Western novels, Mr. Garland, for reasons unknown, abandoned his chosen field. A few years later he gave us *A Son of the Middle Border*, a quasi or actual biography of his own life, his masterpiece at that time. This was followed by *A Daughter of the Middle Border*, a biography of his wife, which was awarded the Pulitzer prize. These remain his best work and are at least a partial fulfillment of the words of a prophet in our own Western country.

When one considers the present output of Western stuff one may well ask, "Is the truth worth while?" Our painters have answered the question. Their work will stand a fire assay. Reviewing the work of Thomas Moran, whose "Grand Canyon of the Colorado" hangs in the national Capitol, a critic said, "The art of such a man, must, of necessity, be as healthy, as sincere and honest as the man himself. . . . I was more than ever convinced that the future of American art lies in being true to our own country."

In sketching the Indian and buffalo, Charles Craig, contemporary to Moran but still living, has added his bit to the truth. Europe and America have contended for the work of this veteran artist, with a rivalry between foreign capitals, such as London and the pre-war St. Petersburg. What Remington did for the old army of the West, Craig, arriving in his chosen field in 1865, did for the plains Indian. His canvas of an old Indian ford, "Apaches Crossing the Rio Grande Del Norte," stands apart from any competitor. When the Santa Fe railway extended its line westward to Dodge City, Kansas, in the early '70's, its construction trains were unable to reach the front for days and days, blocked by the migration of the buffalo to their southern, winter range. One gets a clear conception of these primal scenes from the paintings of Charles Craig. In no other form of art are the myriads of that primitive animal so vividly portrayed.

The work of Charles M. Russell, of Montana, another of the great artists of the West, carries an authority all its own. His mastery of material is the result of first-hand knowledge. In an infinity of detail lies the secret of his success, which cannot be questioned. He was a cowboy once, and no range man can find fault with his scenes of action. Horse and man and atmosphere blend into the perfect picture.

In looking for new material, Russell spent a winter in Mexico. On his return to his home at Great Falls, Montana, he resumed work on the same kind of scenes that had been his subjects for forty years. His friends were disappointed—they had expected something new—and took him to task.

"I know Montana," protested the cowboy artist, in reply. "The pay-dirt hasn't been entirely worked out in the mesas and coulees of this upper country. Why, to get Mexico's colors accurately, I would have to live there twenty-five years. Excuse me, boys, but I'm too old to take in more territory."

Had our authors had the same honesty, thoroughness and knowledge of their limitations, the West today might have had a literature comparable to that of the New England states. The primal things of the old West, it appears, have escaped the attention of our modern school of writers. The late Emerson Hough contended with some bitterness that the very center of the production of Western literature was located at Stamford, Connecticut.

The remedy? Several agencies are at work in every section of the West. In Texas, for instance, the Folk-lore Society, in gathering the state's legends, is lending a valuable aid to a future literature. The schools and colleges also are awake to the importance of the local material and are preparing the way for a literature, which should be as spontaneous as the flora of the plains. Progress toward a truthful and artistic presentation of Western life cannot come from any sources different from these. All that is lacking is the will and the willingness, dowered with a sympathy as true as a mother's love.

"Virgins, Villains, and Varmints"[1]

W. H. Hutchinson*

The basis for this venture is the same as the basis for a back-raise on two pair after the draw—personal opinion. In this case, the opinion has been formed, unconsciously, as the writer has read "westerns," first as an avocation, and later as a vocation. The difference is as marked as that between courtship and matrimony.

In the first instance, you read for the *what* of the story, helping the author sustain the illusion of reality. In the second, you read for the *how* of the story, that you may learn from that author what he or she can teach you about "grabbing the reader by the throat and giving it to him while his eyes pop." This may seem a peculiar exercise. It is an essential if we are to comprehend one reason why the "western" is not only literarily suspect today, but has been a bar sinister on any literary escutcheon for some years past.

The basic fact about the "western," consistently overlooked by those who overlook it, is that it was and is written for the same reason that all other popular fiction, including Charles Dickens' output, was and is written—to provide entertainment for the reader and economic well-being, or a facsimile thereof, for the writer. The "western" was and is a commercial product, a standard brand of merchandise for which the customers ask by name. And when the customers—first editors, then readers—ask for a "western," what do they mean?

Depending upon the capillary attraction of the individual, the "western" label may encompass anything from what Sergeant Ordway did or did not say to Thomas Jefferson down to the latest issue of *Powdersmoke Yarns* in the corner cigar store. The Fur Trade, Gold Rushes, Overlanders, Indians, the whole complex of Bernard De Voto's "theme of wonder," can be lumped geographically as "westerns." For our purposes here, the "western" epithet means only one segment of this complex, the last one in time, the cowboy-free range-horseback yarn, told in

* *HLQ*, 16 (1953), 381–92. © 1953 by *Huntington Library Quarterly*. Reprinted by permission of publisher and author.

fiction form in its primary colors of black and white and blood-on-the-saddle.

Tracing the development of this stylized art form with broad strokes of an opinionated brush, it can be found in the writings and editings of Timothy Flint, specifically in Pattie's narrative. The *Davy Crockett Almanacs* added still-evident genes and chromosomes, as did the frontier-Gothic romances of Mayne Reid. The "yellowbacks" took over about the time of Fort Sumter and held the field until the turn of the century. Aiding and abetting the ancestral strain were certain buckskin extravaganzas, featuring such as Buffalo Bill Cody, Wild Bill Hickok, and Texas Jack Omohundro, that culminated in the long-lasting legends and memories of the "Bill Shows."

For the first decade of this century, the "outdoor-action" story seems to have dominated the contents of such magazines as *Munsey's*, *McClure's*, and *Everybody's*, with writers like Jack London, Joseph Conrad, Stewart Edward White, Rex Beach, and Will Levington Comfort. There were some "westerns" by Henry Wallace Phillips, Owen Wister, White again, and O. Henry, but these and their fellows were not yet marked with the tar brush. They were treated, apparently, as just another branch of the "outdoor-action" school and, as such, they received a fair amount of both space and attention in the current literary journals and supplements. For an opinion, the demarcation point comes in 1912 with a book whose closing and most pungent phrase was "*Roll the stone! . . . Lassiter I love you!*"

Riders of the Purple Sage not only gave Zane Grey his first taste of success after several unremunerative novels, but it ushered in the "western" as we know it today. In passing, it might be pointed out that Grey was ahead of himself, ahead of the form he did so much to implant in the consciousness of three generations of readers, in the implications of his closing phrase above. When Lassiter did roll that rock, he and the beauteous heroine were sealed in a hidden valley, presumably for eternity, with no clergyman in their past, present or foreseeable future. This was a daring development in the current outdoor-action school—made possible by the dread alternative in the plot that the heroine otherwise would wind up as a Mormon plural—but it did not take. The basic ingredients Grey mixed up in *Riders of the Purple Sage* have remained virtually unchanged ever since—virgins, villains, and varmints.

Women in the "western" came as sawdust dolls and the tags used to depict their character were obvious. If the girl wore calico or gingham, even hoopskirts, had hair to her waist when the braids accidentally came unwound, possessed a clear complexion and lustrous eyes, she was Good—lineal descendant of Ouida's idealized English maidens genteelly skirting the whirlpool of life—and the hero would get his just rewards in the end by claiming her hand. If she wore tights and spangles and worked in a saloon, she was Bad and was doomed to a sticky end as an accomplice of the villain or as a lone figure stumbling off into scorching sun or numbing blizzard with only her thoughts of what might have been for protection. As simple as that, but in a sense typical. There were two classes of women in the Free Range days and everybody knew where they stood, which made for an unembarrassed social life all around. It also made it easier for the reader to concentrate on the action-plot without getting petticoats in his mind. Women in the "western" were not typical of the sex any more than the libidinous neurotics or man-eating viragos who populate today's contemporary fiction, even that hailed as "significant," are typical.

If the "western" villain leered and drooled, he was a Heavy Villain, whose slavering approach to the heroine, or the material crux of the plot, was easily predictable. The climax of his career was a matter of physical violence, honorable on the hero's part, generally fatal. If the villain dressed like a parson or gambler, he was a Sneaky Villain to be dealt with, after unmasking, even as the desert sidewinder who rattles not before striking, or if he does, cannot be heard. These two categories applied not only to any Anglo-Saxon cast as the menace, but applied equally well to the Mexican or anyone with swarthy skin, flashing teeth, and silver-mounted costume, who was *always*, the Cisco Kid not excepted, cast as the villain until recent years and the Good Neighbor policy. This type-casting of the *hombre del país* can be attributed to the Texas influence on the folkways of the Free Range, or it can be traced, perhaps, to residual fear of the Spanish Armada and The Inquisition. At any rate, *Westward Ho* foreshadows the role the Spaniard's New World descendants were fated to play in the "western" story.

As to the varmints in the "western," they were largely incidental props. Coyote, lion, bear, deer, antelope, snake, sheep, sheepherders, Indians, canyon, *malpaís*, blizzard, and drouth were inserted as demanded by the plot. Chief among these varmints, for an opinion, was the Hero. No breed of men ever won the West or lifted a mortgage against such odds. Neither Francis X. Aubry[2] nor Louis Remme[3] ever rode so far so fast without saddle boils or a played-out horse. They could fast like a fakir; water-out like a camel; win the Good Girl; spurn the Bad Girl; destroy the Villain; absorb punishment like a Marine Corps legend; and do it all overweighted some forty pounds with assorted hardware, mostly lethal. It would be nice to be like that.[4]

Despite the obvious defects of two-dimensional characters, of insistence on plot, on action-plot, of exaggerated use of horses, hardships, idiom, and costume, no other single segment of the American scene has received the maltreatment, nor commanded the audience, that the "western" has had and held. For example, *Riders of the Purple Sage* sold over a million copies and the total sales of all Grey's works now exceed sixty-eight million. Harold Bell Wright's *When a Man's a Man* sold eight hundred thousand copies. During World War I, His Majesty's government purchased five hundred thousand of William McLeod Raine's cowboy novels for distribution to the troops. When that war ended, the rising tide of chile con carnage became a flood.

The so-called slick paper magazines used "westerns" as they do today. There were "western" novels in both original and reprint editions. Over and above these outlets, there were the pulp magazines, looked down on by any and every right-thinking literary person, carrying little advertising and that of the truss-and-goitre type, but serving the reading needs of millions and requiring more original material at better rates than is the case today, unfortunately. *Argosy* was a weekly then, consuming some six million words of new material a year; *Adventure* was published thrice-monthly, needing some four million words of fuel yearly; *Short Story* was in this bracket, as were others, including *Blue Book*, and while these "books"[5] were balanced as to contents, they used a goodly proportion of "westerns." The bulk of the market for the "western," then as now, was the strictly "western story" magazine, apparently limited only by the press capacity of the nation and their editors' ability to find material for the pages—*Western Story Magazine* (the *satevepost* of its field), *Lariat, Triple-X, All Western, West, Golden West, Cowboy Stories*, and *Ace High* are remembered titles. Added to these predominantly masculine books in the mid-twenties was *Ranch Romances*, pioneer in the "western love" story, where the formula "western" was told from the heroine's point of view, or in such a way as to provide identification for women readers with the story line and the personalities. Additional demand for "westerns" swelled from Hollywood, where pioneers had discovered box-office gold with Bronco Bill Anderson, and went on with William S. Hart, Harry Carey, Tom Mix, Fred Thompson, et al.

With demand established, supply came posthaste, as in any commodity market. Using either the peak-and-valley technique or the steadily rising curve, depending upon story length desired, and using very basic plots, with the skill of the wordsmith making dialogue, character tags, costumes, and settings appear fresh, the production of "westerns" became a business, a lucrative one. There were men working in the field who could produce a half-million to a million words a year, all saleable; one of the best of them, nameless here because of friendship, had a blackboard in his office on which he kept four story outlines going simultaneously, using two secretaries and a dictating machine, since he was running a successful advertising agency on the side. For the classical example, there can be no better choice than the twentieth century's Sir Walter Scott, the Old Master of Thud and Blunder, Frederick Schiller Faust,[6] who produced over thirty million words in his twenty-seven years of writing under a baker's dozen of names, of which three—Peter Dawson, Evan Evans, and Max Brand—were reserved exclusively for his "western" output. He wrote "westerns" for both pulp and slick magazines—and it is well to note here that the major difference between the two is simply that in the slick story, the writer can expect (and the editor is so oriented) more help from his readers in closing the gap between what he means when he writes and what they get when they read.

There have been few major changes in the "western" since *Riders of the Purple Sage*, and all of them have concerned women. One development has been the rise of the "western love" magazines in the pulp field, for which *Ranch Romances*, mentioned earlier, showed the way. These books have introduced a story element best described as "Sally's Sweater."[7] The story opening introduces the heroine galloping across the range, with ample verbiage on the inevitable movement. The story problem, setting, and characters are briefly introduced, and then back to Sally's Sweater. Whenever the action lags, this handy divertissement is introduced again. It is as close, by and large, as the formula "western" has come to permitting raw sex to get in the way of the action.

The other change has occurred in the slick magazines, with Ernest Haycox and Luke Short[8] as its ablest promoters. This departure from the norm involves the use of two women: one Good but tinged with the suspicion of either evil or of primitive passion; the other Bad but so suspect of smoldering fires of real, do-to-ride-the-river-with virtue that the hero spends a lot of his time, and the reader's, trying to sort them out in his own mind. The use of the two women presents another conflict, in addition to the basic action problem of the story, and introduces something of the psychological suspense narrative into the "western" formula which heretofore was simply one of direct issues, decisions, and consequences stemming largely from physical action and always requiring positive action by the protagonist.

It is easy to dismiss the despised "western" as escape trash, and it has been so dismissed ever since the demand and supply thereof engulfed literary people in the twenties. It is not so easy to dismiss the fact that for some forty years the "western," in one form and another, has held its audience. Of the over 1,100 titles published in Armed Services Editions,[9] 134 titles, the largest identifiable bloc, were "westerns." On the evening of December 12, 1952, at a corner newsstand on Colorado Street in Pasadena, it was possible to count thirty-three exclusively "western" pulps together with six "western love" magazines. (The use of reprint material to fill these books is a salient development in the commercial aspects of writing "westerns.") The varnished cover reprints of "western" novels by the various houses in the field, together with the soft-cover originals issued by Gold Medal Books, make an impressive total in any current drugstore or newsstand tabulation. An instructive exercise is to count the number of "comic" books and see how many of them are built around past or current "western" heroes of the motion picture industry. This leads logically to the number of "western" films released, or re-released, annually by Hollywood; the number of "western" radio scripts aired each year;

and now, of course and inevitably, the impetus given "westerns" by the demands of television for material.

The weight of the evidence as to the popular appeal of the "western" is impressive and it is sustained over distance. It seems destined to endure until the last memory of our last, wholly-owned frontier, the Cattle Kingdom defined by Walter Prescott Webb,[10] is obliterated from the national consciousness. The question naturally arises as to what legacy of letters the "western" has left in its piled millions of words to date. The question is not easy to answer. The "western," even more than other popular fiction, is short-lived unless it be between boards, and even then its life expectancy has been short for lack of serious efforts to preserve it. Some of its best examples have been preserved by anthologists—which is another way of saying by reasoned personal opinion, just as is the following selection.

Owen Wister, "A Pennsylvanian writing about a Virginian in Montana," seems to have made the first genuine contribution in this field of American literature with *The Virginian*. Personal opinion would not rate it as highly as some of the others to be mentioned, but as Bernard De Voto, J. Frank Dobie, and Walter Prescott Webb have clearly shown, Wister was the first to catch certain essential juices of the Free Range and bottle them for market in fiction form.

Andy Adams must rank high on any list, although the use of the term "fiction" in connection with Adams' solid narratives seems pure courtesy. *The Log of a Cowboy*, *Cattle Brands*, *The Outlet*, for three examples, are constructed of the minutiae of daily working on the range and trail as meticulously as *la reata* is braided from the hide the braider has known since it first bawled. One has only to compare *The Log of a Cowboy* with Emerson Hough's *North of 36* to feel the difference.

Stewart Edward White's short stories involving Señor Buck Clark; George Patullo's short stories; W. C. Tuttle's "Hashknife and Sleepy" yarns; Harry Sinclair Drago's fiction laid in White Pine, Nevada; and the Mexican Border-West Texas fiction of Eugene Cunningham all deserve to be saved for future generations. So, too, does one of Alan LeMay's many novels, *Painted Ponies*. All the examples in this paragraph represent nothing more nor less than fine fiction, written for entertainment, by master craftsmen who knew how to give their readers the meat in the coconut without asking them to do their own husking.

It is well to point out here that in any form of popular fiction writing, the author knows more about what his audience (market) wants than that audience knows about the accuracy of what it reads. If the author does not know this, he wastes his time, his agent's time, and the time of many editors. This leads to an inconvenient shortness of temper all around. In the "westerns," the men cited above gave accuracy, knowledge, and insight along with their craftsmanship. Since they were competing (some of them still are) in a field where accuracy was subordinate to craft in the marketplace, their actual contributions have been lumped along with the rest of the "westerns." This error is never more glaring than when it is committed with the writings of Eugene Manlove Rhodes.[11]

Rhodes wrote "westerns," insofar as the public and the critics were concerned. Yet it is in the "westerns" of Eugene Manlove Rhodes that you find what Bernard De Voto terms: ". . . the only embodiment on the level of art of one segment of American experience. They are the only body of fiction devoted to the cattle kingdom which is both true to it and written by an artist in prose."[12] Strong words, even from a man who is noted for the pungency, vitality and frequency of his opinions, yet written *con razón.*

The women of his stories (and the best of them have no women whatsoever) represent Rhodes at his worst. If they are young women, they are "infrangibly virginal," and it is extremely hard to find even the suspicion of a Bad Woman in all his writings. Occasionally in his works, an older woman does appear, after years of frontier abrasion have made her "road weary," and in these few instances, Rhodes achieves with women what he did best—"photograph in color, record in faintest intonation."[13] Otherwise, the dolls of his feminine cast contain just as much sawdust as those of any other "western."

In the list of villains that appear in Rhodes, he has both Heavy and Sneaky Villains as heretofore defined, but in their characterizations, he differs from the other practitioners in the field. His first choice for the villain in any story was one of the Sons of Mary—banker, railroad promoter, grasping lawyer, greedy official—those who did not work with their hands for daily bread, and worse, far worse in Rhodes' lexicon, who profited, grew swollen and fat on the lives of those who did work with their hands. It would have been an easy technical trick to two-dimensionalize these characters but Rhodes went to some pains in story construction to show why these villains of his were parasites upon the body of the country that had nurtured them. Such a condition was true to his experience, true to his country and his people, but it made his stories hard to follow;[14] a reader picking up a Rhodes "western" for the first time was apt to react like a pup with his first porcupine. And another divergence from the usual in Rhodes' villains is simply this: he never cast Spanish-descent in the role.

When it came to the varmints, Rhodes again diverged from the formula under discussion. The flora and fauna of his chosen country, the land itself, heaving up and breaking off, eroded, dusty, shimmering in the heat, or shrouded in the mists of too-infrequent rainfall, are integral parts not only of his stories but of the very lives of the characters he took from life, often not bothering to change their names or actual attributes. His people are what they are because of their country; a water hole is not spaced forty miles from the next simply because such an arrangement serves the story needs.

It is these differences from the "western" that give Rhodes his place. There is good reason for these differences, for this place, reason quite apart from "the way his cultivated mind played upon the cowpuncher world."[15]

No other writer of "westerns" encompassed as much first-hand living in the trans-Mississippi region at the time and in the places he recorded as did Rhodes. Born in Tecumseh, Nebraska,[16] he was five-ish when the family removed to Cherokee, Kansas. He had had twelve years of the prairie experience of wind, drouth, blizzards, grasshoppers, and the green buds swelling in the creek bottoms when spring came, before he accompanied his father to the Rio Grande valley[17] in New Mexico in 1881. Thereafter, for twenty-five years,[18] he was a cowboy, only a fair hand;[19] horse wrangler and bronc rider, good at both; miner, freighter, school teacher, dishwasher, road builder, baseball enthusiast, poker player, political fighter, personal fighter, homesteader, carpenter, mason, blacksmith, and rancher who went broke in the losing battle against drouth and cow-country interest.[20] The totality of the Free Range experience found summation in his personal life. What he wrote, he wrote from the inside *out*; he wrote it, almost all of it, far removed from the country he had loved and left for personal reasons.[21] His knowledge was sharpened by the expatriate's longing; accentuated by distance and the years of absence until it came out on paper as the remembered mellow haze of a coal-oil lamp seen through the window when both the world and the man were young and ". . . circles had no centers."[22] Yet upon what he wrote, you may, as an archaeologist, depend.

In *Bransford in Arcadia*,[23] there is a description of a prospector's camp, adit, forge, and every artifact, that can stand for all time as the native habitat of the single blanket, single burro, single jack seeker. In *The Trusty Knaves*, a twenty-horse jerk line string brings an ore wagon and stub-tongued trailer into town just as these outfits pulled in to Lindauer's Store in Deming. In *Beyond the Desert*,[24] the actual search of the El Paso & North Eastern Railroad for good boiler water across the gyp flats between Orogrande and Alamogordo is the basis of the whole plot. There are similar examples in everything he wrote—the people and the land of six New Mexico counties, Socorro, Sierra, Doña Ana, Lincoln, Otero, and Grant, preserved for all time in the clear amber of a joyous, dancing, illuminated prose.

There is one major obstacle in the path of anyone who seeks to read Rhodes today, to hone these opinions against the stone of his own personal experience. It is almost impossible to find him in print.[25] His published books have been pursued for years by "a coterie as select and discriminating as any that ever boosted a tenth-rate English poet into a first-rate reputation."[26] Rhodes, by reason of his prose style, never achieved the mass popularity, with concomitant press runs and reprints, that other writers of "westerns" did—Grey, Mulford, and Raine, for examples. Rhodes never achieved the output, in toto or per annum, that any one of the men mentioned herein achieved; he was a slow worker by nature, writing not just for his market, but writing so that every word would stand up in the minds of those in New Mexico who had known Gene Rhodes as well as Rhodes had known them and their joint country.[27] Yet, if his books, or his stories in frayed copies of old magazines, can be found, they will ring like a shod hoof on *malpaís* in the minds and hearts of anyone who knows the West-That-Was.

There is good reason for devoting so much space to the "western" story, be it written by honest craftsman or native artist. It has been too long neglected for what it is, a common fund of experience for generations of readers. And even you may be surprised at your share in that experience if you recall clearly all the printed words devoured in your lifetime, be that lifetime long or short when you read this opinionated survey of the "western" story in American literature.

Notes

1. Thomas B. Clark first used this title in an article on the Dime Novel in *American Heritage*, NS 3, no. 3 (1952). It seemed equally appropriate to a study of the "western" story.

2. Santa Fe, New Mexico, to Independence, Mo.

3. Knights Landing, Calif., to Portland, Oregon.

4. Which is the feeling the author wanted.

5. Trade term.

6. Killed on the Italian front in 1944 while a war correspondent.

7. The phrase is Alan Bosworth's.

8. Fred D. Glidden, Jr.

9. By the Council of Books in Wartime.

10. In *The Great Plains* (Boston: Ginn, 1931). Chapter X in this work is devoted to the literature of and about the Great Plains and the Cattle Kingdom.

11. His first publication, "Charlie Graham," a poem, appeared in *Land of Sunshine Magazine* for April, 1896. His last was a book review of *Sky Determines* by Ross Calvin in the San Diego (Calif.) *Tribune*, June 24, 1934. Two of his novels, *Beyond the Desert* and *The Proud Sheriff*, were published posthumously after serial appearance in *The Saturday Evening Post* during his lifetime.

12. In his Introduction to *The Hired Man on Horseback*, an informal biography of Rhodes by his widow (Boston: Houghton Mifflin, 1938).

13. Eugene Cunningham to W. H. Hutchinson.

14. As did his trick of breaking his story line to insert an essay that had nothing to do with it. See *Stepsons of Light* (Boston: Houghton Mifflin, 1921), pp. 62–72; reprinted as "King Charles' Head" in a collection of Rhodes' essays, *Say Now Shibboleth* (Chicago: Bookfellows, 1921).

15. J. Frank Dobie in "*My Salute to Gene Rhodes*," his Introduction to *The Little World Waddies*, a Rhodes collection edited and published by W. H. Hutchinson (El Paso, Tex., 1946).

16. January 19, 1869. Died at Pacific Beach, Calif., June 27, 1934.

17. To Engle originally, as best can be determined from the letters and related material in the Rhodes Collection at the Huntington Library.

18. A two-year gap occurred, 1888–90, when Rhodes attended University of the Pacific, San Jose, Calif., now College of the Pacific located at Stockton.

19. Dobie, op. cit.; Carroll McCombs to W. H. Hutchinson.

20. All from the letters or related material in the Rhodes Collection, Huntington Library.

21. There are as many stories *about* Rhodes as by Rhodes.

22. Pres Lewis in *The Trusty Knaves.*

23. *Bransford in Arcadia* (New York: Holt, 1914). Reprinted as *Bransford of Rainbow Range* (New York: Grossett & Dunlap, 1920).

24. *Beyond the Desert* (Boston: Houghton Mifflin, 1934).

25. *The Best Novels and Stories of Eugene Manlove Rhodes* (Boston: Houghton Mifflin, 1949). This collection of Rhodes' works, with an Introduction by J. Frank Dobie, is now out of print.

26. DeVoto, Introduction to *The Hired Man on Horseback.*

27. Letters and related material in the Rhodes Collection, Huntington Library, San Marino, California.

The Themes of Western Fiction

Max Westbrook*

Revolt-and-search has long been a basic motif in American fiction. Typically, the hero rebels against institutional evil and searches for a code or setting that will enable him to express abstract belief. But this is difficult. What can Steinbeck's Jim Casy do when he finds that the religion he has been taught is a mockery, but that he himself is still a religious man? What happens to the Hemingway hero when he finds that the values he believes in are better represented in the bull ring than on the battlefields of Italy? Certainly, the hero cannot stand alone and stoutly proclaim to the world that he will die for abstract truth; a man can't defend the Alamo in the name of a syllogism. And yet, neither can the hero forget God simply because He is not found in the churches or disbelieve in justice simply because it is not found in the socio-economic structure. It is the hero's belief in value which caused him to rebel in the first place; it is the necessity for embodiment which causes him to search.

Naturally there are countless exceptions and variations, but the rebellion against institutions and the search for some embodiment or symbol of abstract value is definitely an important theme, not only in American fiction, but in American literature and life generally. Because this same revolt-search motif is basic to the cowboy story, I think it is a mistake to consider Western fiction merely a product of regionalism. If the cowboy story is examined in the broader framework of the revolt-search motif, its kinship to major American literature, its themes, and its shortcomings can be more fully understood.

The essential idea behind the revolt-search motif is that truth cannot be embodied in an institution or written down in a list of rules. An ultimate truth, however, does exist; and the hero—through his superior insight—has enough intuitive or symbolic understanding of this truth to distinguish him from common men. At least six important themes result from this one idea. First, nature is a better source of truth than man-made—therefore corrupted—institutions. Second, man is evaluated more accurately by his performance in a fist fight than by his performance in a

**SWR*, 43 (1958), 232–38.

drawing room. Third, intuitive knowledge and empirical knowledge are superior to book-learning. Fourth, language—especially institutional language—cannot denote what is truly important. Fifth, the best men are frequently cast out of society because they *are* the best men. Sixth, symbolic action (usually defense of an underdog victimized by institutions) is the most valid expression of value.

Emerson, Thoreau, Melville, Twain, Stephen Crane, Hemingway, and James Jones are just a few of the many American writers who illustrate this viewpoint. Emerson's insistence on "an original relation to the universe" reveals his basic allegiance to the revolt-search motif. Christ in the church, for example, is dead; but Christ in nature, discovered by an individual's insight, is alive. Thoreau's refusal to pay taxes indicates the same general position. Both Emerson and Thoreau are well known for their belief in nature, experience, intuition, their defense of the low and the commonplace (because the low and the commonplace are judged so by institutional categories), and their use of actual things as symbols of higher truths.

Herman Melville's Billy Budd is crucified by institutional laws that are incapable of assessing the natural goodness of which he is symbolic. In Chapter XXXIII of *Moby-Dick* and in the "El" paper (*Pierre*) Melville makes overt statements of the revolt-search viewpoint. Huck Finn's frequently-explicated decision to do the "naturally right" thing by Jim, regardless of what is "conventionally right," illustrates the same inadequacy of institutional rules. Just as Huck sees that society's rules about slavery do not account for what Jim is, so does Stephen Crane's Henry Fleming see that society's romantic concept of war does not account for what war is. At the end of *The Red Badge of Courage* Fleming is a good Emersonian in that he has given over the false concept of Greek heroics and discovered his own individual relation to the universe.

In Hemingway's *A Farewell to Arms* Frederic Henry says that abstract terms such as *glory* and *honor* are obscene because society has taken them over and corrupted them into the counterwords of a hypocritical preachment. Later, Henry bolts from the Italian army when its high officers initiate a sacrificial slaughter of the innocent in the name of honor and loyalty. Prewitt in James Jones's *From Here to Eternity* stands alone, without the aid of established modes of expression, and endures the persecution of military society because of an abstract belief which he is never able to formulate.

Throughout major American literature, heroes rebel against institutions and search for a more meaningful embodiment of abstract value.

In many ways, the West provides an ideal setting for the American hero's revolt and search. Urban rebels must take on characteristics of the very institutions they oppose, for it is difficult to convince readers that an unsophisticated outcast could reshape New York City. One possible solution—the outcast is assigned trivial action which is symbolically important—too often ends in preciosity. The Western setting is an easy solution to the writer's problem. Cowboy heroes can perform courageous acts on the basis of what they are as individuals. They can creditably be very crude of speech and even be praised for it. They do not need institutional accouterments in order to defend homesteads or rescue wagon trains, and homesteads become cities, wagon trains pioneer the founding of states.

Another advantage—the idea that man's relation to values was clear and clean, before urbanization—is illustrated in the preface to Jack Schaefer's *The Big Range.* "I like to write about the wide open spaces when they were still open and their wideness could enter into the people, some of the people, who left life's footprints on them . . ." However sentimental this may be, it is the Western version of Emerson's "Nature." By observing, appreciating, and battling nature, by living out in the bigness and openness of the plains (Schaefer is typical in thinking of nature as the bigness of the plains), man can realize a moral perspective which far surpasses the rote piety of corrupt cities.

Schaefer's "Jeremy Rodock" (Hollywood's *Tribute to a Bad Man*) is his best illustration of the theme of nature. Rodock finally captures a particularly fiendish band of thieves who have painfully crippled a herd of mares and foals as part of an elaborate plan to steal them. Instead of hanging the thieves or taking them straight to the sheriff, Rodock follows the rule of nature. He orders them off their horses, has their boots removed, and begins to herd them at the point of a whip across rugged plains-country to a sheriff who is fifty miles away.

Thus, a legal problem is handled as a moral problem. The two cowardly thieves suffer punishment, the third thief endures a very painful expiation, and Rodock is able to see a greater truth than the inefficient laws of civilization or the brute laws of personal vengeance. Schaefer's theme, then, is that there is a moral value which is greater than anything man can trap and formalize in his earthly institutions but which is attainable through the medium of nature and natural action.

A somewhat extreme version of the theme is found in the frequent, direct association of the hero with the infinite. Because of some deep harmony he has established with nature, he is able to take on certain qualities of that supreme truth which is symbolized by nature. In Owen Wister's "Hank's Woman" the narrator suggests that nature has steeped the Virginian in "that serenity that lifts us among the spheres," that his understanding is "unfathomable." The Virginian's unfathomableness suggests the infinity of truth. Furthermore, the narrator is an educated man, a cultured easterner who is humbly learning about truth and human nature from a cowboy.

Man's organizations, however, are often presented as an unfortunate necessity, as a force which beats down the best men but is necessary because the vast, inferior majority are not capable of rising above just that superficial kind of rote morality which is found in systems and institutions. We see this in Schaefer's *First Blood* when the youthful hero has to choose between personal law and civic law. The problem is caused by mass man's inability to judge in terms of abstract truth; only a select few can see beyond institutional substitutes and they are unable to formulate distinctions for common men. Thus arises the necessity for the monster precedent, and that which man tags law and order becomes a monument to his own shortcomings. The young hero, of course, chooses civic law, a decision which forces him to kill a close friend who is clearly the most "naturally" courageous and honorable man in the area. Conrad Richter's *The Sea of Grass* offers a different handling. The hero, Baron Bruton, is a cattle king; but he established himself in pioneering days, when it was more likely that individual ability would be rewarded. When the homesteaders move in (representing the encroachment of civilization), Bruton and his empire are destroyed. Melville's theory of the "divine inert" (*Moby-Dick*, Chapter XXXIV) is an encompassing explanation of why the best men cannot become institutional leaders.

When the machinery of the protective organization does break down, it is almost always one of the outcast heroes who must come to the rescue. Seldom does reform come from the normal function of an institution. The most frequent exception is the heroic sheriff, but in countless stories he must go outside the law in order to restore justice, as in Eugene Manlove Rhodes's *Pasó Por Aquí.* A. B. Guthrie's *The Way West* illustrates another variant. Hero Dick Summers guides the wagon train, saves it from destruction, teaches its leaders, but is never a member of the group.

Stories of heroes who simply do not fit into the system are even more typical. Sometimes the hero has performed an act of heroism—perhaps the killing of a villain who had cowed the sheriff—that was exemplary in the abstract sense but to be condemned in the social sense. Being an essentially kindhearted man, he may attempt to rejoin society as just another citizen; but duty will soon require him to perform another act that is not justified by man-made rules, and he will be forced to return to his role of the truly virtuous outcast.

Shane is a pat example, but Alfred Henry Lewis' Wolfville series better illustrates the general tendency to portray the truly virtuous as people who do not meet the phony standards of the system. Being outside convention is such a definite characteristic of the Wolfville irregulars—a group of tobacco-chewing, tough-talking softies—that their pattern of life takes on a kind of unconventional conventionality. The essence of the Wolfville attitude is exampled by one basic habit: the men continually talk in terms of an extended metaphor that compares life to a card game. You never *attempt*, *endeavor*, or *try*; you "make your play." A school would not *pay a salary*; it would "win for fifty dollars a week." "Prayin'," says one of the Wolfville gentry, "is like goin' blind in poker. All you do is hope a lot." The language of card-playing, not being sanctioned by proper society, becomes the language of moral evaluation. Bret Harte's stories of the same type are better-known examples of a "regional" theme that is actually national: Damon Runyon's characters are just Bred Harte's tough-talking softies transplanted to Brooklyn. Compare, for example, "The Luck of Roaring Camp" and "Little Miss Marker."

Since institutions are at best a kind of necessary evil and since institutions have a prior claim to language, the Western hero has no words for what is truly important. In addition, glibness, flattery, slogans, moral dicta, propaganda, deceptive legal phraseology, parlor-room patter, grammatical snobbery, and a dozen other institutionalized misuses of language have corrupted it and marked it as something to which the Western hero is fundamentally opposed.

When forced to express something important the hero will often use slang or profanity to take the edge off. Sometimes he will fall back on what is supposed to be an exclusively he-man metaphor, or he may stumble and stammer until another character or the author's interpolations say it for him. Jeff Bransford, one of Rhodes's favorite heroes, is a well-educated man who can speak grammatically perfect English, but the taint of conventional achievement is removed by the fact that he can also talk slang—any time he wants to—and talk it with equal naturalness. Owen Wister's Virginian has a superior insight into Shakespeare, but the brilliance of his analysis is made all right by the poverty of his grammar. In Chapter III of Tom Lea's *The Brave Bulls*, *torero* Pepe Bello says that value to him is "not namable." Walter Van Tilburg Clark dramatizes a more subtle version of the same theme (see especially Chapter I of *The Ox-Bow Incident*, and *The Track of the Cat*, *passim*). The student of major American fiction will be reminded of Billy Budd's stammer, Stephen Crane's heroes who will not speak of their friendship ("The Open Boat"), or Hemingway's idea that the truly important things are beyond words.

One result for the Western writer is that he often tries to accomplish linguistic expressiveness without appearing to do so. Lewis has encountered the particular problem of wanting to say something that is best expressed by "bookish words." His unsatisfactory solution—a typical one—is to indicate mispronunciation through misspelling. In slick fiction the handling is even more clumsy, the assumption being, apparently, that two *pards* and a *dang-blast-it* will legitimatize a folksy speculation on philosophy. A number of Western writers, Rhodes and Wister especially, include some plausible explanation for the non-cowboy part of the hero's vocabulary. Whatever the method, the idea is the same: to be meaningful, expression must be non-institutional.

Likewise, the Western hero tends to reject institutional knowledge and to prefer intuitive knowledge or empirical knowledge, both of which have the advantages of not being dependent on schools, of not requiring a logical formalization, and of constituting a more direct contact between the individual and the truth. The heroine of *The Brave Bulls* asks Pepe Bello how one learns to be a *torero*. "Don't you take any lessons, read any books, practice a lot, to learn?" But the *torero* answers, "You learn all the good stuff from the bulls and yourself while you're standing there." As J. Frank Dobie flatly puts it in *A Vaquero of the Brush Country*, the only school for cowboys is the range itself. Intuition is equally recurrent as a characteristic of the outcast hero. Sometimes, as with the old Indian in Clark's *The Track of the Cat* and the Mexicans in Elithe Hamilton Kirkland's *The Divine Average*, intuition is characteristic of the outcast race. Both intuition and empiricism have permeated Western culture on all levels. Note, for example, the Hollywood hero's "sixth sense," which is simply a folksy version of *intuitive knowledge*.

One recurrent result is the ethical equivocation seen in the handling of such problems as prostitution. If the woman is really a prostitute, the hero will assist her publicly and be kind to her generally, but will not marry her. If marriage does take place, then the woman was probably only *thought* to be a prostitute. In *The Violent Land* Wayne D. Overholser employs both possibilities within a single story. What is not being openly admitted is that there is thought to be some truth in what the institution advocates. Prostitution *is* evil. What the writers are usually trying to dramatize is the idea that going against the rules of propriety proves a sincerity not found in institutional charities. The hero's natural insight enables him to recognize true virtue even when it is hidden behind a pejorative, surface quality that has misled society into a typical error: judging on the basis of what appears to be instead of on the basis of what *is*. In "The Western Bad Man as Hero" (in *Mesquite and Willow*), Mody C. Boatright outlines the same kind of ethical equivocation. The requirements for a bad-man hero are shown to be surprisingly conventional.

There are, however, more legitimate actions the outcast hero can perform and still keep within the limits of the revolt-search motif. The most important of these—fighting against a tyrannical institution—has also been analyzed by Boatright, in "The American Myth Rides the Range: Owen Wister's Man on Horseback" (*Southwest Review*, Summer, 1951). A second permissible action is the defense of an underdog institution. Struggles to save the small cattleman from the big cattleman, or peaceful citizens from hired gunmen, are the most frequently found examples. The hero himself seldom stays to participate in the functioning of that system he has helped to establish. Shane lives among his friends just so long as they are being terrorized by the cattle king. Dick Summers (*The Way West*) guides the wagon train to its destination, then returns to the mountains. Oftentimes, the hero offers rationalizations, but in reality—like Billy Budd and Huck Finn—he is a noninstitutional hero.

A third possibility is based on the hero's code, a code that is not written down, preached, or even taught. Like the Hemingway hero, the Western hero derives his code from experience or simply realizes it through insight.

Further, the code is concerned more with action than with any social, civil, or religious function. That part of the code which is social is usually connected with non-parlor room matters such as drinking, gambling, or a concept of hospitality based on frontier conditions instead of city conditions.

At least one other permissible action requires mention. The hero may fight for an abstract cause if the taint of institutionalism can be removed. He may not fight for honor if honor is represented as being a characteristic of the system. But if his own social group opposes him, or if the odds are so insurmountable that to fight would be to "commit suicide," then the hero may fight for an abstract cause as such. Two Hollywood Westerns, *Stagecoach* and *High Noon*, and Paul Wellman's *The Iron Mistress* are clear illustrations of this principle. In all three cases, society's hypocrisy serves to establish the necessary distinction between an institutionalized corruption of value and the hero's legitimate realization of value.

One of the main reasons why mature Western fiction exists in such small quantity is that the appropriateness of the setting to the revolt-search motif has led to an unartistic literalness. What so many Western writers fail to realize is that actual validity is not synonymous with artistic validity. The fact that many cowboys and gunfighters were tall, dark, and heroic does not mean that an authentic tall, dark hero will be an automatically successful artistic creation. Sentiment, romance, and one-dimensional character portraits cannot be justified by an indignant finger-pointing at history books.

Vernon Young's analysis of *Red River* in "The West in Celluloid: Hollywood's Lost Horizons" (*Southwest Review*, Spring, 1953) is a first-rate explanation. The revolt-search concept may prompt illogical resolutions, but the ending of *Red River* is an aesthetic failure. Hollywood also fails in *The Silver Whip*, its version of Schaefer's *First Blood*. The hero's decision to shoot his friend in order to maintain the law is negated by Hollywood's ever-ready panacea—the flesh wound. *Jack Slade*, a surprisingly good movie, is more creditable. The hero, who is forced to take the law into his own hands because of institutional inadequacy, falls into the fatal sin of excessive violence. In the end he is killed by a more efficient law which he himself helped bring into existence.

"The Tin Badge," the source of *High Noon*, is a perfect illustration of the necessity for representation. The hero and his deputy, lying bloodily in the street, explain the story to the reader. This is the literal approach to fiction, and the fact that many sheriffs did keep their jobs in spite of public indifference and high mortality rates does not change the fact that "The Tin Badge" ends with a tacked-on moral. Perhaps the Western writer is faced not so much with the problem of giving broader significance to a local genre as with the problem of transliterating traditional American themes into artistic form.

History And Theory Of The Popular Western Novel

The Beginnings of Cowboy Fiction

Mody C. Boatright*

I

If the writer seeking a mass audience is to be successful, he must present his characters in relation to the beliefs and values that this audience holds. This does not mean that he must relate them to a consistent social philosophy. For the intellectual constructs of philosophers, historians, and other learned men become fragmented, broken into myths, symbols, and slogans, and reach the masses as a series of tenets and attitudes often inconsistent with each other. It is by appealing to these attitudes, which he may in fact subscribe to, that the writer makes his characters emotionally satisfying to his audience.

The nineteenth-century writer who wished to present the cowboy in a favorable light to a mass audience had to find some way to relate him to popular values. The first attempt to solve the problem relied on a series of beliefs derived, in part through the Romantic Movement, from a primitivistic social theory popular in Europe in parts of the seventeenth and eighteenth centuries. This philosophy held, in brief, that the earlier forms of social organization were superior to later forms. Thus, an agricultural society was better than an industrial society; a pastoral society was better than an agricultural society; and a savage society was best of all. Hence the noble savage.

The good life was a simple life, lived close to nature, in which all man's natural desires were satisfied. Nature itself, whether thought of as natural law or as natural inclination, was a sufficient guide to the good life. Hence there was no need for elaborate instruction in morals. Indeed, man-made moral systems, being largely sophistry and pedantic learning, more often obscured than enlightened. The simple life lived close to nature was conducive not only to virtue, honor, and happiness, but to physical health as well. Man was naturally endowed, too, with a feeling for beauty and defor-

**SWR*, 51 (1966), 11–28.

mity and needed no refinement to respond to the sublime—particularly to the sublimity of nature, which was superior to the sublimity of art.

Civilized man had fallen from his former primitive excellence, and his only hope for redemption was in a return to his early simplicity. For civilization in creating an economic surplus had brought about luxury, with its long train of attendant evils. Luxury had created expensive and artificial tastes and promoted greed manifested in land monopoly, rapine, and fraud. The increasing complexity of society had reduced the freedom of the individual, for freedom was conceived of as consisting in the absence of external restraint, not in the number of alternatives present. Luxury had also created an effete society, governed not by natural human relationships, but by convention, which tended to deprive men of their masculinity and women of their natural social role. The people of the western states should, therefore, be superior to the people of the eastern states.

Many of these ideas are to be found in the writings about the American cowboy. The student of popular culture will not be surprised to find them advocated and contradicted in the same work.

The earliest novel in English I have been able to find with a cattle country setting is William Bushnell's *The Hermit of the Colorado Hills*, published in 1864.[1] This book owes something to Lord Byron and something to Mrs. Radcliffe. The central character, suffering from disappointment in love and remorse for his crimes (his attempt to abduct the woman who had rejected him resulted in her death), becomes the hermit. "Years ago, girl," he says, "I turned my back on my home and swore never to befriend one of my people, even if dying at my door." He nevertheless befriends the girl (he knows by a ring on her finger that she is the daughter of the woman he loved), and thus restores his humanity.

The agents of evil that threaten the rancher are Indians (noble savages occur, but they are rare among the Comanche and Apache), who fear the Hermit, believing that he is a great medicine man in command of supernatural power. The cowboys, consistently called *herders*, play a subsidiary role in the plot, but they are warmly praised for their innocent nobility. They have responded to the ennobling influence of nature.

This chord is struck near the beginning of the story: "What a glorious dream of freedom on the Pampas! Where can the mind, heart, lungs—ay, and the very soul, so drink in a realizing sense of freedom—so full of the perfect expansion that is typical of what we call the infinite."

After a lyric description of the landscape covered with wild flowers, the author proceeds:

> There is no more certain proof to a thinking mind that our good mother Nature intended that the wilderness should be made a home for man—that it should yield bountiful stores of golden grain, and made to blossom like a rose, than the fact that she has created a race of hardy and dauntless men, who throwing aside the trammels of civilized life, and scorning luxuries, boldly compete for the honor of primitive pioneership.

He singles out for special praise Daniel Boone, "nearly forgotten, who planted for the wealth-seekers who followed him to reap."

> Among these hardy and dauntless men are the herdsmen. They are the very picture of health, muscular beasts, daring and graceful as they dash headlong among their unbroken herds. Untrained in schools of fashionable etiquette and effiminacy, uncursed with luxury, conditioned and educated to animal hardships, they get, being with their beasts, truer hearts and a more perfect sense of honor, than many who quibble all a while. . . . There is no half way with the herdsman. Blood alone can pay for blood. Generous to a fault, daring even to rashness, tender hearted even to tears, but stern as death itself, he has made his mark upon the histronic [*sic*] pages of the south-western border, and written his name on the battle fields of Texas and Mexico.

In the use of primitivistic motifs in the interpretation of Western American life, Bushnell was following a long established tradition. His originality consisted in the application of these motifs to the cowboy. In making this application he established a lasting precedent, for in the decades that followed, the conventional *persona* of nature's nobleman would become a man in boots and chaps, armed with a six-shooter and mounted on a western pony.

Bushnell, however, had in this respect no immediate successors. Joseph E. Badger, Jr., a prolific writer for Beadle and Adams, turned to the cattle country in 1879, and in 1884 published his best work on this theme. *The Prairie Ranch; or, the Young Cattle Herders* is essentially a ranch country idyl. As a means of conveying to young eastern readers some idea of how ranching was carried on, Badger has two brothers, Ross and Arthur Duncan, spend the fall and winter on a ranch with their cousin, Walter Harvey, whose mother has died, leaving no white woman in the house.

It is a pleasant visit during which the boys are introduced to the ranch buildings and equipment; witness horsebreaking by an expert Mexican rider named Pedillo; take part in a roundup; witness marking and branding; see the mavericks peacefully prorated among the ranchmen (except one five-year-old bull, whose ownership is determined by a roping contest); go on an antelope hunt; camp out on a fishing trip and are serenaded by coyotes, which, Walter assures the tenderfeet, are about as dangerous as so many rats; go with a herd up the trail, witnessing a stampede on the way; and arrive safely at River Bend, Kansas, where one of the cowboys drinks too much, where Pedillo loses his money at monte, and where the herd is sold for eight thousand dollars in cash.

At one place Badger introduces an incident to satirize wild-west fiction, and since he was one of the most active producers of this fiction, had a predilection for highly complicated, melodramatic plots, and was soon to perpetrate such titles as *Solomn Saul, the Sad Man from San Saba; Big Bandy, the Brigader of Brimstone Butte;* and *Daddy Dead-Eye, the Despot of Dew Drop*, he exhibits a capacity for self-ridicule I have not found among his peers. When Walter comes into camp at night to find his cousins waiting with drawn six-shooters, he says: "I expected to find you hid under your blankets, bewailing the unlucky stars that led you out here to fall untimely victims of the Horrible Howler of the Pathless Plains. I'm glad to see you're better grit."

In *The Prairie Ranch* Badger makes one concession to the tradition of violence. In River Bend the cowboy who drank too much talks indiscreetly about the money Walter is carrying home. This is reported to Walter, and when he and his men are overtaken on the road by a stranger who says he wishes to travel back to Texas with them, they disarm him and hold him under arrest, all of which he takes in perfect good humor. Later they are attacked by four men. They release the stranger, who joins in fighting the attackers, three of whom are killed and the other wounded. They are real bandits. The stranger is eventually revealed as the brother of Walter's father. He had got wind of the planned robbery and had overtaken the cowboys to forestall it. Then, too, he wanted to visit his brother, whom he had not seen in a long time.

These Kansas bandits are the only malefactors in the story. The cowboys are amiable and faithful to their employers. The peaceful division of the mavericks has been mentioned. There is no conflict over grass or water. No Indians disturb the tranquillity of the region. No Mexican bandits attempt to raid the livestock or carry off the women. No rustlers infest the range. The total impression is that of a peaceful community such as the primitivists imagined to exist in pristine times when there was plenty of land and men dwelt in peaceful and harmonious simplicity, uncorrupted by luxury. But in spite of this idyllic quality, we have in *The Prairie Ranch* the most realistic fictional depiction of life in the cattle country before *The Log of a Cowboy*.

Physical health was not the least of the virtues attributed to primitive living. Cowboys of the subliterature of the nineteenth century are never sick, and they recover from their wounds with surprising rapidity. Primitivist thought on this subject received sanction from the medical profession when hundreds of patients, especially those suffering from respiratory diseases, were advised to go West. Examples include Sidney Lanier, Frederick Remington, Owen Wister, and Sidney Porter. The health-seeker became a stock character in Western fiction. His illness might be merely a device to account for his presence in the West, but more often than not he recovered his health and thus testified to the therapeutic qualities of the western climate and way of life.

This is the theme of Edward S. Ellis in *Across Texas* (1894). Herbert Watrous, son of a wealthy New Yorker, suffering from symptoms of "consumption," is advised by his physician to forego entrance to Yale for a year and travel for his health. After considering southern Europe or an ocean voyage, the doctor advises a trip through the American Southwest. Young Watrous is to be accompanied by his friend Nick Ribsam (who in a previous work had hunted moose with him in Maine).

They come to San Antonio by train, where they present their letter of credit to a banker, Mr. Lord, who, coincidentally, is considering the purchase of some ranch property in New Mexico and is preparing to send two of his trusted cowboys to inspect it.

The narrative is mainly concerned with the journey, including adventures with horse thieves and Apaches. Certain chapters, particularly those on Austin and San Antonio, read much like a travelogue. Along the way the men explain their work, and the author intersperses comments in praise of the cowboys. "Men trained in the profession of cowboy think and act quickly." They "were governed by that devotion which belongs to chivalry. There was not one who would not have protected the youth with his life."

But the reader is not permitted to forget the purpose of the journey. The boys had barely reached San Antonio when they were told by Mr. Lord that the city was "a resort for invalids threatened with or suffering from pulmonary weakness, who find the mild equitable climate very helpful. He had known cases in which it had wrought a complete cure." Herbert "showed an improvement within twenty-four hours after arrival in the city of the Alamo."

Climate, however, was only one factor in Herbert's recovery.

> You [the reader] will remember the real cause of Herbert Watrous' journey across Texas, which was to regain his health that was seriously threatened by his bad habits and rapid growth. While he received vast benefit from breathing the pure air of the South-west, it was his forced march, as it may be called, to New Mexico that did the splendid work for him.
>
> The continuous exercise, the crystalline atmosphere, the deep refreshing sleep, the abstention from tobacco [this is the first mention of tobacco, and the only bad habit apparent in the book is studiousness], nourishing food (which, though only partially cooked and eaten at long intervals, was the best diet he could have obtained), in short the "roughing it," in the truest sense, was the "elixir of life," and wrought a change in the young man which, could his parents have witnessed, they would have pronounced marvelous.

II

The Prairie Ranch and *Across Texas* were intended for juvenile readers. In both, events are reported as witnessed by boys of about eighteen years. In neither is there a hero in the popular sense of the word. Before the cowboy could be made the kind of hero the readers of dime novels and popular weeklies had come to expect, he must be given the major role and allowed to engage in activities other than his routine duties as cowhand. It did not require unusual originality to substitute the fighting cowboy for the fighting scout—the most popular Wild West hero of the seventies and eighties. But even this required caution. The writer was confronted by the same problem that had puzzled Cooper and his immediate successors in the treatment of the frontiersman. Assuming that a love interest involving a genteel heroine was essential to the novel, the problem was to provide her with a suitable lover. In the Leatherstocking tales Cooper had introduced a genteel hero and had left the frontiersman, whose role was what Scott called "the principal personage," as distinguished from the technical hero, in celibacy. In *The Pioneers* Cooper had introduced in Oliver Effinghan a gentleman wearing the garb of a hunter, and Edward S. Ellis in *Seth Jones* had made elaborate use of the same device. After many adventures and much mystification, the disguise, including dialect, is thrown off, and a gentleman worthy of the heroine stands revealed.[2]

Prentiss Ingraham in *Crimson Kate, the Girl Trailer; or, The Cowboy's Triumph,* 1881, apparently his first cowboy novel, had employed a modification of this strategy. The hero, Lester Langdon, is a college-educated gentleman from the East who has come to Texas to be a cowboy. He becomes expert in the skills required, but his language, manner, and bearing distinguished him from the native Texans. There is no secret about his background. Early in the story he rescues the General's daughter by killing one of her abductors and roping the horse upon which she is bound. This done, he introduces himself:

"My name is Lester Langdon, and I am but a poor cowboy."

"You are a brave one and a gentleman, be your calling what it may."

Later in the story Lester meets the Hermit, who is really Mabry Monkton, a cousin of the General. "Who are you?" asks Monkton.

"A cowboy."

"You are not one of the rough kind; Texas is not your home."

"No, my home is in the East, but I live in Texas now."

The complicated plot centers around the efforts of Lester's cousin, Loyd Landon, to do away with him and inherit the estate. He brings false charges of murder against Lester, whose commission in the army (granted as a reward for rescuing Lillian) is revoked, and he is sentenced to die. A remark by Monkton further reveals Ingraham's caution. "Don't call him cowboy, for he was regularly commissioned as an army officer and will be again as soon as the truth is known." After many incidents in which Lester proves adept in wearing disguises and speaking the language of those he impersonates, the truth is known and he inherits the estate.

He is not to marry Lillian, however, but Crimson Kate, introduced relatively late in the story. She is a white girl, ultimately revealed as the daughter of Loyd Langdon, long held in captivity by the Indians. She comes to the army camp to warn of an impending attack, led by a white renegade, who turns out to be Loyd. She is an expert trailer and readily leads the troops to the Indian encampment. After the Indians are defeated and Loyd is killed, Lester puts Kate under the tutelage of a governess, and, we are told in the conclusion, eventually marries her.

For the hero of his next cowboy novel Ingraham used a living person, as he had done frequently, particularly in his numerous fictional stories about Buffalo Bill. At the time *Crimson Kate* was published, William Levi Taylor was a cowboy on Cody's Nebraska ranch. He had been born at Fredericksburg, Texas, in 1857, the son of a Confederate cavalryman, who was killed in the war. "I was dependent upon myself," he said, "when ordinary children are still in the nursery." He went to work as a cowhand, and by the time he was fourteen years old was "able to ride and rope with some of the best of them."[3] Like many Texas cowboys of his generation, he followed the cattle industry north and was a cowboy on Cody's ranch when the Old Glory celebration took place in 1882. He was a member of Cody's Wild West from the beginning. His performances gained wide acclaim. He was billed as "Buck Taylor, King of the Cowboys," a cognomen which by 1887 would be an asset on the title page of a Beadle novel.

In *Buck Taylor, King of the Cowboys; or, The Raiders and the Rangers, A Story of the Wild and Thrilling Life of William L. Taylor*, a story parading as biography, there was no reason to conceal Taylor's background. He is presented as a native Texas cowboy with little formal schooling, whose language, however, is as grammatically correct as Ingraham's own. But as a working cowhand he could hardly have had the wild and thrilling adventures Ingraham's readers craved. He must leave the ranch, and for laudable reasons. "His uncle had hoped to keep him upon his large ranch, for Buck soon became noted as the best one of the cowboy herders; but the youth was anxious to get beyond the circle of a ranch's herd of cattle." Therefore at the age of eighteen he takes his "old fashioned rifle," calls his dog named Vermifuge, and mounting his scrawny horse named Snakeroot rides off toward the Rio Grande to enlist in McNally's [*sic*] Texas Rangers.

He is not long in demonstrating his prowess. The ridicule of a veteran Ranger, Sal Bradford, leads to a fistfight in which Buck is victorious, and they become fast friends. Buck wins a shooting match, rides an outlaw horse, and, to secure a better mount than Snakeroot, goes in search of a fine roan mustang that had eluded all efforts to capture him. Buck finds three Indians also looking for the roan. He waits until they have trapped him, then kills two Indians and wounds a third, whom he takes care of until he is able to travel and then sends him away. This is Mad Wolf, a noble savage, who later helps Buck escape from captivity. When Buck returns riding the stallion and bearing two scalps, he is welcomed by the Rangers as a peer.

In the course of the story Buck fights against Indians and Rafael's Raiders, a band of Mexican bandits, who have a spy in McNally's company. This man, really one Rodriguez, going under the name of Roddy Armstrong, thinking he has killed Buck (Buck had removed the bullets from Roddy's six-shooter) has him buried. Buck escapes from the shallow grave, and without food walks nearly two hundred miles to camp. This requires three days. Buck later fools a band of Indians by donning in succession five costumes and riding five different horses. Another example of his cleverness brings on the denouement. Rafael is known to watch the

Rangers through field glasses from his stronghold. Upon Buck's proposal, he and McNally stage a quarrel in pantomine; Buck draws and fires and McNally falls. Buck mounts and flees. Rafael attacks. He is met and many of his men are killed.

When Ingraham turned to Buck Taylor again in 1891 to produce five novels in rapid succession, he abandoned all condescension and made the series in effect a eulogy to the cowboy. Buck enters as an established hero. In *Buck Taylor, the Saddle King; or, The Lasso Rangers' League* (1891), he is described in these words:

> He was in person over six feet in height by several inches, with a slender form, but athletic, broad shoulders, and the very *beau ideal* of a Texas cowboy.
>
> He was dressed in somewhat gaudy attire, with a watch and chain, diamond pin in his scarf, representing a miniature spur, and upon the small finger of his hand was a ring, the design being a horseshoe of rubies.
>
> About his broad-brimmed dove-colored sombrero was circled a miniature lariat so that spur, horseshoe, and lasso designated his calling.
>
> In the belt were a handsome pair of revolvers and a bowie knife, while upon a hook on one side hung a lariat of the very finest manufacture.
>
> His face was one to remember when once seen, beardless, youthful, yet full of character and fearlessness, amounting to reckless daring.

In *The Cowboy Clan; or, The Tigress of Texas* (1891), Taylor and his men

> were proud to be called "Texas cowboys" and knew the country perfectly.
>
> They could follow a trail as well as an Indian, ride even better, throw a lasso unerringly and shoot straight to dead center every time.
>
> A reckless lot of men they were, light-hearted, entirely fearless, generous, noble in the treatment of a friend or fallen foe, and though feared by evil-doers and red-skins, they were admired and respected by the soldiers and the people of the settlements.

In *Buck Taylor, the Saddle King*, Buck admits

> that a great many wicked men have crept into the ranks of our cowboy bands; but there are plenty of them who are true as steel and honest as they can be. . . . We lead a wild life, get hard knocks, rough usage and our lives are in constant peril, and the settling of a difficulty is an appeal to revolver or knife; but after all we are not as black as we are painted.

Taylor and his men are attached to an army post near the Mexican border as "government herders." "I am," he explains, "chief of the cowboys for the Government herd of cattle, only I consented to do a little extra work, you see." This extra work, which is the sole concern of the novels, is pursuing and fighting bands of outlaws who steal and rob and abduct women. There is nothing to impugn the integrity or the efficiency of the army, but the implication is unmistakable that for the job to be done the cowboys are superior to the troopers. This superiority stems partly from their superior knowledge of the country, partly from their superior skill in the use of weapons, including their peculiar weapon, the lasso (it is the means by which Buck kills Tiger Tom), and partly from their greater resourcefulness. Taylor's cleverness matches his prowess. For instance, he is captured by two of the outlaw band. He convinces them that he has gone over to their side and offers them whiskey from a bottle he carried in his saddle bag. The whiskey is drugged and they are soon in his power.

He carried the liquor for just such emergencies, for he never drank, not even a mint julep. His relations with women are scrupulously honorable. He cannot fall in love, first, because even Prentiss Ingraham cannot take wide liberties with the marital facts of a well-known personality, and, second, because he must not marry, but must remain free for further adventures in the sequel.

Ingraham's women, although frequently requiring rescue from the villains who capture them, more often for ransom than for lust, combine the accomplishments of the East with the athleticism of the West. Valerie Tracy, or Trescott as her husband's name turns out to be, was an accomplished musician from a cultured New Orleans family. Indeed, her love of music was her undoing, for it was the fine singing voice of the villain that first attracted her. In *The Cowboy Clan* she plays the guitar and sings, one of her songs being "The Texan Cowboy's" song, probably Ingraham's own composition, only the refrain of which is given:

> Lie down now cattle, don't heed any rattle,
> But quietly rest until morn.
> For if you skeedaddle, we'll jump in the saddle
> And head you off, sure as you are born.[4]

The locally nurtured ranch girl is exemplified by Belle Hassan, described in *Buck Taylor, the Saddle King* as

> fearless as an Indian, and riding like one, a deadly shot with rifle, revolver, bow and arrow, and throwing a lasso unerringly. Belle Hassan was the admiration of all the bold spirits who knew her, and yet under her accomplished mother's tuition, she had become a good student, a devoted reader, a fair artist, and a musician of no mean pretensions, her voice being strangely pathetic and soft in tone.

But in spite of Belle's ability to ride and shoot, she, like many a girl in the Beadle novels, gets herself captured on different occasions by Indians and outlaws, thus providing the hero with opportunities to display his prowess.

Ingraham made no further use of Buck Taylor after 1893, when Taylor left Buffalo Bill's Wild West.[5] He wrote other cowboy novels, including *The Cowboy Clan in Cuba* (1897), in which the cowboys under the leadership of Charlie Chase rescue Lucita and Harry Agramonte from a firing squad. But the works here considered epitomize Ingraham's treatment of the cowboy as a hero. In *Crimson Kate*, 1883, the hero is an educated eastern gentleman who has gone West "a cowboy for to be." In

Buck Taylor, King of the Cowboys, purporting to be a biography, Taylor is described as a heroic character, who has attained on the cattle range the skills that made him McNally's leading Ranger, but he is commended for wanting to be more than a cowboy. It is more honorific to be a Texas Ranger. In the novels of 1891 Buck and his band are proud to be known as cowboys. Their status is above that of soldiers.

The cowboy warrior band appears in the novels of other writers, including Sam Hall (Buckskin Sam), who in *The Brazos Tigers; or, The Minute Men of Fort Belknap* (1882) inserts a defense of Texas cowboys:

> Many of them are now engaged in driving the immense herds of cattle and horses from Texas north, through the Indian Nation, to the great stock markets, and let me say that these so-called cowboys have been greatly traduced by the American press; for as a class, they are noble, brave, and fearless men, liberal to a fault, tender-hearted, and devoted to each other. In fact, few men can be found, who lead a roaming life in nature's garden, who will not divide their little all with anyone who is in need. Fewer still would desert a friend, or take advantage of an enemy.
>
> If, when they reach town, they are poisoned with "prussic acid and bug juice" until they become insane and use the weapons they are obliged to carry, too freely—more in sport than otherwise—it is the fault of the town that permits the sale of the vile poison, more than of the poor fellows, whose protracted privation of continuous watchfulness by day and night, naturally causes them to take advantage of a day's rest to have a free and easy jamboree.

But Hall's concern in the story is not with cowboys having a free and easy jamboree in town, but with them as a band of men fighting Indians and outlaws on the range.

III

The cowboy warrior band, while maintaining its identity, has, like Ingraham's cowboy herders and Hall's Minute Men of Fort Belknap, a quasi-military status and functions under a leader, who overshadows yet represents the group. The lone rider was to emerge in the works of William G. Patten, best known as the creator of Dick Merriwell. The cowboy knight errant is mobile in that he is not committed to a fixed residence and avoids personal involvement with the other characters in the story. As he rides about, he is always ready to take a hand in behalf of the abused and oppressed weak, male or female.

Patten did not create this character overnight, but foreshadowed him in Hustler Harry of *Hustler Harry, the Cowboy Sport; or, Daring Dan Shark's General Delivery,* apparently his first cowboy hero (1889). Harry Hanson, to give him his real name seldom used in the story, "drapped" down from High Notch into Cimarron "on the lookout for sport." He is not long in finding it. He enters a saloon (although he does not drink) and finds the local bully and badman, Hickory Bill, abusing a Negro. He promptly knocks him down and throws him out. The reader is not surprised, for Harry is described as

> a man at least six feet tall and "built from the ground up." Not a thickset, ox-like figure, but one which combined great strength with manly grace. . . . Every limb was rounded and muscular, yet was not overburdened or cumbersome . . . the square, full lower jaw denoted a determined, unswerving nature. His eyes were blue and filled with a half-mirthful yet wholly unfathomable light.

Hustler Harry glories in being a cowboy, declaring,

> "Fact is, if I war rollin' in yeller wealth, I never cu'd give up the range. Just one whiff of the trail, one beller from the hurd, one rattle of long horns set my blood to bilin' and seethin' like I was set fair onto er red-hot furnace an er nigger fireman shovin' in pitchpine an' rosin fer all he was worth."

His ebullience is manifest in frequent boasting reminiscent of the humor of the Old Southwest.

> "I'm er high old maverick fer fun, an' if ye'eve got anything of ther kind in this hyer burgh, u's just trot it out."
>
> "I'm Hustler Harry, ther Hard Nut to Crack from High Notch, an' I'm just a wild maverick on ther stampede w'en I gits ter goin'. If ary of you critters thinks he can put his brand onto me, just let him tackle ther job. I'm hyer ter' muse the congregation."
>
> "I'm Hustler Harry ther Hard Nut to Crack. Yer don't want to try any little tack-hammer on my hide. Bring out yer big sledges, an' git yer lives insured w'en yer tackle ther job."

With the help of Detective Daring Dan Shark, Harry rescues a kidnapped girl and brings the outlaws to justice, but he falls short of being the character at first represented. In the first place, he is not entirely disinterested, for he is accused of being a murderer and the leader of a band of outlaws and must clear his name. (The real villain is his double and half brother.) In the second place, he is not a real cowboy but another Seth Jones, and eventually drops his dialect and tells the girl he loves, "In fact, I tell you the truth when I say that I am a gentleman. In becoming my wife you will not have a common brainless husband. I have wealth to a limited extent. Most men would consider themselves fortunate if they possessed a fourth as much."

Whether the girl would have accepted him without this revelation is not clear, but she does accept him and thus makes him ineligible for further heroic roles.

Patten more nearly approached the cowboy knight in *Wild Vulcan the Lone Rider; or, the Rustlers of the Bad Lands. A Romance of Nebraska* (1890). The technical hero is a genuine cowboy, Paul Rickway, "one of those grand creations of the mountains and the plains, a young nobleman of nature." His rival in love goes under the name of Colonel

Delos Dangler, but is in reality Lyman Mesurado, a cattle rustler. The principal personage, to use Scott's term again, is Wild Vulcan,

> . . . a strange, gloomy appearing man of mystery, the friend of every honest person, the deadly foe of outlaws and hostile Indians. Involuntarily, with a feeling of awe, the cowboys shrank away from the man sitting so silently in their midst. They had heard strange tales of the prowess of the wild man whom the redskins called the Great Thunder. It was said that single-handed he had attacked and destroyed a dozen hostile redskins, by whom he was greatly feared.

The girl, Nida, has to be rescued more than once; first by Paul, who loses her when he is attacked by an Indian, with whom he grapples and rolls into the river and is presumed to have drowned; but frequently by Wild Vulcan, who can be depended upon to make his appearance at critical times. But since it is eventually revealed that the bogus colonel has murdered Vulcan's wife and stolen his daughter, the Lone Rider, like Hustler Harry, is less disinterested than at first appears.

In this respect he differs from Cowboy Chris, the hero of a half-dozen or more Half Dime novels Patten published under the pseudonym of William West Wilder from 1889 to 1899.

In *Cowboy Chris, the Desert Centaur; or Hawking, the Human Hawk. A Story of the Arid Plains* (1897), two men are riding across the plains. One is Reuben Randall, a man possibly in his fifties, dressed as a cowboy and wearing a "Stinson" hat. The other, Christopher Comstock, in his twenties, is a "square-shouldered, finely built man" who has "the appearance of being a perfect *man*, being one of those persons women regard with frank admiration." At a distance they see a man being chased by Apaches. The younger man says, "We must take a hand someway, old man! It is our duty to aid the weaker party . . .," to which the veteran replies. "I reckon it is our duty to send as many 'Paches as we kin to ther happy huntin' ground. We'll be doin' the kentry er mighty big favor. 'Paches an' rattlesnakes is just one and the same."

They take a hand and dispatch "several" Apaches, but they are chiefly occupied in rescuing Bessie Pike.

> "Hear me!" cried out Chris Comstock [when her abduction was discovered], placing his left hand over his heart and lifting his right hand toward heaven, "I solemnly swear never to know rest until I have solved the mystery of Little Bessie's fate and punished those who have harmed her, if she has been harmed."

He rescues her not once but twice and punishes those who have kidnapped her. He finds her father "rough and uncouth," but she seemed "refined as if she was the possessor of some education." He admits to himself that "she is a dear little creature for whose sake I would make any sacrifice, but that is no reason why I should desire to make her my wife. My wife! Ha! ha! ha! I will not marry for years, if ever. I am beginning to taste the sweets of a roving life, and I shall not settle down for years to come."

Besides, Bessie has a worthy lover in Conrad Vincent, whose failure to rescue her was not attributable to any fault of his own.

But Conrad and Bessie are not to marry until the end of the sequel, *Cowboy Chris, the Vengeance Volunteer; or, the Death Hunt Pards. A Romance of Arizona* (1898). Here she is kidnapped again, this time by a villain named Boone, who murders her father and hopes, by forcing Bessie to marry him, to acquire the estate. Boone disposed of, Chris attends the wedding as best man. He is left free to ride forth like a knight of the Round Table, rescuing other Bessies, but with this difference: women will play little part in his roving life except as they provide wrongs to be redressed. Cowboy Chris will have successors.

IV

By the end of the nineteenth century the cowboy had been admitted to the hierarchy of the heroes of the popular fiction of the American West. First introduced sympathetically as a supporting character to the technical hero and as a symbol of primal innocence, he advanced to the leadership of a warrior band (incidentally adding the lasso to the six-shooter and bowie knife as the conventional weapons of such bands), and in the nineties emerged as the knight of the mountains and plains, "whose glory was, redressing human wrong." In none of these roles, however, had he entirely superseded other western heroes. Numerically he was still overshadowed by the scout and the detective.

Nor was the cowboy a hero to all writers who made use of him as a fictional character. David Druid's Sam Strong, who appears in *Sam Strong, the Cowboy Detective; or, The Ranch Mystery* (1891), is not a cowboy at all, but a detective who brings Sikes Bowles and his cowboy band to justice. Of this band it is said, "For with one exception, all twelve men were cowboys, that lawless class of western plainsmen, to whom are chargeable so many deeds of crime and recklessness [that] are perpetrated daily." And Frederick Whittaker's cowboys are wild barbarians from wild and barbaric Texas. In *Parson Jim, King of the Cowboys; or, the Gentle Shepherd's Big Clean Out* (1882), when they reach town "crazy with excitement and drink . . . and firing all round them into the windows of the houses," the townspeople rush into hiding; that is, all except one, a young consumptive from Boston, who is beaten into insensibility for his presumption. The victim eventually recovers to become first a shepherd and then ranch foreman, in which capacity he shows the westerners how a cattle ranch ought to be run.

As Henry Nash Smith has suggested in *Virgin Land*, the cowboy hero was a son of Leatherstocking's, though considerably less garrulous than his forebear. The fiction in which he appeared followed well-established patterns, imitating that of earlier Wild West fiction, among other ways, by references to recent or contemporaneous events, such as border raids on the Rio Grande, trail driving from Texas, fence-cutting, and the Johnson County War in Montana. The action abounds in disguises; doubles, usually brothers or half brothers, are frequent; lost children and missing heirs are found and identified; secret hideouts—usually caves, but sometimes cabins in secluded canyons—are readily available. The plot is a culmination of a long train of events set in motion years before at another place. Except in the juveniles you may expect a woman to be kidnapped, sometimes by Indians but more often by a white man and his minions. His object may be marriage, prompted either by lust or by a desire to secure her property. It may be revenge. It may be to collect a ransom. The abductor is always guilty of other crimes, but he never beats or in any way physically abuses the woman. In my sampling I have found no instance of a rape and only one of seduction. (This is in Wilder's *Nobby Nat, the Tenderfoot Detective; or, the Girl Rancher's Rough Hustle* (1892), where the father of the victim is dead and she has no brother. Her Amazon sister forces a pistol-point marriage, but the girl, always delicate, pines away and dies, but not before the hero has made her a widow.) The final solution always involves violence, usually the death of the villain, though he may be permitted to escape to reappear in a sequel.

Certain taboos are almost universally observed. Good cowboys may enter saloons and take a hand in a poker game, but they never drink, even in a home where mint juleps are served. If they smoke they smoke a pipe or a cigar, never a cigarette. Even with all the kidnapping of women, there is extreme reticence about sex. Lovemaking is restrained. The hero may resort to the deceptions common in the detective story of the period. He may put on a wig and false beard and spy on the enemy; he can disable him with narcotics, and if he is in captivity he may disable or even kill his guard by any means possible; but under other circumstances he must not stab in the back or shoot from ambush. His nobility of character is also reflected in his attitude toward his horse, a noble animal of great speed, strength, and endurance worthy of love. As Joseph E. Badger put it in *Laughing Leo: or, Spread Eagles Sam's Dandy Pard* (1887),

> Only one whose life has been passed for the greater part in the saddle can even begin to appreciate the intense love which one comes to feel for a good horse. To such a man, provided he is a *man*, not simply a brute with half the complement of legs, his horse becomes like a wife and children, so far as love and affection are concerned.

Notes

1. This and several other novels discussed in this essay were brought to my attention by Warren French, "The Cowboy in the Dime Novel," *Texas Studies in English*, 30 (1951), 219–34.

2. For a penetrating discussion of this problem, see Henry Nash Smith, *Virgin Land: The American West as Symbol and Myth* (Cambridge: Harvard Univ. Press, 1950), pp. 59 ff.

3. Don Russell, *The Lives and Legends of Buffalo Bill* (Norman: Univ. of Oklahoma Press, 1960), p. 306.

4. In *Buck Taylor the Comanche Captive; or, Buckskin Sam to the Rescue*, Ingraham writes of the "cattle and horses . . . asleep upon the prairie or grazing upon the rich grass, while about them the cowboy sentinels rode to keep them from straying, either whistling or singing to soothe the dumb brutes"; and in *Buck Taylor, the Saddle King*, Taylor's men sing "The Cowboy Farewell" at the burial of their slain comrades, but aside from those quoted, no words for the cowboy songs are given.

5. Walsh and Salsbury, *The Making of Buffalo Bill*, pp. 254–56.

Origins of the Western

Richard W. Etulain*

In the first quarter of the present century, a new American literary type—the Western[1]—arose. Because until recently historians and literary critics have paid scant attention to popular literature, the Western has received little notice. Those who have chosen to discuss this popular genre have usually dismissed it as literary trash or as a species of sub-literature.[2] This being the case, no one has undertaken a study of the origins of the Western. This paper is a very brief and tentative treatment of the rise of the Western and why it arose when it did.

Some students of popular culture contend that the roots of the Western can be traced back to Homer and other writers of the epic. Others suggest that it owes most of its ingredients to medieval romances and morality plays. And still others argue that Sir Walter Scott, Robert Louis Stevenson, and other writers of historical adventure influenced the shape and content of the Western more than any other source. Each of these arguments has its validity, but the major reasons for the rise of the Western are found in more recent trends in American cultural history. More than anything else the genre owes its appearance to the combined influence of a number of occurrences in the years surrounding 1900. Each of these events or cultural changes may have been largely independent of the rest, but all shared in giving rise to an indigenous literary type.[3]

The appearance of a new hero in American literature—the cowboy—offered distinctive experiences for the author of the Western to portray. As Warren French and Mody Boatwright have pointed out, the cowboy always appeared earlier in a few dime novels but nearly always as a minor figure and frequently in an ungallant role. By 1890, however, the cowboy was beginning to move to the forefront as a western fictional hero. Commencing with the writings of Owen Wister he received a new emphasis. This newly-refurbished hero aided greatly the rise of the Western.[4]

Also, about 1900 there was a revival of interest in the historical novel—one of three such periods in American literary history. Americans

* *JPC*, 6 (1972), 12–17. © 1972 by *The Journal of Popular Culture*. Reprinted by permission of *The Journal of Popular Culture*.

turned to historical fiction as one possible formula for recapturing a past that they were reluctant to lose. Because the Western was to be historical or pseudo-historical, it benefitted from the revival of interest in the historical novel.[5]

Moreover, there was an increased interest in the West during the last two decades of the nineteenth century. A series of critical economic problems brought to mind a sobering truth: the West was filling up; its wide open spaces would soon be gone. Tourists flocked west, and a number published their reactions to the region in such influential eastern magazines as *Outlook*, *Harper's*, *Scribner's*, and *Atlantic*. These same periodicals took more western fiction in the 1880's, and the western pieces became so popular by the middle 1890's that Henry Alden, an editor of *Harper's Monthly*, did his best to keep all of Owen Wister's work in his magazine. Several editors wanted Wister's fiction, and only higher prices kept him in the *Harper's* fold.[6]

The era from 1890 to 1910 has frequently been termed "the strenuous age." The fiction of Jack London, Harold Bell Wright, Stewart Edward White, Rex Beach, and other writings of the rough, virile, and out-of-doors type speak for the age. It was the period of the Spanish American War generation, of Teddy Roosevelt, of militant Anglo-Saxonism. This spirit is found in the Western, particularly in its portrayal of the gallant hero who is always eager to combat any foe, regardless of the odds.

By the early 1890's interest in the dime novel was diminishing. Shortly after its inception during the Civil War, this popular type had turned to the West for several of its heroes—Buffalo Bill, Deadeye Dick, Old Scout, and other frontier worthies. As the dime novel began to disappear, the popularity of its hero fell rapidly. Readers undoubtedly were dissatisfied with a continuous line of heroes who fought off twenty Indians and rescued the heroine, even with one arm badly wounded. They wanted a gallant and strong protagonist but one that was, nonetheless, believable. Eventually, the hero of the Western satisfied both of these desires.[7]

The Western also continued an American melodramatic tradition that had appeared earlier in such sources as the writings of James Fenimore Cooper, the dime novel, and the works of the sentimental novelists. In the post-Civil War period western literature became a recognizable current in the stream of melodrama. The work of Bret Harte, the dime novelists, and the story paper writers firmly established the melodramatic tradition in the literature of the West. As one study of the western periodical literature of the late nineteenth century points out, western writers increasingly utilized vague western settings and general descriptions. And a nostalgic tone crept into western literature. It was as if those who had lived through the previous years were, by 1890 and afterward, looking back and trying to recapture some of their past glory.[8]

Finally, the most important reason for the rise of the Western is the most difficult to describe with precision. This factor is what historian

Carl Becker calls the "climate of opinion" of an era. In this case, it is the predominant mentality of the progressive period in American history.

Several interpreters have described the Progressive Era as a watershed period in the American mind. From the 1890's until World War I a new urban industrial thrust in American society challenged the older mentality of a rural, agricultural America. For Americans who became Progressives, or who shared the moods and feelings of the Progressives, this conflict between the old and the new was a traumatic experience that was not easily resolved.

Many Progressives were forward-looking. Like Theodore Roosevelt, they accepted the new urban-industrial force and advocated a federal government strong enough to deal with the powerful forces that the cities and industrial capitalists had unleashed. These New Nationalists, as they were called, were optimistic reformers and called for strong, new leadership to deal with recent problems.

Another strain of the progressive mind that owed much to Populism is evident in the early ideas of Woodrow Wilson. He too thought that the rise of an urban-industrial America necessitated changes in the forms of government and society. But Wilson and his followers thought the necessary reform was that of breaking up large corporations and of returning to a pre-industrial America, of recapturing Jefferson's agrarian dream. If these advocates of New Freedom allowed themselves to do so, they easily slipped into a nostalgic longing for pre-Rockefeller, Carnegie, and Vanderbilt days.

The same nostalgia that was apparent among proponents of New Freedom was also evident among followers of New Nationalism. In several ways Roosevelt stands as a Janus figure: the venturesome technocrat and yet the advocate of individualism, the product of an eastern-Harvard gentility and yet the westerner and Rough Rider. Other Americans of the era shared Roosevelt's feelings: the desire to hold on to the fruits of industrialism without losing, at the same time, individual freedom. For these persons, the American West was the last frontier of freedom and individualism, and it had to be preserved as a sacred bulwark against profane industrialism.

And thus the West as a physical and spiritual frontier was an important symbol for Americans during the Progressive Era. To lose it or the idyllic existence that it represented was to lose part of their past and to bargain away their future. It is not difficult to perceive how this psychological necessity encouraged authors to devote more attention to the West in their writings. The need and mood were apparent, and writers who were a part of this identity crisis—or at least sensed it—could assure themselves a larger audience if they portrayed the West romantically. So the conflict between industrial and agricultural America and the resultant nostalgia for the past were large encouragements for the rise of the Western.[9]

These trends were John the Baptists in preparing the way for the Western. Such writers as Owen Wister, Zane Grey, and Frederick Faust (Max Brand), sometimes working within the limits of these trends and sometimes pressured into new directions by them, did much to establish the dimensions of the Western. Wister, for example, utilized the new cowboy hero and the Wyoming past and blended them with the necessary ingredients of adventure fiction—love, action, and good versus evil—to produce the first Western in *The Virginian* (1902). He was, in short, the synthesizer of the elements that make up the Western. Following the pattern that Wister introduced, Grey and Brand, though men of lesser writing talents, turned out dozens of Westerns by the end of the 1920's. The roots of the Western, then, were nourished by cultural and intellectual currents that rippled through American experience between the end of the nineteenth century and the Depression.

Roderick Nash, who examines this era's need for wilderness symbols, expresses as well as anyone the cultural-intellectual matrix that helped spawn the Western. He says:

> America was ripe for the widespread appeal of the uncivilized. The cult had several facets. In the first place, there was a growing tendency to associate wilderness with America's frontier and pioneer past that was believed responsible for many unique and desirable national characteristics. Wilderness also acquired importance as a source of virility, toughness, and savagery—qualities that defined fitness in Darwinian terms. Finally, an increasing number of Americans invested wild places with aesthetic and ethical values, emphasizing the opportunity they afforded for contemplation and worship.[10]

What Nash points out—and this is a point that students of American popular culture must keep in mind—is that the origins of a new popular idea or genre are usually tied to specific occurrences in the mind and experience of the era that produces them. So it was with the beginnings of the Western.

Notes

1. I use the term *Western* in a narrower sense than most do who invoke the term. By a *Western*, I mean a novel about the West that follows a recognizable formula—most often that of action, romance, and stock characters. Thus, most of the novels of Zane Grey, Max Brand, Ernest Haycox, and Luke Short are Westerns; but the works of western writers like Willa Cather, John Steinbeck, and Walter Van Tilburg Clark are not.

2. For an example of this negative attitude: "It has been the fate of the American West to beget stereotypes that belong to pseudo art before it has yielded up the individual types that belong to art proper." Robert B. Heilman, "The Western Theme: Exploiters and Explorers," *PR*, 28 (1961), 286.

3. Four books have been especially helpful for the remarks in this paragraph and the paragraphs that follow: Henry Nash Smith, *Virgin Land: The American West as Symbol and Myth* (1950; rpt. New York: Vintage Books, 1957), pp. 88–137; E. Douglas Branch, *The Cowboy and His Interpreters* (1926; rpt. New York: Cooper Square, 1960), pp. 180–270; Joe B. Frantz and Julian E. Choate, *The American Cowboy: Myth and Reality* (1955; rpt. Lon-

don: Thames and Hudson, 1956), pp. 140–79; and G. Edward White, *The Eastern Establishment and the Western Experience: The West of Frederic Remington, Theodore Roosevelt, and Owen Wister* (New Haven: Yale Univ. Press, 1968), especially pp. 31–51. Since this essay was first written, Russell B. Nye's superb *The Unembarrassed Muse: The Popular Arts in America* (New York: Dial Press, 1970) has appeared. The section in his book dealing with the rise of the Western agrees with several of my contentions and adds other helpful information on the nineteenth-century backgrounds of the Western. See pp. 280–304.

4. Warren French, "The Cowboy in the Dime Novel," *Texas Studies in English*, 30 (1951), 219–34; Mody C. Boatright, "The Beginnings of Cowboy Fiction," *SWR*, 51(1966), 11–28.

5. Willard Thorp, *American Writing in the Twentieth Century* (Cambridge: Harvard Univ. Press, 1960), pp. 1–11; Ernest E. Leisy, *The American Historical Novel* (Norman: Univ. of Oklahoma Press, 1950), pp. 9–17.

6. Earl Pomeroy, *In Search of the Golden West: The Tourist in Western America* (New York: Alfred A. Knopf, 1957), pp. 73–111; L. J. Shaul, "Treatment of the West in Selected Magazine Fiction, 1870–1910—An Annotated Bibliography," Thesis Univ. of Wyoming 1954, pp. 50–152. The Alden-Wister relationship and other details about readers' interests in western fiction published during the 1890's is exhibited in the Owen Wister Papers, Library of Congress.

7. Wallace Stegner, "Western Record and Romance," *Literary History of the United States*, ed. Robert E. Spiller *et al.* (New York: Macmillan, 1960), pp. 862–64, 872. For the influences of Buffalo Bill and his Wild West shows, see Don Russell, *The Lives and Legends of Buffalo Bill* (Norman: Univ. of Oklahoma Press, 1960); and Joseph Schwartz, "The Wild West Show: 'Everything Genuine,' " *JPC*, 3 (1970), 656–66.

8. Smith, pp. 88–137; Mary Noel, *Villains Galore* (New York: Macmillan, 1954), pp. 131–32, 149–59; Shaul, pp. 51–52.

9. The previous paragraphs are a product of several sources. The split between past and present that plagued many Progressives is abundantly documented in important books on this era by such writers as Richard Hofstadter, George Mowry, and Arthur Link. I am also indebted to W. H. Hutchinson for suggesting to me several years ago the close relationship between the rise of the Western and the traumas of the progressive period. More recently, this relationship is dealt with in White's *The Eastern Establishment and the Western Experience*; and in David Noble's several books on the Progressives, particularly in his latest book, *The Progressive Mind, 1890–1917* (Chicago: Rand McNally, 1970). Peter Schmitt adds another dimension in his stimulating monograph *Back to Nature: The Arcadian Myth in Urban America* (New York: Oxford Univ. Press, 1969). Finally Roderick Nash and John William Ward suggest that the clash between past and present was a pivotal tension in the twenties. See Nash's *The Nervous Generation: American Thought, 1917–1930* (Chicago: Rand McNally, 1970) and Ward's "The Meaning of Lindbergh's Flight," *AQ*, 10 (1958), 3–16.

10. Roderick Nash, *Wilderness and the American Mind* (New Haven: Yale Univ. Press, 1967), p. 145.

Prolegomena to the Western

John G. Cawelti*

Many of my generation doubtless remember bolting dinner and rushing to the radio to hear the opening bars of Rossini's *William Tell Overture* followed by the thundering hoofbeats of the great horse, Silver. Three times a week, year in and year out, the Lone Ranger rode the radio networks from Station WXYZ in Detroit. Those of us who were true addicts came to know every conceivable regularity and variation within the half-hour program format. To this day, though it has been some twenty years since I last heard the great cry "Hi-ho Silver," I can still remember the shape of the program. I believe I could state almost to a minute the time that elapsed between the opening and the first gunshot, a time that varied little from year to year. In fact, during the several years of my regular listening to the masked man's exploits, I can remember almost no variations in the basic pattern of the program. Everything was precisely worked out from the opening introduction to the last dying away of the Lone Ranger's voice as he, Silver, and Tonto rode away after bringing law and justice into the life of still another Western community. Even a change in commercial became a noticeable and almost disturbing event in this grand stylized parade from beginning, through middle, to end. As I recall my responses to this peculiar work of art, it seems perfectly clear that the compelling thing about it was not so much the particular content of any of the eipsodes—I have long since forgotten what happened on any particular program and doubt that I even paid much attention to it at the time—but the vigorous clarity and the dynamic but somehow reassuring regularity of the form itself.

The Lone Ranger no longer holds the fascination he once did, but he still interests me in a different way—as a cultural phemonenon of some significance. I am not alone in this, for the scholarly investigation of popular forms like the Western has increased greatly in the last two decades from both humanistic and social scientific points of view. Unfortunately, however, this scholarly investigation has little of the vigorous clarity and precision which often characterizes its subject matter. To ex-

* *WAL*, 4 (1970), 259–71. © 1970 by the Western Literature Association. Reprinted by permission of the Western Literature Association.

amine such a collection as the anthology *Mass Culture*[1] is to realize not only that there is no meaningful consensus about an appropriate method of analysis for popular cultural forms, but that there is not even any significant agreement about what they are. Humanists tend to approach the problem from one point of view, social scientists from another. Nowhere do we find a single set of definitions and assumptions within which the diverse insights and methods of the scholars who deal with popular culture can be meaningfully related to each other.

It is my opinion that these difficulties arise directly from a failure to treat popular cultural forms seriously as what they most obviously are: artistic constructions primarily created and used for aesthetic purposes. In this paper, I wish to explore some of the implications of this proposition. I will begin with a general critique of current approaches to the study of popular forms. Then, confining myself largely to the particular case of the Western, I will try to suggest how we might develop a useful method of analysis. Finally, I will discuss the way on which such an analysis can lead to a fruitful procedure for analyzing the cultural significance of popular forms.

Two assumptions about the character of popular culture have been largely responsible for our failure to develop a coherent conceptual system, agreed on by historians, humanists, and social scientists, for the analysis of popular culture. These are (1) that popular culture is not only qualitatively, but generically different from "serious" culture and that, therefore (2) a work of popular culture should be treated as something other than a work of art; that it must be primarily analyzed as a collection of social themes, a hidden ("latent") work of political rhetoric, a concealed bit of psychoanalysis, or an unconscious religious ritual. Let us examine these assumptions more thoroughly.

1. In the first flush of enthusiasm over the great nineteenth century developments in sociology and naturalistic philosophy, many students of literature and art began to interpret all works in terms of some principle of social determinism.[2] This procedure reached its nadir in the pedantic Marxist criticism of the 1930's, when critics reduced great writers like Henry James to object-lessons of bourgeois decadence and applauded the self-conscious proletarianism of such now-forgotten trivia as Clara Weatherwax's *Marching, Marching.*[3] Practiced by men of broad knowledge and love of the arts the social approach to literature was a liberating force which helped rescue the arts from the doldrums of Germanic scholarship and the formalistic didacticism of Victorian gentility.[4] However, the method of direct correlation between sociological reality and aesthetic expression never established itself as a permanently fruitful basis for artistic analysis. Even in the heyday of the social approach to literature and the visual arts, music was always the odd man out. If the principle of sociological determinants of aesthetic expression was valid, music should have been no different from the other arts, yet it was always

evident in this case that a difference in the form and medium of expression vitally affected the method of analysis. In the last two decades, even sociologically oriented students of the arts have reemphasized the independent status of aesthetic expression as a mode of human experience.[5] Though a kind of popular sociologizing and psychoanalyzing persists in the mass media, few serious critics would think of drawing a direct causal connection between some specific social condition or ideology and a novel by Henry James or a painting by Picasso.

However, the tendency toward a simplistic cultural, sociological or psychological reductionism persists unabated in the analysis of such popular cultural forms as the Western because it is easy to assume that the greater simplicity and popularity of such forms reflects a generic difference between the popular work and the more complex serious one. But is a television western really different in kind from any other work of art? Indeed, it is perfectly obvious that the commercial and organizational circumstances under which a television western is produced establish different aesthetic rules and limitations from those encountered by the isolated poet in his garret, or his university office, but why should this lead us to assume that the Western is not primarily an artistic construction similar in nature if not in quality or complexity to a play by Shakespeare or a novel by James Joyce. And if it is an artistic construction, how will we ever arrive at an understanding of its cultural significance by treating it as something else?

2. The consequence of assuming that the popular work is generically different from the serious one is that we must then make it into something other than a work of art. Here we inevitably start riding our own special hobby horses. The theologian sees the Western as a religious ritual, the sociologist as a skirmish in the class struggle, or a hidden bit of political rhetoric, the humanist as a decadent offshoot of some form of traditional culture, the psychologist as a maneuver of the psyche, the anthropologist as a contemporary trope of some primitive myth. We are confronted with an embarrassing wealth of mutually exclusive versions with no way of bringing them together into a single, coherent analysis.

II

An essay on the Western by Mr. Peter Homans suggests a way of resolving some of these difficulties, though, in the end, it too falls into the trap of reducing an artistic construction to a simplistic cultural explanation.[6] Mr. Homans approaches the Western by attempting to understand it as a unified construction before he tries to determine its cultural significance. His method, therefore, involves three main steps: (1) isolation of the characteristic elements—setting, characters, events, themes—of the Western; (2) analysis of the characteristic way in which the Western organizes these elements into an ordered pattern or plot; (3)

determination of the cultural significance of this pattern. Using this approach, Mr. Homans concludes that the basic pattern of the Western is a plot "in which evil appears as a series of temptations to be resisted by the hero—most of which he succeeds in avoiding through inner control. When faced with the embodiment of these temptations, his mode of control changes, and he destroys the threat. But the story is so structured that the responsibility for this act falls upon the adversary, permitting the hero to destroy while appearing to save."[7] This pattern, Mr. Homans feels, is related to the cultural influence of "Puritanism" because it has the same emphasis on the necessity for inner control and repression of "the spontaneous, vital aspects of life."[8] The popularity of the Western, therefore, is to be attributed to its permitting a legitimated indulgence in violence while reasserting at the same time the "Puritan" norm of the primacy of will over feelings. Therefore, Mr. Homans believes there is a connection between the popularity of the Western and the cyclic outbursts of religious revivalism in the United States.

Despite a number of dubious historical generalizations—a much over-simplified definition of Puritanism and a questionable dating of religious revivals, for instance—it seems to me that Mr. Homans' basic approach is unacceptable. He recognizes that the Western is not simply a collection of characters or themes, but an artistic construction which results in "an ordered vision of character, event and detail."[9] Furthermore, Homans points out that the analyst must not only identify typical settings, characters and events, but discover and state their relationship to each other in terms of some "basic organizing and interpretive principle for the myth as a whole."[10] The analyst must, in other words, define the action or plot in Aristotle's sense of the term. A statement of what happens, or a list of characters will not suffice, for events and characters in any dramatic work cannot be correctly interpreted except in relation to the structure of the whole work. Many critics point with alarm to the events of violence which occur so frequently in contemporary popular cultural forms, but simply to count with horrified fascination the number of beatings, murders, eye-gougings, etc. which one can encounter in a day of television viewing will lead to little in the way of illumination. Imagine what a viewer-with-alarm might say about a television program which began with a murder and moved through suicides, poisonings, and suggestions of incest to end up with the screen littered with corpses. Pretty terrible, and doubtless indicative of the alienation, sadism, and nihilism which dominates contemporary popular culture, except that these events were not taken from a television Western, but from Shakespeare's *Hamlet*. The point, of course, is that in an artistic construction, events, even violent ones, take their meaning from the whole structure. There is quantitatively just as much violence in Shakespeare or in *Oedipus the King* (a nice bit of eye-gouging) as there is in *Gunsmoke*, but it does not mean the same thing. In the Western, violence is characteristically the hero's means of resolving the conflict generated by his adversary; in Shakespeare it is the means by which the hero destroys himself, or is destroyed; in the classic detective story, violence is the adversary's means of protection and the hero's clue. In each instance, violence cannot be understood simply as violence, for its meaning depends on the place it plays in the overall structure of the action.

Thus, the first step in the cultural analysis of any artistic construction must be the definition of its elements and their relations. In the case of a narrative or dramatic construction like the Western, the elements are characters, events, settings, themes or ideas, and language, and the pattern is that of a plot or action in the sense of a unified chain of events growing out of the motives and ideas of a group of characters and having a definable beginning, middle and end.

Social scientists may well object at this point that the method of analysis I propose is essentially a humanistic approach and is therefore hopelessly subjective and unscientific, for everyone knows that humanists are continually quarreling over the interpretation of the works of art with which they deal. It is true that to isolate and quantify the elements of a pattern is apparently a more scientific procedure than the attempt to define their complex relationships to one another. But, as I have suggested, such a procedure is so false to the nature of artistic constructions that it is about as scientific as it would be to think one had analyzed an election by counting the number of polling places. Nor is the kind of plot analysis I have suggested as subjective as it seems, for there is the direct empirical test of whether the analyst's model of the plot actually fits the work itself, or, to put it another way, whether the suggested organizing principles actually account for the various elements in the work. A good plot model should provide a basis for explaining why each event and character is present in the work and why these events and characters are placed in the setting they occupy. If some element remains unexplained, it is clear that the organizing principles have not been adequately stated.

III

Mr. Homans' careful discussion of a typical Western plot seems to me an excellent proof that such an analysis can be carried on carefully and objectively. Unfortunately in the case of Mr. Homans' analysis, a confusion between a typical Western plot and *the* Western as a popular form leads to a breakdown in his methodology and finally to an unwarrantedly simplistic conclusion. The reason for this is that there is an important difference from a methodological point of view between *the* Western and say, a novel by Henry James. The latter is a unique construction shaped by a highly individual artist, while the former is a general type with many different particular versions. In studying the cultural significance of a work by Henry James we are dealing with the vision and creative power of a unique individual. In other words, a novel by James is, because of its uniqueness, a type in itself. However, in analyzing a popular form like the Western, we are *not* primarily concerned with an individual work, such as a single episode of *Gunsmoke* or a particular novel by Zane Grey, but with the cultural significance of the Western as a type of artistic construction. This is simply because the circumstances in which a Western is produced and consumed do not encourage the creation of unique individual works of art, but lead to the production of particular realizations of a conventional formula. Therefore the culturally significant phenomenon is not the individual work, but the formula or recipe by which more or less anonymous producers turn out individual novels or films. The individual works are ephemeral, but the formula lingers on, evolving and changing with the times, yet still basically recognizable. Therefore, a popular form, like the Western, may encompass a number of standard plots. Indeed, one important reason for the continued use of a formula is its very ability to change and develop in response to the changing interests of audiences. A form which cannot be adapted like this will tend to disappear. One good illustration of this is the immensely popular nineteenth century form of the moralistic, sentimental novel of seduction which grew out of Richardson's *Pamela.* In the twentieth century the cultural patterns which made this form of narrative meaningful and exciting have changed too much for the form to adapt to them. Other popular formulas, like the Western and the detective story, have thus far proved more adaptable to changing cultural needs.

The trouble with Homans' analysis is that he takes one typical plot for *the* Western. There are many Westerns of the type Homans describes in which an outsider comes into a community, is tempted by evil, overcomes the temptation, destroys the evil and leaves again. On the other hand, there are a good many Westerns in which the central action is the initiation of the hero into the world of men—as in stories of the dude-become-hero variety—or in which the plot hinges on the resolution through violence of a conflict between love and social prejudice—as in Owen Wister's classic *The Virginian.* What we need are plot analyses comparable to those Homans has given us of the several standard Western plots. From such analyses we shall be able to discern more clearly than before the general outlines of the form by discovering those patterns which run through all the types of Western plot. In addition, these plot models would certainly tell us a great deal about the changing significance of the Western, for I have no doubt that, if we were able to classify the types of Western plots, we would find that certain plots have been particularly popular at different times. Being able to trace changes within the form should enable us to discover many important things about changes in the culture which produced it, and there is no better way of defining these changes than through the comparison of plots.

But what of the form itself? What is *the* Western and how can it be objectively defined in such a way that we can relate it to the culture or cultures in which it flourishes? In a sense, *the* Western as a form is simply the sum of the various plots which creators of Westerns have used. Thus, as I have suggested, one way of defining the form is by generalization from careful analyses of the various types of Westerns which have been created. Yet, *the* Western also seems to be something more or at least something different from any or all particular Westerns. Different as they are in characters, events, and even settings, we have no difficulty in recognizing a fundamental similarity between *The Virginian* and *Gunsmoke*. Furthermore, it seems reasonable to predict that if the Western retains its popularity, new versions different in many respects from those known before, yet still recognizable as Westerns, will be developed. It would seem, therefore, that *the* Western is not primarily a set of characters, events and settings, but a set of rules or formulas for shaping many different kinds of material into a certain pattern of experience. If this is correct, a meaningful definition of *the* Western must ultimately take the form of stating, as best we can, a set of rules for the construction of an imaginary world characterized by a certain kind of experience. This fictional world must resemble the world we know at enough points to justify our temporarily accepting it as the real thing. At the same time, however, the world of the formula must have a satisfying clarity and certainty as well as a kind of excitement, suspense, and resolution which remove us from the ordinary world and give us a momentary sense of release from its ambiguities and anxieties. In many ways, it seems to me, the fictional universe of such popular formulas as the Western, the detective story, and the secret agent adventure, resembles the world of a game with its clear opposing sides, restricted patterns of action, heightened suspense and certain resolution in victory and defeat. Perhaps this is why the great spectator sports and the major formula stories form the staples of popular entertainment.

If we follow through the game world analogy, I think we can delineate three central characteristics which most popular formulas must meet:

1) a game must have clearly opposing players—usually in the large spectator sports, two sides. These form basic moral reference points to which the viewer or participant relates with clearly positive or negative feelings. Similarly in most clearly differentiated popular formulas we have sides: a hero or group of good people and a villain or band of evildoers. The relations between these sides dominate the action. 2) A game has a set of rules indicating which actions are legitimate and which are not; only certain moves can take place and they must happen in a certain order and move toward a particular result. Analogously, a formula story has a particular pattern of expectations. Certain situations occur and others are definitely excluded by the rules. For example, in the detective story the criminal

must be detected. To have a still unsolved crime at the end of the book is definitely out of bounds. In the case of the Western, one of the most important rules is that the hero cannot use violence without certain justifications. 3) Finally, a game takes place on a certain kind of board or field whose shape and markings indicate the significance of particular actions. The formula story also depends on a particular kind of setting, an abstracted social structure and landscape which give meaning to particular actions. In this way, the Western hero's relation to the town is analogous to the football player's relation to the line of scrimmage.

Let us now see how these three characteristics might help define the Western formula. First, since a game is basically determined by its board or field, so a popular formula tends to be initially characterized by its setting. Thus, the secret-agent story and the Western differ in that one takes place in a world dominated by the struggle of rival nations and is usually set in a contemporaneous time, while the other unravels itself in an imaginary game world where the fifty yard line is the frontier and the major points of social and geographical topography are an advancing civilization on one side and a savage wilderness on the other. Against this background, a three-sided game is played out. There is the good group of townspeople who stand for law, order, decency, and the whole complex of values associated with civilization; there are the villains who are characterized by their rejection or perversion of these values and by their closeness to the savagery and lawlessness of the surrounding wilderness; and finally, there is the hero whose part is basically that of the man in the middle. Unlike the townspeople the hero possesses or comes to possess the savage skills of violence and the lawless individualism of the villain group, but he is needed by and finally acts on the side of the good group of townspeople. The pattern of expectations which characterizes the Western is too complex to spell out in any detail here, but some of its main lines can be indicated. There must be a series of acts of violence to set the three-sided game in operation and to provoke and justify final destruction of the villain in such a way as to benefit the good group. Usually these acts are worked out in a sequence of chase and pursuit which can make use of the Western field of action and its particular form of movement, the horse, to the greatest extent. Because the crucial result of the game is not the hero's final fate, but the resolution of the conflict between the hero's alienation and his committment to the good group of townspeople Westerns end in many different ways. Sometimes the hero gets killed, sometimes he rides off into the desert, sometimes he marries the rancher's daughter and becomes a leading citizen. As I have already noted, I suspect that important differences in cultural attitude are indicated by changes in the kinds of plot which are the most popular ways of working out the Western formula at different times. It is no doubt significant that the great majority of Westerns in the first 3 decades of the twentieth century follow Wister's *The Virginian* in creating plots of romantic synthesis.

The typical Zane Grey story or pulp western of the twenties and thirties associated the hero's victory over the villain with his assimilation into the developing society usually by marrying the school teacher or the rancher's daughter. After World War II however, the most significant Westerns have dealt with the gunfighter. In the typical gunfighter story the hero's violence, though necessary to the defeat of evil, nonetheless disqualifies him for the civilized society which he is saving. Similarly, in this more recent type of Western, the good group of townspeople is usually presented in a far more ambiguous way, as if there were some question whether they merited the hero's sacrifice.

If we turn from the problem of defining the formula to the question of interpretation, we are now in a position to see why this job is so complex and cannot be reduced to a simple psychological or sociological function as for example in the kind of explanation which states that the Western is "a puritan morality tale in which the savior-hero redeems the community from the temptations of the devil" or such a typical psychoanalytic explanation as "the cowboy myth in its form of manifest denial of the female or mother figure represents the intense childhood desire for her and the fears attending these desires, namely that gratifying these wishes carries with it the implication that she is weak and powerless in the face of father." Not that either of these statements is incorrect. In fact, I am inclined to believe that both of them, along with twenty other such statements I could quote, are right, but only partly so. The Western like any work of art has many different kinds and levels of meaning. If it did not have a complexity of meanings it could not continue to appeal to so many different groups of people over such a considerable period of time. The real problem is how these levels of meaning are connected with each other. If we can arrive at a better understanding of how popular artistic formulas select and integrate a complex of cultural and psychological meanings into an imaginary world, we will have a better understanding of these popular types than if we look for a single sociological or psychological key. Moreover, I think that seeing how popular formulas synthesize and give pattern to many different themes will give us insight into the way in which our culture organizes and unifies diverse values. For example, the Western certainly addresses itself to the problem of individual spontaneity and freedom in relation to social responsibility and discipline, to the opposition between institutionally defined law and the individual's personal sense of morality and justice, and to the relation between nature and society. The dramatization of these conflicts is one of the significances of the Western field of action and the three-sided game described above. If we consider how the Western articulates these values, certain interesting constellations are revealed. First, there is the assumption that law and individual morality, society and nature, social involvement and freedom are opposing values and that these oppositions parallel each other. Second, the Western formula seems to suggest that these opposing values can and must be resolved, but that the resolution can only occur through violence. I'm not quite sure why this is so, but it seems to have something to do with the nature and role of the villain and the way in which he represents some of the same values as the hero. When the hero finally commits himself to the destruction of the villain, he is destroying an aspect of himself. To do so, he must become convinced that the lawless individualism which the villain represents is so dangerous that it must be completely destroyed. If this analysis is at all correct, it suggests that the Western's resolution of the conflict between society and the individual is one in which society demands the destruction of much that is valuable in the individual self and is yet a necessary and desirable commitment because unrestrained individualism is still more frightening.

I hope that these extremely tentative and incomplete reflections have at least suggested that analysis of a popular formula like the Western is a very complex task. Furthermore, I have sketched in only one dimension of the formula, its treatment of the cultural values of individualism, natural spontaneity and social discipline. Many other areas of meaning remain to be explored and related to each other. In addition, I have not satisfactorily dealt with the problem of different versions of the formula, the way in which it has changed over the last century and a half from the Leatherstocking saga, to Wister and Grey's romantic tales of the hero who becomes fully assimilated into the society, to our present-day fondness for elegiac tales of gunfighters who are sacrificed for a society which no longer has a place for them. These changes as well as the different kinds and levels of meaning in the basic formula need to be explored and defined more carefully if we are to arrive at an adequate cultural interpretation of the Western and other popular formulas.

What needs to be attended to, then, is the serious study of the popular formula as a complex artistic structure with many different levels and kinds of meaning. Once the character of these structures has been more thoroughly and completely defined we need to examine with greater care both the many changes which have taken place in these formulas and the different kinds of meaning which they embody. In addition, I suggest that we undertake to make comparisons between the pattern of the imaginary world which defines the Western formula and the characteristic patterns of other popular forms not only from the arts but from other areas of culture such as sports, politics and manners. If artistic constructions are a way of giving shape or pattern to human experience, it is quite possible that we will find reflections of similar ordering principles in other aspects of the culture. Above all, I feel we must get away from the assumption that an artistic form, even a popular formula, is dependent upon some single deeper economic or psychological or social motive, instead of a relatively autonomous means of giving order to a great variety of values and experiences. This is why it is so important to understand a popular formula as an artistic whole. It is the way in which the formula orders and shapes character, action and theme which is of primary importance. If we had a fuller and clearer understanding of the ordering principles which govern the imaginary world of the Western and other popular formulas, we would, I feel, have a better understanding of the patterns of experience which dominate our culture and shape the lives of all of us.

Notes

1. Bernard Rosenberg and David M. White, eds., *Mass Culture* (Glencoe, Ill.: Free Press, 1957).

2. See Hugh D. Duncan, *Language and Literature in Society* (Chicago: Univ. of Chicago Press, 1953) for an extensive bibliography of the sociological study of literary works.

3. The "classic" example of Marxist criticism in the 1930's is Granville Hicks' book on American literature, *The Great Tradition*.

4. Cf. the work of Taine and Brandes in Europe and Parrington in America.

5. An excellent discussion of this point can be found in Lionel Trilling's criticism of Parrington in "Reality in America" reprinted in *The Liberal Imagination*. Both of the two major critical movements of the last two decades, the "New Criticism" of Ransom, Brooks, Warren Blackmur, *et al.*, and the "Aristotelianism" of Kenneth Burke and the "Chicago school" of McKeon, Crane, Olson *et al.*, have had as a major principle the integrity and uniqueness of the work of art.

6. Peter Homans, "Puritanism Revisited: An Analysis of the Contemporary Screen-Image Western," *Studies in Public Communication*, no. 3 (1961), pp. 73–84.

7. Homans, p. 82.

8. Homans, p. 83.

9. Homans, p. 74.

10. Homans, p. 82.

Theories of the Literary Western Novel

The Western Esthetic

Max Westbrook*

When the artist in the West begins the study of his legacy, he finds it is at once the most concrete and the most abstract of any regional legacy in America. He finds himself committed to the land, to an intimate knowledge of nature; and his commitment is specific, detailed. He is obliged to know the color of the hawk's wings, the name of the small cold lake farther up the mountain, and how to catch the trout which swim there. Without such experience and knowledge, he is a tourist, a dude. He is bookish and in disgrace. Along with an inherited duty to know and to respect the land comes the onus of the American dream—and with an insidious twist. The West, in the vision of so many of its artists, has the obligation to restore, or at least to husband, the American dream *after* it has already been corrupted in the East, the South, and the Midwest. Frederick Jackson Turner's famous thesis on the frontier, in fact, may be more applicable to Western literature than to Western history. Certainly, a substantial number of Western writers believe that Western experience (Westering, a way of life, whatever one's geographical fortunes may be) is the nation's best chance of healing the wounds caused by the Puritans when they made us feel ashamed of our bodies, afraid of the voice that comes from our dark and inner selves, apologetic for our worldly ambitions. Western writers have thus faced anew the ancient and sometimes American hope—the effort to discover the unity of body, soul, and land.

Between values and action, however, there is need for the stuff of continuing history. The nostalgic regionalist and the minor local colorist aside, a regionalist seeks that excitement which comes from realizing that what his countrymen have done is not yet known and will never be fully known so long as the study of the past continues to shock with new revelations about the meaning of today and to inspire fresh hopes and untold fears for the future. For the New England regionalist, Puritanism is but one of the forces of a continuing history which stretches from the landing of the *Mayflower* to the present, or at least to World War II. The mean-

**Walter Van Tilburg Clark* (New York: Twayne, 1969), pp. 39–53.

ings of Southern history—whether praised, damned, or evaluated judiciously—are intrinsic to the most contemporary Southern imagination.

I The Loss of Historical Continuity

The Western imagination, by contrast, is denied a historical continuity. The artist looks to a heritage which has neither continued nor declined. It has stopped. He is caught, as it were, with his abstractions in his hand. He finds it difficult to write fiction in which the meanings of the past are brought to bear on contemporary problems. The history of the American Indian in the West may seem a rich source for cultural and literary purposes, but contemporary economics and politics in the West are not shaped by that history so much as by the energies of a Westering Babbitt who came from a bordering culture. The cowboy experience, in which profound ethical problems were realistically related to the economy of a burgeoning society, once spread its influence over a large area. But the cattle drives lasted only a brief time—a quarter of a century at most—and they ended abruptly. It was much the same with trapping, buffalo hunting, and gunfighting. Even the frontier farmer has not been found to exercise a relevance in the contemporary Western civilization he helped make possible, at least not in the way that antebellum slave holders are relevant to the contemporary South or seventeenth-century Puritans to twentieth-century New England. The Western artist—wanting to avoid the various forms of disunity he associates with Eastern and Southern decadence, hoping to exploit in living and in writing the lessons in unity he feels in the vastness and the weight of nature in the West—is covetous of action. Yet the kind of action he values seems to have taken place in the past, seems available today only in weekend sports, in a summer and suspect ranch, in sublimated forms that lack connection with socio-economic realities.

The problem of historical continuity gives rise to another problem, one which does not lend itself to neat explanations. The artist in the West finds himself in a strained relation with his national heritage. He is aware of the obvious economic and cultural importance of the West to the nation as a whole, and there is ample evidence also of his realization that the Western writer's search for continuity is not unlike the early New Englander's search for a history which—at least until the Civil War—had not yet been running long enough to *be* a history. Furthermore, all serious Western artists that I have read reveal their interest in the national—indeed, the universal—implications of their insight into regional experience.

The larger affinities of the Western writer, however, are subject to frustrations. The centers of literature and learning have long been in the East; and, although the South and the Midwest have won some respectability, a serious artist in the West may find himself, at any moment, slandered by Eastern and uninformed generalizations. Serious Western writers, it is true, are accustomed to having their best works blurred with the films of Roy Rogers. One can make a family joke of that kind of thing. Surely, it will pass, one can say. But beneath the lack of understanding lies a fundamental difference between the Western artist and the national culture of which he considers himself an alien member.[1]

That difference can be stated. Varying segments of the American culture recognize a meaning which cannot be assessed by the rational faculty. This non-rational meaning may be associated with religion, with the human spirit, with insight or sensitivity, with nature or the soul, or with what we may call "intuitive knowledge." In the East, the Midwest, and the South, intuitive knowledge is, most characteristically, a property of the conscious mind. In the Western esthetic, intuitive knowledge is a property of the unconscious mind. An intuition in the service of the conscious mind may have primarily an ethical function and thus acquire the prestige of philosophy without the formulations of philosophy. Hemingway's heroes, for example—most clearly his early heroes—are capable of moral insight apart from the offices of a rationale. Jake Barnes' efforts in brotherhood in *The Sun Also Rises* are dependent on his intuitive ability to sense the needs of his fellow man, and his efforts are meant to represent genuine ethical values. Yet Jake's metaphysics consists of little more than a vaguely serious wish that he could be a better Catholic. Frederic Henry in *A Farewell to Arms* is sensitive to the feelings of the Priest; and it is manifest that his sensitivity is a virtue, a genuine virtue, not an illusion. Yet his comments on ultimate reality, both before and during Catherine's dying, are unremittingly negativistic. A firm stance on metaphysics, in fact, is usually associated with insensitivity and, therefore, with villainy. Hemingway's early heroes are forced to make-do with a code, with ethical values discovered by the individual's insight and lacking the sanction of metaphysical formulation.

II Two Types of Intuition

Characteristic Western heroes may or may not have the Hemingway type of sensitivity; but, in either case, their intuition is grounded in the unconscious mind and carries metaphysical implications. The two types of intuition are not always and rigidly separated, but the distinguishing Western viewpoint is that to make intuition the property of the conscious mind is to assign to reason the impossible task of contacting ultimate reality. Since metaphysics is primary to ethics, since it is the intuition and not the reason which can contact the real, the man of conscious intuition is thought to have taken the only means of getting beyond reason and to have confined it to the service of reason.

Conscious intuition is obviously a non-rational mode of apprehension, but the insights it produces are within the compass of the rational mind. While it would be impossible, for example, to make a rational explanation of the bullfight substitute for the ability to see and to feel its meanings, as Jake Barnes cannot with words make Robert Cohn see and feel, it is nonetheless true that a rational explanation of the values of the bullfight is sufficiently clear to the reason. The insights of unconscious intuition, by contrast, are offensive to reason when rendered into words. The man of reason is free to dislike Jake Barnes' intuitive appreciation of bullfighting, but his values require him to approve of Jake Barnes' distinction between the good will of Romero and the corrupt will of bullfighters who seek praise for a courage they do not have. In Walter Van Tilburg Clark's *The City of Trembling Leaves*, however, Tim Hazard's intuition can be formulated only in terms of friendly and unfriendly gods; and the formulation contradicts reason's requirement that knowledge be consistent and coherent according to rational standards.

The artist in the West faces, therefore, difficult problems from within and from without, problems which push him to bold and—sometimes—strained efforts. He feels an obligation to be, as it were, both Whitman and Dreiser at one and the same time. He believes in the sacred unity that can be apprehended only by the unconscious intuition, and he recognizes the lot of the democratic American, the man committed to a conscious and self-conscious struggle on behalf of the individual in a land that is holy and yet profane, potentially sacred yet suffering from massive exploitation. Differing versions of the Western esthetic—from the most successful to the most stereotyped—can best be understood, I think, in terms of their varying methods of handling or evading this difficult problem.

Central to the approach of the more successful Western writers is a belief in "primary realism," a term Clark has used to describe the recurrent human experience C. G. Jung calls "archetypal."[2] This realism is deeper than that of the "narrow factualist" whose refusal to accept the archetypal forces and wonders of life causes him to define man as merely a product of environment, despite the fact that a "product" does not develop an ulcerous guilt, or go trembling into puberty, or feel the mystery of woman, or the awesomeness of God, or the necessity of a Christ, or the terror and beauty of death. Rejecting such spiritual cowardice, Clark holds that man's beliefs must accommodate both the brute force of nature and the affirmation of nature. A realist supposedly bases his belief on what is, but the *is* of the universe includes the brutality and indifference which so impressed the naturalist, as well as the empathy and meaning which so impressed the romanticist.

"Primary realism," based on archetypal realities which are deeper than either the facts or the theories of modern man, is thus inclusive without being eclectic. It is man's intellect which presumes to separate dream from fact, which insists that man must pay allegiance to one or the other. It is man's insistence on rational understanding which drives him into the dark corners of existentialism, where he must leap, apologetically, into a pretension his reason cannot fuel into faith, or else do without God, do without the sense of any meaning to human existence.[3] Intuition must serve the unconscious mind, Clark believes, because it is the intuition—and not reason—which has the toughness to sense the infinite variety of man and his universe. To put intuition in the service of reason is to imprison it in an intellect which demands consistency on its own terms. To seek a unity which betrays the variety of man and his universe is to run the supreme risk, is to be fatally unrealistic.

III "Primary Realism" and the Critics

Clark's "primary realism" and the broad tradition of Western sacrality, of which it is a part, have not won favor in prestigious literary circles; the praise that has been won is usually tainted with apology, with attempts to justify a given work as good history or good craftsmanship and thus of merit despite its being Western.[4] The most notorious voices of Western criticism, unfortunately, have not done much to help the general understanding of the literature whose cause they support. One well-known but partisan critical study of the tradition of sacrality is *Start With the Sun* by Karl Shapiro, James Miller, and Bernice Sloate. The book condemns the Puritans for separating man into flesh and spirit, praises Whitman for celebrating the wholeness of man and for exhorting Americans to return to the primal and generative source of life, and accuses T. S. Eliot of disrupting Whitman's healthy direction and returning American literature back into the old sickness of Puritan separativeness. But this accusation judges Eliot according to the standards of a tradition quite different from the one to which he gave allegiance, an embarrassing error for critics busily protesting the tendency to judge the Whitmanian tradition according to the standards of Eliot and the "New Criticism." More importantly, this is to ignore the fact that the *donnée* in American history is an extreme self-consciousness forced upon us by our constitutional claim that we would prove to the world the worth of individual man; and, further, no defender of sacrality should fault Eliot for facing honestly the barrenness of American individualism and the isolation that resulted or for his working out a resolution which can accurately be called a rediscovery of the establishment sacrality of high church and cultural traditions.

Even less helpful is the venture into criticism by an artist whose fiction is a major part of modern sacrality: D. H. Lawrence's *Studies in Classic American Literature.* Lawrence's adherence to the sacred tradition is unmistakable, and his pronouncements often carry force. He repeatedly emphasizes his belief that the unconscious is primary to the conscious, and he holds that to believe only what the intellect can grasp is to deny forces and meanings that cannot be denied. Yet he shows no understanding of American individualism, and he argues so dogmatically for the unconscious that he falls into the very divisiveness he is attacking. Lawrence, an extremist, chides Melville for an interest in reform of naval injustices. There is certainly a good deal of the perverse in Lawrence, a childish desire to shock the establishment out of its Babbittry; but *Studies in Classic American Literature* does little to help our understanding of the place of ethics in sacrality or of sacrality as a literary tradition.[5]

Closer to Clark's vision and closer to the center, I think, is John Steinbeck's theory of "non-teleological" thinking.[6] Steinbeck shows more sympathy for the American born into self-consciousness, and he is fully aware of the capacity of man to corrupt any tradition into tyranny. Basically, Steinbeck argues that ethical principles are primarily the product of reason and culture. As such they are not teleological. This does not mean that man should be non-ethical or unethical, but that there is a deeper reality to life, that man's reasoning about ethics is not a way to get at primordial reality. Man's reason turns him back upon himself, takes him away from teleology. There is, Steinbeck believes, another way to think.

This other way of thinking—a belief in the possibility of knowing through the unity of thought and things—is more than anything else the common denominator among the differing versions of sacrality. Real knowledge is said to be knowledge in things, not in words *about* things. Those who think only with their intellect—or with the emotional refractions of intellect frustrated—can believe in a benevolent God, an indifferent force, or in no God. The intellect simply cannot encompass all three. Yet man has the capacity, through the offices of the "little man inside" (the voice of intuition in the service of the unconscious), to sense God and no-God, to see in the things of life an unreasonable variety—if only he will admit that heresy into the court of his own intellect.[7]

IV Five Basic Beliefs

At least five characteristic beliefs follow from this central principle of the unity of thought and things. First, there is no answer of the type demanded by the intellect. For the sacred man of the American West, it is presumptuous to think an individual's intellect can formulate the infinite. Second, the end hoped for is not a state achieved but an attitude—felt but never owned—toward a reality which touches but which is never confined by the intellect. Third, what is commonly called evil is an intellectual confusion of forces which are an intrinsic part of man and nature; and it cannot be exorcised by the pathological flagellations of the intellect. These forces—brute drives, if you will, but not evil—can be appeased, shaped away from destructive action, only through the individual's courage to be human, to listen to those archetypal meanings which are given voice through the unconscious. Fourth, the Christian God is a concoction of the rational mind, an illusion of man's desire to have a comforting and personal attention from on high; for only the intellect could propose a God so out of keeping with human nature as the Christian God. God, to the sacred imagination, is plural, various. He includes both the non-rational cruelty of the Old Testament God and the love of the New Testament God. Man's intellect cannot conceive His face, but man's unconscious can sense His generative, primordial force. Fifth, the hope of man is to establish contact with the original, the source, to "start with the sun."

Clark's own version of these characteristic beliefs is distinguished in part by his awareness of the total American experience. The Clark hero is American, specifically, in that his heritage includes the Puritan scar. He too has been rent asunder, at least damaged or endangered, by the inheritance of a noisome consciousness—which may explain Clark's interest in and sympathy with the self-tortured and overly-analytical heroes of Henry James.[8] The need—and it is shared by Clark's ineffectual saints—is to heal the wound, to make of one's self a whole man restored from an inherited disjointment of body and spirit, an inherited separativeness from nature. It is in this sense, and in this sense only, that Clark's affinity for the nonintellectual can be understood. His heroes feel the weight of the American experience from Puritanism toward the American dream and into the barrenness of the individual ego. Not even the boy hero is free, pure, natural; even he is analytical, and consciously so.

It is fitting, therefore, that Clark's heroes do not deny the intellectual responsibilities of the ego they are born with and do not wish to banish. And it is fitting that one of Clark's favorite words is "balance," a sign of the precarious and yet historically realistic type of unity in which he believes. If the Clark hero can accept the burden of ego and yet hold the arrogant ambitions of the intellect in check, then perhaps he can touch primordial realities beyond the intellect, perhaps he can learn to walk quietly on this earth, attentive and respectful. Perhaps he can exorcise the evil of man's separation from nature and heal the psychic wounds of our modish severance of body from soul. If he can realize the balance that is in things, then unity will occur; and *occur* is the precise word. The rational faculty, of course, is offended by this word; if man respects a claim to ultimate reality without understanding the process of the claim, how is he to distinguish the genuine from the bogus? But here again, advocates of sacrality reply, is the arrogant intellect, insisting that it must know the workings of the primordial, betraying man's unconscious ability to distinguish between the authoritative voice of the primordial and the whims of personal bias. The rational mind can neither trace nor understand the workings of ultimate reality, but the unconscious can sense its authority.

The significance of the word *occur* in Clark's world view can scarcely be overestimated. When Clark added the ego to his concept of sacrality, he brought in also the will, a sense of individual responsibility that is different in kind from the role of the will in Oriental or primitivist sacrality; and the will is necessarily a function of the conscious mind. Clark grants, furthermore, the legitimate place of the will in the balance that he seeks; but he believes in the necessity of a partnership of faith between unconscious intuition and the reason. How the conscious reason and the unconscious intuition can form a partnership is, obviously, beyond the understanding of our rational minds. Thus a state of unity is a value which occurs. It may be sought, both by the advisory voice of the conscious mind and by the substantive voice of the unconscious intuition; but it cannot be programmed. It is an exercise in dedication, with full attention to the demands of the workaday world, and the disciple need not know its mystery. To ask for more is to ask that the real submit itself to the intellect's ability to name the real, is to limit nature to man instead of opening man to nature. Thus Clark finds a kind of answer in the process of questioning. Answers tend to close the matter and they invite smugness, but the man who questions may keep his mind open and his intuition alert.

The discipline of man's unconscious intuition is the topic of Chapter 6, but the role of faith in sacrality must be mentioned here. From the viewpoint of Western writers like Clark and Steinbeck, the Christian intellect has vitiated faith. The modern emphasis on reason (that which is within the area of human understanding) has left no meaningful place for faith (that which is beyond human understanding). Faith has come to be for the modern Christian not a vital mode of touching God but a cover-up for reason's inability to go all the way to God. When reason runs out, the Christian hides behind claims of faith; but he turns to cries of "faith" only as a last resort, only when his more admired reason has run into a chasm it cannot cross. Thus the modern Christian, according to practitioners of Western sacrality, is hard put to answer the child's question: why have faith in the Christian God rather than in any other God? And it is difficult to show the child how belief in the Christian God is any more than a cultural preference.

Faith, in the sacred tradition, must have ontological rather than merely cultural status. For sacred man, faith obtains to ontological status quite simply because the primordial speaks to the unconscious intuition with authority, with primordial authority.[9] The man of reason finds it difficult to hold such a position, for he has given a primary role to the individual ego; and if faith comes in the authoritative voice of God, how can the goodness of the individual be required? What virtue is there for a democratic individual in obeying the voice of absolute authority? The answer, according to the man of sacrality, is that man's individual virtue is a necessary condition of his hearing the voice. For the man of reason, faith is a dishonored prop to the limitations of reason; and the burden of ontological validation rests, impossibly, on man's rational capabilities. For sacred man, the validation rests in the only place possible—in the primordial source—and man's role in the act of faith is to have the goodness and courage to hear and to heed.

None of this should suggest that religion for the sacred man is an easy thing. Clark is typical of Western artists at their best in his emphasis on balance; and balance—if it is to be realistic—is maintained in tension. To lose that tension is to lose all. On one side, the Clark hero finds the primitive, the innocent, the animal—that which enjoys the most unaffected contact with nature. On the other, he finds the intellectual and the materialist, those who have lost the capacity for generative action. The hero's quest is not a search for compromise, not a reasoned balance between the spiritual and the practical; rather, the quest is for a unity of thought and things, a dedication to learning how to think through the language of both the things of nature and the things of man.

V The Ancient World and the Modern Intruder

But the hero's land—as nature or as civilization—has not been given to him in primitive innocence. The land has come into the hero's touch already tainted by history, as the hero himself is tainted by history. The American West is not—in the vision of its major contemporary artists—a land one grows up in. It is a land one goes to. The land, after all, belonged to the Indian before the white man came to exploit the West. For the white hero to appropriate Indian (or primitivist) traditions as a means of belonging to the land would be for him to take a conscious and therefore an intellectual and doomed approach to sacrality. Since Indian traditions are not intrinsic to the white man's own history, the appropriation would be calculated more than felt.[10] The Indian does in many stories teach the white hero, and he is certainly more worthy than men satiated by societal values; but primitive cultures cannot provide a unity with land for those Western writers who accept the mind as well as the body, the curse as well as the accomplishment of civilization.

Clark's hero, for example, even when born and raised on the land, is an initiate, a man on the edges. He is the intruder into someone else's nature, the outsider come into the domain of offended gods; and some of his judges watch his entrance with love, some with malevolence. No associations can be fixed. The soul is not just the center of goodness—limp, white, defenseless, and pure—but seems to house also some most unholy energies. Reason is only relevant at times, and it lacks the ability to pick those times. God is not necessarily good or evil or even attentive. In the soul, in reason, God, land: in all areas the hero finds good, evil, and irrelevance.

The intellect cannot maneuver through such irrational possibilities. Only the unconscious intuition—the raucous and disturbing homunculus of man's inner self—can face such perverse realities and such multiplicity without panic. Still, man does have ethical obligations to his profane and divisive history, to his time and his place, else his allegiance is without language, is abstract. The Western esthetic thus includes a characteristic belief in an ethical obligation which has no intellectually recognizable connection with the real. The ethical is typically associated with linear history and with the intellect, perhaps with a folk-sense of fair play and with local ground rules; the real is associated with the dark and primal self of man's inner being. A formulated connection between the two would have to be a rational one, and the rational mind cannot cross from profane history into the cycles of primordial reality except as empirical observer.

For most Americans and for modern man generally, this is heretical. In European and American civilizations it has been customary to ground ethics in reason, or to blur the traditional distinctions of philosophy and to locate the ethical in church-born habits or, even more loosely, in cultural stock-responses. When grounded in folk terms, ethical principles are normally granted metaphysical prestige without metaphysical responsibility. Since modern man is reluctant to advocate an ethic he cannot understand with his reason, and since man's reason cannot create beyond itself, modern man has made for himself an ethical code that lacks authority. And the incestuous process of man's reason continues, doubling back on itself: the assignment of metaphysical prestige to an ethic of reason has caused modern man to create a god who is merely a man of superior reason. But when this superior man-god is given the responsibilities of the real God and asked to provide and to constitute a rationale for the neighborhood's code of fair play, the illusion is shown to be so feeble that sophomoric questions are adequate to place the man-god in metaphysical jeopardy: if man should be ethical (love his neighbor), why should not God also be ethical, why should He in His omnipotence create horrors for innocents? It follows for the man of reason that if there is no God, man must then find some other rationale for ethical belief; but the average man is not tough enough in his mind to go all the way with philosophy and not bold enough in his soul to accept the shock of sacrality. Modern man, therefore, is left dangling with his man-god and his doubts.

In their own individual ways, Clark and at least a dozen other successful Western American novelists have answered that the questions themselves are wrong. The essential connections of man and his universe are not subject to the verbal abstractions of the intellect. If we insist on confining knowledge to rational knowledge, then we can know nothing beyond our own powers to create; and man has created neither himself nor his universe, neither his reason nor his "little man inside." Western artists do not propose a formula—they would not be worth study if they did—but they do offer a direction, a possibility. If we reason about our place in linear time and learn to intuit with the unconscious our more fundamental place in primordial time, we have the possibility of maintaining an individual ego while feeling the generative power of our archetypal selves.

VI The View From the Unconscious

It is not appropriate, I assume, to conclude this chapter with a necessarily truncated presentation of the obvious qualifications. Andy Adams and Charles Siringo, typical of the authentic cowboy narrative, and Owen Wister and Eugene Manlove Rhodes, representative of romantic Western fiction, are clearly different from Walter Clark, John Steinbeck, Frederick Manfred, Vardis Fisher, Frank Waters, and several others I take to represent—not a dogmatic school—but an intrinsic tradition of Western literature. To do justice to variant versions of this tradition—Willa Cather's *O Pioneers!*, which is a curious use of sacrality as a better means to fulfillment of the Protestant ethic, or Wright Morris's *The Field of Vision*, which is a fascinating use of sacrality as a means of explaining how we have come to be in a wasteland—would require a scope far beyond that of the present study. It is appropriate, I think, to conclude with some tentative suggestions.

At least three conclusions seem justified. First, the emphasis on thought and things as a way of knowing has caused many Western artists to write each book as if it were a unique project. When the "things" change, so must the thought, the tone, the atmosphere. The author's voice behind the work may seem different in each work by that author. Critics who speak for a profane culture—with a firm belief in getting somewhere, amounting to something—want their art to reflect an economic psychology; and thus they are inclined to feel that an artist who does not start from youthful rebellion and move toward the resolution of old age is groping, has not found or fulfilled himself. Clark's three novels, for example, seem on first reading to have been written by three different novelists or by a single novelist who cannot resolve his artist's vision. Clark, however, is not attempting to move from one point in linear time to a culminating point in linear time. Steinbeck's capacity for treating each work as a separate entity has caused him to search for the sentimentality or idealism or harsh realism which he finds in the "things" of a given work; he does not view character and event from a predetermined metaphysics within the compass of the conscious mind. The primordial reality he seeks is deeper and more flexible. This has hurt his reputation with Eastern critics more attuned to the kind of continuity and consistency—found in Hemingway, for example—that is prompted by a devotion to linear time.

Second, the belief in unconscious intuition causes a basic shift from the norm in the relation of a hero (or of a character who is right in a given instance) to his author. The fallacy of message hunting granted, it is still more legitimate to associate the values of Hemingway with the values of his hero, or the values of Sinclair Lewis with the obvious implications of his social satire than it is to associate the values of Clark with those of Arthur Bridges in *The Track of the Cat* or the values of Steinbeck with those of Danny in *Tortilla Flat*.The reason is that writers who ground their art in conscious intuition must strike a more intimate relation between this intuition and ultimate reality than writers who feel that the conscious intuition is primarily social. Western writers do create heroes whose values are close to their own, but if you believe that reality is primordial then you believe that reality is less the property of any man's vision—including your own; you feel a certain generosity about man's theories, a generosity that would be a moral irresponsibility in a man who binds his ontology to the free will and responsibility of the individual's conscious ego.

Third, a writer who believes in sacrality takes an approach to actuality which is disturbing and confusing to the expectations of readers accustomed to the art of a profane world view. The sacred man holds that it is necessary to ground one's self in the discipline of actual events, as does the writer of a profane tradition. But actuality to a sacred man is more real than expected in that it can manifest the primordial—tangibly—and yet less real than expected in that actual events are but the ephemera of the day, are not required to have a fidelity to conscious intuition sufficient to constitute a possible mode of apprehending ultimate reality. Belief in the integrity of natural objects is a necessary condition for belief in the free will and in the responsibility of the individual's conscious mind; and this view holds at least from Emerson to Hemingway. In the sacred world view, however, the voice of homunculus may speak a lie—in terms of reason's standards—which is the closest thing we know to the real and primordial truth.

Since Western writers are committed to their own time and yet believe in sacrality, the burden of the reader is to heighten his sensibility, to prepare himself for reading both the ritual swim of *The City of Trembling Leaves* and the shocking realism of the hanging in *The Ox-Bow Incident*. Both a capacity for naked purity and a capacity for brute murder are within each one of us, the Western artist believes. If we are to read him well, we must use our reason; but each reader must bring with him also his own homunculus.

Notes

1. For an interesting and informative presentation of the ideas and attitudes of Western novelists, see John R. Milton, ed. "The Western Novel: A Symposium," *SDR*, 2, no. 1 (1964), 3–36. The novelists interviewed are representative of those I refer to as central or intrinsic: Frederick Manfred, Frank Walters, Walter Van Tilburg Clark, Vardis Fisher, Harvey Fergusson, Forrester Blake, Paul Horgan, and Michael Straight.

2. *The City of Trembling Leaves* (New York: Random House, 1945), p. 14. Especially relevant also is Clark's discussion of the "nuclear"; see pp. 200 ff. in the same novel. The standard reference for Jung, of course, is "Archetypes of the Collective Unconscious."

3. I was impressed by the clarity and forcefulness of Mircea Eliade's explanation in his *Cosmos and History: The Myth of the Eternal Return* (New York: Harper, 1959), p. 156. The chapter on "The Terror of History" is especially interesting.

4. For examples of reviewers who feel Clark's power and praise his narrative ability but who dislike and misread what makes him Western, see the following: Hamilton Basso, "The Great Open Spaces," *New Yorker*, 4 June 1949, pp. 76, 79; Vernon Young, "An American Dream and Its Parody," *ArQ*, 6 (1950), 112–23; Jean Garrigue, "The Watchful Gods and Other Stories," *New Republic*, 25 Dec. 1950, p. 20.

5. Further difficulty, I realize, will be caused by the fact that for some readers I will seem to be talking about the values of Jean-Jacques Rousseau or Paul Gauguin or Jack Kerouac while stubbornly refusing to admit it. I can only hope that in the process of the book *Walter Van Tilburg Clark* the differences will become clear. Basically, Clark does not advocate the escapist return to nature of Rousseau, the pure forms of Gauguin (who wished to close his eyes to what was in front of him in order to see the essence), or the antiintellectualism of Kerouac. The best Western writers generally are neither nostalgic nor inspirationalist. Sacrality, I hope to show, is a good deal more tough-minded than what passes in the marketplace for practicality and realism.

6. John Steinbeck, *The Log from the Sea of Cortez* (New York: Viking Press, 1962), pp. 132–35. Steinbeck also agrees with Clark, D. H. Lawrence, and others that thought comes afterwards: "Only at the last when the move is mounted and prepared does thought place a roof on the building and bring in words to explain and to justify." See *The Winter of Our Discontent* (New York: Viking Press, 1961), p. 91.

7. See "The Writer and the Professor," *Chrysalis*, 1 (1962), *passim*.

8. This point will also be discussed in the chapter on *The City of Trembling Leaves* (hero Tim Hazard is fascinated by Henry Adams) and in the concluding chapter. Note, also, the relevance of Davies in *The Ox-Bow Incident* (New York: Random House, 1940) and Art in *The Track of the Cat* (New York: Random House, 1949).

9. See, for example, Jung's explanation of the authoritative voice of the unconscious in his *Psychology and Religion* (1938; rpt. New Haven: Yale Univ. Press, 1963), p. 49. See also the first essay, "The Autonomy of the Unconscious Mind." An explanation from a different viewpoint is C. S. Lewis, *The Abolition of Man* (New York: Macmillan, 1947), especially chapter ii.

10. The following, from "Archetypes of the Collective Unconscious," is directly comparable to Clark's own thinking: "If we now try to cover our nakedness with the gorgeous trappings of the East, as the theosophists do, we would be playing our history false. A man does not sink down to beggary only to pose afterwards as an Indian potentate. It seems to me that it would be far better stoutly to avow our spiritual poverty, our symbollessness, instead of feigning a legacy to which we are not the legitimate heirs at all. We are, surely, the rightful heirs of Christian symbolism, but somehow we have squandered this heritage. We have let the house our fathers built fall into decay, and now we try to break into Oriental palaces that our fathers never knew." Quoted from *The Basic Writings of C. G. Jung*, ed. Violet Staub De Laszlo (New York: Modern Library, 1959), p. 298.

Frontier and Region in Western Literature

Richard W. Etulain*

A perplexing problem facing the serious student of western American literature is the imprecise terminology of the field. Is there any difference, for example, between the Western and the western novel? What is a western writer? Is Thomas Berger a *western* novelist? What, if anything, distinguishes local color work from regional writing? Even more vague are the numerous meanings attached to the word *West*. Does the term indicate a geographical area—that is, a frontier, a region, or a section? Is it an experience? Or—as Henry Nash Smith has shown in *Virgin Land*—is the idea of the West hopelessly entangled with a conglomeration of symbols and myths?

This paper will focus on two terms used frequently in describing the West—*frontier* and *region*. I use the word *frontier* to describe the trans-Mississippi experience of the nineteenth century; and by *region*, I mean the post-frontier era, the West as a settled and civilized community. I do not wish to be held accountable for these hazy and inadequate definitions beyond the scope of this paper. It is impossible to explain with exactness the termination of the frontier West and the beginning of the regional West, although most historians agree that the transition occurred sometime between 1890 and the New Deal era. The conscious acceptance of the ending of the frontier, however, may have been even later. (Interpreters of western literature seem to be in agreement with these dates. An examination of what commentators have said about the literary West indicates that by 1930 critics began to show much more interest in western literature as the product of a region rather than of a frontier.) My purpose here is to center on what western writers have said when they have dealt with these years of change in their fiction.

Since, however, two well-known treatments of this transitional era have been discussed elsewhere, they need only be mentioned briefly. The most obvious of the literary reactions to the coming of the regional West is the refusal to accept the transition and to hang on to the frontier. This

* *SwAL*, 1 (1971), 121–28. © 1971 by *Southwestern American Literature*. Reprinted by permission of *Southwestern American Literature*.

nostalgic longing for the past is particularly evident in the Western. Much of the formula fiction of Zane Grey and Max Brand is shot through with a crippling nostalgia for an older, more idealized West.[1] A second approach to the frontier-region theme is that discussed in Harold Simonson's *The Closed Frontier: Studies in American Literary Tragedy.*[2] For many persons, including several prominent writers, the terminated frontier was a dire note to be sounded in their writings. The open frontier—and all the highly-charged emotions associated with it—had to be forgotten, and this was tragic. This feeling of fatalism is what Simonson tries to show in his examination of the writings of such authors as Mark Twain, Ole Rolvaag, and Nathanael West.

A third avenue of western writers to this era of metastasis needs to be examined. I have chosen four pieces to illustrate this approach. Two writers— John Steinbeck and H. L. Davis—lived through part of this era and pictured it in the thirties. Two other novelists—A. B. Guthrie and Wallace Stegner—have dealt with the subject in novels published in the early seventies. These four examples provide an interesting contribution toward understanding an important theme in western literature.

John Steinbeck's "The Leader of the People" has been frequently interpreted as an example of his non-teleological thinking or as an indictment of a modern West that produces men who lack the manly virtues of earlier frontiersmen. Other commentators stress the author's use of the initiation theme in Jody's gradual perception of what his grandfather represents.[3] These views add to one's understanding of Steinbeck's short work. I have no quarrel with them, but another theme deserves further attention.

Nearly every critic who has studied "The Leader of the People" has commented at length on the author's use of the word "Westering" and on Grandfather's speech about the " 'whole bunch of people made into one big crawling beast.' " Grandfather adds: " 'it wasn't getting there [the West Coast] that mattered, it was movement and westering.' " When Jody speaks of being a leader like his grandfather, the old man answers, " 'There's no place to go. There's the ocean to stop you. There's a line of old men along the shore hating the ocean because it stopped them." Those who employ this last quotation to argue that the story is most of all a lament for the passing of the frontier have a strong point; but they are incorrect in stressing it as Steinbeck's *major* idea, for Grandfather then says:

> "No place to go, Jody. Every place is taken. But that's not the worst—no, not the worst. Westering has died out of people. Westering isn't a hunger any more. It's all done. Your father is right. It is finished."

Grandfather argues that even though the frontier is gone physically, the spirit of the frontier—that is, "westering"—need not have died, even though it has. As he tells his grandson, " "I tell these old stories, but they're not what I want to tell. I only know how I want people to feel when I tell them.' " What he wants is for his listeners to *feel* the "westering" spirit and to be driven into action by it, but it is evident that Jody's father has neither heard nor understood what his father-in-law is trying to communicate. For the old man, there could be continuity from the old West to the new West through "westering," the adventuresome spirit that impelled men to lead others and that drove entire groups across the nation. But no one comprehends this point, and thus a contribution that the frontier west could make to the regional west has been lost.

A similar point is suggested in the writings of H. L. Davis. Davis, who grew up on one of the last frontiers in the Pacific Northwest, was related to the well-known pioneer Jessie Applegate and was personally acquainted with many men who homesteaded in northeastern Oregon. Most of Davis' earliest sketches and stories published in H. L. Mencken's *American Mercury* center on the first years of the twentieth century, the era in which northeastern Oregon passed rapidly from a frontier into an area populated with small towns.

Davis also used this setting for part of his first novel, *Honey in the Horn*, which won the Harper Prize in 1935 and a year later the Pulitzer Prize. The teenage hero of the novel represents a relationship between past and present. Clay Calvert symbolizes youth coming of age, and his initiation is played out against a setting that is struggling out of pinafores into maturity. The author carries the young hero through a series of adventures, in picaresque form, which are revivified because the Oregon frontier is rapidly falling away, and small communities are springing up to dot the landscape. Clay gradually learns what it is to be a man; he cannot revert to his boyhood but must accept the new responsibilities thrust upon him. At the same time he must not forget what his past has taught him.

Counterposed to Clay is Uncle Preston Shively, who is probably modeled after Jessie Applegate. Uncle Preston's life is mired in the past, and he spends most of his time writing a history of frontier Oregon. Even when his life and property are threatened, he chases away all signs of the present to chronicle such notable events as a listing of the territorial land laws. Unlike Clay, Uncle Preston lives in the past, will have no part of the present, and surely is not interested in running lines of meaning between the two. One of Davis' favorite techniques is to employ an older and more experienced person to teach a young initiate. In *Honey in the Horn*, this theme is given a reverse twist: here Clay learns the necessity of joining past and present for an understandable future, but this lesson comes in spite of the actions of his teacher, Uncle Preston, who wishes to avoid present manifestations of his past experiences.[4]

A. B. Guthrie has remarked in a recent speech that he is "divided between backward and forward," that for him "Every choice entails an onus. Every gain is at some loss. Every change leaves its regrets. Progress weeps while building on toward a future bright or blind." These words are an apt introduction to important ideas in Guthrie's latest novel, *Arfive*, which completes his ambitious tetralogy about the West developing "from fur hunter to Ford."[5]

Set in the opening years of this century, the novel chronicles the tail end of Montana's frontier era and the beginning of its towns. *Arfive,* in fact, is set in the twilight zone between past and present, and this time scheme allows Guthrie to ponder the changing West as it canters into the future.

Two major characters shoulder most of Guthrie's thematic concerns. Benton Collingswood, mid-western, puritan, and academic, comes to Arfive, a small Montana town, as the schoolteacher. He is so hogtied with moral strictures that he is beside himself when confronted with prostitution, sex deviance, and adolescents learning the alphas and omegas of the birds and bees. Collingswood fears innovation; he is afraid that change will bring uncertainty and perhaps chaos. On the other hand, Mort Ewing, who has grown up in Montana and has seen it develop, accepts change as inevitable. Yet he is no do-gooder; his feelings are summed up: "a man could stand up for improvement and sit down for reform" (p. 50).

Guthrie is interested in showing the "civilizing" of Arfive in the two decades previous to World War One. As it moves from an isolated, crossroads hamlet to a small town with churches, new schools, and cars, the author takes pains to show how the East (represented in the backgrounds of Collingswood) and the frontier (illustrated in the beginnings of Ewing) are John the Baptists for the town's arrival as a settled community. Eva Fox, who had madamed the local sporting house, becomes the proprietor of a successful restaurant, but she is never allowed entrance to the town's polite society. Some Indians and old trappers of the area are likewise excluded by the local Comstocks. But others like Ewing, through their pragmatic and diligent pursuits, are accepted as town leaders. These changes come slowly; there is no yawning chasm of discontinuity between past and present, and the product of these changes is not merely produced by the new setting but is an amalgamation of foreign (eastern) and familiar (western) influences.

It is Collingswood's gradual, reluctant acceptance of change that contains the central point of the novel. He thinks about the youthfulness of Montana, how only "two lifetimes took a man back to Lewis and Clark"; and he wonders what the future will bring. A friend tells him " 'Change is the order of nature. . . . It is in our nature somehow to resist while forwarding it. What comes comes, to our dismay or delight or more likely both, and both diminished.' " Collingswood reflects on this advice and finally acquieses: "So be it. Change. Push, man. Sing hello and sigh good-by" (pp. 99, 101). Guthrie sums up this feeling: "I accept the fact that progress leaves us no retreat. We can only insist NO UNDUE HASTE. We can only try to guide it. We can't stay it. Neither should we."[6]

Wallace Stegner's major theme in his most recent novel, *Angle of Repose*, adds another dimension to the frontier-region theme. In this work, Stegner is most interested in the question of perseverance—why a marriage has lasted nearly sixty years in spite of large differences of background, personality, and experience. In dealing with the theme of perpetuity, Stegner raises several important points about the influence of the past upon the present. It is partially because of these provocative points that *Angle of Repose* is an important western novel, more important than *Little Big Man*, it seems to me, because the novel deals extensively with the West (past and present) and also because it probes the meaning of western experience as a product of native and alien influences. More than a comment upon the West, the work is a product of a superb mind attempting to understand its own western experiences and those of other westerners.

The major characters—Oliver and Susan Burling Ward—are man and wife trying to accommodate themselves to one another and to the West in the late nineteenth century. The trials of acclimation are pictured against a changing West, a section that is struggling to rise on its new and shaky legs. The action takes place in a series of tableaux that picture the West rushing from frontier to region: from California and Colorado mining camps to Idaho irrigation settlements and finally, to complete the cycle, back to California mining towns. The dimensions of the lives of Susan and Oliver are greatly magnified through their reactions to their evolving environment. For Oliver, every change, every failure, is another step toward what he believes will be eventual success. He stubbornly holds on to the belief that he will be an integral (and a valuable) part in the West's movement toward civilization.

Susan has much more difficulty in adjusting to the changing West. At first, she sees the West as a rustic and picturesque wonderland (and her local color writing betrays these superficial observations), but the possibility of living the rest of her life in the West is, for her, a chilling prospect. The region is too crude and uncultured. Susan is, as Stegner told John Milton, like other "*eastern* characters who are going to have some of the refinement ground out of them" before they can adjust to the West. Stegner adds:

> It's a Willa Catherish kind of theme. She [Cather] keeps pointing out that the frontier breaks the really refined. . . . The frontier was a brutalizing experience, but it also could be, for people who weren't broken by it, an experience which changed them in other ways. It could be a coarsening experience but also a strengthening one. So I've got some genteel-tradition folks who are going to have to develop a few callouses.[7]

Stegner used Lyman Ward, the grandson of Oliver and Susan, as a narrator, and his position as both observer and participant, cements the narrative together. Lyman, who writes from the perspective of a man living in 1970, faces several problems: his marriage is a failure, he has trouble understanding radical ideas of his son, and his health is failing. Frustrated by the shortcomings of his own life and the perplexities of his milieu, he hunts among the biographical remains of his grandparents for answers to his questions about stability in personality, marriage, and civilization. As one might expect, there are no easy and explicit answers. But for Lyman there are some hints.

He realizes that his grandmother learned that living in the past was impossible. She also comprehended that her inordinate attachment to genteel culture and Victorian sensibilities was wrong, that she had to change and adjust to her new circumstances. She realized, no doubt as most immigrants have, that a new environment rarely called for or accepted the wholesale continuation of old life styles. Instead there must be adjustment and change. Some traditions would and could continue, but others had to be thrown out—and totally forgotten. The narrator specifies these ideas of compromise in the geological term "angle of repose," which indicates the angle of slope at which rocks cease to roll. Susan's life came to that angle, and Lyman seems to realize in the final pages of the novel that his grandmother succeeded because her life had been one of compromise, amalgamation, and acceptance. She learned from past experiences and realized that the juxtaposing of the old and new was the key to meaning for her life.

Having announced the texts of my sermon, let me—belatedly—give a gloss on the scriptures. These four examples illustrate an alternative to viewing the ending of the frontier either nostalgically or tragically. Instead, they suggest that the frontier experience has varied lessons for modern westerners. The message may be the need for the "westering" spirit of John Steinbeck or the necessity of leaving off the past that H. L. Davis talks about. The contribution may also be that of A. B. Guthrie: the importance of accepting change without mistaking innovation for moral decay. Finally, as Wallace Stegner remarks, scratch a westerner deeply enough and one is likely to find an easterner with callouses reluctantly gathered in frontier experiences.

These writers agree on one explicit point: Americans can and ought to learn from the past. There are more obvious links between the past and present than Americans have sought or looked for. Other similar points are suggested. Why is it that students of the west so seldom view wholly the development of their region? Many historians never venture beyond the 1890s to study the twentieth-century West, while scholars of literature, once so intent in studies of frontier literature, have done little recently with that period and seem immersed in scrutiny of later western writing. In both cases, the meaning of the West has been amputated and seen only in part. The West is neither frontier nor region alone; it has been both, and its largest meaning will be found in seeing relationships between these two eras.

Another point is closely related to the ones suggested above. Why have interpreters spilled so much ink in trying to show what is unique about the West and its literature? Perhaps, as historian Earl Pomeroy has suggested,[8] the most important questions about the American West are ones of continuity: how has the West repeated the experiences of others, Europeans and Americans? This idea, if broadened, argues that those of us interested in western American literature might make larger contributions if we pointed out continuities of theme, structure, and attitudes common to writings about our region with those produced by other Americans. Again Wallace Stegner is a pathfinder. He has said recently: "This is what I would really like to see some western writer manage to do, to put together his past and his present. . . . "[19] In *Angle of Repose* he has done just that; he has pointed the way—in content and method. One only hopes that future discussions of western American literature will follow his paradigm and discover the important continuities between frontier and region.

Notes

1. Richard W. Etulain, "Origins of the Western," *JPC*, 6 (1972), 12–17.

2. *The Closed Frontier: Studies in American Literary Tragedy* (New York: Holt, Rinehart and Winston, 1970).

3. Joseph Fontenrose, *John Steinbeck: An Introduction and Interpretation* (New York: Barnes and Noble, 1963), pp. 63–64; Peter Lisca, *The Wide World of John Steinbeck* (New Brunswick, N. J.: Rutgers Univ. Press, 1958), pp. 105–107, comes closest to my point argued above. For a dissenting view on these ideas, see Donald E. Houghton, " 'Westering' in 'Leader of the People,' " *WAL*, 4 (1969), 117–24. See also an answer to Houghton: Robert E. Morsberger, "In Defense of 'Westering,' " *WAL*, 4 (1970), 143–46.

4. For an excellent summary of Davis' ideas about the past, see Paul T. Bryant, "H. L. Davis: Viable Uses for the Past," *WAL*, 3 (1968), 3–18.

5. "Author Guthrie—'going toward the sunset,' " *The Exponent* (Montana State University), 2 April 1971, p. 5.

6. "Author Guthrie," p. 5. One can easily make a case that a major theme in Guthrie's Western tetralogy is this ambiguous response to progress.

7. John R. Milton, "Conversation with Wallace Stegner," *SDR*, 9, no. 1 (1971), 54.

8. "Toward a Reorientation of Western History: Continuity and Environment," *Mississippi Valley Historical Review*, 4 (1955), 579–600.

9. Milton, p. 53.

Can the Western Tell What Happens?

Don D. Walker*

Can the Western tell what happens? A quick and easy answer to this question is yes if one supposes that the literary work we call the Western can deal with the present and not merely with the past. Down in my country within the past year, a so-called group of hippies or some of Nature's children—what they were called depended on who was doing the naming—set up their tents—or teepees—on some public land. It happened that the land was also rangeland, and thus there was an immediate conflict of interests, although no one argued that the hippies were about to eat the grass the cows were supposed to chew. One can easily conceive a Western using this conflict, a Western set in 1972, with so much of the Now in it that surely it would tell what is happening.

The classic Western, however, has been set in an earlier time; it has involved mountain men who wear buckskin and shoot muzzle-loading rifles, buffalo hunters who drive their wagons across vast grasslands where millions of buffaloes still roam, and cowboys who ride horses instead of pickup trucks, who carry six-guns instead of terramycin trouble shooters, and who prefer a Bull Durham to a Camel with a filter. But surely one cannot insist that the Western be historical in this way; surely the genre is big enough to include a work like *The Last Picture Show* as well as works like *Lin McLean* and *The Log of a Cowboy*. Yet insofar as the Western does stick to elements of the past, the question remains: can it tell what happens? Does a work about fur trading in 1824 or buffalo hunting in 1868 or trail driving in 1884 tell only what happened? Or can it tell what happens?

Many readers and critics are of course content to believe the Western tells what happened. Interested in the western past, not the western present, they value any work which recreates that past in a way they trust is authentic. In this recreation history and literature supposedly complement each other. History depends closely upon the evidence of documents, the field work of trail tracing and campsite location, the study of

**Rendezvous*, 7, no. 2 (1972), 33–47. © 1972 by Don D. Walker. Reprinted by permission of Don D. Walker.

such western artifacts as rusty traps, branding irons, and antique barbed wire. Literature depends on a close detailing of places as they were and experiences as they could have happened. The imagination functions only in imitation of what history offers. Any creative venture beyond what seems historically probable is regarded as an unfortunate lapse into legend, myth, and fiction. Much western fiction is thus secretly ashamed to be fiction.[1] And one of the most praised western novels is barely a novel at all.[2]

The result of this assumption of a close relationship, if not identity, between history and literature is a shared commitment to matters western. Western novelists are deeply interested in western history; indeed they are sometimes historians as well as writers of fiction. Western historians admire western literature, providing of course it is properly historical. They praise *The Log of a Cowboy* and *The Big Sky*; they have doubts about *The Virginian*; but they don't have to worry about *Catlow* and *Border Breed*. Even the literary people don't believe in that sort of stuff. Historians and literary critics join in the happy camaraderie of regional discussion. In their formal moments, they organize workshops and centers for Studies of the American West.

A less happy result, however, is the blurring of important differences between history and literature. I would not argue for the value of differences as differences, although a rigorous taxonomy of intellectual disciplines is perhaps always needed, especially when a 20th-century neo-organicism is every day homgenizing the life of the mind. During the past decade, ecology, theology, sociology, literature, etc. have tended to become a vast intellectual mush, bland to the taste although supposedly rich in the vitamins of relevancy. However, I would argue for the value of literature as literature. And the relationship with history has been one-sided and vitiating to that value. In the companionship of the Muses, Clio has been stronger than the rest of the girls put together.

If we take a couple of examples from fiction and history, we can see how little difference may seem to show between them. In one of the chapters of *The Big Sky*, A. B. Guthrie tells how Boone Caudill sets a beaver trap. In one of the chapters of *Bent's Fort*, David Lavender tells how Tom Smith helped to amputate his own leg after he had been shot by Indians.[3] Both accounts are rich in the concrete detail which appeals to the senses as well as to the mind; both order this detail in the sequence, pace, and rhythms of the actions themselves; both consequently have a vivid and compelling immediacy. Knowing Guthrie's careful research on trapping beavers, the reader can say, I'm sure that's just the way it was done. Turning the pages of Lavender's history, the reader can say, it's just as exciting as a novel.

In spite of what might be called novelistic features, Lavender's work remains nevertheless a history, at least in intention. A note makes this entirely clear: "My reconstruction is not authoritative, merely an effort to piece together what might have happened."[4] The historian cannot know exactly what happened, but he can carefully, responsibly recreate the event as it probably took place. The probability here is the historian's probability: given all that we can know from the documents, given what we can find out about the particular time and place, given what we can extrapolate about a particular historical person, this is what might have happened. There is no intention on Lavender's part to establish a probability transcending a very fixed resultant in historical time and space.

A similar kind of intention seems to move Guthrie's account of setting the beaver trap. Boone is not a historical person; the particular place and exact time of the setting do not come from any historical sources; one supposes that the same kind of setting could have taken place in any one of fifty or more years and on any one of hundreds of creeks and rivers of the West. Even so, the writer's purpose is historical. One can argue, I suppose, that Guthrie does his job so well, renders the setting with such concrete immediacy that we do not so much know about an event a century ago as imaginatively experience it now. One can argue that here is the universal experience of setting a beaver trap. But surely this is to exaggerate the reach of the novel, or at least this particular part of it. For can one with any seriousness talk about the human universals in setting a beaver trap? One can note that wading in ice-cold water knots the muscles now as it did in 1830 and as it will in 2030. But does literature exist to give us such transcendent truths? No, setting a beaver trap belongs to history. If that history becomes sensuous by virtue of its having a novelistic texture, it is nevertheless history.

Many readers interested in the West are of course content that the novel tells what happened. Indeed western literary criticism has for a long time been dominated by the historian's way of judgment. A few examples will show my point. More than seventy years ago, Arthur Chapman, writing about "The New West and the Old Fiction," predicted that "some keen-eyed genius, who recognizes the theatrical untruth of the accepted school [of western literature], will catch the interesting phases of actuality. Then we shall get some capital stories of the big mines with their complicated machinery and of the ranch, minus the cowboy and the roundup." "The actual people of the West," he went on, "will be introduced in fiction, and the change from artificiality to reality will be welcome, especially on the sundown side of the Missouri River."[5] Chapman assumed that literature is a sort of mirror, with literary reality dependent wholly on its capacity to reflect accurately what is out there objectively in the West. Just about seventy years later, Edward Everett Dale, in an introduction to Harry Chrisman's *Fifty Years on the Owl Hoot Trail*, observes: "It [Chrisman's book] gives to the reader a more authentic understanding of ranch life and the *social history* of the American frontier than he is likely ever to get from fiction or so-called 'Westerns'. "[6] Westerns are thus supposed to give authentic understanding of ranch life and the social history of the frontier. Finally, lest Chapman and Dale lack sufficient reputation as literary critics, I cite the authority some regard as the very Aristotle of western letters. Bernard DeVoto wrote of Eugene Manlove Rhodes: "The pattern of thought and feeling in his books is that of the era he wrote about. It is the record of the deposit which experience in the range country left on the minds of those who underwent it. I am willing to let that define realism in fiction."[7] Rhodes is an important writer, then, because he tells us what happened: he gives such past experiential facts as how water in barrels on a cook wagon stank when carried fifty miles and left under the desert sun and how cowboys believed in the genuine gentility of women and acted accordingly.

Without questioning the value of such information, one can nevertheless insist that the giving of such information is not the special—indeed the high—function of literature. However much it may help to tell what happened—to be historical—literature must aspire to tell what happens. Otherwise, it fails finally to be literature at all.

The distinction I am making here is of course an old one, at least 2300 years old. Aristotle, in his *Poetics*, wrote: "It is not the function of the poet to relate what has happened, but what may happen. . . . The true difference [between history and poetry] is that one relates what has happened, the other what may happen." Poetry here may be taken for literature in the imaginative sense, the Western under question thus being in this context a form of poetry. The substitution of *what happens* for *what may happen* follows Northrop Frye's paraphrase, and I trust does no violence to the essential meaning. Thus, again following Aristotle, when we say that the Western can tell what happens, we mean that it can present universal human meanings, that it can deal in what, in the Aristotelian context, would be called poetic truth, as different from historical truth. Shifting the question from *can* to *how*, one asks more specifically: how can a story configured out of elements taken from a previous century reveal a truth about human life today? How can pieces of history be put together to reveal meanings that really have no historicity at all? An adequate answer here requires a consideration—a fresh reconsideration—of some old problems in the relationship of literature and history.

No historian, I assume, any longer believes that history can be completely objective. He can have before him the account ledger of a fur trading company; he can hold in his hands a rusty beaver trap found on some mountain river; he can locate and photograph the site of a particular rendezvous. In the method of an archeologist he may even dig around and find a piece of charcoal from a fire now more than a century and half old. All of these bits of evidence are objects. A rusty trap has all of the hard reality of a lump of ore going into an assayer's mortar. Yet when these objects are taken together, in the construct we call history, they are mixed with elements that can only be called subjective. Or perhaps one should say that the matrix in which they are held in meaningful coherence is irreducibly subjective.

Nevertheless, the historian's commitment is outward, to that world of the past. He rightly assumes that the reality he seeks to define is grounded in something back there, that however epistemologically he may be mixed with that reality it is yet conditioned more by the objective world than by his subjective presence. In the object-subject relationship, it is the object that is more important. His activity as historian points toward the object.

Of all this one needs to be reminded preliminary to considering how history can be objective in another, quite different way. Suppose the mountain man is conceived less as a hard-bitten man in pursuit of another beaver hide than as a man in pursuit of that time and place, that virgin valley, *in illo tempore* in which goodness had its beginning. This primitivistic mountain man may carry beaver traps; he may be dressed in greasy buckskins; as he heads out for Eden he may even start from St. Louis. But clearly his reality is not grounded in the historian's object. Professors Phillips, Hafen, and great researchers like them can never find him in the archives. Pile up the documents to the library ceiling, and still he is not there. Conception here is less a passive structuring of idea under the pressure from the supposedly objective data than an outward thrust of imagination organizing the data to embody an inner meaning.

While the novelist may freely and knowingly conceive in this way, the historian would supposedly suppress such an assertive imagination. Yet historians do not always meekly await the meaning of their evidence. Or speaking another way, like novelists, they are men with active minds and imaginations: they sometimes presume an inference. The inference of course is rigorously objective—at least they hope it is—a piece of zinc dropped into hydrochloric acid; inference: hydrogen will bubble up.

Take an instance from the history of the fur trade. When the Lewis and Clark party was returning home down the Missouri, it met a pair of trappers on their way back to the beaver streams. John Colter decided to join them, even though he had now been away from civilization for more than two years. Nicholas Biddle, when he noted Colter's decision, observed: "The example of this man shows how easily men may be weaned from the habits of civilized life to the ruder but scarcely less fascinating manners of the woods." Colter without reluctance went back "to the solitude of the woods." This was written in 1814. More than a century later, when Burton Harris wrote his book on Colter, he corrected Biddle's version. Biddle, he noted, "endowed Colter with a reputation for being callous and devoid of normal human feelings." However, the evidence suggests, concludes Harris, that Colter's action was nothing "more than the action of a man taking advantage of an excellent business opportunity."[8]

As a historian, one easily agrees with Harris that Colter was less fascinated by the manners of the woods than by the prospects of some marketable beaver skins, but surely Harris partially misreads Biddle. Biddle's Colter is not so much callous and devoid of normal human feelings as he is converted to a primitivistic way of life. He has made the Rousseauistic choice that supposedly lay open to any man in the wilderness. *Ruder*, in Biddle's text, does not mean what it usually means today but what it meant say in the poetry of Wordsworth. And *solitude of the woods* is less a term to indicate loneliness and isolation than a poetically charged conceit of romantic primitivism.

The obvious and easy historical conclusion to draw here is that Biddle's Colter is not historical while Harris's is. Colter as object was probably simply a trapper in search of furs. However, history is never as simple as this. There is another dimension, with another sort of object, that must be taken into account. Shall we assume that Biddle engaged in a bit of personal, idle dreaming when he thought about Colter? Or shall we suppose that his mind, like other minds of his time, held active structures that put the evidence together in certain ways? Is not the idea of primitivism as much an object, though vastly more difficult to deal with, as is the profit motive of a trapper named Colter? But here of course the center of focus shifts from the mind (or behavior, for historians tend to a sort of behaviorism) of Colter to the mind of Nicholas Biddle. Colter becomes not the prime object, hard and meaningful in itself, but the correlative of another object, the primitivistic idea in the mind of Biddle. Colter of course is still an object, but he is the object as representation, not the object as final meaning.

Now I assume the historian does not consciously configure his objective data to make it represent his ideas. In his sophistication, he is aware that this may happen, that he may write metahistory instead of history; consequently, he struggles to escape his subjectivity. He may indeed at times seem to refuse to think at all, and he is sometimes so spooky of literary dangers that he avoids imagery as he would avoid disease and he reduces his prose to the flat matter of fact for fear a style will play tricks on him.

The novelist, however, is an animal of another species. If he believes in anything, he believes in the power of the creative imagination. He does not sit quietly in his study waiting for the documents to tell him the truth. It may be that he puts his ear to history as Howells said he should put it to nature, but confident novelists are likely to make discoveries in another way. We usually call it insight, and what we mean is a clarification, an understanding, a moral and esthetic ordering that is unashamedly subjective. Unlike the historian, the novelist deliberately manipulates the data of his imaginative world to make it persuasively represent a meaning which issues from himself, not from the documents.

What is the nature of this meaning? How is it validated? How does it differ from the cranky assertion, the claim which is delusion? For one supposes that the novelist, whether he deals with the social world of *The Financier* or the personal world of *The Stranger*, is concerned with meanings that are not idiosyncratic. Even though the novelist may stop short of universals, he nevertheless aspires in his novel to win the assent of a great many readers. Writing a novel is in a sense an act of public communication. And one can say that insofar as meanings and the novelistic strategies by which they are presented and argued are shared by a community of minds such meanings have a kind of objectivity. A novel's meanings may not have the total acceptance of a geometric proposition, but they also cannot have merely the private "truthfulness" of a paranoid fear. Nevertheless, whatever their ultimate public acceptance, initially they are private. They are born in the subject or at least they have their ground there, and no amount of seemingly impersonal, detached form should disguise this fact. The notion of the novel as autotelic is not ultimately satisfying, for whatever the esthetic independence of the text, that text does not wholly establish its own end. The formal ends of a novel may of course be criticized as ends, but they must also be considered means toward some larger literary end for which one needs a bigger word than esthetic. One may study and delight in the design of *The Ambassadors*, but ultimately one ponders the human condition of Strether. Of similar limitation is the term *ontological* when it is used to modify *criticism*, when it is used to suggest a *being* in the work of art and independence of the *being* in the artist. One would hope that all great novels, including western novels, are ontological in the sense that they seek an ultimate ground of being, but this is quite different from saying that a novel *is* as a poem *is*.

One comes, then, to the question: what is the nature of the truth which the novel speaks? What kind of truth is signified by the verb *happens* rather than the verb *happened*? Aristotle called it the universal as opposed to the particular. As he said, "Poetry tends to express the universal, history the particular." This may be, as scholars have long insisted, too simple a distinction. Poetry, certainly the novel, does express some of the particular,[9] and history, certainly from the eighteenth century on, has tried to express some universals. Yet it still remains true that poetry deals with meanings that happen, with truths that were true in the past, true in the present, and possess the predictive virtue of being true in the future. History, on the other hand, while it may suggest tentative lines of development for the future, does not justify itself for its predictive possibility.[10] It is on the whole content to find the truth of what happened. The statement history repeats itself is a popular naive notion to which no sophisticated historian can adhere. If in a sense life repeats itself, it is poetry rather than history which seeks to define these recurring patterns of the human condition.

The novelist deals, then, with meanings which do not possess historicity in the usual sense at all. I say usual sense, meaning that they do not derive out of particular times, places, particular clusters of events. If the novelist narrates how the beaver trap was set so that it snapped on a hind leg rather than a foreleg, so that the beaver could not free itself so easily by self-amputation, he is dealing with an idea having historicity. Trapping experience over the years in the fur trade led to this bit of "theory." But if the novelist recognizes that man is a divided being, sometimes pulled between the polar attractions of free isolation and ordered community, he deals with a human meaning of a quite different sort. This sense of man may be poignantly acute at one time, only vaguely present at other times. One sees it actively present in the Romantic period, scarcely stirring in mid-eighteenth century, say in the world of Benjamin Franklin. And yet one cannot really trace its origins, its waxings and wanings, to historical causes. One tends thus to conclude that such division is in some way inherent in the nature of man.

How is it inherent? Unfortunately our anthropology[11] is inadequate to give this question final answer. Man seems inherently to seek rebirth, to find again that innocence which he knows to his pain he has lost. We describe this need in various ways: a need to return to the womb, to nature, to Eden; but whether we use the language of psychoanalysis, romantic philosophy, or biblical myth, whether we call the human structure assumed to fix this need a psychological complex, an archetype, or a myth, we agree that we are speaking of a human reality that cannot be got at by a scientific clinical empiricism or a mathematical rationalism. And it cannot be accounted for in the usual historical analysis. Even though one cannot claim that it is universal—today we are rightly spooky of such absolute notions—he can insist on an existential validity broad enough to satisfy the writer's hope of general truth. If it is not essential to man, it is present in the condition of his existence.

If such a meaning is mythic rather than historical, we arrive then at the obvious conclusion that for the poet myth is finally more important than history. The mythic patterns—or let us call them archetypal patterns—do repeat themselves. They *happen*. They have their own validation in the way in which they intensely and yet comprehensively (thoroughly) contain the critical tensions of a human situation. Their economy escapes analysis. A library of criticism will not add to the power of the story of Abraham and Isaac.

Yet western writers have again and again been warned to avoid the mythical. The mythical West, they are reminded, is not the historical West, and to live imaginatively in the mythical West is to live some sort of falsehood. Truth lies only in the historical West; that is the real West. In that West only lies the possibility of a literary realism. The dogma goes on and on, as if this way lies the literary promised land where great works spring from western minds, where every writer who can tell a cow from a crowbar can be a Faulkner. But all of this is a naive and misguided gospel.

Recently a well known western writer offered a hundred dollars to anyone who can give documented proof of a walkdown in western history. I do not have the full statement before me, but I assume he implies that writers should avoid the climatic gun play in their fiction because one cannot document it in history. If my assumption is correct, then here is yet another instance of confusing history and literature, of failing to distinguish between what happened and what happens. Suppose an enterprising researcher digs deep and long in the files of the *Trail End Gazette* and comes up with a seemingly accurate story about two cocky cowboys facing each other down on September 22, 1886. This may earn the hundred dollars offered; it may provide an interesting if obscure note in the history of the cattle trade; but what does it have to do with literature? In any kind of literary criticism worthy of the name, the walkdown has been suspect not because it couldn't be footnoted from history but because it was used in a dehumanized oversimplification of the dramatic forces and personalities involved. If the shoot-out is grounded in persuasively delineated conflicts between men, if this violent confrontation yields significant results in the definition of man locked in tragic predicaments, then it needs no other literary justification. If a suggestive model cannot be found in history, then it will need to be invented by the novelist.

The falseness, indeed the silliness, of the argument from history can be emphasized by another, imaginary offer. Sometime in the third century B.C. a Greek writer announces that he will give one hundred drachmas to anyone who can supply documentary proof that someone in Greek history married his mother, killed his father, and then put out his own eyes.

But if history does not provide the ground of the novelist's truth, it may nevertheless provide the means by which his truth is articulated. What happened may be useful in telling what happens. The critic can therefore suggest that the writer continue to be interested in the history of the West; that interest can fill the reservoir or give substance to the fountain (I do not wish to argue the absolute rightness of any metaphor) out of which the novelist works. If history does not offer the truths which he seeks to present, it does offer a richness of setting, incident, patterns of human response from which the novelist may build his work.

How then does the novelist use history? How does he use what happened to tell what happens? How does he use the mode of history to deal with that which is non-historical?

The fundamental line of difference between history and the novel has no doubt been obscured by the fact that a work of history sometimes reads like a novel and a novel often has features which one can call historical. The way in which the historian imagines in a novelistic fashion has already been considered, but the historical features of the novel need to be more carefully noted. If the eighteenth century was the first period of extended concern with the nature of history, it was also the period when the novel came to full maturity. It was no accident of titlemaking that some of the first great novels were titled as histories. A title like *The History of Tom Jones* signifies the literary intention to deal with a man through a course of time; it indicates the writer's conviction that the way to define him is to develop his meaning in sequential experience. Such sequential experience plotted over the years can of course be called a history. A great many novels have this sort of historical design.

Such design, however, does not mean that these novels are historical in the historian's sense. The data out of which the novel's world is rendered, while they may be the hard facts of history, needn't be. An imagined fact, if it works persuasively in the novel, is just as good as the non-imagined fact. It may be the historian's fact that many cowboys did not carry six-guns or that some of the six-guns they did carry were actually five-guns. This is no better for the novelist than the "fact" that most of them carried at least one gun and sometimes two. Of course the novelist may want to write another kind of novel and have no guns at all. I am assuming for many kinds of dramatic situations that guns are as necessary to the western writer as swords were to Shakespeare. Further, the ordering of the data, the determination of the sequential patterns, owes nothing to what any group of documents may say. Order is arranged to satisfy dramatic needs interior to the novel. Of course if the novelist wants to fasten his imagined world onto the historical world, he'll have to respect this outer history. He cannot have the War of 1812 fought in 1843. Finally, and most important of all, there is the difference in ultimate claim of meaning. That which seems in its texture and time-design a "history" is not after all saying, this *happened* to this man in the years 1830 to 1860, but rather, this *happens* to men when they are placed in certain kinds of situations and forced, by themselves or their surroundings or both, to solve the human problems that confront them. Solutions here are not the particular solutions of history but insofar as possible the universal solutions of poetry.

If such consideration answers the question how does the novel resemble history, it does not wholly tell how the novel uses history. Here the focus may appropriately be established within the context of criticism of the Western. Why should the Western, which aspires to be poetry, to tell what *happens*, be so seemingly dependent on history, which tells what *happened*? I say *seemingly dependent* because, as I have tried to point out, the necessity of history is more apparent than real. The usefulness of history is another matter.

The answer here can best be given by some examples showing how nonhistorical insights into the human condition can be effectively, indeed powerfully, presented in the body of history. One can rightly call this history the objective correlative, with the reminder once more that the objectivity of the literary structure is the objectivity of means, not the objectivity of ends.[12]

Any thoughtful analysis of man's relationship to law reveals a complex set of impulses, ideas, loyalties. Most, if not all, men feel an obligation to some general principle of right or that which is the accepted norm of sanctioned behavior. This feeling may spring from the pressures of something called conscience or superego or conditioned social habit; the novelist can start with his awareness of its recognized presence in the personality. The general principle may be the universal morality of natural law, in which case man may feel its demands even though he is a hundred miles from any other man; or it may be the community of common or civil law in the close context of which he feels his loyalty. Again the metaphysics of the principle may be left to the philosophers; the novelist begins with his conviction that such principles do bind men.

At the same time, however, men are persons of impulse, of intensely motivated actions which do not have their sanction in a general moral principle at all. If a father revenges the death of a son, or a brother the death of a brother, this can be called an action grounded in loyalty, but it is the loyalty of blood; it conflicts with a higher loyalty to law. Thus there may be in the same person a tearing division of obligation, an acute tension between loyalties. One can talk about such a predicament in abstract philosophical terms; one can try to get down into the special intimacy of it, the existential situation itself, by some sort of concrete, phenomenological analysis; but the truth remains that the only way to deal with it both at the level of logical discourse and at the level of full particularity is through the literary work. For what is being articulated here is not really an idea at all but a human situation. Its full existential reality can be rendered, but it cannot be talked about. Or at least the philosophical paraphrase is not the whole truth intended.

If the novel is to try to deal with this truth, it obviously needs a time and a place where both loyalties can be persuasively established. The West, it seems to me, provides that time and place. The historical social facts of thinness of population, the absence of strong social cohesion, the tenuity of any lines of legal authority, these and other factors created a situation of moral and legal uncertainty. Thus western history provides an objective correlative by which this truth can be imaged.

I am not prepared, however, to assert that this truth has been powerfully imaged in any single work. For one reason or another, the western writer has been content to stop short of the full thrust of this dramatic possibility. In some instances he has settled for the standard, the expected, the neatly completed formula, as if he has believed that his readers want only the action, the outline of meaning, and not the full and complex statement.[13] In some cases he has been imaginatively timid because he has supposed he must have the backing of history. Nevertheless, a number of

Westerns have helped us see the importance of this happening and the rightness of the West as its imaginative locus.

An example is Will Henry's *Who Rides with Wyatt*, a popular Western first published in 1955. If it fails to go much beyond the standard pattern of fast-paced action, it at least suggests the sort of work I have in mind. The Wyatt here is of course Wyatt Earp, the historical lawman and gun fighter. A long shelf of books and articles have dealt with Earp or with Wyatt and his brothers, and the central biographical question remains: was Wyatt Earp a good lawman heroically embodying the needed civic virtues of social order or was he in his sheer dependence on violence, the use of his gun or the butt of that gun, really no better than the frontier hoodlums he brought to justice or to the ends of his own vengeance? This, I repeat, is the biographical question, but it is not a novelistic one. If the novelist is seeking to answer the question what happened to Wyatt Earp, he is really writing a kind of history or at least he is moved by the historian's purpose. If on the other hand he is exploring imaginatively the predicament of a lawman acting extra-legally for personal reasons, then he is showing what happens. The historical Earp and his world of Tombstone merely provide a good objective configuration. If this is rendered fully and deeply, the novel makes its own case. That is enough. No claim of historical support need be made. No claim of historical truth need be argued. I would add, however, that if I were writing the novel, I would avoid giving my central figure, however many of his parts are derived from history, a historical name. Even with a hero like Earp, who exists in considerable degree in the freer realm of legend, the writer takes on some of the burdens of biography. The novelist has enough burden without taking on the added, and irrelevant, burden of biography. The result, as in the instance of Henry's novel, is likely to be neither responsible biography nor fully realized fiction.

Earlier I mentioned the anthropological conviction that man is a divided being, blessed (or cursed) with a sense of freedom and a profound feeling of dependence, with the need to be himself in absolute self-reliance and the need to rest his egoistic drives in the bosom of society, with the desire to flee to Eden and the hope to accept the burdens of his fallen state. Again, such division, the awareness of it, the tensions it draws, may be more evident in one time than in another, but the anthropologist nevertheless assumes the division is inherent in the condition of man and therefore nonhistorical.

Here, too, the historical West offers an appropriate imaginative locus. The geography of the historical West contained islands of cohesive society, for example, Santa Fe and Taos, later Salt Lake City and Virginia City; but between these islands there were vast spaces of social emptiness or at least extreme thinness where a man might approach the polar opposite of a social existence.[14] Furthermore, the historical West held a variety of men representing a whole spectrum of commitment to or rejection of civilized settlement. There was little if anything primitivistic about Captain Lewis, David Thompson, or even Jedediah Smith; still one can perhaps attribute to other men a degree of fascination with the wilderness. The loners of the fur trade, men like Colter, Glass, and Bill Williams, may have acted out of a greater need for self-reliant wilderness freedom than for social togetherness. We cannot really know, for the biographical data are too few and too superficial.

But even when we do not and cannot know, we are invited to make some guesses. Inescapably we are struck by the facts that some men of the West led advancing settlement and then fled the very settlement they had sponsored. Starting with Boone, the frontiersman seemed sometimes to be an ambiguous mix of civilized and primitivistic values.[15] If one says, as I have already said, that Jedediah Smith was civilized rather than primitivistic, he must still account for the fact that Smith chose to live and die in a world of relative social emptiness. His biographers have not even begun to solve the puzzle of his thoughts (which of course are too few) and actions. But here the novelist sits ready to take the actions, the hints of attitude, the experiences to be gone through and interpreted, and give them a meaningful coherence. He starts with the questions why do men behave in these strange ways? Why do they seem so divided in their purposes? But these are questions about what happens, not what happened.

A considerable number of western novels deal with this human predicament of being caught within the conflicting pulls of the free wilderness and settled civilization. Sometimes the presentation is highly superficial. The mountain man comes out of society, still carrying its values, and goes out into the West. After a sufficient number of adventures—buffalo hunts, encounters with grizzly bears and Indians—after eating boiled dog and raw buffalo liver dipped in bile, perhaps after a wilderness attachment to a penny-skinned squaw, he comes back to civilization to marry the genteel heroine. Here the split is radical and complete. Indeed we seem to have two characters with the same name, there being no center to hold the two parts together. The civilized "vestiges" do not function in the wilderness, and the primitivistic accretion during the western adventures seems to be left behind, like the beaver traps, when he goes east across the Mississippi. Equally superficial is the version which sends the mountain man, alone on his mule, off into the never-never wilderness, there supposedly to live happily ever after on his pemmican and mountain air. But to *live* in this literary sense is not to exist in any viable and relevant human condition. This is western phantasy, not fully realized western fiction.

What is needed is of course a novel which establishes a center, a center showing both impulses, recognizing both needs, and holding the tensions between them. This means a highly complex literary conception of character, as complex in its way as James's conception of Lambert Strether or Faulkner's conception of Quentin Compson. An Andy Burnett, a Johnny Christmas, a Sam Minard will not do.

Even Harvey Fergusson's Sam Lash does not wholly fulfill our critical hopes although of all literary mountain men he perhaps comes closest to a matured realization. The first part of *Wolf Song* makes Sam a mountain man, independent as a wild animal, happy in the rough life of the senses. Then his human "flaw" is revealed in his attachment to Lola. Never again can he find the freedom, the primitive wholeness he felt as a mountain man, although for a brief time he seems to have regained it. Ultimately he comes home to civilization, but to an important extent this home is a trap. However much he may love and belong to Lola, she remains his antagonist. So at the end of the novel, though Lash and his woman are together, the tension, the ambiguity remain.

Other examples of the novelist's insight objectified in literary history could be given, in fact a whole range of discoveries about the human condition. Some themes obviously need another sort of configuration. If the novelist is concerned with the tight, deterministic hold of social environment upon men and women, as in Crane's *Maggie* and Dreiser's *An American Tragedy*, he will probably not turn to the historical West.[16] If he is interested in the burden of the past upon man, as in some of Faulkner's novels, he will turn to an imaginative world which is saturated, perhaps haunted by its history. The West provides neither social nor historical density. But to the gifted novelist able to escape the tyranny of factual history, able to cure himself of a nostalgic fascination with a colorful place and time now gone, it offers an abundance of materials out of which to speak his truths. He can, if he believes in his vocation as writer, if he trusts the rightness of his imagination, tell us what happens.

Notes

1. Nothing spooks the average western buff quite like the word *fiction*. The popular magazine *True West* prominently features on its cover the words *No Fiction*. One supposes that without this warning readers might pay good money for writing which is *not true* and that further they might innocently be led into the deceptive world of fiction. The general assumption seems to be here that a reader cannot tell the difference between fact and fiction, that history and fiction have no interior signs of structure, style, or theme by which the reader can tell the one from the other.

2. Andy Adams' *The Log of a Cowboy*.

3. The language of critical discussion here seems to maintain the usual difference between a novel and a work of history. Indicating action in the novel, we say Boone *sets* the trap. Describing action in the history, we say Smith *helped* amputate his leg. Conventionally we use the present for the novel, the past for the work of history. My point, however, is that such conventional differences are really superficial. Boone's pastness here is just as certain as Tom Smith's.

4. *Bent's Fort* (Lincoln: Univ. of Nebraska Press, 1972), p. 403.

5. "The New West and the Old Fiction," *Independent*, 9 Jan. 1902, p. 100.

6. *Fifty Years on the Owl Hoot Trail* (Chicago: Sage Books, 1969) p. xvi. Italics are Dale's.

7. "The Novelist of the Cattle Kingdom," Introduction to *The Hired Man on Horseback*, by May Davison Rhodes (Boston: Houghton Mifflin, 1938), p. xxviii.

8. *John Colter, His Years in the Rockies* (New York: Charles Scribner's Sons, 1952), p. 37.

9. Perhaps much of it. John Crowe Ransom noted that the poem, a configuration claiming universality, "consisted actually, and notoriously, of particularity." "Criticism as Pure Speculation," in Donald Stauffer, ed., *The Intent of the Critic* (Gloucester, Mass.: Peter Smith, 1963), p. 109.

10. Even if the rule of phase did apply to history, my point would not be altered. If, as Henry Adams suggested, history has gone and is going through certain changes of phase, with consequent acceleration, this historical process is repeatable only in theory. Supposedly on another planet where there is life, the same curve of acceleration might happen again. If the historian asserts that he deals with what happens, and what happens is that a civilization will change from steam power to electrical power to atomic power, he doesn't end up with an insight he can use many times. More useful might be Turner's theory of political reversion in the social thrust west beyond settlement. However, Turner's description of successive reversions on successive frontiers suggests a similarity of social condition more apparent than real. Only by simplification, only by unburdening history of its accumulating deposit of experience, could one assert that the self-reliant frontier democrat of Nebraska was the same as the self-reliant democrat of the upper Ohio Valley. To ignore the accumulation of additional experience is unhistorical indeed. There was perhaps too much of the transcendentalist in Turner just as there was perhaps too much of the rationalist in Adams.

11. When I use the term *anthropology*, I mean of course philosophical anthropology.

12. In using the term *objective correlative*, I am adapting for my purposes a concept first made critically well known by T. S. Eliot. However, I am not therefore insisting on the rightness of Eliot's own use. In "Hamlet and His Problems," Eliot wrote: "The only way of expressing emotion in the form of art is by finding an 'objective correlative': in other words, a set of objects, a situation, a chain of events which shall be the formula of that *particular* emotion; such that when the external facts, which must terminate in sensory experience, are given, the emotion is immediately evoked." *Selected Essays of T. S. Eliot*, new edition (New York: Harcourt, Brace, 1950), pp. 124–25. While the western novelist may use a set of objects, a situation, a chain of events from history, I would not want to call his configuration a *formula*; his work does not represent his meaning as H_2O represents water. I would not assume that if the Western is constructed of certain elements in a certain proportion that a definite meaning will necessarily be generated. And certainly what is evoked is not just emotion. Further, even if we can define the evoked meaning as some sort of esthetic entity fusing both emotion and logical statement, I do not suppose that meaning resides only in the sensibility of the critic, evoked there by the instrument of the novel.

13. By *statement* I mean of course the novelist's presentation, not the scientist's or the philosopher's logical discourse.

14. Here I am not writing as a cultural geographer or sociologist of the West. I am aware of the facts that in any comprehensive study of the early West all sorts of qualifications need to be taken into account. There is the fact of Indian society itself; if the mountain man gave up white society for life as a white Indian he did not necessarily give up a sense of belonging to a cohesive group. There is the fact that the fur trade—and even more so the cattle trade—was in many ways a collective enterprise. Alexander Ross, for example, gives no sense of the primitivistic motives that may have moved men in their role as trappers and hunters. Even Bill Williams was sometimes a member of a group trading organization. And Hugh Glass has been elevated to literary heroism not simply because he survived alone in an almost

unbelievable crawl but because he forgave those who had abandoned him. Certainly the act of forgiveness assumes a sense of brotherhood, if not community. Nevertheless, one can assert that if any man ever tried out the possibilities of being alone, it was the mountain man, the historical mountain man.

15. See Henry Nash Smith, "Daniel Boone: Empire Builder or Philosopher of Primitivism?" *Virgin Land: The American West as Symbol and Myth* (Cambridge: Harvard Univ. Press, 1950), pp. 51–58. Mix is probably the wrong term here although in somes instances the two sides, the two interests may have no organic unity within the person. I am of course assuming the possibility of such a unity, a personality that whatever its conflicting pulls, its inner tensions, remains a unified, if complex, personality. In speaking of man as divided in this way, I do not mean to suggest that he is schizophrenic.

16. It is possible of course that he could use a special part of the West, say the human ant hill of Virginia City, Nevada.

CRITICAL ESSAYS ON INDIVIDUAL WESTERN NOVELISTS

Early Western Novelists

Emerson Hough and the Popular Novel

Delbert E. Wylder*

With perhaps the exceptions of *Heart's Desire* and the later *John Rawn*, it is almost impossible to conceive of Emerson Hough having contributed very much to the development and depth of either regional Western literature or to American literature in general. But Emerson Hough *was* popular. His historical romances sold well, beginning with the successful historical novel *The Mississippi Bubble*—and both *North of 36* and *The Covered Wagon* not only were translated into foreign languages but have remained in the popular realm of paperback books even until the present. *The Covered Wagon* has even been condensed into a Classics Comic book without, one might suggest, a great deal of loss to any content other than that of a great deal of "authentic" detail about the trip West. Hough and his writing, then, serve as an apt illustration of some of the difficulties and dangers implicit in the study of the popular novel. More important, I think that a look at some of his works might indicate certain research approaches that might well be applied in a valid study of the popular novel and place that type of novel in its proper perspective. It seems to me that a distinction must be clearly made between the popular novel and the "literary" or "elitest" novel.

Several years ago, John G. Cawelti asked an important question about the popular Western novel. "Why," he asked, "should [we] assume that the Western is not primarily an artistic construction similar in nature if not in quality or complexity to a play by Shakespeare or a novel by James Joyce?"[1] Cawelti's question in a sense provides its own answer. We should *not* assume that the popular Western is *not* an artistic construction, for it does have form and structure, characters, tone, and other elements that make up the novel. What does concern the critic, and the teacher it seems to me, is that one of the primary concerns is, in fact, the matter of the quality and complexity (or rather the lack of quality and complexity) in the popular Western novel. Hough provides an exceptional example not only of the simplicities and inaccuracies that are innate in the

**SwAL*, 2 (1972), 83–89. ©1972 by *Southwestern American Literature*. Reprinted by permission of *Southwestern American Literature*.

popular approach, but also of some of the dangers implicit in teaching the popular novel without making some important distinctions.

Despite Emerson Hough's claims to literary excellence, he was a popular novelist, and his adherence to the superficial realities of life in the West (or the Midwest or South, for that matter) only thinly disguised his inability to cope with the deeper realities of the Western experience. In 1906, Andy Adams wrote Hough that

> Russell of Montana, among the artists, may continue to please a few of us old boys, but Remington, with his bad men, holds the center of the stage. The second winning of the West—for truth—is on, and I extend my hand in congratulations.[2]

This letter came after Hough's *Heart's Desire*, and Adams had good reason for extending his hand. Unfortunately, Hough's later Westerns developed a new pattern, partly because Hough was writing too fast and partly because he wanted to make more money. After what Hough considered to be the financial failure of *Heart's Desire*, he returned to a pattern or formula that had resulted in, for him, a financial jackpot with *The Mississippi Bubble* and at least a winning combination of elements in *The Law of the Land*. Of the ten Western novels he wrote (*The Girl at the Half-Way House*, *Heart's Desire*, *54-50 or Fight*, *The Magnificent Adventure*, *The Sagebrusher*, *The Covered Wagon*, *North of 36*, *Mother of Gold*, and *The Ship of Souls*), the last eight qualify as "formula" novels by Cawelti's list of characteristics. All of them, first and foremost, have two sides, and the sides are readily identifiable as the hero versus the villain. In each novel, the game has at least one, if not more, clearly defined set of rules, and finally, the "game" takes place, as Cawelti has it, "on a certain kind of board or field whose shape and markings indicate the significance of particular actions."[3] This board, I take it, has to do with situational contexts.

Of the eight novels, the three that are most obviously Western are *The Way of a Man*, *The Covered Wagon*, and *North of 36*. In each novel, there is a specific hero figure, his heroine, some other rather close friends on one side; the other side is represented by a true scoundrel with his cohorts. The game, of course, is always won by the hero. Because of some type of strange misunderstanding (the hero usually has been thought a cheat or a thief, or even dishonoràble in his relations with women), the heroine is at least temporarily sympathetic to the villain, who is just subtle enough not to twist his mustaches in public. The many good, but very gullible people who will eventually be won over by the sterling character of the hero are also initially sympathetic to the villain.

The rules are definitely established early in the novels, and the most important one in the Hough novel is that the hero, as in an Alger novel or one of Dryden's Heroic plays, must start at a disadvantage. Furthermore, it is forbidden the hero to explain his difficulties, for a chivalric code of honor even more restrictive than Almanzor's or Aureng-Zebe's does not allow him to complain or to explain, except to himself. He must prove his worth through action. Another rule, evidently, is that the heroine must be innocent enough to be unable to judge character or to understand human motivations, especially the masculine variety. And she also must have a heart that dominates her head, since any serious breach of emotional faith in the hero would be unforgivable.[4] The heroine of *The Covered Wagon*, for example, must remain in love with the hero even while she is preparing to wed the villain.

On the third point, the setting of the American West either during a period of expansion (as in most) or when that expansion must be protected (as in *The Sagebrusher*) is the game board. The object of the game is generally to prove that the Anglo-Saxon race is the superior race and that its expansion cannot, nay should not, be stopped. This is true even of *The Sagebrusher*, a novel of World War II in which the Germans (also, strangely enough, Anglo-Saxons) attempt to blow up a dam in the United States—and, as a matter of fact, are successful. Hough solved the problem of competition between Anglo-Saxons by having the espionage activity carried out by Jews in the hire of the Germans.

Another problem that might have been more difficult to handle, had Hough tried, was the fact that some of the elements in the game were in direct conflict with the others. One of the most important elements was the hero's code. It becomes, even in the West, the symbol of a civilization. Hough's idea of the Western code is a curious mixture of Southern chivalry and Victorian genteelism. It centers around blood (or family), sensitivity, and response to outside hostile influences, protection of ladies (as distinguished from females), and a stoicism that includes, of course, bravery in the face of danger and a straightforward honesty. It was a reflection of his own code which, he once said, he got from his father. As he wrote to George Bird Grinnell, "My old Virginia daddy taught me that none of our family could ever welch on an obligation, ever offer discourtesy when none was carried to him, or ever forget to challenge an affront when it was known to be such."[5] His protective attitude toward women was evidenced when he once detected a slight to his wife and demanded that the chairwoman of an Indianapolis ladies club survey all 400 members of the club to discover whose husband it was who had slighted his wife "Lotty." His bravery he tried to demonstrate in all of his rather dangerous field trips in the West. He endowed all of his heroes with very much the same type of code. It is, of course, a code that represents a highly civilized control, through family tradition, of sex, aggressive drives, and fear. It is highly territorial in nature, setting up personal boundaries that cannot be breached, as well as restrictions upon the encroachment of the territory of others. It also involves, as an inner-directed code, the concept of guilt for self-punishment of a failure to operate within this rather idealistic structure. Hough's heroes seem almost masochistic in light of their ability to punish themselves even if they have done nothing wrong but have only seemed to.

On the other hand, Hough was convinced of the superiority of his own race. Manifest destiny was to him not so much a religio-political concept as a biological-political concept. In one sense, of course, Hough was dealing with a truth. He sensed what Conrad knew, and what the new biologists are now discovering, as Desmond Morris puts it—"that man is the most opportunistic of the predators." Thus, Hough saw the expansion of the Anglo-Saxons almost as the expression and fulfillment of the laws of nature. Not only were the fittest to survive, but they were destined to dominate completely. This theme runs not only through his histories, as in *The Passing of the Frontier*, but in almost all of his novels as well. One of his early "Southerns," for example, is titled *The Law of the Land of Miss Lady, Whom it Involved in Mystery, and of John Eddring, Gentleman of the South, Who Read its Deeper Meaning.* The novel concerns an uprising by blacks in the South, the settling of the uprising by violence on the part of whites, and the eventual trial of the whites and their acquittal after a declamation (certainly not a plea) from John Eddring.[6] Late in the novel, Eddring finds himself protecting a young lady and her female escort on an island. The "deeper meaning" he "reads" while he is protecting the females.

> In the night the wild life of the forest went on. The barkings and rustlings and splashings still were heard, and the great cat called again. But all these savage things went by, passing apart, avoiding this spot where the White Man, most savage and most potent of all animals, had made his lair and now guarded his own.[7]

At the end of the chapter, having heard the wind whispering "Only the strong. Only the strong," Eddring's heart "throbbed steadily. Peace came to his soul now as never before; since now he knew that he was of the strong, that he was ready for life and what combat it might bring."[8]

Now that was a Southern. In Hough's Westerns, the Indians fill the position of the blacks. Hough was extremely careful to be true to reality in his description of the American Indian, and he was less prejudiced about Indians than he was about either Jews or blacks. Note in this letter to Samuel Merwin of *Success* magazine, for example, he doesn't mention Indians. "If we could wipe out all the Jews, Negroes, Immigrants, and Labor Unions in the world, we would have a fairly decent country to live in. . . ."[9] As a matter of fact, Hough once wrote to William Griffith at *Collier's* that "The Fact is, we are about as savage as the Indians, and a close parallel can be drawn between our respective manners and morals."[10] As a muckraking journalist, Hough once investigated and exposed a leading Oklahoma senator for his manipulation of funds intended for the Indian reservations, and he knew many Indians and was a welcome guest to many of them. However, this is not quite Hough's expression in the novels. The Indians had to be, in the formula novel, clearly evil. They are savages, but evil ones. The white men are good savages. After several battles with the Sioux in *The Covered Wagon*, a novel in which the Indians are always referred to as savages, we find this strange description of the white encampment:

> And that night, in the two separate encampments, the white nation, in bivouac, on its battle ground, sat around the fires . . . till near morning, roasting boss ribs, breaking marrowbones, laughing, singing, boasting, shaking high their weapons of war, men making love to their women—the Americans, *most terrible* and *most successful* of all savages in history.[11]

This, in short, is a hymn of praise, and it comes from the narrator who usually praises fair play, genteelism, and delicacy of feeling.

I am not trying, here, to denigrate Emerson Hough as a man. He was a racist, it is true, and he passed his racism on to a good many readers. He was also one of the first and most effective of conservationists, protecting the buffalo and other endangered animals—and the forests. What I am concerned with is his novels. What he has here, of course, is a fine human paradox—the stuff of great literature. But he has written a simplistic formula popular Western in his desire, as he once wrote a reader, to entertain. "If I have forced you," he wrote, "and some others to take an interest in the affairs of that day, and if I have perhaps entertained you for an hour or so, I have fulfilled my function as a novelist."[12] There is nothing here about the truth of the human heart nor of any other truth, nor is there any statement about the complexity of life. On the other hand, we can all remember a British "frontier" novel that employs this same strange paradox—the civilized code and savagery. But the author, Joseph Conrad, and his narrator Marlowe are both aware of that human paradox. They know of the truth of Kurtz's discovery of "The Horror" discovered beneath the code of civilization and the great irony that keeps Marlowe from confessing truthfully the last words of Kurtz to his Intended. Marlowe's reaction to the great lie is to expect the house to collapse, that the heavens would fall upon his head. And Marlowe continues: "The heavens do not fall for such a trifle. Would they have fallen, I wonder, if I had rendered Kurtz that justice which was his due?" The answer to such a question is open to the reader, but the question is concerned with the basis of civilization. Conrad, in *Heart of Darkness*, may not be as true to physical reality (that is, then, authenticity) as Hough in his more carefully researched novels, but Conrad is far more concerned about the greater truths that it is the province of literature to examine. Elitest culture it may be, but it is superior in the quality and complexity and the basic honesty of its writing.

I am not suggesting here that Popular Culture is not a valid field of study. In fact, it seems to me that the implications here are that the study of popular culture in a serious fashion is almost essential in a complex society. It is an important part of a humanistic curriculum for many of the reasons John Cawelti suggested. Most importantly, I would suggest that, taught in relation to elitest literature, it can be especially illuminating.

However, there are many more ways in which the study of the popular novel can contribute to the education of the contemporary student. A colleague of mine at Southwest is, for example, studying the relationship of the Western formula to the popular fiction of space exploration and is finding a number of similarities.

Some of the terminology used in this present paper suggests that a sociological study of the popular novel might be in order, applying the concepts of tradition-direction, inner-direction, and other-direction in much the same way that Riesman, himself, does in his analysis of the children's books "The Little Engine that Could" and "Little Toot." The socio-psychological approach could also be adopted to the study of the popular Western. After all, there is another sense in which we can talk about "game" techniques—that of transactional analysis as described in Eric Berne's *Games People Play*, and as practiced and discussed by his many followers. "A game," Berne explains, "is an ongoing series of complementary ulterior transactions progressing to a well-defined, predictable outcome." Actually, there is nothing more predictable than the outcome of a popular Western. Berne also points out that "Every game is basically dishonest, and the outcome has a dramatic quality." The peculiar dishonesty of the popular novel in its vision of life, despite its drama of violence, seems particularly appropriate in an analysis of contemporary society, especially when humor is now being used so frequently to mask both the dishonesty and the violence, as in Portis' *True Grit* and Friend's *The Scalphunters*.

The "game board" almost always involves land, or territory, and the examination by the new biologists of what Robert Ardrey called "the territorial imperative" may, when applied to Western novels, indicate something about man's territorialism as it changes from the popular novel of one century to that of another century. The popular Western may also be studied as the continuation of a folklore tradition, finally gone commercial.

In short, there are many ways to approach the study of the popular Western. Always, however, it would seem to me that the researcher should keep in mind exactly what he is dealing with. He is dealing with the formula novel and, to use terms from transactional analysis, the writer of the formula novel assumes the Parent role with the reader assuming the role of Child. He is like Polonius talking to Laertes, perhaps. The creator of "elitist" literature assumes the Adult role and presumes that the reader will also take the role of the Adult. The formula novel essentially says, "The World is simple. People are simple. Life is simple."[13] The formula novel can end with speeches such as Will's in *The*

Covered Wagon, "Dear girl, you need never be afraid anymore," or Dan's in *North of 36*. "Why there is a new world, after all! We are the very first. There is no past."[14] Literature, on the other hand, suggests not only quality but all the complexities and contradictions that could lead Kurtz, when he glimpsed his own soul, to cry "The Horror," and the study of literature hopefully results in an understanding like Marlowe's—who did not have to experience the fall himself in order to understand it.

Notes

1. John G. Cawelti, "Prolegomena to the Western," *WAL*, 4 (1970), 262.
2. Andy Adams to Emerson Hough, 19 January 1906.
3. Cawelti, p. 268.
4. In his first novel Hough had put himself into an extremely difficult position, and he was careful never to do it again. Mary Ellen Beauchamp, having plighted her troth to a young Confederate who was killed in the Civil War, vowed that after his death she would never marry. She manages to hold to her promise against the pressures of a former Union soldier in the *Great American West* for almost 300 pages. At the end of the novel, after she has left to live once again in the South, the hero manages to find her. Strangely, she no longer resists, and the novel can be concluded.
5. Emerson Hough to George Bird Grinnell, 7 February 1906.
6. It is quite clear in the novel that the whole trial is a mockery. John Eddring had no chance of being convicted by a white jury.
7. Emerson Hough, *The Law of the Land* (Indianapolis: Bobbs-Merrill, 1904), p. 310.
8. Hough, *The Law of the Land*, p. 311.
9. Emerson Hough to Samuel Merwin, 19 June 1908.
10. Emerson Hough to William Griffith, 22 October 1908.
11. Emerson Hough, *The Covered Wagon* (New York: Appleton, 1922), p. 236.
12. Emerson Hough to Mr. Trist Wood, New Orleans, La., 23 August 1909.
13. Hough, *The Covered Wagon*, p. 379.
14. Emerson Hough, *North of 36* (New York: Appleton, 1923), p. 429.

Two Heroes in One: Reflections on the Popularity of [Owen Wister's] *The Virginian*

Donald E. Houghton*

Owen Wister's *The Virginian* is not only the most widely read of western novels, it well may be the most widely read American novel ever published, and new editions continue to appear. The reasons for the popularity of this novel since it first appeared in 1902 continue to elude us. That *The Virginian* is a "western" explains only in part its amazing durability, since we forget most western stories as quickly as we do other popular fiction. Reviewers and critics have pointed out that the novel is a mixture of many things, but so are a great many popular novels long since forgotten. If we could identify more precisely than we have so far the source of the novel's unique staying power, we might understand a little more about Americans themselves and more specifically about American attitudes toward that frontier experience which is so central in American history and folklore.

The explanation I wish to offer here of the novel's great appeal is that Wister presents his readers *two* quite different but equally appealing Virginians in *two* quite different but equally appealing success stories, and he does this in such a way that the casual reader is not aware that there are two stories, each with its own hero and each hero possessed of quite different values. In story number one, Wister's Virginian is a romantic primitive who rejects traditional values of civilization in favor of a free life next to nature. In this story the Virginian's ultimate triumph is primitive and violent: he kills his adversary in a shoot-out. On the other hand, in story number two, the Virginian readily accepts society and civilization and is quite ready, even eager, to accept changes that Eastern culture and technology bring about in the West. In this second story the Virginian's triumph takes the form of a gradual advance from cowhand to partner on a cattle ranch and marriage to a refined young woman from a good New England family. Wister thus brings together in a single novel two Virginians, one who succeeds in terms of Western values, the other in

**JPC*, 4 (1970), 497–506. © 1970 by *The Journal of Popular Culture*. Reprinted by permission of *The Journal of Popular Culture*.

terms of Eastern values. Whether deliberately or inadvertently, Wister manages his material in such a way that the reader feels that both Western and Eastern values emerge triumphant. In a single novel Wister combines the basic ingredients of both Cooper and Horatio Alger, Jr.

One indication that the novel splits into two stories is the way in which Wister alternates between the first person point of view and that of the omniscient author. For most of story one, which presents the Virginian as a natural man, Wister uses a first-person narrator. Story number two, which concerns the Virginian's courtship of schoolteacher Molly Stark and the Virginian's progress toward financial security, is told primarily from the point of view of the omniscient author. Like Wister himself, the first-person narrator is a temporary visitor from the East, but again like Easterner Wister, he is not antagonistic to the West and its ways. On the contrary, from the opening of the novel, the educated, literate narrator, although "green from the East," quickly makes clear he feels that the West is superior to the East and he sets about westernizing himself as soon as possible, using the Virginian as both his mentor and model.[1]

This narrator of story number one falls in love with the wide open spaces with their "pure and quiet light, such as the East never sees," this "land without end, a space across which Noah and Adam might have come straight from Genesis."[2] Inhabiting this great uncivilized, unsettled land is nature's noblemen, the cowboys: "Daring, laughter, endurance—these were what I saw upon the countenances of the cow-boys. And this very first day of my knowledge of them marks a date with me. For something about them, and the idea of them, smote my American heart, and I have never forgotten it, nor ever shall, as long as I live. In their flesh our natural passions ran tumultuous; but often in their spirit sat hidden a true nobility, and often beneath its unexpected shining their figures took on heroic stature." And the best of the cowboys was the Virginian. "He was not more than six feet. . . . But in his eye, in his face, in his step, in the whole man, there dominated a something potent to be felt, I should think by man or woman." Something of a vagabond, the Virginian has visited Texas, New Mexico, Arizona, California, Oregon, Idaho, Montana, and now Wyoming. "Everywhere he had taken care of himself, and survived; nor had his strong heart yet waked up to any hunger for a home."

Although the Virginian apparently has sex enough on his rare visits to town, it is mother nature who is his mistress. He loves to go to his secret island in the middle of a mountain stream: "So many visits to this island had he made, and counted so many hours of revery spent in its haunting sweetness, that the spot had come to seem his own. It belonged to no man, for it was deep in the unsurveyed and virgin wilderness; neither had he ever made his camp here with any man, nor shared with any the intimate delight which the place gave him." At these times he sheds the last vestiges of civilization: "Then, when at length he had ridden abreast of the island pines, he would ford to the sheltered circle of his campground, throw off the saddle and blanket from the horse's hot, wet back, throw his own clothes off, and shouting, spring upon the horse bare, and with a rope for bridle, cross with him to the promised pasture. . . . And while the animal rolled in the grass, often his master would roll also, and stretch, and take the grass in his two hands, and so draw his body along, limbering his muscles after a long ride." The Virginian describes his feelings: "Often when I have camped here, it has made me want to become the ground, become the water, become the trees, mix with the whole thing. Not know myself from it. Never unmix again."

It is not surprising then that this Virginian of story one shares with the other cowhands a dismay at the news that some of the young men in the area are marrying and raising families: " 'Jim Westfall!" exclaimed the Virginian. 'Him a fam'ly man! Well, if this hyeh Territory is goin' to get full o' fam'ly men and empty o' game, I believe I'll—' " He feels a chill at the news that a schoolhouse is soon to be built nearby. "It symbolized the dawn of a neighborhood, and it brought a change into the wilderness air. The feel of it struck cold upon the free spirits of the cowpunchers, and they told each other that, what with women and children and wire fences, this country would not long be a country for men."

The drama of story number one emerges from the friction between the Virginian and the villainous Trampas. The Virginian makes Trampas look bad when in a card game Trampas says, "Your bet, you son-of-a—." The Virginian cooly removes his pistol from its holster, and holding it unaimed, says to Trampas these now-famous words: "When you call me that, *smile.*" Trampas is responsible in part for the estrangement between Virginian and his friend Steve. It is Trampas who is responsible for involving the naive and foolish Shorty in rustling. The tension between the Virginian and Trampas reaches a climax when Trampas, after drinking too much, tells the Virginian he has until sundown to get out of town.

Despite the good Bishop's advice to avoid the showdown with Trampas and despite Molly's warning that the marriage is off if he meets Trampas, the Virginian, in true Western fashion, follows his feeling that a man must do what he has to do. "I am going my own course," he says to Molly. "Can't yu' see how it must be about a man?" Author Wister steps in at this point to reenforce the Virginian's decision to have it out with Trampas: "It had come to that point where there was no way out, save only the ancient, eternal way between man and man. It is only the great mediocrity that goes to law in these personal matters." The Virginian, of course, is the quicker draw and kills Trampas. So ends Wister's story number one, a "Western" story.

Since the second story which emerges from the novel presents the Virginian as quite amenable to Eastern ways and values, the use of the same first-person narrator whose hero is the "untamed" Virginian of story one posed some problems for Wister. In addition, a first-person narrator who was only an occasional visitor to the West could not very well keep in close touch with the progress of or be witness to the more intimate details of the Virginian's courtship of Molly Stark, which is central to story number two. Unaware of or unconcerned by the inconsistency or possible confusion occasioned by abrupt changes in point of view, Wister tells most, but not all, of his second story from the point of view of the omniscient author.[3]

The Virginian of the second story is hardly recognizable as the same man Wister gives us in story one. In place of a "wild man" we find a steady worker on Judge Henry's ranch, an establishment "notable for several luxuries." The Virginian thinks of quitting this job, not to live a freer life but to avoid a foreman who is blocking the Virginian's advancement. This situation is soon rectified, however, and the Virginian gradually moves onward and upward toward a better paying position with more responsibilities.

At one point the Judge gives the Virginian the title of "temporary foreman" and the responsibility of supervising a large crew of cowboys who assist the Virginian in taking two ten-car trainloads of cattle to the Chicago market. The Virginian performs the task well, and on the journey from Chicago back to the ranch, he keeps the wild and unpredictable cowboys on "the narrow path of duty" and prevents their drifting off to the towns along the way or to the gold fields. On this journey, the Virginian bests Trampas, not with shooting irons but by telling a better tall story than Trampas could think up. All of this takes place in the caboose of a freight train.

When the Virginian reports back to the ranch, the Judge rewards him with the foreman's job. "It meant everything to him: recognition, higher station, better fortune, a separate house of his own. . . ." The Virginian vowed to live up to the trust put in him: "He was foreman now. He had said to Judge Henry, 'I'll try to please yu'.' And after the throb of emotion which these words had both concealed and conveyed, there came to him that sort of intention to win which amounts to a certainty. Yes, he would please Judge Henry!"

On another occasion the Virginian of story number two gives the shiftless Shorty a scolding for not handling his money more wisely. The Virginian points to himself as an example of a hardworking, prudent man: "And now I have got savings stowed away. If once yu' could know how good that feels—." The Virginian tells Shorty he ought to have invested his money in land. "But never mind that. . . . Take my land away to-morrow, and I'd still have my savings in the bank. Because, you see, I had to work right hard gathering them in. I found out what I could do, and I settled down and did it. Now you can do that too."

In story one, marriage, children, and schools are anathemas to the cowboys, including the Virginian, who makes up a dirty song about taking the teacher down to the schoolhouse to teach *her* a thing or two. In story two, however, the Virginian begins in a gentlemanly way to court Molly as soon as she arrives in the West. When Molly says early in the novel, "I don't think I like you," the Virginian replies, "You're goin' to love me before we get through." Molly does eventually love the Virginian, but not until after he works long and hard to become more civilized and thus more worthy of her. Under her tutelage he improves his spelling and penmanship and fills in other gaps in his education by reading Molly's books, the works of Scott, Browning, Dickens, Austen, and Shakespeare.

After he smooths some of his rough edges and improves his economic position, Molly agrees to marry the Virginian. She worries a little about how he will be received by her family and her Eastern friends. When the Virginian volunteers to write a letter to her mother explaining the situation, Molly wonders, "Suppose he should misspell a word? Would not sentences from him at this time—written sentences—be a further bar to his welcome acceptance at Bennington?" But the Virginian is now quite up to the occasion. Both Molly and he write to mother, and it turns out that at letter writing "The cow-puncher had greatly excelled the schoolmarm!" Molly has worried needlessly: "She should have known that he would indeed care to make a good impression. . . ."

When the time comes to purchase the wedding and engagement rings, the Virginian insists on nothing but the best: "Rings were to be had in Cheyenne and a still greater choice in Denver; and so far as either of these towns his affairs would have permitted him to travel. But he was set upon having rings from the East. They must come from the best place in the country. . . ." Some time later when Molly tells him that she is certain that he likes good clothes better than she, he discloses that he has an Eastern tailor. Near the end of the novel, the Virginian reveals to Molly the degree to which he has come to accept Eastern values: "Why, I have been noticing. I used to despise an Eastern man because his clothes were not Western. I was very young then, or maybe not so very young, as very—as what you saw I was when you first came to Bear Creek. A Western man is a good thing. And he generally knows that. But he has a heap to learn. And he generally don't know that."

The climax of Wister's story two follows hard upon the climax of story one. After killing Trampas in the street, the Virginian goes back to the hotel to announce the news to Molly:

"Yu' have to know it," said he. "I have killed Trampas."

"Oh, thank God!" she said; and he found her in his arms.

Since Molly here seems to have capitulated to a primitive Virginian and his code, the reader may feel that the scene at the hotel shows the victory of Western values over civilization and consequently is part of story one. Wister himself seems to believe this: "He had come to her from a smoking pistol, able to bid her farewell—and she could not let him go. At the last white-hot edge of ordeal, it was she who renounced, and he who had his way." But Wister here is either confused or trying to hide the fact that he has all along been trying to pass off two different Virginians as the same man. The truth is that Virginian number one leaves the novel at the moment he kills Trampas.

Wister knew as well as anyone that if a victory of a primitive hero and his way of life is to be convincing in fiction, the hero's story must end at the moment of his triumph. To follow a Western hero in time is to run into the facts of history, which facts reveal all too clearly the inundation of the West by the East and the destruction of everything the Western Virginian of story one believes in and lives for. In *his* novel, however, Wister could and did take his story beyond the shooting, and he could do so without running the risk of turning the triumph of Virginian number one into a defeat. When the Virginian goes back to the hotel to see Molly, the reader need not feel that all the untamed Virginian stands for is after all doomed because of the presence of civilized Easterners like Molly. Wister has all along given us both a Western and an Eastern Virginian. At this crucial moment in the novel, Wister does what he has been doing throughout the novel: he shifts from one Virginian to the other. The man who was willing to give up Molly in favor of shooting Trampas was the Virginian of story one. In shooting Trampas he is true to his values and then drops from the novel to live with other cowboys in legend and myth. The man who goes back to the hotel is Virginian number two, the man with the good job, land of his own, and money in the bank, not to mention an Eastern tailor and a taste for the classics. He returns to the hotel to marry the woman who will mother his children and manage his home. In a few years, Wister tells us, the Virginian's hard work and his investment in real estate pay off. "But the railroad came, and built a branch to that land of the Virginian's where the coal was. By that time he was an important man, with a strong grip on many various enterprises, and able to give his wife all and more than she asked or desired."

As the split in his novel reveals, Wister was as drawn toward civilization and progress as to a simple life in the wide open spaces. His visits to the West were always merely visits. Educated in Europe and at Harvard, Wister apparently enjoyed drinking claret with his sophisticated friends, William Dean Howells, Rudyard Kipling, and Oliver Wendell Holmes, Sr. and Jr., quite as much as sharing a bottle of whiskey with his cowboy friends in Wyoming. The man who had studied music in Paris and had played his own compositions for Franz Liszt enjoyed his fame as a writer quite as much as the experiences which provided material for his stories.[4]

This is not to say that Wister did not love the West as much as he suggests he does in story one of *The Virginian* and in much of his other writings, but to underscore the fact that, like most Americans, Wister was drawn toward both the primitivism of the West and the civilization of the East. Wister's moving back and forth between East and West over a period of fifteen years suggests that he did not want to choose one world to the exclusion of the other, and for a few years, until the West filled up, he did not have to.

When Wister came to write *The Virginian*, he split his novel into two stories with two heroes perhaps in an unconscious effort to avoid the hard reality he knew from experience, that the values of primitivism and the values of civilization are incompatible. To the extent that the reader of *The Virginian* is unaware of what Wister has done to avoid the complex issues raised by the conflict between East and West, the novel creates the happy illusion that we need not give up one world to gain the other. The novel makes the unsuspecting reader feel that the best of both worlds can exist in one place, at one time, and in one man.

Notes

1. Wister worked into *The Virginian* seven short pieces about the Virginian he had published earlier in *Harper's* and *The Saturday Evening Post* between 1893 and 1902. Three of these were written from the point of view of the first-person narrator and four written from the point of view of the omniscient author. When these early pieces were incorporated into the novel, Wister did not rewrite them to establish a consistent point of view.

2. All quotations from *The Virginian* are from the Riverside Edition (Boston: Houghton Mifflin, 1968), ed. Philip Durham.

3. Wister apparently understood the importance of choosing a satisfactory point of view for his stories. As early as 1894, after gathering much information in Arizona concerning the Earp-Clanton feud, he wrote in his journal: "I have heard enough to make something interesting out of that business. I am puzzled how best to tell it. Whether impersonally . . . in good English, or else to put it in the mouth of a local narrator. In this way I could gain humor, and in the other I suppose the tragic parts would go better." See Fanny Kemble Wister, ed., *Owen Wister Out West: His Journals and Letters* (Chicago: Univ. of Chicago Press, 1958), p. 213. But Wister was reluctant to revise his work. He wrote to his mother in 1902 concerning his progress on *The Virginian:* "It is the revision and interpolation that I do certainly hate. If you look at this sheet of paper you'll see cuts—knife cuts. Those are where I have sliced my short stories and pasted them in pieces with the interpolations between." *Owen Wister Out West*, p. 15.

4. Strangely enough, Wister's daughter has said that Wister never talked about the West with his family: "I never heard him say a single word about the fifteen years spent mostly in hunting big game and collecting material for his books. Perhaps it was because by the time we were old enough to hear about them, those years were long past." *Owen Wister Out West*, p. 24. In any event, from 1918 until the end of his life, Wister spent part of every year not in the West but in Europe, where he studied the cathedrals and started a book about French wines.

The Classic Generation of Western Novelists

The Primitive World of Vardis Fisher: The Idaho Novels

John R. Milton*

With the subjects and themes of advanced society (at least in the last two or even three volumes of the Vridar Hunter tetralogy), Vardis Fisher is not at home. He is more vivid and more significant and more understanding when he deals with the primitive world, the "animal" world. This may be the result of his Idaho environment and of the primitive conditions under which he lived as a boy; but there is more to it than that. Fisher seems to think that man is still an animal in many ways, subject to non-reasonable pressures and to fears and prejudices which keep him from being a truly civilized creature. This is perhaps a rather obvious condition in man, one which need not be stressed. Nevertheless, there is considerable difference in the contemporary treatments of this condition in fiction. The eastern, or metropolitan, writer of recent times has tended to gloss over the historical reasons for this condition, even ignoring more than he should the deep moral responsibilities in which man has failed. It is too easy to blame a person's immediate social environment for his development, and to excuse his actions on the grounds of pressures brought to bear upon him in his business or his suburban community. Fisher probes back into man's psychological history, into his very origins, to find not excuses but reasons for his behavior. That man is still an animal, subject to primitive urges and irrational reactions, is one of the suggestions we are left with at the end of Fisher's monumental work, *The Testament of Man.*

Fisher finds barbarisms in modern society, as any perceptive sociologist or anthropologist can. From the autobiographical materials in the Idaho novels it is evident that the young Vardis Fisher was shocked and disturbed by the cruelties of men as well as by the harshness and indifference in the natural world. His later research for the twelve-volume *Testament* was undertaken in order to explain those cruelties and to provide some kind of answer to the questions raised in the Vridar Hunter

**MQ*, 17 (1976), 369–84. Portions of the essay have also appeared in John R. Milton, *The Novel of the American West* (Lincoln: Univ. of Nebraska Press, 1980).

tetralogy. Fisher also used the method of relating in vivid detail the barbaric nature of man, presumably to shock the reader into an awareness of the problem. One illustrative passage, from *Tale of Valor*, will be sufficient to indicate the kinds of details Fisher chose:

> He had seen famished wolves at a carcass, and jackals, but they had not been so savage in their blood-and hunger-lust as these creatures before him, tearing the spleen apart with their two filthy hands, the liver, kidneys, the lungs, the guts, while blood gushed from the corners of their mouths and their eyes rolled in rapture as, choking and gasping, they wolfed it down. The one who fascinated Lewis most was a scrawny bowlegged brave who managed to possess nine or ten feet of the small intestine and now wed it into his mouth and down his throat, his cheeks and tongue sucking it in, his throat muscles rising in blood-filled rolls, as his two hands squeezed down the tube, forcing the contents out at the other end. In what seemed to Lewis only a few moments the long piece of gut disappeared. (p. 249)

Fisher is not in favor of this primitive behavior, and yet he almost seems to enjoy describing it. His extensive use of animalism in the *Testament* series is designed to show that man has not been able to free himself entirely of his primitive origins, that even in the twentieth century he is socially and morally crude. The intention is to teach, to show that man need not be captive to his origins, that he has the ability and the power and often the will to be something higher and better than mere creature. It is obvious that certain parts of the history of the American West lend themselves easily to this particular theme. What goes wrong, as in the passage above, is the tone; Fisher goes beyond a literal description of the animalism and adds either irony or humor. Irony would work if it did not seem to be so purposive, as it often does in Fisher; humor could be employed as a relieving device, but it is not always used in that way in Fisher's novels. Perhaps Fisher exaggerates to the point of humor because this is the only way in which he can endure the barbarisms of which he writes; or perhaps he gives in to the impulse to shock his readers, partly for his own enjoyment. Sometimes it is hard to tell. We know that, as a person, he was sensitive enough (although he wore a cynical surface) to be terrified, even while fascinated, by the cruelties which man commits upon his fellow men.

Cruelty is a major theme throughout Fisher's work, appearing in such variations as the results of animalism and emotionalism, in men preying upon other men, and in a fear of the unknown which gives rise to inhuman behavior in the name of religion. Fisher believes that man has the intelligence to overcome his animalism and emotionalism, and his superstitions, but that he has refused to take this step forward; therefore, Fisher is often bitter and antagonistic against the human race, adopting the role of the village atheist in order to prod, to criticize, and to condemn. He attacks stupidity and callousness, and he revels in the gore of barbarism, all the while trying to protect and nourish his own sensitive soul.

One sympathizes with the man (and cries out for all men) after reading his Idaho novels, especially the Vridar Hunter story.

Vridar is the oldest child of Joe Hunter, an early settler in the Idaho benchland, a simple but hard-working man who is married to a puritan. Vridar is caught between the rigidity of his mother's beliefs and his father's easy lack of belief. His father ignores him and allows him to run loose, while his mother frightens him and tries to confine him within narrow moral limits. The frontier life in Idaho is brutal, wild, and animalistic. Vridar is an overly-sensitive boy who is constantly afraid of life and who is not loved by anyone. *In Tragic Life* is an episodic story, running in chronological order but leaving huge gaps in the life of Vridar. This does not matter, because Vridar's life is all of one piece and representative incidents and influences serve as well as the complete story. The treatment of the boy's life is extremely realistic, sometimes raw and shocking in its descriptions of a crude environment, but always the writing is terribly honest, sharp and clear, and occasionally figurative. Vridar is, in this volume at least, completely believable, contrary to the opinion of a *Time* magazine reviewer who had obviously never been west of Manhattan. Some of the minor characters are grotesques, but in their context, and from the boy's warped point of view, they work well and are successful within the author's intentions.

Vridar's childhood is tragic, in the sense that he is beset by every fear that it is possible for a child to know. The rest of his life seems to be governed by the first eighteen years. Whenever Vridar seems prepared to face life without fears, and with love, something turns up in his non-Idaho world which has direct correspondence with the pressures and cruelties of his childhood environment. In *Passions Spin the Plot*, Vridar takes his grief and fear with him to college in Salt Lake City. His life at college is both pathetic and humorous; Vridar is the victim of his extreme shyness, his sensitivity, his deep concern with morality, and his fear of the fierce competitions and dishonesties of life. This is a dark book. Vridar is, by most standards, mentally unbalanced. He sees all life as evil and purposeless. Read out of context, this novel is hopelessly grim; but it helps to establish Fisher's thesis that man is constantly under the control of senseless fears, whether in the Idaho wilds or in the city. Vridar is the product not only of his Idaho environment, but also of his entire culture and of his race. Although he is an exaggerated character, he is true to his prototype, and he is to be considered as representative of the men who are victims of their cultural history. This includes almost everyone.

The "love story" of Vridar and Neloa Doole is the wildest and most frustrating in American fiction. Neloa makes love indiscriminately to other men, acting from a natural and animal-like impulse. She ignores Vridar for years after he has fallen in love with her and finally marries him for what seems to be a matter of convenience more than anything else. Vridar the idealist, the romantic, is tortured by Neloa's lack of concern for him, but he must marry her anyway. Like Philip, in Somerset Maugham's *Of Human Bondage*, who felt compelled to return again and again to Mildred, the "vulgar slut," so Vridar must have Neloa although he loathes her and can find no reasonable purpose in loving her. In a symbolic sense, Neloa is dark and mysterious Woman, an archetypal figure out of the primitive mists, and her power over Vridar is simply that of woman over man. Taken by itself, the relationship between Vridar and Neloa makes a powerful story, one of the most fascinating episodes in Fisher's work; but the conflict is never resolved, and the relationship ends rather meaninglessly (Neloa commits suicide) except for the slight turn which it gives to the growth of Vridar.

We Are Betrayed, the third volume in this series, finishes Vridar's years at college in Utah. His motto at this time is that "Honesty has to pay its price. It used to pay in hemlock or hanging. Now it pays in isolations. . . ." Vridar thinks that he is learning to be completely honest, and thus different from the people around him; but he is little more than a youthful idealist trying to play the role of the realist. And the closer he comes to what he considers realism, the more absurd he becomes. He has several, indeed many, honest characteristics, but they are exaggerated to ridiculousness. In typical youthful fashion he addresses himself to the exhortation, "To thyself be true," and then proceeds to destroy (in his own mind) everything that has been built up in the past two or three thousand years. Much that is in our traditions may deserve to be destroyed, or relegated carefully to its historical place, but to have the cultural and religious structure of the world annihilated in one novel is, I think, going beyond the bounds of plausibility.

Vridar now, in rapid succession, serves time in the army, becomes a bootlegger and a friend of whores and pimps, becomes a father, and begins graduate study in English at the University of Chicago. While in Chicago, he spiritually deserts his unfathomable part-Indian wife and falls in love (intellectually) with Athene Marvell, an educated girl who is completely different from Neloa. Neloa drinks poison and Vridar goes to pieces, first in the hospital and then in the morgue:

> Her eyes were closed. There was a smile on her white face and it was the smile that he had known and loved; and there was brown stain on her lips, her chin; but he did not see the stain. "Neloa?" he said.
>
> Then he heard a sound and listened for a long moment, with wonder taking him: and he screamed, so sudden and terrible was his joy. "Neola, I knew you wern't dead!" He bent over her. . . . He bent lower, his face close to her heart; and in this body he worshiped, looking so queenly under the white gown, he heard a strange gurgling. Swiftly he touched her hand and it was like ice; her white cheek, her throat; and shrank back, horrified. . . . He buried his face in her hair, smelling of it, until he felt again deeply, that she was not dead. . . . A man knocked on the door. . . . He crossed the room to the door and stopped and looked at her again; and all the anguish of his heart broke into a cry. He ran back and put his arms around her and knelt, with his cheek to her cold cheek. And he was still there, kneeling, holding her close, when two men came and led him away. (pp. 365–66)

And a little later Vridar vomits as the body of Neloa is put into the furnace at the crematorium. But first he has vowed, in her name, to finish his work and to be honest with himself and others. Unfortunately, honesty by itself is not literature, not even realistic literature, and the force of Neloa's death and of the heightened writing (as in the passage above which tells of her death) is lost in Vridar's foolishness and in Fisher's determination to make literature out of what he considers truth. Truth figures prominently in this novel and in the one which follows, but it is never identified and never given life. It is the truth of the scholar's facts, not the truth of humanity. Fisher, of course, frequently tended to think that the two were the same.

No Villain Need Be concludes the tetralogy. In the first volume Fisher was a novelist; he produced a powerful and effective piece of fiction with the action, characterization, scene, and strong sense of conflict which we expect from fiction. Gradually, through the next three volumes, fiction gives way to a kind of loosely-dramatized exposition. In the last volume there is almost no action. Through endless conversations, Fisher presents all of his ideas in encyclopedic fashion, thinking them through as he goes along. The novel is tedious, and it resolves nothing. Fisher later was aware of this, although he occasionally pointed to an anonymous reviewer or two who thought this volume was the best of the four. At the end of the novel, he pleads for "thorough exploration first, and then a tradition leading to, and finally resting upon, the inviolable responsibility of leadership." He indicates that Freudianism and Marxism have something to contribute, but does not make clear what that is or to what, exactly, they are to contribute. Fisher was not a politician; he might have liked to be a psychologist; he probably was more than anything else a moralist. But he too was dissatisfied with the conclusion of Vridar's story and he wrote the entire *Testament* series in an effort to resolve Vridar's problems.

Long before the job was accomplished, however, he created a fictional community in the Antelope Hills section of Idaho, a community made up of the relatives and neighbors of Vridar Hunter. As seen in *Toilers of the Hills*, this is a community of silences, loneliness, vast indifference, terrible mystery, and, sometimes, madness. This is the region that made Vridar into what he was, but seen from a different point of view. The chief character is Dock Hunter, one of Vridar's uncles, who brings his second wife, Opal, to the Idaho benchlands. She comes reluctantly, he eagerly. Dock believes in the promise, half-myth and half-truth, that "next year will be the year." His one aim is to conquer the land, and he works hard and cheerfully while his wife bears children and decays. There is a good deal of hope at the end of the novel; Dock seems to have overcome the arid land with his formula for dry-farming. But Opal has grown old in the meantime, although she is only thirty-one; the land has taken its toll on her. The final effect is that of tragi-comedy.

Fisher paints a vivid picture of the harshness and the beauty of the land. It is within this juxtaposition (almost a paradox) that the mystery of life is to be found, and Fisher is at his best in dealing with this mystery. His descriptions of nature are frequently magnificent. The people are a little less than magnificent; most of them are weak people with enough flaws to keep them from struggling on a high plane. A few of them survive the land and the climate with some kind of grace. But they are a people without tradition, without a legitimate place on the frontier, because they have brought almost nothing with them, and it is already too late to carve an empire out of a frontier which has vanished, leaving behind only a vague tradition of hope and courage. These people are in every way isolated, by circumstances as well as by the land:

> And everywhere were silences, strangely apart and alone: the small green silences in coves along their way, the round silence of each hill or the flat silence of each plain, great solitudes that filled the sky and lay over the mountains and beyond. There seemed to be no sky, Opal thought; only thin dusty air no bluer above than below, only whitish altitudes as far up as the eye could see. (p. 4)

Opal subconsciously realizes that there is no longer a rainbow with a pot of gold at the end. That search has ended, leaving only the backwash, the poor farmers struggling to conquer a land that is hardly worth the taking. In some respects Fisher is here a western Erskine Caldwell. The difference is that he lacks Caldwell's grotesque humor, although he touches upon it in some ways, and he pays more attention to the qualities of the land—in a regional sense of emotional response to it:

> His mind groped for words that would make her understand the mystery of there (mountains), the deep living power of them, almost the intelligence of them. Between all these and himself, he admitted, there existed a kinship, something for which he could find no words, a feeling of love sometimes, or of fear and wonder. (p. 100)

It is the cyclical drama of nature with which Fisher finally commands our attention here:

> Upon them, in the fall of the year, and upon Dock most of all, there fell a silence, and into their eyes there came the fear of men haunted by the ruthless power, unseen and beyond control. But with the awakening of another spring they gathered hope again and marched with greater courage into the long hard work of another year. . . . And it was at this that Opal wondered most, at the fierce silent drama between these men and the hills. (p. 251)

At the last, Opal becomes reconciled to the land and to her house. She and Dock, uncomplex but endurable, discover "houseness" in a new and traditionless land of limited opportunity.

The achievement of "houseness" is the theme of *April* also, although the method of this novel is somewhat different from the rest of Fisher's work. Kitty Weeg and her daughter, June, are removed from the real world, having taken refuge in the romantic world of books—cheap romantic novels. Of Kitty it is said, "Of the mad and terrible and beautiful world she knew nothing. . . ." In the midst of human and natural conflict

> . . . Kitty Weeg was as serene as the white dishes in the cupboard, for she did not, June realized, live in this world at all: she ate and slept and combed her hair and went now and then to the spring for water or to the cellar for a jar of fruit; but she had escaped into a world of books, and she lived within the romantic legends of love and despair, hope and triumph. (p. 197)

And Kitty comes to nothing, as, perhaps, most people come to nothing. By the end of the novel she has been forgotten. The story belongs to her daughter, for a long time enmeshed in her mother's romanticism. June is a stout and homely girl of twenty-four who should have married long ago. She has been courted, in a way, since she was eleven by Sol Incham, another homely and lonely person. June spurns him because he is not as dashing and romantic and gallant as the characters in her mother's novels. Sol is merely honest, steady, good, and sincere. June tries instead to find some kind of perverse satisfaction in three other people: (1) a new hired hand, William Wallace Argyll, a young and slender man who thinks he is a poet, and whom June baffles with her play-acting, her pretenses at being another girl, named April, who is something like the girls in the cheap novels; (2) an old maid, Susan Hemp, with whom June thinks she has affinities, though Susan always throws June out of her house; (3) Virgin Hill, the most beautiful girl in town, very popular, to whose house June goes one day so that she can just look at her, observe her, and admire her, and whom she insists on kissing on the mouth before she leaves, to see what it is like to kiss a beautiful girl. The atmosphere of this novel is unreal, except that it is grounded in the usual people of the Antelope Hills area, people who figure in the Idaho novels, and also in the land itself which is very real even though seen frequently through the romantic eyes of June. Sol, too, is very real. But a partial mystery surrounds June, Kitty, Susan, and Jon Weeg. Herein lies, presumably, the "fable" of the subtitle of this novel.

June is one of the many "little" people in the world. She is not important enough to achieve great victories, nor can she be the material for tragedy. Her problems are little ones, her successes are little ones, and she can at best gain a small satisfaction from life. *April* is like Frederick Manfred's *The Chokecherry Tree* in which the chief character lives in the shadow of the giants, just as the chokecherry tree grows beneath the cottonwoods. The life of the "little" person is warm and humorous in many ways, even though plagued with the cruelty of gossip and human weaknesses. *April* is the most cheerful of all Fisher's novels, and he said that it was his favorite. June gradually abandons her romantic notions and comes to accept Sol:

> In the course of time he fell upon the subject of his empty house and this became for her a symbol of his need: something empty and unused, a loneliness waiting for a woman, for gentle ways to smooth it into beauty and repose. The house haunted her. (p. 67.)

And so June becomes a "little hero" by conquering that house, by cleaning it and cooking a meal for Sol who finds her there and is finally accepted by her. The charm of *April* shows up in striking contrast to the tragedy which is *Dark Bridwell.* The land is the same; the people are part of the same community, but the relationship is physical only. A great spiritual gulf separates these two novels.

Dark Bridwell is, I am convinced, not only Fisher's best novel (although it is only his second out of twenty-six) but one of the masterpieces of the American novel. It is a true tragedy of the end of the American frontier; it achieves the status of myth, although firmly anchored in the Idaho soil; and Charley Bridwell, through his peculiar strengths and weaknesses, becomes an American Lear. Fisher's own weaknesses as a writer are held in check more successfully in *Bridwell* than anywhere else, and although the people and incidents are similar to (in many cases the same as) those in the early part of the Vridar Hunter story, they take on a deeper significance in *Bridwell* and are shaped more artistically and more powerfully.

The story is told through three characters: Charley Bridwell first, then his son Jed, and finally Charley's wife Lela. There is some overlapping of incidents because of the three views, but the story does not falter; in fact, it proceeds so inexorably that it seems pulled by fate, a dark fate in spite of Charley's cheerfulness. And brooding over the whole story is the author. He does not interfere or intrude, and his presence is felt in the way that a supreme but disinterested intelligence is often felt by sensitive people. This particular point of view serves to achieve, for the reader, the correct distance between himself and the material. The reader is drawn into the story by its immediacy and reality, but he is also aware that he is confronting a work of art. Control of distance is a refinement of the central intelligence of Henry James and is, I think, one of the major technical achievements of twentieth-century fiction. Although it has its origins, I suspect, in *Madame Bovary*, it is to be found more in American fiction than European, and more often in western American fiction than eastern.

Charley Bridwell is a child of nature. He drinks a great deal and indulges in "unpitying devilries," but he is lovable. He takes what he can get and gives what he has. He is completely at one with nature, fearing nothing, daring everything, but content to let things take their natural course. He is not ambitious, and he is not without tenderness; yet, like an animal with a short memory, he will disregard his own family unless they are in physical danger. He is deeply affected by his natural environment, although his reaction to it is a primitive one. When he watches the forces at work in the swift rapids of the river, similar forces well up in him:

> And as Charley watched, there came upon him that strange and deep emotion that always took him by the throat when he saw life wrenched into blind violence. It was a lust to kill, as if through murder he would have to seek his way to peace. It was a black power that gripped him and made him do brutal or reckless deeds. He had little strength against it; and if he did not abuse man or beast, drawing from savagery an aftermath of calm, he had to give himself to some fierce experience. (p. 51.)

In this particular instance, he dives recklessly from a high bank into the boiling river, disappears from sight until Lela faints from fear, then appears with a devilish grin on his face, "triumphant . . . a river demon." Charley is a man with a place but without a time; he is a mountain man born too late. The frontier, the life of the wilderness, is gone forever, and Charley cannot adjust to even the meager society of rural Idaho.

Neither is Charley able to adjust to his natural environment entirely. He does not fear a dangerous and busy life, but neither does he want it. He prefers peace and solitude and serenity, and thus appears lazy to his family and his few friends. Like an animal, he would reconcile himself to nature, but to a mystical aspect of it, not to all the particulars. On the other hand, Lela hungers for the dangerous and busy life but is afraid of it. And so the two people are at cross-purposes with each other and also within themselves. The river becomes a symbol of these differences:

> Charley hated it. He hated the river's senseless going to an unknown and futile end, the loud tongue of its monologue, its grotesque buffoonery, its crazed barnstorming on its way to the sea. And its stage-struck gestures, its steady infernal booming, awakened a cruel hunger that had stood unused in his being. He stepped out of long indolence, feeling the great surging of life, yet despising it. How, he wondered, could a man rest in peace, when Nature dramatized even the melting of snows? (p. 98.)

The description of the river is significant, because it is also the description of Charley. In a way, he is nature, or natural man, and when he hates the river he hates himself. He senses that he is possessed by some kind of dark and primitive evil (perhaps ignorance), but he can do nothing about it. He even breeds another like himself, his son Jed, who can with fascination study a snake:

> Though they were enemies, the spirit of this snake was his spirit; their two souls reached back anciently to the same dark source. Their ancestry was the same wilderness of desire. (p. 167.)

And so Charley and after him Jed symbolize the dark origins of man, the primitive spirit, evil in its ancient sources of ignorance, base desires, and lack of intelligent control. Yet Charley is capable of tenderness, and Jed is capable of turning against his father.

Lela finds something else in the river:

> It was a tireless hunger, ancient but forever young, baffled but forever seeking, as if under the earth's calm surface there was a great unrest, out of which it came eternally, speaking the language of life. Night and day . . . she heard the sound of its travel . . . until life spun within her like an eddy of feeling isolated from all meaning, condemned to a timeless fever of striving, but exiled from all change. (pp. 271–72.)

She never finds what she is looking for, because Charley is always there to frustrate and thwart her desires, but the river remains a "symbol of the up-reaching life, and its going [gives] her strength." Like the white whale in *Moby Dick*, the river is whatever man makes of it; it is a mirror in which each person sees himself. Like Ahab, Charley Bridwell hates what he sees. But, like King Lear, Charley is blind to the dangers around him, blind through vanity, and this blindness leads to his defeat.

Two people hate Charley. One is his son Jed, named after a man whose teeth Charley once kicked out. The other is a sheepherder named Adolph Buck. Adolph runs off with Charley's daughter, and Jed takes away Charley's wife. Charley, the man for whom truth lay in "the lurking sunlit vision, standing in all the accidents of ill luck and chance," finally becomes the object of a hatred which rises to the level of myth and destroys him.

Jed has inherited both the Bridwell lust for devilment and the deep brooding intensity of his mother. The latter gives him the sensitivity to see that his father is cruel (though perhaps innocently) to Lela; the former charges him with the desire to excel his father's "cunning ingenuities." The mixture makes Jed into a strange boy, intensely cruel, yet often likable, shaped not only by his blood-inheritance but also by his environment:

> Everything around him . . . invited him to solitude or to reckless deeds. The great mountains, the untamed headstrong river, the wild animal life and the lonely blockade of winter months—he felt the power of all these, and their ruthlessness, and their savage ways. (pp. 151–52.)

Jed leaves home when he is fourteen. During the next nine years Charley becomes lazier and more cruel, neglecting Lela while she bears several more children and is slowly and spiritually starved. She is isolated in the wilderness with a man who is little more than the wilderness himself. Then, in an archetypal pattern, Jed returns to take his mother away. The final scene in the novel is one of the largest, wildest, and most significant in American fiction. Charley, in an animal rage, turns on Jed and almost kills him, but Lela beats Charley senseless with a club and goes off with Jed. Another son waits for Charley, thinking that he too will leave with them, but Charley remains, and in madness he drinks and raves, curses and laughs like a devil, and tries to come to terms with his grief. He cannot change, and in the morning he walks away, never to be seen again.

And yet his ghost remains with us, just as the ghosts of primitive man still walk beside us and ride in us whenever we succumb to the dark forests and the strange madness of our savage origins. We have made some progress; Jed, although evil himself, is less so than Charley. For a time he exceeded even Charley in cruelty, and I see this as an oblique reference to such things in man's history as the Inquisition, with which Fisher deals in *My Holy Satan* (1958). But somehow there is progress, increased love and rationality, making its way through the primitive evils. The shadows remain, but the river finally flows on, taking Lela and her children with it.

The shadows and the potential light, the barbarisms and the struggle toward rationality, the cruelties and the occasional hope through the beauties and the mysteries of nature—these permeate all of Fisher's fiction. Some of his later work is heavy with exposition and autobiography, presumably the result of his increasing impatience with superstition, ignorance, and fear, all of which he tried valiantly to overcome. While his life work rarely swerved from its predetermined course, established by his youthful reaction to the Idaho wilderness, the early and archetypical *Dark Bridwell* remains his most artistic blending of the literally real and the mythical. From the American western experience comes the universal story of mankind.

Bibliography

Fisher, Vardis. *April*. Caldwell, Ida.: Caxton, 1937.

———. *Dark Bridwell*. Boston: Houghton Mifflin, 1931.

———. *Tale of Valor*. Garden City, N. Y.: Doubleday, 1958.

———. *Toilers of the Hills*. Caldwell, Ida.: Caxton, 1928.

———. *We Are Betrayed*. Caldwell, Ida.: Caxton, 1935.

A. B. Guthrie's Vanishing Paradise: An Essay on Historical Fiction

Donald C. Stewart*

In October, 1949, A. B. Guthrie, Jr., told Harvey Breit that he wanted to write "a series of at least four panels on the Western movement. In them I want to try to interpret American life to the American people. . . . You know about my first two books. The third will be the story of a cow camp and/or gold days. . . . The fourth will be the interior Northwest from the turn of the century to the present."[1]

The Big Sky (1947) had been a stunning literary success. *The Way West*, just published at the time of this interview, was to win him a Pulitzer prize. He eventually wrote the other two books he had projected, *These Thousand Hills* (1956) and *Arfive* (1971), but they are decidedly inferior to their distinguished predecessors.[2] Despite their differences in artistic merit, however, all four works sustain Guthrie's deep affection for the Northern Great Plains, the territory now of Nebraska, the Dakotas, Wyoming, and Montana. In all but *The Way West*, Guthrie's principal locale is North-Central Montana, specifically the valley of the Teton River and the territory around his boyhood home, Choteau, Montana. The effect of the four books is to see a curtain raised and then lowered on a succession of historical occasions, each one incorporating and adding to the previous one. What are the changes which occur as one epoch succeeds another? What are Guthrie's feelings toward these changes? These are the questions this essay attempts to answer.

The Big Sky begins in 1830 in the hills and timber of Kentucky. Seventeen-year-old Boone Caudill escapes an angry father, the law, and the ant hills of civilization and heads for lands west of the Mississippi. The novel continuously celebrates the plains and mountains of the upper Missouri in their pristine beauty. As such, it is the touchstone for the succeeding novels which show this savage paradise steadily corrupted by the advance of civilization. It is marvellously appealing country, but one never is allowed to forget that the trappers who adore it accept, without

**Journal of the West*, 15, no. 3 (1976), 83–96.

questioning, its constant danger, from Indian, wildlife (the everpresent rattlesnake and the grizzly bear), and weather:

> Boone hitched himself closer. "It's fair country up there, I reckon."
>
> Summers looked at him, and his mouth made a small smile. "Wild. Wild and purty like a virgin woman. Whatever a man does he feels like he's the first one done it. . . ."
>
> The hunter's voice picked up the thread of his thought. "I seen most of it. Colter's Hell and the Seeds-kee-dee and the Tetons standin' higher 'n clouds, and north and south from Nez Perce to Comanche, but Got almighty, there's nothin' richer'n the upper Missouri. Or purtier. I seen the Great Falls and traveled Maria's River, dodgin' the Blackfeet, makin' cold camps and sometimes thinkin' my time was up, and all the time livin' wonderful, loose and free's any animal. That's some, that is."
>
> "Lord God!"
>
> "A man gets a taste for it."[3]

The entire second section of *The Big Sky* is dominated by the exhilaration of Boone and his friend, Jim Deakins, as they ascend the river. As the primitive beauty of the country increases, so does their anticipation of danger from Indians, a danger which terrifies the French boatmen but excites the Americans. Their mentor is Dick Summers, the veteran mountain man, whom Guthrie eventually uses to connect three eras: the period of the first wave of trappers, after Lewis and Clark's ascent and return on the Missouri; the period represented by *The Big Sky*, the last dynamic era for the trappers and the beginnings of the trails west; and the period of westward migration, particularly to Oregon and California which occurs in *The Way West*.

The French fur traders with whom Boone, Jim, and Summers ascend the river are annihilated by Indians and only the three Americans escape into the trappers' life. For Summers it is a second youth, but his growing nostalgia and his perception of the inevitability of change color the middle section of the book:

> It was known country to Summers, the Wind Range, and the everlasting snow fields and the Grand Tetons that could come into sight soon, was known country and old country to him now. He could remember when it was new, and a man setting foot on it could believe he was the first one, and a man seeing it could give names to it.

He concludes, however, that the change in the country is as much a change in himself as in the external changes wrought by the increasing numbers of people coming into the area. For Boone and Jim the country is as new and as wonderful as it was for him earlier. This particular theme is developed in the novels which follow *The Big Sky*. When Lije Evans of *The Way West*, Lat Evans of *These Thousand Hills*, and Benton Collingsworth of *Arfive* first see this Western high country, they respond to it with the same intensity as did their predecessors.

Guthrie purposely set *The Big Sky* between 1830 and 1843 because it permitted him to capture the end of the trapper era and the beginning of the westward migrations which are occurring as the book ends. These intrusions into the High Plains and Central Rockies are bitterly resented by the trappers, none more frustrated than Boone's Uncle Zeb who, as early as 1830, was lamenting the demise of the Western wilderness:

> "She's gone, goddam it! Gone!"
>
> "What's gone?" asked Summers. . . .
>
> "The whole shitaree. Gone, by God, and naught to care savin' some of us who seen 'er new. . . ."
>
> "This was man's country onc't. Every water full of beaver and a galore of buffler any ways a man looked, and no crampin' and crowdin'. Christ sake! . . ."
>
> Summers gray eye slipped from Boone to Uncle Zeb. "She ain't sp'iled, Zeb," he said quietly. "Depends on who's lookin'."
>
> "Not sp'iled! Forts all up and down the river and folk everywhere a man might think to lay a trap. And greenhorns coming' up, a heap of 'em—greenhorns on every boat, hornin' in and sp'ilin' the fun. Christ sake! Why'n't they stay to home? Why'n't they leave it to us as found it? By God, she's ours by rights." His mouth lifted the bottle. "God, she was purty onc't. Purty and new, and not a man track, savin' Injuns', on the scoop of her."

Uncle Zeb is right, of course. At that moment they sit in the shadow of Fort Union, the American Fur Company's elegant post at the junction of the Missouri and Yellowstone Rivers. In a decade, the Blackfeet Indians, the trappers' most feared enemies but also a source of the exhilarating danger in their lives, will be decimated by smallpox and reduced to pitiful remnants of their former selves. Steamboats will be plying the Missouri to the Platte River, and Jim will be upsetting Boone with talk of "new forts along the river and new people moving out from the settlements and the farmers in Missouri palavering about Oregon and California, as if the mountains were a prime place for plows and pigs and corn." Only Dick Summers is able to accept the changes, unpalatable as they may be, as inevitable.

The non-trappers coming into the big sky country are the apostles of progress. And no one states the case for this kind of "progress" more objectionably than Elisha Peabody, an Eastern entrepreneur who seeks a northern route through the mountains:

> "I'm not interested in beaver. I've told you that. It is development I'm interested in, future development. You appear to think, because the Indians haven't made use of the great Western country, that nobody can."
>
> Peabody took a deep breath, as if to make sure he had wind enough for his argument. "When country which might support so many actually supports so few, then, by thunder, the inhabitants have not made good use of the natural possibilities." His wide eyes looked at Boone, earnest and polite but not afraid. "That failure surely is justification for invasion, peaceful if possible, forcible if necessary, by people who can and will capitalize on opportunity."

This is the baldest statement of the conflict between the Abrahamic concept of land use employed to justify exploitation of natural resources and extermination of less civilized races set against the concept, only in very recent years coming into popularity, of man living in and not dominating the biotic community. It is not clear whether, in 1947, Guthrie had been schooled in the land ethic preached by the great American conservationists of the nineteenth and early twentieth centuries, but the portrait of Peabody is sufficiently uncomplimentary that one suspects he did not approve of the laissez faire materialism which governed the actions of those leading the westward expansion a century ago.

Guthrie does not close his eyes to the culpability of the mountain man, however. He reveals him as a too often willing accomplice in the destruction of the land he loved.

> "I don't guess we could help it," Summers answered, nodding. "There was beaver for us and free country and a big way of livin', and everything we done it looks like we done against ourselves and couldn't do different if we'd knowed. We went to get away and to enj'y ourseles free and easy, but folks was bound to foller and beaver to get scarce and Injuns to be killed or tamed, and all the time the country gettin' safer and better known. We ain't see the end of it yet, Boone, not to what the mountain man does against hisself."

Guthrie explicitly stated that he had intended to show the mountain man "for what he was, or what he seemed honestly to have been—not the romantic character, the virtuous if unlettered Leatherstocking, but the engaging, uncouth, admirable, odious, thoughtless, resourceful, loyal, sinful, smart, stupid, courageous character that he was and had to be."[4] It was inevitable that he would be the destroyer of the paradise which he had entered. The reasons may not have been completely clear to Guthrie, however. Several readers of the novel point out that while the mountain man may have fled a corrupt civilization which he despised, he carried the corruption of the civilization he escaped with him. He thus becomes the first corrupting influence on the wilderness.[5]

In *The Big Sky*, then, Guthrie created a savage but enormously attractive paradise, corrupted in part by the mountain man himself, but made even more vulnerable to the corruption of an advancing civilization by the mountain man's complicity in destroying the land he loved. We must look closely at the next three books, therefore, to determine exactly how, and in what ways, this paradise was lost.

The immediately observable changes in the country of the upper Missouri River over the three books which succeeded *The Big Sky* are the physical changes made by man himself. In *The Way West* there are not many. The Oregon Trail, although it represents a significant and eventually lasting road through the paradise of the mountain men, in 1845 still shows the country dominating men. There are graves along the trail, many of them unmarked, like those of the trappers who "went under." There are landmarks also to which the pioneers cling for security: Chimney Rock, Scott's Bluff, and Independence Rock, in which many, like Brownie Evans, chisel the record of their passing. In spite of these feeble assertions by man attempting to convince the great Western wilderness that his passing is to be noticed, the wild wins. The flowers are abundant, buffalo, antelope, and rattlesnakes, one of which takes a life, still exist in profusion. The wilderness's final triumph is that the pioneers, who begin with wagon-loads of possessions, gradually give them up as the trail takes its toll. Beside one heap of family goods is a laconic sign: "Help yourself," the pioneers' grudging acknowledgement of the price the wilderness is exacting for this intrusion upon it. The mountain man and the Indians, by contrast, always travelled light, taking their living from the land. The endeavor of the pioneers is not a total loss, however: "The natural surroundings awaken feelings of awe in travelers of sufficient sensitivity which, in turn, heightens their respect for each other. . . . Furthermore the environment presents both a threat and a promise. The obstacles are formidable and difficult, perhaps impossible to overcome, but those who accept the challenge and struggle manfully but respectfully with nature to achieve their objectives in the end will somehow become 'great' in the process."[6]

When Lat Evans of *These Thousand Hills* comes to Montana from Oregon in 1880, the country, while still wild, is tame by the standards of 1837 or even 1845. Here a ramshackle town, saloon, and house of prostitution represent the beginnings of civilization, intrusions upon Boone Caudill's paradise. The Indians, also, are generally a sorry lot—they camp near white towns to trade, primarily for the debilitating alcohol—the last of the great Indian wars of the Northwest being over. Ironically, Miss Fran's house at Fort Benton is the best looking structure in town. For Tom Ping, Lat's sidekick, it calls up recollections of the bigger Kansas towns. It is unlikely that Kansans of that era would have enjoyed that kind of distinction.

Fort Benton, the head of navigation on the Missouri River, is now a bustling river port: "Lat looked out to the river and the levee and the cargoes piled there. Except for them, this Front Street hardly had another side, the town was hunched so near the bank. A crew was working around the steamboat, shuttling back and forth with packs of hides and robes and sacks of ore or wool and barrels of some kinds of gray stuff for the East."[7]

Lat wins enough money in a horse race (he has been given a stake by a prostitute with whom he had become personally involved) to buy some cattle and borrow money for a ranch he wants to develop. He leaves Fort Benton for Tansytown, which we may assume is an early version of Choteau:

> Take away the saloons [Gilt Edge, the Lally Cooler, and the bar at the Jackson Hotel] and there wasn't much left, just the mercantile company with the post office in it, the hotel, McCabe's barn, the blacksmith shop, a meat market of sorts, Bob Reed Saddles and Harness, a couple of shacks that did for offices—all pressed against the board walks that the townspeople had pitched in

> to build along the main track. Back of these, now in sight and now out, sat the homes, built mostly of log. Callie's house [the prostitute who'd now become a madam], put up by an overblown booster who'd been forced to sell it, looked big by comparison. Not much of a town, even counting the bars.

Still, it represents a significant intrusion upon the wilderness treasured by Boone, Jim, and Dick Summers. And it grows. As the book progresses, Lat prospers on his ranch. The settlers come in, the land is enclosed, cattle replace the once plentiful buffalo, wolves, and antelope which either get exterminated or driven into more confined areas.

Unfortunately, Lat Evans does not at first perceive that Montana's early appeal for him—openness, vast spaces, chances—are the very things he, as a respectable citizen, will eventually take away by closing in and taming the land.[8]

In *Arfive*, Guthrie's name for Choteau, we get occasional glances back to earlier times, to the era of the mountain man, the pioneer, and the early cowpunchers, but a more vivid focus on what the Montana High Plains country has on it now that was absent decades ago. At a railhead thirty miles east of Arfive we encounter a smoking train, a junky railroad barn which passes for the station, cowboys loafing at a bar, and a derelict Indian.[9] Arfive itself, according to Rancher Mort Ewing, has "two general stores, a good restaurant run by a Chink name of Soo Son, a butcher shop, harness and saddle shop, blacksmith shop, Woodmen's Hall and three saloons, one of them named the Family Liquor Store, and a "hotel, which ain't as bedbuggy as some."[10] This latter-day Tansytown also has a house of prostitution and a church with a resident minister. In subsequent years it will acquire a new courthouse, a new grade and high school, a bank, a second store, resident doctor, dentist, and lawyer, some land locaters, a commercial club, telephone systems, separate post office, electric lights, a railroad spur from Great Falls—in short, everything, no matter how primitive at the time, which brings Arfive into the twentieth century. Still the broad expanses of land and the great sky exist. What, then, is lost? Everything. Once a road penetrates a wilderness and a town is built, the wilderness is gone. The savage Eden of *The Big Sky* has been permanently defiled.

This paradise is lost in more subtle ways, too. The attitudes brought by the people who cross and eventually settle in this portion of the High Plains are not compatible with those of the native inhabitants or of the trappers. Dick Summers, the mountain man turned guide of the pioneers in *The Way West* observes that "these were different from the mountain men. These couldn't enjoy life as it rolled by; they wanted to make something out of it, as if they could take it and shape it to their way if only they worked and figured hard enough. They didn't talk beaver and whiskey and squaws or let themselves soak in the weather; they talked crops and water power and business and maybe didn't even notice the sun or the pale green of new leaves except as something along the way to whatever it was they wanted to be and to have."[11] The Oregon pioneers are thus the philosophical descendants of Elisha Peabody of *The Big Sky*. Tadlock particularly resents and dislikes Dick Summers who is for him "Undisciplined. Unsystematic. Accustomed to living without purpose, like a savage." Unfortunately, while Tadlock may represent the wave of the future, his virtues, those of the man of affairs in a civilized society, are not useful in an unstructured situation like the trek along the Oregon Trail. Summers is more flexible and adaptable to the needs of the moment. Tadlock cannot even look on buffalo herds or land without thinking that some management is needed. Lije Evans, the eventual leader of the wagon train, has a more aesthetic response to the land, but his feeling is mixed with a patriotic joy which would never have occurred to the mountain man.

The keen nostalgia for things lost is expressed through Dick Summers, again the character Guthrie uses as a point of reference between different eras. He laments the passing of the buffalo and the beaver, of the days of his youth and the Indian girls he had known:

> The country, like himself, when he saw it first, young and wild like himself, without the thought of age. There wasn't a post on it then, nor any tame squaw begging calico, but only buffalo and beaver and the long grass waving in the Laramie bottoms. The wind had blown lonesome, the sound of emptiness in it, the breath of far-off places where no white foot had stepped. A man snuggling in his robe had felt alone and strong and good, telling himself he would see where the wind came from. . . . In not so long a time now people in the mountains would be living on hog meat, unknowing the flavor and strength of fleece fat and hump ribs. Unknowing, either, how keen an enemy the Rees and the Blackfeet were. He almost wished for the old Rees, for the old Blackfeet that the white man's pox had undone. They had given spirit to life; every day lived was a day won.

Lat Evans of *These Thousand Hills* responds to the wilderness and openness of Montana four decades later, but he has too much of the entrepreneur in him to leave the land alone. It is grass land on which cattle can be fed. And he will collect and feed those cattle eventually. He has none of Tadlock's personal irascibility, but he has all of Tadlock's ambition and passion for management.

Mort Ewing of *Arfive*, Lat Evans' logical successor in Guthrie's next book, is a successful rancher, but some of the old trapper values survive in him. He can respond to the wind, the sky, and the blue lift of the Rockies. Although drawn into the affairs of the town continuously, he feels most in tune with himself and the land when he is out on the open range away from civilization.

No idea which both the pioneers or the settlers bring into the Western wilderness is more inappropriate or unintelligible than the idea of property. The trappers, of course, accepted the Indians' values: the only thing wrong with stealing was in getting caught. But the Oregon pioneers are constantly upset by the Indians' theft of their goods. Suspected cattle-rustling causes Curtis Mack of *The Way West* to shoot a Kaw Indian, an incident which leads to some uncomfortable moments for the wagon train. Later in the book, a contention which has been steadily building between Lije Evans and Tadlock eventually boils over when Tadlock attempts to lead the hanging of a Snake Indian youth for petty theft. He is trying to impose white man's rules in a situation where they are not so much inappropriate as simply inapplicable. Evans understands this; Tadlock does not. Lije is forced to make his point by beating Tadlock physically.

The single most ugly episode in *These Thousand Hills* involves the hanging of some rustlers by a lynch mob. Lat Evans is an unwilling partner in the affair which he sees as more of a vendetta than an attempt to bring about justice. But again, the problem arises because of the white man's whole notion of property and the severity of the penalties he is willing to levy against those who transgress against this notion. The rustling episode is particularly sad when set beside the world of *The Big Sky* which had abundant buffalo and unlimited space. The white man is condemned on two counts: (1) for destroying nature's bounty; (2) for importing his own property and attempting to develop and sell dearly the surplus he creates.

Preachers and orthodox Christianity are corrupting influences, also. Jim Deakins of *The Big Sky* asks many thoughtful questions about the nature of God, but he is succeeded in later books by a succession of Methodist circuit riders who doubt not that they have the answers. Brother Weatherby of *The Way West* is anthropologically ignorant and stupid. He tries to convert the Sioux without any notion of the manner his teaching will be transformed by them into the terms of their culture.[12] When Dick Summers interprets for him, the preacher is shocked to learn that the Indians have no word for soul and thus no means of comprehending the idea that their immortal souls must be saved, at least in Christian terms.

Brother Van, the Methodist preacher of *These Thousand Hills*, is a comic figure. His empty rhetoric exhorts the Lord to lead sinners to righteousness, and he blesses everything that comes into his mind: the territory of Montana, the good people, mothers and fathers, the lame and the halt, the little children. But Guthrie tells us that "underneath the long coat and stout trunk it enclosed, Brother Van's legs appeared thin."

Despicable for his pious sanctimoniousness is John Wesley Harrison of *Arfive*. He is thoroughly bigoted, boasting that Arfive has good solid American names, "hardly a Roman in the lot and not a black man in a hundred miles"; he finds conducting funeral services for a prostitute extremely distasteful (an interesting comment on his knowledge of the company Jesus kept); and he stalls the Mort Ewing and Juliet Justice marriage until he learns that neither has been divorced because the church "has convictions in that direction." One is compelled to observe that in all three of the books succeeding *The Big Sky* the white man's rigid, uncharitable religion has little place in a region in which white men and Indians once accommodated themselves to each other very comfortably, except when they were at war, in terms both understood and accepted. In a region exploding with the vigor of wild untamed nature, it is ascetic and life-denying.

The pioneers and the settlers are most off key, however, in their attitudes toward bodily functions and sex. On the Oregon Trail there are big arguments about the propriety of using buffalo chips for fuel, as if there were any choice. And the book has several references to the devious and comic methods the pioneers use, particularly women, to avoid being detected while urinating or eliminating. There were no problems for trappers and Indians who responded to nature's call whenever and wherever it came.

Sexual frustration is the constant preoccupation of many of the men on the Oregon Trail and in the later books. The trappers of *The Big Sky* responded to their needs by turning openly to the Indian women. But in *The Way West* Curtis Mack commits adultery with Mercy McBee because he has a frigid wife. Joyce Sheridan, the respectable wife of Lat Evans in *These Thousand Hills*, implies by her behavior that sex is somehow not nice. Unlike Boone's Teal Eye, who joins in openly and willingly, she is full of indirection; "It wasn't yes, and it wasn't no, neither one, because she was of gentle birth, out of Indiana, out of Earlham College, because she was herself." Lat might have thought also because she was conditioned by a society in which women denied physical love as anything other than something vulgar to be tolerated with fortitude. Old Man Godwin of *These Thousand Hills* sums up the oldtimer's dilemma succinctly: "Oh, I s'pose I understand, but it wasn't until white wives and picket fences began comin' in that a man got damned for actin' like a man."

The people of *Arfive* are even more genteel. They are divided over the appropriateness of calling a natural feature "Titty Butte" or "Breast Butte." The prostitutes who, in the previous era, would have roamed the streets, are now conveniently out of sight, even when they eat behind a curtain at Soo Son's restaurant. Eventually, they will be gone and their madam will have turned into the respectable proprietor of the restaurant.

To Schoolmaster Benton Collingsworth's credit, it must be said that his basic humanity wins out over society's ideas of respectability early in the book. He hedges, then decides to accept into his school Juliet Justice, an eager orphaned student, who had been tainted by contact with Eva Fox's house of prostitution. Under pressure from Mort Ewing, he consents to admit her. He then knocks the sheriff's deputy flat on his back for an indelicate remark about the new pupil. Eventually, his behavior alienates some of the town's despicable "respectable" folk. To his wife, Benton says, " 'Before you, you see not only the preacher's doubt and the storekeeper's discard, but also the ne'er-do-wells' choice and the saloon owner's friend'.

> "What, Benson?"
> "Maysie, I've swapped constituencies."

Paradise, then, has been lost. The savage, wild, and vital world of *The Big Sky* has been tainted by the marks white civilization puts on it and by the attitudes which the settlers bring into it. All is not lost, however. In a very special sense, the physical characteristics of this vast country endure. For example, Guthrie's characters, in all four books, are remarkably consistent in their response to the big sky. Boone sees "the sky above, blue as paint, and the brown earth rolling underneath, and himself between them with a free, wild feeling in his chest, as if they were the ceiling and floor of a home that was all his own." Fifteen years after Boone Caudill crosses the Platte and comes alive with the sight, Lije Evans responds in a similar manner:

> He couldn't believe that flat could be so flat or that distance ran so far or that the sky lifted so dizzy-deep or that the world stood so empty. . . . He thought he never had seen the world before. He never had known distance until now. He had lived shut off by trees and hills and had thought the world was a doll's world and distance just three hollers away and the sky no higher than a rifle shot.
>
> He said, "By God, Dick! By God!" and Dick nodded, knowing how it was with him, and silence stronger than any sound closed in on the words as if he had broken the rules of speaking.

Although Lat Evans of *These Thousand Hills* is more taken by the scope of the immense grass-lands than are his predecessors, he too, responds to the sky:

> Farther than a man could think, beyond buttes blued by distance, floating in it, the earth line lipped the sky. And hardly anything, any living thing, to see. Wolves, coyotes, and prairie foxes, gophers and the like of these, which didn't count. Now and then a bunch of antelope. No buffalo so far. Cattle to be counted on the fingers except back on the Sun where early ranchers had scattered a few. Beyond them, here, just emptiness and open sky.

Even in *Arfive*, the sky, the predominant image in all of Guthrie's work, prevails. Benton Collingworth thinks that "more than anything else, though, it was the size of this world, the generosity of it, that won a man over, that made him want no other. Depth of sky, reach of miles, elbow room for mind and muscle. Here was a country to live in."[13]

There are but two instances in the four books in which the vastness of Montana's land and sky are sources, not of joy and exhilaration, but of dread. Lat's wife, Joyce, prefers the hills and trees of Indiana and is frightened by the big sky and the open land: "There's just distance, so much that there's no place to go. . . . The sky is so high, and the mountains so cruel, and all the land is so bare." During her first pregnancy she is even more terrified and beat down by the land and the sky. In *Arfive* Jay Ross's wife comes to a point where she can stand it no longer. She decides she must leave: "I could never get used to the sky here. It is bottomless and without end in any direction, and I feel so—flung out, I guess you could say, so bare and so scattered."

With the vast sky, Montana has the ever-present wind which the early trappers and then the pioneers and cattlemen enjoy. But the women cannot tolerate it, and it proves a source of embarrassment to Benton Collingsworth of *Arfive* because it takes his hat off and sends him on an embarrassing public chase. There are two kinds of wind: the steady currents from the northwest which in winter blow such cold and storms that they pierce even the heaviest clothing people of the area can muster; the chinook which comes from the south, warm, and melts the ice and snow.

Guthrie almost ignores the seasons. Spring and summer are mentioned only casually and the fall, when the sun's warmth is mellow and the wild fruit is ripening, only a bit more. The winter, however, gets attention in all books but *The Way West*. It freezes the trappers coming over the mountains in *The Big Sky*, kills the cattle and sheep of *These Thousand Hills*, and continues its vengeance against the people of Arfive. No matter that civilization has arrived by the time of *Arfive*. The Montana winter freezes the grease so hard that cars won't start, the outside water pumps have to be thawed twice a day, the cows are in danger of having frozen udders, and chicken eggs freeze almost immediately after they are laid. At forty-eight degrees below zero, life struggles.

The rivers of the great Western plains country are respected by all generations of those who enter this land. The trappers and the traders of *The Big Sky* use them as landmarks and roads, but they must also battle the spring floods. The Missouri is, for them, a devil of a river with its currents, dams, and debris. The pioneers of *The Way West* mark their progress by the rivers they cross: the Kaw, the Wakarusa, the Little and Big Vermillions, the Big Blue, the Platte, the Sweetwater, the Green, and that last and most difficult river, the Snake. The rivers of mountain country, however, are places for pleasant idylls, the Bear Valley for the Oregon travellers, the Breast River for the trappers and, later, for Benton Collingsworth. He camps and fishes where once Boone Caudill made love to his Indian wife, Teal Eye.

It is the land itself, however, that endures beyond anything man can do to it. Its immensity, its scope, and the sense of freedom and exhilaration it gives to all the generations of men who come upon it lift them out of themselves. Boone Caudill:

> "Christ, but it's fair country, Dick! Mountains to the west, and the valley and plains rollin' away."

Jim Deakins is more philosophical than Boone:

> The feel of the country settled into Jim, the great emptiness and age of it, the feel of westward mountains old as time and plains wide as forever and the blue sky flung across. The country didn't give a damn about a man or any animal. It let the buffalo and antelope feed on it and the gophers dig and the birds fly and men crawl around, but what did it care, for being one with time itself? What did it care about a man or his hankerings or what happened to him? There would be other men after him and others after them, all wondering and all wishful and after a while all dead.

The Oregon travellers pass through this great region, rarely stopping to reflect on it. They are preoccupied with the trail, with the daily chores of cooking, setting and breaking camps, tending to the bare necessities of life, and just surviving until they reach their destination. They look beyond the big sky country to the Pacific Northwest and probably do not reflect upon the country through which they have passed until years later, in the quiet and solitude of their established dwellings, they take time to ponder the difficult journey which brought them to Oregon.

Even though he will enclose parts of it, Lat Evans' love for this country is as intense as that of his predecessors:

> The Tansy. The Sun. The Missouri, better called the Smoky Water, as the Indians called it. The Goose Neck. The Knees. The Judith. The Musselshell. The Dry Forks. The Marias. The Crocondunez near Fort Benton. The Freeze-out. The Two Medicine. Names strange to Ma but wild and sweet on the tongue. Far-ranging names that acquaintance with the country made better. A hundred miles behind him, when he turned to look, he could see the mantled nipples of the Sweet Grass Hills.
>
> Names and places, and things no words could tell. Spring in Montana. Summer. Fall. The look of the ranges, bench on bench. The month of the wild rose. The time that cactus flowered. Everywhere the grasses straight or blowing.

Benton Collingsworth of *Arfive*, although he possesses an Abrahamic concept of land use, thinks that "Here was the country to live in. All right. Be sensuous: it was a land a man wanted to wake up with." He feels keenly the sense of its recent history, the former presence of Indians, trappers, cowpunchers, all celebrated in Guthrie's previous books.

Arfive provides Guthrie with the modern perspective. He can show us the railroad and the automobile, noisy intruders upon Boone Caudill's paradise. He can show Mort Ewing, thinking that the horticultural niceties of the University of Montana campus do not appeal to him as much as "a reach of raw land" or the tumbleweed.

That it may have been Guthrie's implicit intention to preserve in all his works the sense that Montana's vast territory is a force bigger than man comes through very strongly in a graduation address he gave at the university in July, 1949:

> Maybe its space and climate that gives the Montanan his humor, his readiness to accept, his unwillingness to exaggerate self. Montana is mighty

> country—bad lands, high plains, foothills, mountain spurs, mountains, valleys. It is rugged. It possesses a grim beauty. Any way the eye looks it is filled with nothing, said an Easterner who couldn't see. The grandeur, the unpredictability of the place, make self-concern incongruous.[14]

Montana is still sparsely settled. Approximately 700,000 persons are spread across its 147,000 square miles. Its two largest cities, Great Falls and Billings, barely exceed 60,000 persons each. Guthrie's boyhood home, Choteau, had 1,586 people in 1970. To the trappers, this would still have been an ungodly intrusion of greenhorns upon the land they loved. The roads, the enclosures, the permanent dwellings, and the civilization brought by those who displaced the Indians would have been unpalatable. The savage paradise which Lewis and Clark first penetrated in 1804–1805 is gone. But by modern standards the Montanan still has more sky, land, and space than most Americans. And as Dick Summers so rightly observed, to the young, the first experience of this country is as exhilarating as it was to the generations who came into it long ago. But make no mistake about it. Paradise has been lost, and not in terms of land enclosures, disappearing native animal populations, mining of the earth, and dominance of civilized attitudes. For a time in the early 1960s the grimmest realities of the twentieth century came with a silent vengeance right into the land where Boone Caudill once asked Teal Eye to be his squaw. Guthrie: "If I had a choice, I would choose Choteau for the years of my boyhood, unchilled, as I am chilled now, by the presence in Teton County of eighteen Minute-Man bases, eight of them within fifteen miles of the town."[15]

Notes

1. Harvey Breit, "Talk with A. B. Guthrie, Jr.," *New York Times Book Review*, 23 Oct. 1949.

2. For discussion of the relative merits of Guthrie's books see James K. Folsom, *The American Western Novel* (New Haven: College and Univ. Press, 1966), p. 66; Vernon Young, "An American Dream and Its Parody," *ArQ*, 6 (1950), 114; Richard Cracroft, "*The Big Sky:* A. B. Guthrie's Use of Historical Sources," *WAL*, 6 (1971), 175; Wallace Stegner, Foreword to the Sentry Edition of *The Big Sky* (Boston: Houghton Mifflin, 1965), p. ix; John Williams, "The 'Western': Definition of a Myth," *Nation*, 18 Nov. 1961, p. 405; Dayton Kohler, "A. B. Guthrie, Jr., and the West," *CE*, 12 (1951), 254; Orville Prescott, *In My Opinion* (Indianapolis: Bobbs-Merrill, 1952), pp. 140–45; David Stineback, "On History and Its Consequences: A. B. Guthrie's *These Thousand Hills*," *WAL*, 6 (1971), pp. 179–80; Edmund Fuller, *Man in Modern Fiction* (New York: Random House, 1958), p. 105.

3. A. B. Guthrie, Jr., *The Big Sky* (Boston: Houghton Mifflin, 1947), pp. 74–75. All subsequent quotations from the novel will be from this edition.

4. A. B. Guthrie, Jr., "The Historical Novel: Tramp or Teacher?" *Montana: The Magazine of Western History*, 4, no. 4 (1954). See also Guthrie, "The Great Rockies," *Holiday*, Aug. 1963, p. 29.

5. See Folsom, p. 69, and Frank Goodwyn, "The Frontier in American Fiction," *Inter-American Review of Bibliography*, 10 (1960), 365. See also Jackson Putnam, "Down to Earth: A. B. Guthrie's Quest for Moral and Historical Truth," *NDQ*, 29, no. 3 (1971), 50.

6. Putnam, p. 52.

7. A. B. Guthrie, Jr., *These Thousand Hills* (Boston: Houghton Mifflin, 1956), p. 76. All subsequent quotations from this novel will refer to this edition.

8. See Stineback, pp. 182–83. For a dissenting opinion see Putnam, pp. 53–55.

9. The image of the railroad as a violator of wild and virgin country is not new by this time. Ruskin had expressed it for Englishmen nearly a century earlier in *Fors Clavigera*, chapter V, where he describes the destruction of the rocky valley between Buxton and Bakewell. See Charles Harrold and William Templeman, eds., *English Prose of the Victorian Era* (New York: Oxford Univ. Press, 1938), p. 1023.

10. A. B. Guthrie, Jr., *Arfive* (Boston: Houghton Mifflin, 1971), p. 9. All subsequent quotations from this novel refer to this edition.

11. A. B. Guthrie, Jr., *The Way West* (New York: Willian Sloane Associates, 1949), p. 51. All subsequent quotations from this novel will be taken from this edition.

12. An informative gloss on Weatherby's attitude is Somerset Maugham's short story "Rain" and its missionary, Mr. Davidson.

13. Of particular relevance to Collingworth's response is information Guthrie has given about his father's first morning in Montana in 1901. He had gone out of his house and, surveying the immensity of the land into which he had moved, said, "By George, I'm free!" *The Blue Hen's Chick* (New York: McGraw-Hill, 1965), p. 2. Guthrie even has the protagonist in "First Principal," a short story based on his father's work as a school principal in Choteau, respond to the immensity of the Montana sky. *The Big It and Other Stories* (Boston: Houghton Mifflin, 1960), p. 90. The sky image is present in Guthrie's magazine articles, also. See "The End of Their Wanderings: Choteau, Montana," in Thomas C. Wheeler, ed., *A Vanishing America: The Life and Times of the Small Town* (New York: Holt, Rinehart and Winston, 1964), p. 155, and "Montana," *Holiday*, Sept. 1950, p. 47.

14. A. B. Guthrie, Jr., "Twenty-six Years After . . ." (Missoula: Montana University, 12 July 1949).

15. Guthrie, "The End of Their Wanderings," p. 163.

Change of Purpose in the Novels of Louis L'Amour

John D. Nesbitt*

The novels of Louis L'Amour, like the novels of many another paperback Western writer, sing their author's praises on every front cover. The slogans range from "A Classic of the West" to "America's Fastest-Selling Western Writer" to "World's Bestselling Western Writer" to the imperious "World's Greatest Western Writer." L'Amour's recent surge in popularity, occasioned by a strong publicity push by Bantam in the fall of 1975, has brought more of his books than ever before onto the new and used book racks. He now is, indeed, the best-selling and fastest-selling writer of them all. His books serve the worthy purpose of whiling away the hours behind the walls of a prison,[1] in a military barracks, on the banks of a river when the fish are slow to bite, or on a creaky camp cot in the lazy hours between the morning and the evening hunt. It is commonly acknowledged that any book by "Looie" is bound to be good reading, even if a casual reading of ten or twenty of his sixty-some books does not resist the old "read one and you've read 'em all" criticism.

To the person who reads with a slightly less abandoned mind, and to the critic who does not dismiss L'Amour with ridicule and contempt, L'Amour's novels are not just the same old story with the hero of each new volume given a different name and a different colored horse. His books have changed over the years, independently of story lines or plot formulas, according to an apparent change in moral and historical purpose. L'Amour's career can be divided into three phases—early, middle, and recent—and the novels from each phase reflect a change in his use of historical detail accompanied by a change in moral focus. L'Amour is such a prolific writer of short and often similar novels that it seems justifiable to discuss his works by the handful. Since he has no single *magnum opus*, nor even "major" and "minor" works, this essay will discuss groups of novels from each of the three phases of his career.[2]

L'Amour's career as the novelist we know today began variously and gloriously in 1953, with the publication of *Hondo* and *Showdown at*

WAL, 13 (1978), 65–81.

Yellow Butte. Prior to that he published a volume of poetry, *Smoke from This Altar* (1939), several Hopalong Cassidy sagas under the pseudonym "Tex Burns," and a multitude of short stories. A few of the short stories have been reprinted in *War Party* (Bantam, 1975), but for the most part we know L'Amour's productions from 1953 to the present date. From 1953 to 1957 he published novels with no fewer than six presses; the copyrights have since been obtained by Fawcett and Bantam, the two main purveyors of L'Amour novels today.

The novels of this early phase are entertaining in their unbridled violence, their directness of moral utterance, and their frequent (if pedantic) tidbits of Western lore and trivia. As one L'Amour critic has put it, "a certain amount of humor is unavoidable,"[3] and the simplicity of these books is diverting. Two of the novels from this period, *Utah Blaine* (1954) and *Showdown at Yellow Butte* (1953), reflect L'Amour's simplest use of history and his most direct statement of morality. (Both of these were also originally published under the pseudonym "Jim Mayo," but now appear under L'Amour's name.) In both of these books, history is the setting but not the subject. Historical range wars such as the Lincoln County War and the Mason County War, and mention of contemporary gunfighters such as Clay Allison and Wild Bill Hickok, constitute the backdrop of the land wars of these two novels. In addition, we are treated to details about pistols, rifles, and shotguns that were used during that period of time. But neither of these books attempts to articulate or depict history itself; they are, as Henry James said of romantic fiction, "at large and unrelated," isolated excursions into a fictional and stylized Wild West. Out of these two conventional stories of the struggle for land come the expected moral conclusions: it is wrong to defraud the government of land, it is wrong to grab land from honest homesteaders, and it is wrong to settle the land without having reverence for it. It is right to love the land, to care for one's horse, and to give up the driftin' life in favor of settling down to married life and ranching. And along the way we learn a little lore as well, such as "Man freezes mighty quick, drinkin' whisky," and that a man can boil water in a cup made of birch bark. All in all, the lore, the trivia, the historical detail, and the morality, along with the numerous shootings and fistfights, add up to pretty light material—even for L'Amour.

In his other novels of this period, L'Amour's fiction takes on more purpose in depicting time and place and in expressing morality. *Hondo* is his best-known novel of the early phase, and one of his best-known overall. Its popularity is due partly to John Wayne's performance in the movie by the same name, and perhaps to Wayne's endorsement on the front cover of the book. It reads, " 'Best Western novel I have ever read'—John Wayne." Wayne's blessings aside, however, *Hondo* is a more substantial piece of entertainment than the two "Jim Mayo" books. As in the other two, the historical and geographical touchstones are spare. The setting is more than functional, however, in the dimensions that it takes on. The desert, with its historical endowment of hostile Apaches, pervades all that takes place in the actions and thoughts of the main characters. Hondo Lane's guiding principle is to understand the desert, to know it, and to survive wisely in it. As the narrator observes, "One cannot fight the desert and live" (p. 102). Hondo's outlook, then, is a moral framework for information that would otherwise be gratuitous. In *Hondo* we learn, as we often do in L'Amour novels, how to build a fire that won't be seen. We also learn, as we do elsewhere, that Apaches eat mule and horse meat, but not pork or fish. Where in other contexts this information is thrust in irrelevantly, here it sustains the prevailing sense of the desert and the need to live thoughtfully in it. Similarly, when Hondo teaches the boy, Johnny, to find water by following the bees and the quail, the reader does not get the feeling he is being lectured to. Elsewhere in the novel, though, L'Amour is merely grandstanding, as when he deluges the reader with information on how to track the squirrel, the badger, the wolf, the coyote, the dog, and the cougar. Angie Lowe's reflection that mountain men liked panther meat the best, and Ed Lowe's recollection that longhorns "had been known to whip grizzlies," also exemplify Western lore that is invested with less meaning and incorporated with less grace.

L'Amour has his ups and downs in conveying moral statements just as he does in presenting details. Some of his pronouncements are tolerable, and even entertaining, as when Hondo tells Angie that "People learn by gettin' bit" (p. 19) and that "Handsome woman like you, walks with her head up, ought to kiss a man before she dies" (p. 37). Other moments are less charming, such as when Hondo ruminates on his life while he waits for death in the Apache camp: "A man needed something on which to build. A man without a woman, without a home, and without a child was no man at all" (p. 110). Equally sententious is the narrator's sermon as Company C rides out to meet an ambush: "No man knows the hour of his ending, nor can he choose the place or the manner of his going. To each of us it is given to die proudly, to die well, and this is, indeed, the final measure of the man" (p. 38). In this novel the highest values are to survive with honor, to pass on what one has learned, and to die well. Like the characteristic L'Amour hero, Hondo doesn't die, but he does prepare to die well when he is faced with what seems to be certain death.

The values embodied and enacted by early L'Amour heroes are essentially those of the individual on the borderline of civilization. The hero is neither alienated nor isolated, since nearly every L'Amour plot involves the hero in someone else's complications. The opening up of the West nourishes the bullies, landgrabbers, and robbers, while the dangers of the frontier bring out the weaknesses of men who cannot cope and who expose virtuous women to the threat of hostile Indians and unscrupulous white men. It is noteworthy that in the two "Jim Mayo" books L'Amour puts all the adversity in the hands of the power-hungry landgrabbers. In the other novels from this early period, the hero must deal with Indians, cowards, and the environment as well. Even if the morality is rather blunt, it arises out of settings that have more dimension and more convincing detail than in L'Amour's truly hack novels.

The "Jim Mayo" books and the more fleshed-out novels of the early phase still share a broad central characteristic. In the context of historical conditions and touchstones, the footloose hero becomes civilized into a settler. Although L'Amour reiterates his American myth of domesticating the wandering fighting man, these early novels do not constitute—individually or collectively—an *apologia* for Westward settlement. That ambition would come later. For the present, he satisfied his reader with conventional plots, each cut loose and detached from the other, and "at large and unrelated" to any historical vision.

L'Amour's middle phase reaches from the late 1950's to the early 1970's and includes over half of his sixty-odd novels. This phase continues some of his established patterns, and lays the foundation for his later ambitions and purposes. Accordingly, the novels divide mainly into two groups. There is the continuing march of stories about the wandering hero who gets involved in other people's scrapes, and who meets a woman who will walk beside him and not behind him.[4] Except for an occasional exception such as *Kiowa Trail* and *The First Fast Draw*, these novels are narrated in the third person as the early novels are. Also like the early novels, these novels have a different name for each new hero, as if to offer up an eligible bachelor for each new plot. From a survey of these books it would seem that nothing could shake L'Amour's fell purpose of domesticating tall, tough, broad-shouldered, fast-drawing men about thirty years old. But then there is the other group of novels, the ones with the same family names and the same men cropping up time and again. These books are almost all narrated in the first person, and refer to incidents (sometimes footnoted) that take place in other novels in the group. While L'Amour continues producing the good old standbys in the middle phase of his career, he is apparently working, simultaneously, on a sort of interlocking family mythology. For what purposes, his later phase will tell.

In the good old standbys of this period we are treated to the L'Amour fare of variation and repetition in plot structure that we have come to expect and enjoy. In addition, a new dimension appears in several of the heroes in this group of novels. The hero is often a gentleman, and has been to Europe prior to knocking around on the frontier. The continental finish offers a less rough-hewn morality to be expressed through the hero, and it adds a new set of historical details that place L'Amour's stories in a broader historical context. Besides the regular trivia of how buffalo wallows became gullies (*Kilrone*, p. 24, and *Under the Sweetwater Rim*, pp. 21–2), or how only the earliest forts had stockades, there is the additional feature of a frontier frequented by people who talk of Sir Walter

Scott and Tennyson. Thus the titular hero of *Kilrone* (1966) has won a rapier duel in Paris, and can listen intelligently to Major Paddock's wife talk about Zola.

Val Darrant, the hero of *Reilly's Luck* (1970) who grows up alternately in the West and on the continent, takes in an even broader swath of history than the earlier heroes did. He learns that Apaches never attack at night, and that a Spencer .56 fires a slug as big as a man's thumb. He also reads Scott and Tennyson, and stays up late reading *Faust* only to have Byron's *Manfred* recommended as better reading. He also learns to wrestle, box, and fence, and enjoys early-morning Innsbruck in a little cafe where "Goethe used to come to sip wine" (p. 43). To round out his worldwide training he goes horseback riding in New Mexico with a boy his own age named "Billy," and hunts buffalo with a "tall young man named Garrett." On top of all this, Wild Bill Hickok gives him a pistol—a Smith and Wesson Russian .44, as the L'Amour reader might expect. L'Amour lays it on pretty thick in this novel, to be sure; touches like the Hickok and Garrett scenes are in bad taste, and the novel does not succeed as historical fiction. On the other hand, it should be appreciated that L'Amour has stepped out of his old formulas and has tried putting historical material to a new use. Even if he does seem at times to share with Will Reilly "a ready memory for facts gleaned from histories and almanacs" (p. 21), his attempt at recreating an historical milieu, as in the opening paragraphs of Chapters 23 and 27 where he describes Denver and Durango, is more ambitious than the mere introduction of fact and trivia. The intrusion of the Hickok and Garrett material is offset somewhat by these other touches of historical color.

In *Under the Sweetwater Rim* (1971) L'Amour returns to the dashing cosmopolitan Army officer for his hero. Lieutenant Tenadore Brian, age thirty and broad-shouldered, finds himself rescuing the captain's wife and the major's daughter from the Wyoming wilderness and from a brutal band of post-Civil War border riders. The situation and the main character are reminiscent of earlier works: Brian lives on jerky, hardtack, and coffee; he finds game and shelter for his dependents; and he outfights and outmaneuvers (and kills) the border riders who had threatened the virtue of the women in the wilderness. (They had also tried to get away with sixty thousand dollars in gold.) What makes this novel different from the earlier ones is the character of the hero. He has a more detailed past than the earlier heroes, and he deliberates on the heritage of an immigrant grandfather who had fought in the Revolutionary War. Also unlike the earlier heroes, he does not settle down on that ranch with trees and running water. Instead, he continues his calling of active soldiering on the frontier, despite his gentlemanly finish and his slim chances of promotion. The key here is L'Amour's new measure of the hero, anticipated in Tenadore Brian and drawn out at length in later novels. Each man has his part in the destiny of American civilization, and the purest moral act is to fulfill that part. Therefore, Brian stays on in service: "This was a country. No wonder the Indians were prepared to fight for it" (p. 181). And the novel ends with Major Devereaux's reflection, "Damn it, the man was a *soldier*" (p. 182).

While L'Amour was working his way towards new moral vistas, he was creating a new race of heroes as well. The Sacketts are, we are told time and again, "fierce fighting men" from the hills of Tennessee. Being a fighting man is central to all L'Amour heroes, but the Sacketts are of a breed all to themselves. For one thing, even though one of them may get married and settle down, there is every possibility that he will re-appear in another Sackett novel. *Sackett* ends with William Tell Sackett's marriage, but in a later novel *(The Sackett Brand)* L'Amour kills off Tell's wife and frees Tell for all sorts of new adventures in later novels. Similarly, *The Daybreakers* ends with Tye Sackett's settling down:

> We found our home, and we graze and work our acres, and since that day in the street of Mora when I killed Tom Sunday I have never drawn a gun on any man.
>
> Nor will I. . . .

The ellipsis which closes the novel serves the additional purpose of keeping the story open-ended. And sure enough, Tye Sackett has his hog leg back on his hip in *The Sackett Brand.*

The stories are open on the other end, too, with one novel making reference to events that took place before—events that are narrated in other Sackett novels. Thus in *The Sackett Brand* we are even given a footnote (p. 14) to *Sackett*, and in *The Sky-Liners* we find a footnote (p. 2) to *The Sackett Brand.* In addition, there are hundreds of cross references and reminders among the many novels of this group. After a while the L'Amour enthusiast smells a rat. L'Amour is not merely writing several stories about the same character as he did in his salad days with Hopalong Cassidy; he is putting together an assembly of interlocking stories about an extensive and ever-extending family. No longer is the reader set free with each new novel, to be entertained with a story "at large and unrelated" to all others. Each Sackett novel carries with it the burden of attachment to all other Sackett novels, and sooner or later the reader is obliged to feel that he is piecing in a larger story.

At about the time the reader is getting into more than he bargained for, he is also being treated to some of L'Amour's least successful narration. These novels are narrated in two ways: entirely first person, and alternating between first and third person. *The Daybreakers* is characteristic of L'Amour's first-person narration. His Sacketts invariably say "taken" for "took," as in "I taken my hat off my head" or "I taken out of there." Other trademarks such as the redundant pronoun ("Me, I don't know" and "Cap, he just looked at me") abound in this novel also. It is not the ungrammatical nature of a Sackett's narration that gets tiring, but L'Amour's narrow range of reproducing the texture of vernacular. Grammatical problems complicate matters, of course, since we don't always know whether L'Amour or Sackett should be the object of our smile: "Crawling to the rim of the buffalo wallow my eyes searched the terrain before me, dancing with heat waves" (p. 70), and "Looking down the table at her my heart went out to her" (p. 120). If one ascribes these errors to an inarticulate narrator who is just learning to read and write, one wonders how to deal with a sublime paragraph like the following, presented through the same unlettered narrator:

> It was a sea of horns above the red, brown, brindle, and white-splashed backs of the steers. They were big, wild, and fierce, ready to fight anything that walked the earth, and we who rode their flanks or their drag, we loved them and we hated them, we cussed them and reviled them, but we moved them westward to what destination we knew not. (p. 9)

One could conclude that L'Amour is not as concerned with narrative purity as Henry James or Wayne Booth would wish.

The alternating narration of *The Lonely Men* has its drawbacks as well. One would think that L'Amour alternates his narration in order to have Tell Sackett narrate tersely and inarticulately, and leave the more garrulous business to the usual third-person narrator. But the separation of narrative effect is not maintained. On the second page Tell observes, in the very words of the usual L'Amour third-person narrator, that the Apaches were "the greatest guerilla fighter the world ever saw," and that he (Tell) "searched the terrain for something at which to shoot." It seems that L'Amour merely follows a personal convention in having the Sacketts tell their own stories. Since the narrative texture is not at stake, he goes outside their point of view for expediency in giving the circumstances of the plot. So, in the second chapter, the narration shifts to third person to inform the reader of details that Tell must be in the dark about. Writers like John Seelye and Jack Schaefer create narrators who tell much more than they understand at the time, but L'Amour doesn't try for that effect. Nor is he concerned with the sophisticated use of alternating narration that Dickens achieves in *Bleak House.* Rather than attempt narrative integrity *or* complexity, he follows the easiest trail in order to tell the story. As a consequence, the reader may become impatient, and his impatience may well vitiate the entertainment that is sought so expediently and that is usually the reward of a L'Amour novel.

The obscure motives behind the family web of the Sackett stories and the dawning morality of *Under the Sweetwater Rim* come to light in *Sackett's Land.* In the "Preface" to this book, L'Amour reveals the purpose (and status) he claims for himself. After some preliminary philosophizing on history, he discloses his design:

> Some time ago, I decided to tell the story of the American frontier through the eyes of three families—fictional families, but with true and factual experiences. The names I chose were Sackett, Chantry, and Talon.
>
> . . . . . .
>
> Story by story, generation by generation, these families are moving westward. When the journeys are ended and the forty-odd books are completed, the reader should have a fairly true sense of what happened on the American frontier. (v-vi)

Apparently, then, the first-person narration of the Sackett stories is not an arbitrary choice. Telling "the story of the American frontier through the eyes of three families" is meant to give conviction and immediacy to L'Amour's version and vision of the American frontier.

L'Amour's ambitious declaration of purpose comes at a key point in his career. At this same time (1974–5) several changes were taking place in L'Amour's status. Bantam changed the covers on his novels, and the price. Books that were previously priced from forty cents to ninety-five cents jumped to a dollar and a quarter and a dollar and a half. Although Bantam has changed its covers and upped its prices on several authors, in L'Amour's case the change coincided with other new developments. The slogan changed from "Today's Bestselling Western Writer" to "The World's Bestselling Western Writer." In October of 1975, with the publication of *The Man from the Broken Hills*, Bantam declared in full-page advertisements that "Louis L'Amour takes over as Bantam's #1 author, surpassing John Steinback, Emilie Loring, and others." In the next year and a half he enjoyed enormous publicity on television and in newspapers. Also during this time, Fawcett brought out a complete line of all nine of their L'Amour novels—with new covers on some, and new prices on all. The "Jim Mayo" books, unheard of for nearly twenty years, now stand side by side with *Hondo* and others.

All of this information tells us more than just the fact that L'Amour is making a decent wage. (Decent enough, incidentally, to re-create an 1865 Western town.) He has changed from a successful writer to a self-appointed chronicler of the Western movement. Consequently, his recent books are less autonomous than even the early Sackett sagas, and in no way as unfettered as the earlier stories about the tough man of the frontier. In the later phase, where characters and plots are spun for a grander web, L'Amour is a self-styled historian and apologist for Western settlement.

Sackett's Land (May 1974) and *Rivers West* (March 1975) were obviously written to fit into the overall design. The former tells the story of the first Sackett to come to America from Wales in 1599, and the latter tells of the first Talon to come from Canada in 1821. In these two novels and in other novels of this period, we learn that the Sacketts are fighting men of Welsh descent, the Talons are builders of French descent, and the Chantrys are scholars of Irish descent. In an article published in 1972,

Ernest L. Bulow anticipated this one aspect of L'Amour's later fiction: "It is vital for the writer of popular fiction to conform to popular taste and to keep up with shifts in public sentiment. . . . It is predictable that L'Amour will produce some ethnic heroes in the near future or lose his standing."[5] By producing these two immigrant heroes, heroes who saw that their destinies were to help build and settle America, L'Amour coordinated his ethnic appeal with a larger trend in popular sentiment: the bicentennial fever. In his three bicentennial families he established a fairly comprehensive ethnic and occupational range for his chronicles.

L'Amour's new mode could be maintained by his established conventions of plot and character, which could be modified with bicentennial history and morality. In Barnabas Sackett we see once again a stalwart young man itching to "go wild upon the world" (p. 9), a man eminently capable of killing fish, geese, deer, Indians, and white men in order to succeed in his venture. Also like other L'Amour heroes, he is successful in finding shelter, good at reading sign, hungry for knowledge of history and literature, and deeply desirous of dying well when the time should come. And like previous first-person narrators, he is sententious. He tells his patron:

> "Yet when two peoples come together that one which is most efficient will survive, and the other will absorb or vanish . . . it is the way of life.
>
> "The Indian must not lose pride in what he does, in his handicraft, for if he loses pride he will no longer build, his art will fail him, and he will completely be dependent upon others." (p. 168)

What is new about the Sackett narrator is that he is now a mouthpiece for his author's moral version of history.

Jean Talon, like Barnabas Sackett and the putative descendants of both, is handsome, honest, and strong. (When the time comes, he also holds his knife cutting edge up, a heroic feature dating as far back as *Hondo.*) Another index of his heroism is his fever to go West; but he is more intense than previous heroes in his fever to see the new land settled and governed properly. Early in his travels Talon learns, in a philosophical discussion with the landlord of an inn, that "none of us is free of responsibility," and that "good government is everybody's business" (pp. 23–24). Where the earlier L'Amour hero opened up the country for those who would follow, the new hero follows his own personal destiny to help found a culture. Talon is a builder by heritage, and since he works with timber he is "a man who likes order" (p. 123) and who doesn't believe in wasting God's trees on bad building (p. 95). It is fitting, then, that such a man should come upon a plot to usurp the Louisiana Territory, to undermine order, and to despoil the land. L'Amour's reconstruction of history and his propensity for moralizing come together strongly and overtly in this novel; one purple passage in particular shows how Talon (and the novel) is a vehicle for conveying L'Amour's urgent purpose:

> "We're all Americans, I think," I said quietly. "But I have asked myself that question. I am a man who believes in order. A stable government is the responsibility of all men and women everywhere.
>
> "Revolution, for whatever reason, is self-defeating, for violent revolution results in violent reaction. Oddly enough, the worst reaction usually comes from within the revolution itself, and the first casualty is the revolutionary. Look what has happened in France, for example. Those who created the revolution, those leaders of revolution, all were victims of it. And who reaped the benefit?—Napoleon.
>
> "Peaceful change is the healthiest change, but if you will look closely you will see what the so-called revolutionary who deals in violence wants is simply violence. He is unhappy with himself, believes himself incapable of coping with the situation as it is, so tries to disrupt it. He wants violence to relieve his own anger and pent-up hatred." (pp. 112–3).

This is, indeed, a far cry from *The Sackett Brand*, where "Forty gunslingers from the Lazy A have got Tell Sackett cornered back under the Mogollon Rim" (quoted from the back cover).

Ironically, L'Amour "deals in violence" as much as, if not more than, the revolutionaries he deplores. His novels that deal in violence, *Rivers West* and *Sackett's Land* not least among them, are far more entertaining in their fistfights and gunfights than in their philosophical cant. And the fruits of L'Amour's research still evoke some interest. For example, we can appreciate the archaic flavor of his heroines' names (Abigail and Tabitha) as part of his new mode of historical detail. In *Sackett's Land*, descriptions of Durango and Santa Fe are replaced by details quarried from Elizabethan England: the Globe Theatre, St. Paul's Walk, highwaymen, pirates, and taverns. The Long Branch Saloon is, for the nonce, the Tabard Inn. But if we were a little uneasy when Val Darrant met Pat Garrett and Wild Bill Hickok, we cringe when Barnabas Sackett goes to watch Shakespeare's plays. (Thankfully, he does not meet the bard.) In *Rivers West* L'Amour has "worked up" his history, too. We get a contemporary portrait of Pittsburgh and St. Louis, we learn that travelers in New England were expected to carry their own bedding, and we have a keelboat described and a sawyer defined. We are even told what kind of moccasins the Omaha wore. But too much is too much. Details that formerly might have offered a bit of historical verisimilitude (or at least momentary diversion) now cumulatively assert the veracity of L'Amour's historical overview. Where we used to smile at being informed, as in a passage on the culinary preferences of the Apaches, we now grimace at history being filled in for us pedantically, detail by detail, as part of an overbearing design. L'Amour the historian goes too far in these two novels, in that the narrative is constantly cloyed with historical detail and circumstance; and L'Amour the moral historian simply overdoes it in justifying American settlement as justice and democracy in action.

Following these two grandaddy novels, L'Amour's later phase has continued to produce stories about his bicentennial families, and about unrelated heroes. *The Man from the Broken Hills* and *Over on the Dry Side* (both published October 1975) advance the family sagas and blend the ethnic and vocational elements of the original families into new characters. As he did in his middle phase, L'Amour lards his family stories with references to events and family members that the reader is likely to read of elsewhere. Milo Talon, the hero of *The Man from the Broken Hills*, is half Talon and half Sackett. He makes one mention of his cousin Tell, and frequent mention of his brother Barnabas. The brother is of course named after the grand sire from Shakespeare's time, and has lived in France with Talon relatives. When Milo mentions that Barnabas will import some European cattle to mix with the Texas longhorns, the reader is as much as guaranteed a future novel in which manifestations of European culture will blend into the cattle empires of Texas. In the final pages of the novel Milo Talon remains a bachelor like some of his Sackett cousins, but he receives a letter that bodes well for future romance with China Benn; quite possibly, that romance will appear in a later volume.

The hero of *Over on the Dry Side*, Owen Chantry, also fits into the grander web of characters. His brother Clive, mentioned throughout the novel but dead from the opening chapter, happens to have been a builder as well as a scholar. Consequently, mention of a Chantry ancestor visiting the Gaspé Peninsula (whence came Jean Talon in *Rivers West*) makes the reader wonder what other future connections are in store.

As extensions of L'Amour's family plan, then, both of these novels fit into his monomythic rendition of American settlement. They also display the extremes in narrative quality that emerge from the master plan. *The Man from the Broken Hills* has a successfully created narrator. The speaking voice lapses occasionally, but for the most part Milo Talon's narration is evenly textured with humor and vernacular. He does use the inevitable "taken" for "took," and he does "shuck" his Winchester a little too often; still, he maintains a smooth and casual tone, and delivers some pretty good lines. L'Amour achieves a narrator who is also an engaging character and who, unlike previous Sacketts and Talons, can tell a complimentary story about himself without boasting or apologizing. And since Milo is a tolerable narrator, L'Amour's stream of cowhand lore arises comfortably out of the narration. So we don't have a narrator continually thrusting in gratuitous information, even though we do have quite a few narrative digressions on the cowpunchin' trade. In addition, we don't have a narrator who is obliged to tell us time and again what a crack shot and devastating fistfighter he is. L'Amour's success in this novel is partly owing to his creation of a new variety of hero. Milo Talon talks his way out of more jams than he shoots or punches his way out of, and his genial nature even colors the narration of one of his few shooting scrapes.

> There were two of them, and I wanted an edge. I didn't know whether I needed it or not, but I wanted it. They had taken money to kill, and they would not welsh on the job.

"We taken this money," Laredo said, "an' we got to do it."

"You could always give it back."

"We done spent most of it, Milo. We just ain't got it no more," said Laredo.

"Well, I could let you have a few bucks," I said quietly. "I could let you have . . . Let's see what I've got." I moved my right hand as if toward my pocket and when they went for their guns I was a split second ahead of them.

Sonora's gun was coming up when I shot him. Sonora was on the right. It is an easier move from right to left, so I took him first. (p. 196)

Despite his own protestations that he doesn't want to be a hero, Talon is the hero who saves the day and settles the range feud. His virtue as a fictional character is that he is less emphatically heroic than earlier L'Amour heroes. He is still a medium for L'Amour's urgency to give details of the West and to impose a simplistic interpretation on civilization, but because he is a more moderate and offhand narrator than his forefathers Jean and Barnabas, he carps appreciably less.

As observed above, L'Amour's choice of narrating his family chronicles in the first person is apparently a conscious and purposeful choice. While he achieves enjoyable narration in *The Man from the Broken Hills*, he does the opposite in *Over on the Dry Side*. As in *The Lonely Men*, the narration alternates between first person and third person, with many of the same flaws. The first-person narrator has a dangling modifier (p. 59), but he's just a sixteen-year-old kid. Then the third-person narrator has one just like it, four pages later. Add to that a misplaced modifier and a misplaced packhorse, and a few other minor confusions in logistics, and what results is a tedious story that serves as a vehicle for L'Amour's characteristic lectures. Entertaining narrative effect is lost in favor of flat introduction of historical details and moral speeches. The reader is left with the impression that L'Amour's fiction sometimes rises above and sometimes sinks below his avowed purposes.

For the reader who is not entirely in sympathy with the new demands placed on him—the demands of piecing together family chronicles and American history, all fraught with significance—L'Amour continues to produce the good old standby stories. In the flyleaf of *The Man from the Broken Hills* L'Amour is quoted in a passage that incidentally illuminates his non-family novels of recent years: "What I hope is that 150 years from now a person could draw a true picture and understanding of the Old West—the country, the people—from reading my books." In *Where the Long Grass Blows*, L'Amour portrays an historically interesting West without presenting urgent messages that would get in the way of his perenially most successful work. In this novel the story of the range war is revived. Like *The Man from the Broken Hills*, the novel introduces information on how cattlemen used the range, how they discreetly stole from one another, how they conducted their roundups, and so forth. The information is more appropriate and interesting than the rundown on Elizabethan décor in *Sackett's Land*, and L'Amour succeeds at presenting material that bears upon the story line and is not inserted simply for the reader's edification:

> Land was of no value without water, and he who controlled the water controlled the land. Longhorns could graze a day or two from water, walking in for a drink only occasionally, if water was scarce. The vegetation they ate gave them enough moisture to get along, although they preferred to drink every day or twice a day. (p. 26)

This is not to say that in these books L'Amour achieves realistic fiction and the texture of historical reality, while in the Sackett-Talon-Chantry volumes he doesn't. L'Amour's strong suit has always been entertainment and his fiction entertains the reader with action, dialogue, description, *and* information. When the information advances rather than impedes the entertainment, the book is more successful and less pretentious.

L'Amour has updated his use of the reliable old plot formulas, and not just in his use of historical detail. An interesting if not thoroughly tasteful twist is that the villain in this novel is an opium smuggler as well as a cattle rustler. Again it is interesting to recall Ernest Bulow's prediction that L'Amour's fiction would conform "to popular taste and . . . keep up with shifts in public sentiment." When L'Amour is not producing immigrant heroes and their democratic descendants, he is producing a hero who recognizes the smell of opium and who is less violent and uptight than the old hero. Bill Canavan shares with Milo Talon an avoidance of fistfights and gunfights, and an ability to be amused and whimsical at his own predicament. Canavan is also a new creation in that he is motivated by cupidity. He enters the scene in order to get his own generous slice of the pie, and to profit from the bigger ranchers' fighting it out. His motives are not base or un-democratic, however, since he has bought some of the range quietly beforehand, and has filed claim to another large portion. L'Amour tempers Canavan's motives further with some familiar morality, when he has Canavan muse that "The country had needed discovery, had needed opening up. But now that was done and it was time to build" (p. 123). Like the hero of the early phase Canavan is in love with the land, and he undertakes to cultivate it; unlike the family saga heroes, he is not burdened by a sense of heritage and destiny that urges him to beat his Bowie knife into a ploughshare. The new L'Amour hero is temperate in his behavior as well as in his motivation—he is only obliged to get into one fistfight and one gunfight in order to achieve his ambitions.

After this cursory survey of L'Amour's career, and particularly in light of the novels produced in the last three years, it is interesting to consider what we can continue to expect of L'Amour. It is a safe bet that his family chronicles will continue, with their attendant lessons in history and morality, possibly until the "forty-odd books are completed."[6] It is equally probable that he will maintain his readership with further variations on the old standby conventions, and we may be presented with more works like *The Rider of Lost Creek* (1976) that seem to be reworkings of much earlier manuscripts. Now that L'Amour is approaching the age of seventy he may slack off writing new novels, and produce from a backlog of recent and not-too-recent manuscripts. At any rate we can expect many more productions within his established range of fiction. Inelegancies of grammar and punctuation may well continue, accompanied by a not-so-rigorous control of narrative point of view. We will be wrong to expect high art or exquisitely crafted fiction. But we will not be disappointed if we expect a continuing variety of entertainment from an author who has regaled us with "stories that take off like a bullet"[7] for a quarter of a century.

Notes

1. An article in the *San Francisco Chronicle*, 22 Dec. 1975, reads: "In some prisons, according to the legend, you have to trade five other books for one L'Amour. . . . But except for some scholars doing dissertations, the literati generally seem to ignore the Los Angeles-based author."

2. See below for a list of titles, dates, and publishers of the works discussed.

3. Ernest L. Bulow. "Still Tall in the Saddle: Louis L'Amour's Classic Western Hero," *The Possible Sack*, 3, no. 8 (1972), 2.

4. See *Kilrone* (New York: Bantan, 1966), pp. 53–54, for one of L'Amour's many uses of this trope.

5. Bulow, p. 8.

6. "Preface" to *Sackett's Land* (1974; rpt. New York: Bantam, 1975).

7. Quoted from the back cover of L'Amour's most recent and most colorful Bantam editions.

Louis L'Amour Novels Cited in Text

Hondo. New York: Fawcett, 1953.

Showdown at Yellow Butte. 1953; rpt. New York: Fawcett, n. d.

Utah Blaine. 1954; rpt. New York: Fawcett, n. d.

The Daybreakers. 1960; rpt. New York: Bantam, 1971.

Kilrone. New York: Bantam, 1966.

The Lonely Men. 1969; rpt. New York: Bantam, 1971.

Reilly's Luck. New York: Bantam, 1970.

Under the Sweetwater Rim. New York: Bantam, 1971.

Sackett's Land. 1974; rpt. New York: Bantam, 1975.

Rivers West. New York: Bantam, 1975.

The Man from the Broken Hills. New York: Bantam, 1975.

Over on the Dry Side. 1975; rpt. New York: Bantam, 1976.

Where the Long Grass Blows. New York: Bantam, 1976.

Walter Van Tilburg Clark's Ambiguous American Dream

L. L. Lee*

"The fat dream," Arthur Bridges calls it in *The Track of the Cat.* "We've gone from ocean to ocean, . . . burning and butchering and cutting down and plowing under and digging out, and now we're at the end of it. Virginia City's where the fat dream winked out. . . . Even a good dream, backed up, turns nightmare, and this wasn't a very good one to start with. A belly dream." Explicitly, Arthur is talking about that American dream of conquering the American land in order to create the good, i.e., the abundantly material life—the dream indeed not just of American capitalism but of "modern" man. But Arthur is also speaking of other dreams, of the American Dream, and for the moment he is his creator's, Walter Van Tilburg Clark's, voice.

What one means by the American Dream depends, of course, upon the speaker. But in every man's definition and in every artist's realization of the Dream must appear the American land, sometimes a new Eden, sometimes something very near to Hell, sometimes mother and destroyer both, almost always a great ambiguity. Moreover, in every definition, the question of what man, or rather the white man, has to do with the mystery of nature must be asked and explored. And, finally, one must say what man has to do with man as they live together in that land.

One can generalize: in his literature at least, the white man in America has rarely been at peace with his landscape, especially with the new, untamed land. He has either conceived of the land as something to defeat or something to be feared, often the two together. He has been fascinated by the land, but he has seldom been at ease in it, even when it is Zion. Leslie Fiedler has said, and surely he is right, that a major act of some American writers has been to substitute "the symbol of untamed nature for that of corrupt civilization, as horror and threat."[1]

Too, wherever he has gone, the white man has carried with him a controlling set of attitudes: nature can be overcome only by the violent efforts of the individual, and, in the face of nature, all men are equal. In

**CE*, 26 (1965), 382–87.

other words, we can say that the American believes in democracy and in individualism (that these two attitudes are often contradictory does not disturb the Dream too much).

It is in response to some such feeling about the relationship of man to nature and of man to man that Walter Van Tilburg Clark has built his fiction. Clark's work is a criticism of the American Dream—not directly, through satire, and not entirely, for Clark accepts much of that dream, but indirectly by giving a statement of value of his own. He is, despite his surface simplicity and occasional sentimentality, a notable ironist.

At bottom, Clark is a moralist. But he does not preach a social system, unless a kind of anarchy be a social system. He addresses himself to the individual: we must love one another, and nature, or die. Nature must not be considered only as something to be overcome and made useful; it is for men to live in, to be *alive* in. The orthodoxies of America, the Puritan Jehovah or the god of money, are anti-life. When Grace Bridges cries out to her mother, "You and your God don't hear little jokes [that tell the truth about life]. And Curt [her brother] and Father don't even have a God, not any kind. Only money," she too speaks for Clark.

All men as living creatures are equal, Clark has agreed (*The Oxbow Incident* is a bitter indictment of social inequality as well as of injustice). But men are good, and so valuable, only if they live in the right way. That right way is to live almost as a holy fool with high moral courage in and with the natural world and with other men. Above all, man's way with man corresponds to his way with nature. This statement is, I suggest, the key theme of Clark's fiction: one side of it may be more important than the other for any one work, but both sides are in every work.

But if Clark is a moralist, he is also a realist. As Frederic Carpenter says of one of Clark's heroes, Clark himself shows his maturity by "recognizing and accepting . . . the radical imperfection of things."[2] The good men of Clark's fiction are not the new Adam; Clark is not so innocent as to believe that the American can remain innocent nor does he believe that the world has been reborn in America. He says, rather simply, that man should be good but that evil exists.

And evil can be anywhere. For Clark, the natural world is usually a good, but is also a mystery, a sometimes terrifying mystery. The natural world can offer images to live by; it can give and restore human integrity; it can be fulfillment if one comes to it as a worshipper, with love but also with awareness. I use the word "worshipper" deliberately. Clark's fiction is filled with the gods of nature who are to be recognized as gods. They are not the devices of bad poetry or mere abstractions; they are true images of man's sense of the real powers of nature. To quote Richard Chase (who is speaking not of Clark but of Twain's river and Melville's whale), Clark's gods are "not only genial, sustaining, and nourishing but also sinister and dangerous."[3]

These gods are more than the "subconscious and irrational motives which govern the individual," as Carpenter would have them.[4] They exist in the natural world as well as in man. Clark's "nature," then, is divine, but we must remember that the divine is also inhuman.

It is in some of the short stories, in the novelette "The Watchful Gods," and in *The Track of the Cat* that Clark most clearly presents his view of the ambiguity of the American landscape. Now, it would be untrue to insist that Clark is talking only about man's relationship with nature in these works; the gods, the good and the evil, are often obviously within the characters. But it would be equally untrue to say that the natural world is nothing but a stage, for the natural world *is*, it is an actual being as well as a subjective symbol.

In "The Watchful Gods," the young boy, Buck, is initiated into adulthood, into the "radical imperfection" of the world of manhood. Given a twenty-two by his father, Buck goes on a hunt and kills a young rabbit. With the killing, he suddenly becomes aware that the world has changed: the "bright gods" of the natural world, the little sprites who are the "gods of life," almost disappear into the "dark spirit" of the fog and of death. Life and nature are no longer simple and beautiful things. Buck remembers an encounter with a rattlesnake and thinks, "The snake was the defender of the rabbit. It followed that the powers of light and darkness were not wholly and always opposed to one another." And, toward the end, Buck, arguing out his problem with his gods, conceives the "judge-god" as "an attentive and two-sided thinker." Having lost his innocence, Buck has become aware not only of the ambiguities within himself but also of the ambiguities within the universe. There is a positive element here: the boy can no longer live in the ordered world of childhood, but he has become aware of the saving grace of irony.

The Track of the Cat is Clark's most ambitious treatment of the complexities of the world. The black mountain lion is a manifold symbol, at once real cat and also nature, nature good and evil. But the cat is also, as Carpenter suggests, the "subconscious motives" which drive the individual. More, at times it seems pure evil itself, outside as well as inside man. To the old Indian, Joe Sam, the cat apparently is "the whole business of [the Indians] being run out by the white man, the end of things. . . . " But Joe Sam also seems to think that the cat is trying to "clear" everybody out of the country, "especially white men."

The actual mountain lion is an insane killer: it slaughters the cattle without need for food; it kills Arthur Bridges with a cold cunning. It is, then, an aspect of nature as non-human, indifferent to human values. In a way, it is one side of the actual American land.

But the beast that "killed" Joe Sam's wife and daughter (and which Joe Sam both fears and seems to cooperate with) is something more. It returns with the first snow of winter and can be held off only by the proper ritual, that is, the completed carving of the mountain lion that Arthur makes each fall. Joe Sam is thinking as a primitive thinks, but he is right. The beast, the force, exists. Arthur fails to finish in time: he is killed by the actual lion; his brother Curt burns the unfinished carvings Arthur has made, including the one that might "as well be God," and he too dies, driven over the cliff by the mountain lion that may exist only in his mind; the destroyer of the land is destroyed by the land—and himself. The physical mountain lion is killed, but, as Carpenter says, "the real evil remains: the symbolic black cat, like the symbolic white whale of a century before, remains in the nature of things to trouble men's minds."[5] The symbolic black cat is the symbolic American land, remaining as "horror and threat."

But if nature, the American land, represents horror and threat, i.e., death, it also represents life. As Harold, the youngest of the good Bridges (Clark perhaps too neatly balances three Bridges against three) observes Gwen Williams, the young woman he is going to marry, he thinks of her as a priestess of life, a priestess of the God of Life as opposed to the God of Death. And "she wants what Arthur wanted." What Arthur wanted was the unspoiled natural world. Too, Gwen embodies the principle of fertility; she and Harold will carry on life.

In *The City of Trembling Leaves*, Clark gives this other side of nature a fuller exposition. Nature here is usually benign, beautiful, solacing, and alive (this is no reversal; nature is still ambiguous, she could be beautiful and solacing in the other works too). The hero of the book, Tim Hazard, asks about Henry Adams:

> Why, all through the two great books, is there nothing about a mountain, a river, a tree, a flower, a bird, fish, snake, animal, star, unless they're in stained glass? How, for instance, could Adams wander all over the tremendous west and tell us nothing but what he had thought in Washington, D.C.? . . . "Adams, weren't you in love with a stained-glass Virgin?"

The questions are important beyond their criticism of Adams: Hazard is saying that nature is life and meaning, that excessive intellectualism is an anti-life orthodoxy. One must experience nature, not use it only as symbol and idea.

As his mother is dying, Tim takes her to Lake Tahoe; sitting on her blanket and looking at the lake, she asks, "I wonder if heaven could be any better than this, Timmy?" It is ironic, but not bitterly ironic, that the dying woman should say this of the continuing natural world. For Tim, trying to explain the effect of that natural world upon him and her, says,

> You become just yourself, fitted perfectly into your place in everything . . . as if you had discovered what you should always be, but can't because the affairs of human beings keep pecking at you, or there are walls, all kinds of walls, which shut out the greater, non-human part and keep the balance wrong in the mind. Anyhow, it's as close to religion as any experience I know. She had it that afternoon. . . . For her to rest, there had to be a positive feeling . . . that something much bigger and stronger had taken hold, and for one Sunday afternoon, at least, she believed that.

The cities of America are, obviously, denials of the land, destroyers of the land, although Hazard admits that houses are "a matter of people, not of buildings." But the mining towns of Nevada leave ugly scars; Los Angeles is inhabited by such dead esthetes as Mr. Hule; the center of Reno belongs to death. A city without trees, for instance, "is drawing out of its alliance with the eternal, with the Jurassic Swamps and the Green Mansions, and in time it will also choke out the trees in the magic wilderness of the spirit."

The city will crush even the good man. The apartment of the Briaskis in Reno seems "like a bit of transplanted moribund city . . . . there seemed to be a thin, gray film over life. . . ." The Briaskis love music, which is one of the ways of preserving or recapturing the magic wilderness of the spirit, but they are too involved in the city life of mankind to be saved. People caught in a dead tradition, they have lost nature. (This relationship between music and nature is expressed in the structure of *The City of Trembling Leaves:* the novel has the "form" of a musical composition— Tim Hazard finally succeeds in writing a symphony with the same name as the novel and so closes the book on an affirmation—with the theme of trees announced in the first section of book and symphony appearing again and again.)

It is the white man, the builder of cities, living usually as the outsider on the land, who is most endangered by the powers of nature. The white man is the man of organization, of groups, not yielding himself to the natural world. He is not a true individual, despite all his shouting about individualism. Jacques Barzun remarks disparagingly of some of the nineteenth century ideas that underly our civilization: "A modern, industrialized, democratic nation must therefore be a compact herd—of rugged individualists."[6] Clark illustrates these contradictions in the American position on individualism when he speaks of "dreamers, or, as Tim would call them, primary realists, and factualists, or secondary realists. . . ." The dreamers are the real individuals, the others are simply members of the mob.

It is this lack of real individualism in the white man that has most disturbed Clark. The white man has acted only to gain power in his group and to gain power over things: this is a violent and false ethic. It is what has led to the rape of the land and to the cruelty of one man to another. From Tetley in *Oxbow* through the corrupt Criasi in *Leaves* to Curt Bridges in *Cat* and perhaps the father in "The Watchful Gods" runs the line of his destroyers, both of land and of other men.

On the other hand, the true individual is not a seeker after power. It is only by opposing the American dream of success, by cutting oneself off from the crowd and the crowd's values, from the hunt for money, that one can be really complete. The individual, then, is likely to be a lonely man; he does not fit into the social organization. Sometimes Clark presents him as the artist, always a figure on the fringes of the community. (In an odd way, Clark's artist is a conservative; he wants to hold on to the still unravaged land and the human values of the past, if not to the nineteenth-century American capitalism that is destroying them.) The true individual has only the power of his integrity—which does not always suffice; he needs, also, moral and physical courage.

The purest example is Arthur Bridges of *Cat*. Arthur is a dreamer (an actual dream of his begins the book), an idealist, but he is neither out of contact with the real nor is he a fanatic. He is also a man of peace. He will not quarrel even with Curt, although this is not because he lacks physical courage. To quarrel would solve nothing. Yet he is regarded by Curt, and his mother and father, as rather spineless and a bit silly. His father attacks him for believing in "back to nature, and it's a sin to make an honest dollar, and so on," and for seeming to prefer literature to "usable information." But here is Clark's point: the man with "backbone," the man of will, usually expresses only the will to power. To such a man, only the "usable" is important; it helps you get ahead. An American without ambition, without this will to power, is almost automatically weak in the eyes of his society.

The composer, Hazard, and the painter, Lawrence Black, of *Leaves* are Arthur's true brothers. These two, especially Black, do not fit into the "American way." Black can be seen, indeed, as almost insane. But in Clark's system of values, Black is a man who, rejecting the money values of his society by refusing to paint simply to sell, is seeking the "magic wilderness of the spirit." Black dreams the true dreams.

The storekeeper, Davies, of *Oxbow* is very nearly at one with the three above; he is the only person in the novel who really struggles for the lives of the men who are hanged. Art Croft, the narrator, at least comprehends Davies' position, although he himself lacks moral courage. He thinks, "Most men are more afraid of being thought physical cowards than moral ones." But he will not follow up his own insight with any action.

It is through these people that Clark demonstrates his grasp of the realities of America, for his true individualists are seldom successful; Clark does not offer "poetic justice." Davies is overwhelmed by the lynchers; he lacks the physical courage that is a necessary part of moral courage: "I had everything, justice, pity, even the backing—and I knew it—and I let those three men hang. . . . I didn't want it to come to a showdown. . . . The most I hoped was that something would do it for me." Black is almost destroyed by his wife, who wishes "to possess and control" him. Arthur is used by his family and, with a sad irony, killed by an element of the nature he loves.

The Oxbow Incident is Clark's best known novel; it is also the one most directly concerned with man as a political animal, that is, man as member of a community. And nature seems almost ignored except as setting, as stage. But stages, certainly, are always symbolic, for they can suggest the attitude of the author of the drama. The stage does so here; nature functions as a symbolic comment upon men's actions. The novel begins in the sunlight, in the beginning warmth of spring, but the main action takes place at night and in the cold. Nature, and so, Life, in a sense withdraws. The cold and the darkness symbolize the lynchers' being outside of nature as well as their own inner coldness and darkness. The hanging at dawn, then, is not just a simple reversal, i.e., death occurring just as the day is reborn, but is also a deliberate assault by the lynchers against the continuing processes of nature.

Oxbow is also the most ambiguous of Clark's treatments of the American scene: not in its protest against injustice, certainly not in its obvious protest against racism. But it is ambiguous in that it is concerned with ambiguities: how does one arrive at justice—and can man arrive at justice anyway?

What is justice to be based upon? Davies answers that it comes from the law, and that the law is based upon the majority will. This is good American doctrine. But every reader will note that Tetley goes through certain forms: he holds a kind of trial, and the decision is based upon the votes of the majority. That majority, though, is not of a group of individuals, but of a "pack" (as young Tetley calls them), men more afraid of being thought physically afraid than they are afraid of committing an injustice. And the action they perform is manifestly unjust, that is, it is wrong. The men are hanged to satisfy Tetley's lust for power, and the group of "rugged individualists" surrenders to him.

Clark is indeed talking about more than a Western lynch mob; he is talking about the whole American society or, rather, the whole human society. And the horror lies in the irony: it is far easier to understand and forgive the brutal actions of slaves than it is to understand and forgive the brutal actions of men who think themselves free and act as slaves. Here is Clark's most explicit criticism of the American Dream: the forms of law will not suffice if they are not based upon true individualism. And these Americans are not individuals nor are they concerned with individuals.

Tetley is even less free than the rest. His mind is sick, obviously; but, worse, his actions are rooted in a rigid code of honor (he is a type southerner) which would not let him be human even if he were otherwise capable. Such a code excuses violence and sadism in the name of manliness. Manliness here is beastliness, or perhaps as Mark Twain would have it in *The Mysterious Stranger*, "humanness."

In short, Clark is saying that man will not have justice until certain external codes, the killing hand of the past that denies the individuality of each person, are forgotten (man must not, of course, reject those elements of the past that raise the spirit). And justice will only exist when it is exercised by individuals, not by packs. The individual is one who understands others and his natural world and is willing to live and to let live. Stated this baldly, Clark's themes are romantic, romantic in a way that has been under considerable attack these past fifty years. But he does not present them as simply answers. Evil does exist; but man should not surrender just because he may not win. One certainly should not accept the death of the spirit merely because such a death is an order, a material order. For, if the fat dream is ended, there are other dreams.

Notes

1. Leslie A. Fiedler, *Love and Death in the American Novel* (New York: Criterion Books, 1960), p. xii.

2. Frederic I. Carpenter, "The West of Walter Van Tilburg Clark," *EJ*, 51 (1952), 65.

3. Richard Chase, *The American Novel and Its Tradition* (Garden City, N. Y.: Doubleday Anchor Books, 1957), p. 144.

4. Carpenter, p. 68.

5. Carpenter, p. 67.

6. Jacques Barzun, *Darwin, Marx, Wagner*, rev. ed. (Garden City, N. Y.: Doubleday, 1958), p. 99.

The Inception of a Saga: Frederick Manfred's "Buckskin Man"

Russell Roth*

In the years between *The Giant* (1951) and *Lord Grizzly* (1954), Frederick Manfred did a great deal of reading, not all of it historical accounts of the life and times of Hugh Glass.[1] Among the books he read were D. H. Lawrence's *Studies in Classic American Literature*, William Carlos Williams' *In the American Grain*, and the novels of William Faulkner, all of which for various reasons he had not got around to before.[2] That he was impressed by these authors is shown in the epigraphs from Lawrence in *Lord Grizzly* and *Conquering Horse* (1959), and the dedications of *Morning Red* (1956) to Faulkner, "neighbor living down the valley a piece and also a son of the Father of the Waters," and of *Riders of Judgment* (1957) to Williams, "who is hacking out a new road up ahead, all the while singing his come-on song."

Lord Grizzly was, of course, the first of the Buckskin Man Tales to be written. With the publication of *Scarlet Plume* (1964) and the final volume of the series, *King of Spades* (1966), their author made explicit, in introductory pages in each book, the "program" of the tales: "1. *Conquering Horse*—Indian pre-white times in 1800 2. *Lord Grizzly*—Mountain man times in 1823-24 3. *Scarlet Plume*—Sioux Uprising in 1862 4. *King of Spades*—Black Hills justice in 1876 5. *Riders of Judgment*—cattleman times in 1892." It is mainly a chronological sequence, as stated, nor are there any repeating characters to link the separate tales. Yet, a deeper reading, on the thematic level, of this program is possible, beginning with the epigraph of *Conquering Horse*, a quotation taken from Lawrence's study, "Fenimore Cooper's Leatherstocking Tales":

> When you are actually *in* America, America hurts, because it has a powerful disintegrative influence upon the white psyche. It is full of grinning, unappeased aboriginal demons, too, ghosts, and it persecutes the white men like some Eumenides, until the white men give up their absolute whiteness. America is tense with latent violence and resistance. The very common sense of

* *SDR*, 7, no. 4 (1969–70), 87–99. © 1969 by *South Dakota Review*. Reprinted by permission of publisher and author.

white Americans has a tinge of helplessness in it, and deep fear of what might be if they were not common-sensical.

Yet one day the demons of America must be placated, the ghosts must be appeased, the Spirit of Place atoned for. Then the true passionate love for American Soil will appear . . .

This goes far beyond the story of *Conquering Horse*, and even beyond the purview of the tales. There is nothing in the book that indicates that Redbird's band of Yankton Sioux are, or will be, "unappeased aboriginal demons"; the concept does not occur until *Scarlet Plume* and *King of Spades*, and then without the scope of the epigraph's implications, and it has vanished by *Riders of Judgment*. But it does remind, especially in conjunction with the emphasis on "American Soil," that Manfred, who always plans his work well ahead, had projected the writing of "an Indian book" as early as the gestation period of *Lord Grizzly*, but under the title *Green Earth;*[3] and that his first book, *The Golden Bowl* (1944), and his third, *This Is the Year* (1947), both focus on the "dust bowl" conditions that afflicted "Siouxland" in the 1930s.

In this sense, *Conquering Horse* looks forward, but it also has a curious sort of tie to Lawrence's subject, the Leatherstocking Tales. For, whether by happenstance or not, the setting of "Indian pre-white times in 1800" overlaps the last in narrative order of Cooper's five tales, *The Prairie*, which has as its setting the Great Plains in 1804. Likewise, while it is natural that the Sioux of *Conquering Horse* would be fighting their traditional enemy, the Pawnees, it is of special note that Natty Bumppo lives in honor and dies among the Pawnees in *The Prairie*, and that the originally No Name hero of Manfred's tale has the "true way" of his vision-quest pointed out to him by an older, friendly Pawnee, Sounds the Ground As He Walks.

The transition is symbolic, for though Manfred is very unlike Cooper, the Buckskin Man is a recognizable sequel to the Leatherstocking explicated by Lawrence. In terms of Lawrence's reading of *The Prairie* as depicting a "pioneering brute invasion of the West, crime-tinged," Chingachgook is to No Name/Conquering Horse and Scarlet Plume as Natty is to Hugh Glass and Earl Ransom. The difference is that the myth of the new essential American that Lawrence found in Deerslayer, "an isolate, almost selfless, stoic, enduring man, who lives by death, by killing, but who is pure white," is in Manfred no longer myth but reality, and without those prettinesses and evasions that Lawrence complains of in Cooper. Also, because they are real, there is psychical movement in Manfred's characters; all of his white protagonists, except Cain Hammett, are engaged in that "great and cruel sloughing" of "the old European consciousness" that, according to Lawrence, is necessary before the "American-at-last" can emerge.

This is, at base, the unifying theme of the Buckskin Man Tales: the search for the true self in a context of an evolving and generic *American* self. The search is portrayed in *Conquering Horse* in its ritualized, prewhite form in America through No Name's quest for the vision that, by tribal rule, will confer upon him an adult identity. In *Lord Grizzly*, mountain man Hugh Glass, who has otherwise adapted to his milieu and thus seemingly "found" himself, still has to discover his surprising capacity for forgiveness. The sloughing here of an overly assumed pre-Christian ethic is matched in *Scarlet Plume* by the necessity for Judith Raveling to learn from the Indians, before the white man's eye-for-an-eye and ironically Christian-approved "justice" takes her Yankton paramour from her, what a total love involves. In *King of Spades*, Earl Ransom is presented with a choice of selves through a choice of love objects: the one equated not only to the mother but to all traditionally white and ultimately European ideas-in-practice, the other "A white girl, Indian raised" whom he finally rejects.

Ransom is an example of Lawrence's ophidian metaphor of consciousness-sloughing: "Sometimes snakes can't slough. They can't burst their old skin. Then they go sick and die inside the old skin. . . ." Ransom is the first of the Buckskin Man Tales' white protagonists to die. But he is also the first to be tempted by material wealth and its concomitant power, which enter the series with the 1876 Black Hills gold rush setting of *King of Spades*. The blocking by these new obstacles of the road to the true self that the tales indicate all Americans must follow shapes the conflict in *Riders of Judgment*. As with Ransom, it is the encroachments of Mammon that must be confronted by Cain Hammett who, in the opening sentence of this final volume on the Buckskin Man, comes "riding down through a cloud" above the timberline in the Big Stony Mountains of Wyoming.

Hammett is not a romantic hero. He is, rather, "a knobby-muscled fellow. His movements, though quick, were blunt. His face was rough-cut, as if slapped into form with the side of an ax. He had a black walrus mustache, and it gave his face a weathered walnut hue." He "rode very light, for all his blunt body. He rode with much of his weight in the stirrups, knees taking up the spring, making it easy on the horse." This is "the man who alone," as he is later to be eulogized, "overthrew the feudal system of the old frontier and turned the cattle kingdom into a free country." He is cool and brave, but nearly colorless, dressed in black. He likes a song that "has got judgment in it. Man judgment and God judgment." His is a spirit which, obviously doomed, thinks, " 'Taint possible. I will be alive tomorrow." But he is killed: "He fell with the Winchester gripped tight in his hand."

It is the antithesis of the pulp and movie "western," but this is realistically rendered 1892. "He shed his blood that men might once again learn that you cannot force a free people to accept something they do not want," says the Reverend Creed. The words are reminiscent of Faulkner's backcountry whites of the same period in *The Hamlet*, whose attitude was not "*What must I do*, but *What do you think you would like for me to do if you was able to make me do it.*" And still, this is a spiritual victory bought sooner or later at tangible loss, and there are new worlds a-coming in which the victory will not seem so clear. For after the small independent cattle spread comes the farm; and after the farm, the dust bowl. *This Is the Year* reads naturally out of *Riders of Judgment* and links the Buckskin Man Tales to the rest of the body of Manfred's work.

II

Of *Lord Grizzly*, William Carlos Williams wrote: "I have never in a lifetime of reading about our West met with anything like it. It is a primitive account—so is the *Iliad* or the *Odyssey*." It "seems to me a very moving and authentic story of a bear of a man such as we, at best, sprung from." One of the models available to its author at the time of the writing was the portrait in Williams' *In the American Grain* of that "great voluptuary," Daniel Boone, who saw that the task was not to *be* an Indian, "but to be *himself* in a new world, Indian-like." Nor was this the only model: paralleling the myth of the new essential American unearthed by Lawrence in the Leatherstocking Tales, *In the American Grain* presents an historical cavalcade of Eric the Red, Cortez, the French Jesuit Pere Sebastian Rasles, Boone, and Aaron Burr leading to a similar construct. However, traces of Williams are harder to find in the Buckskin Man Tales than the presence of Lawrence. This may well be because his book followed Lawrence's by three years, being something of a conscious adjunct to it.[4] Yet, as is demonstrated by the dedication of *Riders of Judgment*, Williams is important to Manfred.

What he supplies, in a sense, is an American writer's corroboration of the "outsider's" evaluations of Lawrence. For example, the epigraph of *Conquering Horse* is underscored by Williams' statement in his chapter on Ponce de Leon: "No, we are not Indians but we are men of their world. The blood means nothing; the spirit, the ghost of the land moves in the blood, moves the blood. It is we who ran to the shore naked, we who cried, 'Heavenly Man!' These are the inhabitants of our souls . . ." And again, in his chapter on Champlain, he says: "The land! don't you feel it? Doesn't it make you want to go out and lift the dead Indians tenderly from their graves, to steal from them—as if it must be clinging even to their corpses—some authenticity . . ." Daniel Boone is a prototype of Hugh Glass:

> With the sense of an Indian, Boone felt the wild beasts about him as a natural offering. Like a savage he knew that for such as he their destined lives were intended. As an Indian to the wild, without stint or tremor, he offered himself to his world, hunting, killing with a great appetite, taking the lives of the beasts into his quiet, murderous hands as they or their masters, the savages, might take his own, if they were able, without kindling his resentment . . . Possessing a body at once powerful, compact and capable of tremendous activ-

> ity and resistance when aroused, a clear eye and a deadly aim, taciturn in his demeanor, symmetrical and instinctive in understanding, Boone stood for his race, the affirmation of that wild logic, which in times past had mastered another wilderness and now, renascent, would master this, to prove it potent.

This is also Deerslayer. Williams' analysis of the Puritans, which has been criticized for being overly negative, is likewise an extension of Lawrence, as well as an attempt at putting in their proper place the Pilgrim Fathers ("fiery particles," "blind seeds," as opposed to Lawrence's "black, masterful men"), which has its echoes in Manfred's analysis of Christianity-in-action, in *Scarlet Plume*. "Never could they have comprehended," writes Williams of the Puritans, "that it would be, that it WAS, black deceit for them to condemn Indian sins, while *they* cut the ground from under the Indian's feet . . .The immorality, I say, of such an attitude never becomes apparent to them. . . . they instituted courts— but in themselves they were like pebbles."

Scarlet Plume is the Buckskin Man Tale in which the largest number of Williams and Lawrence insights can be felt to converge. One page after the passage in Lawrence's study of Hector St. John de Crevecoeur which Manfred chose as an epigraph for *Lord Grizzly*, the following, from Crevecoeur's *Letters From an American Farmer*, is quoted by Lawrence:

> By what power does it come to pass that children who have been adopted when young among these people (the Indians) can never be prevailed upon to readopt European manners? Many an anxious parent I have seen last war who, at the return of the peace, went to the Indian villages where they knew their children had been carried in captivity, when to their inexpressible sorrow they found them so perfectly Indianized that many knew them no longer, and those whose more advanced ages permitted them to recollect their fathers and mothers, absolutely refused to follow them, and ran to their adopted parents to protect them against the effusions of love their unhappy real parents lavished on them!

Lawrence likes this "picture," but insists here and in his study "Fenimore Cooper's White Novels" that between white and Indian there can be "no reconciliation in the flesh." For

> Supposing an Indian loves a white woman, and lives with her. He will probably be very proud of it. . . . He will submit to her, if he is forced to, with a kind of false, unwilling childishness, and even love her with the same childlike gentleness, sometimes beautiful. But at the bottom of his heart he is gibing, gibing, gibing at her. Not only is it the sex resistance, but the race resistance as well.

And so it is in general with Manfred's Scarlet Plume, who says to Judith Raveling at the end of their idyl: "My heart does not run with white blood. Nor does your heart run with red blood. The two can never be as one. . . . You are a woman from the other side and I have done my people great wrong in lying beside you skin to skin. You stole my heart and I could not stop myself."

Judith reacts to this repudiation, as to the days of intimate living that have preceded it, in keeping with Williams' critique of "the spiritual barrenness of the American woman" in the chapter of *In the American Grain* titled "Jacataqua": "They are our cattle, cattle of the spirit—not yet come in. . . . At best they want to be men, sit and be a pal. It's all right. How could they do anything else with the men brutally beaten by the life. . . . Yes, it's a promising country. It's what the French say of our women in Paris: *promising* young women. . . . I wish they could live at home." Judith, of course, cannot live at home, by choice, after Scarlet Plume; symbolically, she is "A wild white swan with a broken neck."

In *King of Spades*, Williams does not figure, but there are reminders of Lawrence, in addition to the example of the sloughing metaphor already noted. The first of these is what Lawrence calls "the incest problem" in his discussion of Poe's "The Fall of the House of Usher": "Incest-desire is only one of the modes by which men strive to get their gratification of the intensest vibration of the spiritual nerves, without any resistance." This, in turn, harks back, not only to the sex and race resistance between white and Indian lovers, but to the "latent resistance" of America itself in the epigraph to *Conquering Horse*. A second reminder is the Erden Aldridge sequence, which has its points in common with Lawrence's description of Melville's sojourn among the Marquesans in *Typee*: "Paradise. He could even go stark naked, as before the Apple episode. And his Fayaway, a laughing little Eve, naked with him, and hankering after no apple of knowledge, so long as he would just love her when he felt like it. . . . Then why wasn't he happy. . . ?" A final reminder is the functional similarity of character Sam Slaymaker to Lawrence's evocation of that "real epicurean of the moment," Doctor Long Ghost, in Melville's *Omoo*.

Melville and Whitman, it should be added, have been favorite authors of Manfred's for years. Thus, Williams' view of Whitman as having had "to come from under and through a dead layer of unrelated culture stuccoed upon the primitive destiny of the land" could hardly have been missed by Manfred; especially as Williams elaborates this view, in his chapter on Poe, into an esthetic for American writers:

> . . . the desire to have "culture" for America by "finding" it, full blown—somewhere . . . could be no more than a pathetic reminiscence. It had NOTHING of the New World in it. Yet, it was bred of the wish to bring to the locality what it lacked.
>
> What it lacked, really, was to be cultivated. So they build an unrelated copy upon it; this, as a sign of intelligence,—vigor. That is, to bring out its qualities, they cover them. Culture is still the effect of cultivation, to work with a thing until it be rare; as a golden dome among the mustard fields. It implies a solidity capable of cultivation. Its effects are marble blocks that lie perfectly fitted and aligned to express by isolate distinction the rising lusts which threw them off, regulated, in moving through the mass of impedimenta which is the world.

> This is culture; in mastering them, to burst through the pecularities of an environment. It is NOT culture to *oppress* a novel environment with the stale, if symmetrical, castoffs of another battle . . .

The "marble block" metaphor was to find further application twenty years later, in Malcolm Cowley's historic introduction to *The Portable Faulkner:*

> All his books in the Yoknapatawpha saga are part of the same living pattern. It is this pattern, and not the printed volumes in which part of it is recorded, that is Faulkner's real achievement. Its existence helps to explain one feature of his work: that each novel, each long or short story, seems to reveal more than it states explicitly and to have a subject bigger than itself. All the separate works are like blocks of marble from the same quarry: they show the veins and faults of the mother rock. Or else—to use a rather strained figure—they are like wooden planks that were cut not from a log, but from a still living tree. The planks are planed and chiseled into their final shapes, but the tree itself heals over the wound and continues to grow.

Manfred is not likely to have missed this passage either, his reading of Faulkner that took place during the same period that he was reading *In the American Grain* having begun with *The Portable*. Both passages have pertinence to his own work as it has developed: a development that could only have been guessed at between *The Giant* and *Lord Grizzly*. Yet, this was the interval that marked the inception of Manfred's Siouxland saga.

III

The publication in 1966 of *King of Spades*, its author's sixteenth book as well as the last volume of his Buckskin Man Tales to appear, was greeted with little serious critical or popular attention. The situation was curiously like that of Faulkner in 1942, the year of his sixteenth book, *Go Down, Moses*. Faulkner also was mostly neglected, both by critics and public. He, too, was typed by many as a "regional" writer, his Yoknapatawpha County making such the same "local-color" impression as Manfred's Siouxland. Faulkner's *currente calamo*, as one rare sympathetic reader called it, tended to draw the same sort of "official" disapproval as Manfred's rougher-hewn, neologistic style. And both have been shockers: *Sanctuary*'s corncob rape and the idiot-and-cow sequence of *The Hamlet* have more than their equal, for a less restrictive era, in the seventy-page description of a frontier massacre which opens *Scarlet Plume* and the detailing of the oedipal mother-son relationship in *King of Spades*.

There are other parallels. As Faulkner is considered in the South to be a "western" writer, so Manfred in the North is definitely a "western" writer. Both authors are examples of Henry James's "solitary worker," whose "Great things . . . have usually been done with double the pains they would have cost if they had been produced in more genial circumstances." Both are epic, bardic writers: what Cowley has termed Faulkner's "double labor" of the imagination, "first, to invent a Mississippi county that was like a mythical kingdom, but was complete and living in all its details; second, to make his story of Yoknapatawpha County stand as a parable or legend of all the Deep South," has been independently accomplished in form and intent for his own Iowa-Minnesota-South Dakota-Wyoming area by Manfred out of its native materials, "worked with until they be rare."

In 1951, after Manfred's first seven books, it would have been difficult to predict this outcome. The only clues were *The Golden Bowl*, which in retrospect stands as something of an epigraph for the entire body of his work, and *This Is the Year*, which at that time was still the best-known of his books despite the intervening "World's Wanderer" trilogy, as it was then called,[5] of *The Primitive* (1949), *The Brother* (1950), and *The Giant*. Manfred's other books were *Boy Almighty* (1945) and *The Chokecherry Tree* (1948). The trilogy had been poorly received by the reviewers and its author's next two book-length manuscripts, *The Mountain of Myrrh* and *The Rape of Elizabeth*,[6] were rejected by his publisher, with whom he soon parted company. This was a period of stock-taking and of self-examination. Manfred had come to a major watershed of his career. Either he would continue along the lines that had made it tempting to label him "a second Thomas Wolfe," or he would strike out in such a direction as had been mapped in the early pages of *The Golden Bowl*:

> Here, long ago, it was only a path which curved to a creek. On this path, mule-eared jackrabbits sometimes leaped out of the tall prairie growths to sit in the open sun, ears keen to the wash of the wind in the grass . . .
>
> And other creatures shared the path with the wild life. The pattering of feet and the beating of horses' hooves on the drum of the earth frightened the animals. First it had been the friendly talented Arikaras, then the imperial Dakota Sioux, silent and hawk-nosed, who swiveled along the path, looking ahead, watching the horizon, ears sharp for the sounds of stealth . . .
>
> Eventually the white man came and looked at the land with long eyes . . .

These were riverheads Manfred had not yet explored. But among his papers, dating back to 1944, were notes on the Hugh Glass story which concluded: "*—see Cowhand novel plot. Maybe this could be part of it.*" Ten years later, after the acceptance for publication of *Lord Grizzly*, Manfred told an interviewer "His work was cut out—a half dozen or more novels still to be written, all of them fitting a pattern he had thought out years before."[7] However this may be, under pressures nearly as heroic as those endured by Hugh, Manfred began the preliminary research for *Lord Grizzly* in the summer of 1952. The writing began in March, 1953. The Buckskin Man Tales had been launched . . .

At first glance, there is nothing of Faulkner in them, and this is true insofar as any direct or even indirect "borrowings" are concerned. Manfred's reading of Faulkner, when he finally came upon him, was not of a repository of literary craft, some of the odds and ends of which might be adaptable to his own work, but of a like-minded "neighbor," as the dedication of *Morning Red* expresses it. He was delighted to find that this neighbor had already successfully done what he, Manfred, wanted to do: that is, to write about a past beyond his own firsthand knowledge as convincingly as he was able to write of what he had personally observed; and, further, to relate this "historical" writing to his "contemporary" production in some kind of meaningful matrix. Faulkner's example was a not often encountered inspiration: the Indian stories, "The Bear," *Absalom, Absalom!* all showed how, in Cowley's words, a number of closely interconnected story-cycles can be kept in balance, with each book like "a chord or segment of a total situation always existing in the author's mind."

Manfred was to handle this differently, in a more linear and less "all-at-once" way. His books are not so much planks cut from a still-living tree as they are the tree itself. In this also perhaps "strained figure," *The Golden Bowl* is the root, far more substantial than its physical dimensions would imply; the Buckskin Man Tales, the trunk; and *This Is the Year*, the beginning of the branching into the novels, the short stories, the poems, and what Manfred calls the "rumes." Such a schematism suggests why the trilogy, appearing before the tales were written, seemed somehow unprepared for thematically: it could not be read in the historical context out of which Manfred writes. That context, while it owes much to Faulkner in spirit, is a development largely in terms of the area which it analyzes as well as describes. The ideological line is from *Conquering Horse* to *This Is the Year*, which makes the "branching" books that follow, in Lawrence's characterizing phrase for Whitman, "post-mortem effects."

In other words, there is an historical and social critique implicit in Manfred that has its basis in the progression from green earth to dust bowl. It is announced in *The Golden Bowl*, delineated in the tales, and exploded in final portentous cataclysm in *This Is the Year*. "Where to now? Where?" asks Pier Frixen as his house lies "cleavered beneath the skies." His fate is a judgment. And if Manfred makes it plain that he will endure, it is not so plain that he will prevail. For Pier, it must be noted, represents both a new European grafting on the essential "American-at-last" and another instance of Earl Ransom's betrayal of the Spirit of Place: "For what? For money. For gold." Thus, among the post-mortem effects of this latest death of the land are a boy with ravaged lungs, a doomed wanderer in the cities, and the ill-assorted and always in-some-way-maimed protagonists of all the novels.

Recently, at least two reviewers of *Apples of Paradise* (1968) remarked what one of them named "the curious imperative" of Manfred's characters "to be barren."[8] The phenomenon is a striking feature of the stories, and culminates in the latest novels in Garrett Engleking and Kon and Karen Harmer. It is almost as though this unfruitfulness is Manfred's equivalent for the soullessness that Lawrence means by "post-mortem effects." The same incompleteness of the person is present, despite its justification by the characters themselves: "It's all right, my husband," says Karen. "Nothing could be helped. . . . We all have a perfect right to be what we are and to have happen to us what happens to us." Manfred obviously feels these losses at the same time that he somewhat ironically depicts the effort of his creations to put a good face on what is, in effect, an inner desolation that accords with the pillaged land surrounding them.

For nature *is* despoiled in Manfred, human nature most of all, as in Faulkner's passage beginning, "Dispossessed of Eden. Dispossessed of Canaan, . . . He used a simple egg to discover to them a new world where a nation of people could be founded in humility and pity and sufferance and pride of one to another." And now this nation is accursed. Manfred's saga not only bears witness to Lawrence's warning that "one day the demons of America must be placated, the ghosts must be appeased, the Spirit of Place atoned for," but, in the Buckskin Man Tales, it reveals some of the major precipitants of this necessity to atone. It takes a view with which more Americans of this era are becoming familiar, and against the causes of which massive movements for change are beginning to build. As a result, although the road has been long and hard and increasingly dusty, there is reason to believe that Manfred's days of prophesying in the wilderness are past.

Notes

1. For a listing of a few of the "some 80 books and articles" on Glass and the life of the mountain man that Manfred read in preparation for the writing of *Lord Grizzly*, see Russell Roth, "Is Manfred the Midwest's Faulkner?" *Minneapolis Sunday Tribune*, 1 Aug. 1954.

2. The main reason he had not read Faulkner was the negative assessment of the future Nobel Prize winner in *Writers in Crisis* (Boston: Houghton Mifflin, 1942), by Maxwell Geismar, a critic Manfred respected. The "impressionistic" Lawrence and Williams books, published in the early 1920s, were out of critical vogue in the Humanist, Marxist, and New Critical periods that followed.

3. Personal knowledge of the present writer, to whom *Conquering Horse* is dedicated.

4. *Studies in Classic American Literature* was published in 1922; *In the American Grain* in 1925.

5. It was revised and reissued in one volume, *Wanderlust*, in 1962.

6. These were later combined and rewritten to form *Morning Red.*

7. Roth, "Is Manfred the Midwest's Faulkner?"

8. Russell Roth, "Same Furies Haunt Troubled Hearts in 'Apples of Paradise': 30 Years of Manfred," *Minneapolis Star*, 26 March 1968.

[On Jean Stafford's *The Mountain Lion*]

William T. Pilkington*

Jean Stafford's *The Mountain Lion* is an authentic example of a rare but legendary kind of book: the neglected classic. Miss Stafford was born in Covina, California, the daughter of a writer of "westerns" (her father, John Richard Stafford, composed western stories under the pseudonyms Jack Wonder and Ben Delight). Part of the author's youth was passed in the Colorado mountains, but most of her mature life has been spent in the East and in Europe. The East, particularly New England, is the setting for much of her fiction—the excellent novels *Boston Adventure* (1944) and *The Catherine Wheel* (1952), as well as many of her short stories. Miss Stafford's most effective literary use of the land of her origin, the American West, is *The Mountain Lion*, first published in 1947. *The Mountain Lion* is a compelling and beautifully wrought story. Put simply, it is one of the masterpieces of recent American fiction and certainly ought to be more widely known and read than it currently is.[1]

As a novel of the West, *The Mountain Lion* is strikingly dissimilar to most western fiction, for it portrays the region in a thoroughly ambiguous and ironic way. Miss Stafford's uncertain feelings about the West seem in part a result of personal experience, in part a reflection of the attitudes of two of her favorite American writers (mentioned in the "Author's Note" that precedes her *Collected Stories*): Mark Twain, who could never quite decide how he felt about the frontier of his childhood and young adulthood, and Henry James, whose ambivalent view of the New World forms the thematic core of some of his best fiction. In her own experience of the West, Miss Stafford was very early presented with an uncomfortable irony. Her father's mythic West, which she describes (again, in the "Author's Note" in the *Collected Stories*) as "noble" and "wicked," had been reduced, by the early decades of the twentieth century, to a considerably "tamed-down" replica of what it had apparently once been. She found little in the landscape, says the author, or in the rudimentary socie-

*"Introduction" to *The Mountain Lion* (Albuquerque: Univ. of New Mexico Press, 1977).

ty it supported, to interest her, and consequently she "hotfooted it across the Rocky Mountains and across the Atlantic Ocean" as soon as she could.[2]

Irony is unquestionably an element of Miss Stafford's depiction of the West in *The Mountain Lion*. The children, Ralph and Molly Fawcett, at first see the Colorado mountains as "frightening," as wearing "peril conspicuously on their horny faces" (p. 95).[3] It is not, however, the rigors of nature that make the western environment dangerous and "frightening"; rather it is the humans who inhabit that environment. The mountain lion that supplies the novel with its title, the last of her species in an area that had once been home to large numbers of such beasts, is a much diminished version of the savage animal that the word "lion" connotes. She looks like an "overgrown house cat" (p. 170), and, appropriately, Uncle Claude gives her the familiar name Goldilocks. Moreover, the mountains themselves are scarcely the threat to humans they must have been a century before; they are now an acceptable scene for pleasure-seeking—hiking and horseback riding, reading and picnicking. Indeed, lurking beneath the horizon, barely out of sight, are those fashionable ski resorts that will one day adorn their slopes.

Elegy, not fear, it seems, is the proper note to strike in a description of the western landscape of the late 1920s, the novel's chronological setting. The gods identified with that landscape are dying gods. Grandpa Kenyon, the man of nature who expires at the beginning of the narrative, is called at one point a "god of September, surrounded by the gold, autumnal light" (p. 55). References to Goldilocks lightly suggest that she is a kind of lonely, hunted deity of the mountains. Her rare appearances are like epiphanies, fleeting reminders of what had been: she was sighted once during the Christmas season as Ralph and Molly are looking for a Christmas tree; on another occasion they catch a glimpse of her on an Easter Sunday.

In *The Mountain Lion*, then, the land has been conquered, and the real danger is the people who inhabit the land, who persist in behaving as if they were living in the nineteenth rather than the twentieth century. In Colorado, Ralph and Molly discover a human society notable for its disorderliness, a society in which "lawlessness" (of a somewhat picayune kind: horse-thieving, making bootleg whiskey) "seemed natural" (p. 97). The westerners in the novel continue to live by the dictates of the "western myth," even though the myth, if it ever had any relation at all to real life, is most certainly anachronistic by the 1920s. Uncle Claude and, to some degree, Grandpa Kenyon fit the mold of the mythic cowboy, a man of nature, adept in his use of weaons, more at home with his horse than with women. The womanless cowboy riding the open range is an appealing and romantic figure, but in reality he was often a most pathetic person. Uncle Claude, for example, is a sad case of arrested development: "He had never grown up . . . his men indulged and protected him like an innocent" (p. 199). Grandpa Kenyon gets along well with the children because, like them, he is "shy and gawky" (p. 26). The cowboy's stunted concept of masculinity is simplistic to the point of absurdity. Ralph learns that the best course one can follow, in order to be thought a man, is "to go unnoticed by having no shortcomings" (p. 168), thus avoiding the ridicule Uncle Claude heaps on any suspected weakness or vulnerability. The cowboy's childish obsession with guns also plays a role in the story's development; it is, in fact, a partial explanation for the tale's bizarre and violent ending.

Contrasted with the elemental life the Fawcett children experience in Colorado is the kind of life usually associated with the "civilized" East: an existence bound by tradition and by the observance of minute social distinctions. In the novel the setting for that life is St. Louis, the family's ancestral home which Mrs. Fawcett remembers with much nostalgia, and California, which seems "a separate thing like Florida and Washington, D. C." (p. 8), and is not, therefore, a part of the "wild West." Mrs. Fawcett honors, above all else, "ceremony" (p. 147). She suffers with much pomp and circumstance the annual visits of her stepfather, Grandpa Kenyon, not because she likes the old man but because those visits have become customary. Surrounded by a "toy-like" (p. 56) walnut grove, the house in Covina is a shrine in which Mrs. Fawcett worships the household gods that have been transported from St. Louis to California, the holy relics associated with her real father, Grandfather Bonney: "the portrait of her father, his books, and the man himself, a heap of dust in a graceful urn . . ." (p. 23). Justifiably, Ralph and Molly rebel against this prim and proper, this polished but limited world that their mother and her allies, the unspeakable Follansbees, have created. Most of the humor in the novel—and *The Mountain Lion* is a very funny book, reminiscent in a way of that archetype of American humor *The Adventures of Huckleberry Finn*—derives from the children's stratagems to escape the boredom and hypocrisy that Mrs. Fawcett attempts to impose on their lives.

One successful stratagem they employ is to retreat into a private place of their own making. In such a place Ralph, with the rigid integrity of childhood, divides the human race into two opposing camps: "Kenyon men" and "Bonney merchants." Grandfather Bonney had been fat, bald, jovial, the owner of a button factory, a paradigm of social grace and impeccable manners. He had supplied his daughter with a model of how life ought to be lived; as a result the children despise the word "Bonney" and all that it represents. Grandpa Kenyon, on the other hand, is closely identified with the natural order. He looks like "a massive, slow-footed bear" (p. 33). Ralph thinks of him, after his death, as "a big river" (p. 48) run dry, its waters having emptied into the ocean. He is a rugged individualist, a man's man, someone who knows "the habits of animals" and subjects himself to "the government of the seasons" (p. 114). To the view of a child the cleanness and simplicity of Grandpa Kenyon's world are understandably attractive. With the passage of time and acquisition of knowledge and experience, however, Ralph realizes that the Kenyon world is not the Edenic paradise it appears to be, that it is as flawed as the world of his mother and real grandfather. Only Molly remains adamant. She will recognize no defect in Grandpa Kenyon; to the end he is "the only hero of her life" (p. 165).

If East and West form a crucial set of opposites within the novel, then so do the conditions of innocence and experience. Looked at from one angle, *The Mountain Lion* falls into that familiar category of American fiction, the initiation story. It is, however, an initiation story with a twist. Ralph's rites of passage are fairly conventional. As is often the case in stories of this type, Ralph's approach to the threshold of adulthood takes the form of a confrontation with evil—or, at least, what he perceives to be evil. Not surprisingly, sex is the "evil" fact Ralph must come to terms with. He thinks of his entry into the complications of adult sexuality as "going into a tunnel with no end . . ." (p. 59). Once he is inside the tunnel, "his guilt started and the world was spoiled" (p. 186). Like most initiates in American fiction, Ralph will no doubt grope his way through the tunnel. He will survive, reconciling himself to the presence of "evil" in his life, but he will do so with a continuing sense of loss—a regret that there are snakes in Eden, that childhood's lovely innocence has to end.

Molly's, however, is an altogether different story. Molly is a memorable and disturbing character, a child who consciously and willfully clings to innocence and refuses, like Huck Finn, to be tainted by the corruptions and compromises of adult life. The central fact about Molly is her physical ugliness. She has "thin, freckled arms" and an "ugly little face framed by black hair with which . . . nothing could be done" (p. 92). Isolated and lonely because of her appearance, she finds refuge only in books and in the company of Ralph. During the six years covered by the narrative—a time span which includes what she believes to be Ralph's defection to Bonneyism—Molly becomes harder and more intent on her disastrous course. She is determinedly "misanthropic at the age of twelve" (p. 144). Ralph begins to see her as a "forthright monster" (p. 165), increasingly "bookish and unhealthy" (p. 168). By the end of the novel it is no longer possible to think of Molly as a female Huck Finn; she has been transformed into a young Miss Watson, complete with exacting Victorian morality.

Throughout this transformation, however, the reader's understanding of and compassion for Molly never waver. She cannot, after all, be blamed for what she is, since she did not make herself. Nevertheless, the damage has been done. The scars of ugliness and isolation are irremovable. Spurred by her unattractiveness and assisted by her intellectual precocity, she erects a psychological defense so impenetrable that eventually nothing touches her, nothing reaches the shriveled heart that must hide somewhere within her. Innocence becomes a shield, donned as protection against the outside world, other people, even her own body. The condition in which Molly finds herself at age fourteen is one that can be maintained only at an enormous cost, both to herself and to those around her. Had she lived, she would have become something dreadful. Ralph wants to kill Goldilocks, the mountain lion, "because he loved her" (p. 218)—a paradox he never bothers to explore. Perhaps his lingering love for his sister—as she dies, he "kissed her blood-salty lips" (p. 230)—in some similarly paradoxical way accounts for his shooting Molly. The shooting is of course accidental, but saying that does not explain away all the strangeness of the occurrence.

Molly's violent end is disconcerting, even shocking. In terms of the imperatives of characterization, however, her death seems necessary. When she stands before her mirror and wishes she had long, golden hair like that of her sisters, then shortly thereafter adds her own name to the list of "unforgivables," Molly commits the final act of withdrawal. Her alienation is so acute that it amounts to a death of the heart, a circumstance that her physical death can only validate. Thematically, also, Molly's death seems appropriate, for the world does not easily accommodate such awesome precocity combined with such ferocious innocence as those which Molly cultivates. She and the mountain lion must both die because both are misfits who somehow threaten to disrupt the delicately balanced social arrangements that encircle them.

Like *Huckleberry Finn*, *The Mountain Lion* is, on one level, a simple book, filtered, as it is, through the consciousness of childhood. It may be read, and read with pleasure, as merely a humorous story about children topped off with a dollop of horror (not, it should be said, a particularly unusual blend in American fiction). When probed, however, Miss Stafford's little classic unfolds a rich complexity, a multiplicity of provocative and suggestive meanings. Some of those meanings may be grasped by careful reading and reflection. Ultimately, though, *The Mountain Lion*, like all great fiction, effectively conceals the secret of its emotional power. The book is simply there, to be read and enjoyed, and then reread—a monument to the writer's mysterious ability to transmute the raw materials of experience into lasting art.

Notes

1. Useful discussions of Jean Stafford's fiction, with emphasis on *The Mountain Lion*, are Louis Auchincloss, *Pioneers and Caretakers: A Study of Nine American Women Novelists* (Minneapolis: Univ. of Minnesota Press, 1965), pp. 152–60; Stuart L. Burns, "Counterpoint in Jean Stafford's *The Mountain Lion*," *Crit*, 9, no. 2 (1967), 20–32; and Blanche Gelfant, "Reconsideration: *The Mountain Lion*," *New Republic*, 10 May 1975, pp. 22–25.

2. Jean Stafford, "Author's Note," *Collected Stories* (New York: Farrar, Straus and Giroux, 1969).

3. Jean Stafford, *The Mountain Lion* (1947; rpt. Albuquerque: Univ. of New Mexico Press, 1977). All page numbers cited in the text are to this edition.

Tragedy and Western American Literature: The Example of Michael Straight's *A Very Small Remnant*

Don Graham*

In Western American literature as in American literature generally, tragedy is a very troublesome concept. Used carelessly as it has been by both critics and novelists, the term slips into meaning merely "sad" or "calamitous" and has no more precision than it does in the daily press. For instance, in a representative attempt to discuss tragic elements in *The Ox-Bow Incident* a recent critic writes: "Because it is placed on the frontier and exploits the conflict between law and extra-legal justice, a conflict inherent in the frontier saga, it is Western tragedy."[1] The problem with such a statement is of course all too plain; innumerable formula Westerns exploit exactly the same conflict. Are they therefore to be labeled tragic? Obviously not. In the same article, this critic makes a better case for another famous novel, *The Big Sky*, calling it a "more successful tragedy and one more central to the Western mind" (p. 247). But the spirit of *The Big Sky* is more elegiac than tragic. Guthrie's novel approaches tragedy, it is true, especially in its assignment of responsibility to Boone Caudill for the passing of a wild, free life; but this judgment comes too late, after the fact, and without a fully developed sense of the inexorable causality of tragedy.

In one of Harvy Fergusson's best novels, *Grant of Kingdom* (University of New Mexico Press: Albuquerque, 1975 [1950]), we can see the term being misapplied in still another way. James Lane Morgan, a first person narrator looking back at the life of the founder of the empire, speaks of Jean Ballard's fate as a "tragedy" (p. 94). When we look at that fate, however, tragedy seems inaccurate. External forces—a rapacious new capitalism and Ballard's failing health—undo the man and his empire. Neither of these causes is truly tragic, because neither is rooted in the character of the hero.

*UDQ 12, no. 4 (1978), 59–66.

It should be clear by now that an Aristotelian conception of tragedy governs the distinctions I have made above. This is not to say that every Western work has to be judged by this standard; a powerful novel such as Vardis Fisher's *In Tragic Life* insists upon its own definition of tragedy and develops the tragic sense without formal grounding in the Aristotelian tradition. But in the absence of some other compelling tragic vision, Aristotle provides a very useful traditional model. Certainly in the case of the novelist Michael Straight, the Aristotelian mode of tragedy is the exemplary and liberating form. In both of his novels, *Carrington* (1960) and *A Very Small Remnant* (1963), Straight found in Aristotle and classical tragedy usable models for the events he had painstakingly researched. There is ample evidence of Straight's avowed intentions, especially with regard to *Carrington*. In a long interview with John R. Milton, he explained how he imposed Aristotelian form upon the raw historical data:

> And I found that the story I had pieced together into a half-formed pattern was the same story, in terms of form and outline, that Aristotle had set forth as the model for classical tragedy: the story of the man on whom many men depend; who is finer than the average, and who means well; but who is brought down, to the common loss, because of some deepseated, irremediable flaw, within himself.[2]

Straight also applied Aristotelian principles to organize the narrative into three units: reversal, recognition, catastrophe (p. 144). *Carrington*, in short, is virtually a textbook demonstration of the utility of the Aristotelian model to Western subjects.

The second novel, however, is the more interesting case and follows the Aristotelian model less closely, almost we might say less rigidly, but with very impressive results. In this first person account of the events surrounding the Sand Creek Massacre, Straight has fashioned a peculiarly American version of the tragic pattern. It should first be noted though that the author himself has declined to call his novel a tragic work. Asked by Milton whether, like *Carrington*, *A Very Small Remnant* was also a tragic novel, Straight replied, "It is not strictly a tragedy" (p. 156). Yet he then observed that there is one story in the novel "which is tragic in the purest sense" (pp. 156–57). He is referring to Soule's story, but Soule, all the evidence in the novel indicates, is flawless. He is as heroic as Hector in *The Iliad* and expresses through his undaunted courage the absolute ideal of total renunciation. Soule gives up success, marital happiness, and a promising future to testify against Chivington and thereby assure his own death. Soule may represent the heroic tradition, but that is not the same as being a tragic hero. Thus Straight's observation about Soule seems to be at considerable odds with his view, quoted above, that the key to tragedy is the tragic flaw.

Of course the real test of a work's tragic status is the work, not the author's external explanation. By the crucial standards of plot and character, *A Very Small Remnant* stands as an innovative adaptation of Aristotelian precepts. We must begin with plot, in Aristotle's judgment the single most important element in tragedy. The novel is divided into five "parts," possibly to correspond with the traditional five-act division in tragedy. An outline of the principal action in each part reveals a rough approximation of the familiar pattern of opening/rising action/climax/falling action/denouement (which in turn contains the three-part scheme of reversal/recognition/suffering). Schematically, the action breaks down thus:

I	II	III	IV	V
Conversion of Wynkoop; peace plans set in motion.	Wynkoop escorts Cheyennes to Denver; Wynkoop relieved of Ft. Lyon command; massacre occurs.	Official inquiry; Soule's death; Wynkoop's new knowledge.	Second treaty; Wynkoop becomes Indian agent.	Foreshadowing of second massacre of Cheyennes; Wynkoop's uncertainty.

The fundamental plot element, the reversal, occurs at the end of Part II, notice, which results in a curve of action slightly in advance of the movement in the classical model. Fully aware of the importance of reversal, Straight has remarked: "The first ingredient of tragedy was, for him [Aristotle], *Peripeteia*, the reversal of fortune. Wynkoop suffers this same reversal at Sand Creek."[3] Straight's adaptation of reversal results in a foreshortening of this turning point and an extension of the drama of recognition, which begins in Part III and extends through the rest of the novel. Similarly, the motif of suffering is likewise extended. A depiction of the curve of ascending/descending action in *A Very Small Remnant* looks like this:

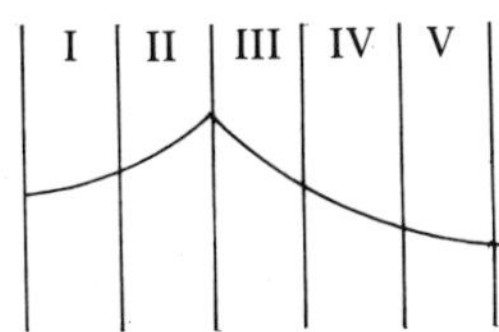

There remains one point to be made about the plot. In arguing that his novel is not a tragedy, Straight justified his position thus: "Wynkoop is defeated, at the end, but balance has been restored, in Denver, and within the time limits of the story, whereas in *Carrington* the balance is restored only in the epilogue, forty-two years after the story is concluded" (*Three West*, p. 156). Although it is true that things in Denver seem right, that orderly government and not the usurping tyranny of Chivington is in control, Wynkoop himself is in a state of great uncertainty; and looming in the near future, as allusions make clear, is the massacre at Washita, the next Sand Creek. Also, one may wonder about the accuracy of Straight's observation concerning the lack of stability and order at the end as an element of classical tragedy. Both *Oedipus* and *Hamlet*, for example, are quite clear about the reestablishment of normal government and order at the end of the play. In regard to plot, then, *A Very Small Remnant* is recognizably classical.

Although Aristotle emphasizes the supremacy of plot, even to the point of insisting that there can be tragedy without character, most later commentators have stressed the importance of character—that is to say, of a protagonist with a flaw. What often results is paraphrases which conflate Aristotle's definitions of plot and character; here is my version: in a tragic work something dreadful and of great magnitude must occur and must be rooted in the actions of a noble-minded though imperfect individual. In other words, in tragedy there is a complicity between a man and his fate, though in many instances the line where responsibility ends and fate begins may be virtually impossible to determine.

In *A Very Small Remnant* we may at first not discern how any character meets the requirements. Soule, whom the author finds tragic, I have already disallowed by virtue of his perfect heroism. Chivington might also seem to be a possibility, since he is a leader of men who brings down ruin upon many others and finally upon himself, but Chivington too is disqualified by opposite qualities from those of Soule. Chivington is totally self-absorbed, driven by angers he cannot even begin to comprehend, and by blind ambition. Moreover, he is rendered as being totally incapable of understanding anything about the nature of guilt or responsibility. Straight's original conception of the Sand Creek materials, he has said, was to cast Chivington in the major role in an opera (*Three West*, p. 149). Abandoning that idea, he turned to the novel, only to realize that Chivington was "too dark, too destructive" to serve as the principal character (p. 149).

This leaves the narrator, Wynkoop, as the only candidate for tragic hero. And Wynkoop too might seem an inappropriate choice. Certainly Straight's comments on how he views his narrator suggest no tragic model. Wynkoop, he says, is "simple, decent . . . modest" (p. 153). Continuing, Straight describes Wynkoop as representing a "predominant strain in the American character":

> In his innocence and his strength and his goodness, his capacity to cause suffering by his lack of understanding, and his determination to redress wrongs, he is a restrained hymn of praise to American life. (p. 155)

Even in Straight's praise of Wynkoop's decency and fundamental goodness, however, there is one dark strain: "His capacity to cause suffering by his lack of understanding." It is precisely this tendency, apparent throughout the novel, that makes Wynkoop a tragic figure, a tendency which we must label a particularly virulent species of American innocence.

There is a direct causal relationship between the massacre at Sand Creek and the actions of Edward Wynkoop. The chain of interrelated events begins when the novel opens. Wynkoop, an exterminator pledged to kill Indians, changes radically and returns to the best, natural impulses of his being, impulses that have been subverted by his role as a soldier and officer. Instead of ordering the old Indian One-Eye shot or refusing to receive him, the woman, and the boy, Wynkoop hears their story and is literally transformed by the suffering and dignity of their experiences. He undergoes a conversion, and from this moment on Wynkoop is pledged to achieve a state of peace between the Cheyennes led by Black Kettle and the citizens of Colorado, presided over by Governor Evans and his military commandant, Colonel J. M. Chivington. Through a series of negotiations, first between Wynkoop and the Cheyennes, then between the U.S. Army and the Cheyennes in Denver, Wynkoop arranges for the Indians to be placed in his care at Fort Lyon. He does so with an enthusiastic, winning, and confident trust in himself, his fellow officers, and the powerful men in Denver. His trust is extremely naive, however, and open to criticism for its lack of awareness of the subtleties of power, the lengths to which devious men will go to attain their private goals. Wynkoop, a retrospective narrator looking back upon his past hopes and defeat, is also very much an ironic narrator, a point that the careful reader does well not to overlook. There are several signs along the way, between the meeting with Black Kettle and the climactic event at Sand Creek, that Wynkoop's naiveté, his innocence, blinds him to facts that a more toughminded figure would have recognized. On the way to Denver, for example, the despised Indian agent Colley tells Wynkoop bluntly that both Evans and Chivington are not interested in peace and, further, that Wynkoop's actions will make Evans into a liar and Chivington into a joke. After Colley's outburst, Wynkoop remarks:

> "That's enough!" I said, rising. Colley was an Indian Agent and a thief; they were fine men; my superiors, and my friends.[4]

In the rush of his optimism for a peace settlement, Wynkoop believes that good intentions, embodied in his and Black Kettle's actions, are bound to insure success.

In Denver Wynkoop fails to appreciate further signs of powerful forces at work against his plans for peace. The first is direct advice from an old friend, Harry Richmond. Richmond tells him that the authorities put the bodies of the Hungate family, slain by Indians, on public display to inflame the populace. He warns Wynkoop to "turn back" (p. 62). The second sign, indirect but much more sinister, comes from Chivington himself. Trusted by Wynkoop, Chivington manipulates the naive junior officer into disclosing important tactical information about the arms and future whereabouts of the Cheyennes. After hearing Chivington talk about torturing a Sioux brave to extract information, Wynkoop answers several ominous questions about his Cheyennes (Chivington calls them "those Indians of yours" [p. 87]). He promises Chivington to bring the Cheyennes close to the fort and describes their limited weaponry. Ironically Chivington is suspicious of Wynkoop, not the other way around, and thus he is not satisfied with Wynkoop's Horatio Algerish "I'll do my best" (p. 87). It is here also that Chivington proclaims Wynkoop "his boy" (p. 87). Not only is Wynkoop totally unsuspecting of any ulterior motives in Chivington's questions, he is completely confident of the future as he returns to Fort Lyon to begin the peace: "Pride filled my days" (p. 89).

One more scene prior to the massacre establishes beyond a doubt Wynkoop's causal relationship with the reversal and his complicity with fate. Relieved of his command at Fort Lyon, Wynkoop assures Black Kettle that the new commander, Major Anthony, can be trusted. Even after Anthony announces new policies—removal from near the Fort to Sand Creek and surrender of weapons—Wynkoop restates his faith to Black Kettle. The dialogue is worth quoting:

> The meeting ended. I was reassured. I told Black Kettle: "You can trust Major Anthony."
>
> Black Kettle shook his head. "Major Anthony has red eyes."
>
> "It's not his fault. They were made red by the scurvy."
>
> "We do not like his eyes" (p.99).

Black Kettle is right; Wynkoop is wrong; and over a hundred and fifty of Black Kettle's people pay a heavy price for Wynkoop's blind trust.

So Sand Creek, the work of Colonel Chivington, is also the work of Major Wynkoop. At Leavenworth, where Wynkoop learns what has happened at Sand Creek, he undergoes a period of personal despair and blames himself for the massacre. He reviews the telltale signs: "Cursing my blindness; cursing my simple faith. Cramer had warned me; Colley had warned me; even Chivington's actions were revealing, if only I had understood" (p. 109). Here Wynkoop clearly acknowledges his crucial role in the events of Sand Creek. He thinks: ". . . Black Kettle and his band were at Sand Ceek, dead because they had trusted in me" (p. 110). He also realizes his true relation to Chivington: "I understood his feeling of affection for me: I had served him well. I had brought the Indians in and left them helplesss. I had laid them like a sacrifice at his feet" (p. 110). Later, he knows that other people also realize his precipitating connection with the massacre; Coberly's daughter, who becomes Soule's wife, tells him: "You were the one who started it all" (p. 149).

The recognition, the necessary change from ignorance to knowledge, is not accomplished in Wynkoop's immediate reaction to Sand Creek, in his awareness of his "blindness," his "simple faith." On the contrary, naiveté and innocence continue to characterize many of his actions subsequent to Sand Creek. Wynkoop's faith in the simple power of truth, for example, sustains him just as earlier his faith in the peace settlement had. When he launches into the plan conceived by Cramer to hold an official inquiry into Sand Creek, Wynkoop is certain that Chivington will be stopped, that the truth will prevail. He is right, but again at a cost he fails to reckon. General Curtis, his commanding officer, warns him explicitly: "Be careful, Wynkoop, lest you place more lives in jeopardy" (p. 113).

Soule's fate illustrates further Wynkoop's characteristic predilection to hold a dangerously simple faith in the inevitable triumph of what is right. Besides believing in the truth, Wynkoop also believes in the Government, as earlier he had believed in his superiors. He tells Coberly, who is fearful of what might happen to Soule: "The Government will protect its witnesses" (p. 148). But Coberly still has doubts, having heard rumors that Chivington has offered a reward for a dead Indian or a white man who defends Indians. Wynkoop overlooks this warning, as earlier he had overlooked portents about Sand Creek. Wynkoop trusts too easily; he lacks, in the purest definition of innocence, an adequate knowledge of man's duplicity, of his simple capacity for doing evil.

The best example of Wynkoop's lack of knowledge about man's nature is his assessment of Soule's future after the hearings are concluded. He thinks:

> It seemed to me that for Soule the danger had passed. His testimony was taken and could not be erased. No end could be served by harming him, save vengeance. And vengeance would be an act of madness—so I told Soule (p. 175).

In a few days, of course, Soule is shot by an assassin. Wynkoop should have a deeper awareness of sin than he does; he should know that in human affairs acts of madness are always possible.

After Soule's death, Wynkoop again undertakes to negotiate peace with Black Kettle's Cheyenne. In a meeting with Black Kettle, he gives an accurate statement of the precise nature of his responsibility for Sand Creek: "I knew nothing. And, like a fool, I suspected nothing; nothing at all" (p. 210). Following these new negotiations, Wynkoop is faced with another choice about his future, about how he is to live with the knowledge of complicity. General Sanborn offers him a promotion to full colonel in the Regular Army, but Wynkoop declines. He prefers instead to serve the Indians another way; he becomes an Indian Agent, the most despised position on the frontier. It seems clear, however, that Wynkoop is really serving himself, and in an unhealthy way. Powerless as an agent, he can do nothing to improve conditions for the Cheyenne. All he can do is suffer, and this sackcloth-and-ashes role marks the lowest point in Wynkoop's stature in the novel. We see his self-serving acceptance of empty martyrdom clearly in the scene in which he tells his wife Louisa of the General's offer and his refusal. Instead of telling her immediately, he plays coy, leading her on, building up her excitement about more money, status, and a chance to leave the arduous frontier for a more comfortable life in civilized country.[5] Obviously in this scene (Chapter 31, pp. 218–221) Wynkoop relishes his role of self-sacrifice. The only trouble is that he is demanding that others suffer with him, his wife, his two children. Moreover, he could have more influence on Indian policy as a colonel than as an agent. Though he realizes that he has hurt his wife unnecessarily, he still poses this absolute condition as explanation for his action: "I started it all, and I have to finish it. They need me, and there is no one else" (p. 220). Here again we see something terribly dangerous in Wynkoop's brand of moral innocence. He had rather be right and lose than work realistically within the complex bureaucracy of the Army. There is a time for absolute heroism, as evidenced by Soule's example, but Wynkoop, the innocent and moralistic hero, has made another wrong choice.

The novel ends on a note of moral uncertainty on Wynkoop's part. He has accomplished nothing as an Indian Agent, and Black Kettle and his band are encamped on the Washita, awaiting, though they do not know it, Custer's attack. Sand Creek recurs, but that lies in the dark future just beyond the novel's end. Wynkoop is left brooding once more upon the degree of responsibility he must bear for his innocent complicity with fate. He thinks:

> Was our failure certain, from the start? I was mistaken, I know, in persuading the Indians that they could place their trust in us. And I was mistaken later on, in thinking that we would honor the commitments that we made (p. 232).

These are the mistakes of a good heart and mind, but one too innocent, too trusting. Had Wynkoop possessed a more realistic understanding of the dark motives of other people and had he not overestimated the integrity of his own moral nature, events might have been different. This is always the mystery in tragedy, the commingling of a well-intentioned but imperfect character with a fate he partially creates and partially receives.

The Western writer who seeks to produce tragic literature has at least three options open to him, only two of which seem valid. He can go his independent way, like Vardis Fisher; he can write elegy and call it tragedy; or he can find in classical tragedy, as Michael Straight has, forms and themes which lend themselves to reinterpretation of Western materials from an unparochial historical perspective.

Notes

1. Levi S. Peterson, "Tragedy and Western American Literature," *WAL*, 6 (1972), 246–47.

2. John R. Milton, ed., *Three West: Conversations with Vardis Fisher, Max Evans, Michael Straight* (Vermillion, S. D.: Dakota Press, 1970), p. 135.

3. Michael Straight, "Truth and Formula for the Western Novel," *SDR*, 2, no. 1 (1964), 90.

4. Michael Straight, *A Very Small Remnant* (1963; rpt. Albuquerque: Univ. of New Mexico Press, 1976), p. 52.

5. I wish to thank my colleague, Max Westbrook, for calling my attention to this interesting and important scene in the novel.

Contemporary Western Novelists

The Novels of William Eastlake

Delbert E. Wylder*

It seems to be a maxim in the publishing industry that all books written about that territory west of Kansas City and east of the California state line are to be called "Westerns," and that they shall all be treated in very much the same manner. Usually it is their fate to go from a first hardbound edition to paperback and then to be forgotten completely. The lesser ones start out in paperback. Newspaper reviewers write a paragraph or two about them. Literary critics do not bother with them. Like the stereotyped television gunslinger, the novel with a Western setting can seldom live down its reputation. On occasion one does—for example Walter Van Tilburg Clark's *The Oxbow Incident*—and for a time it is treated by critics and the reading public as "literature," but a sudden rash of movies and TV dramas about lynchings soon destroys, or at least tarnishes, the reputation of a successful work. In a sense, it is unfortunate that all three of William Eastlake's novels have been set in the West, more specifically the Southwest, even more specifically New Mexico and the surrounding areas. *Go In Beauty* and *The Bronc People* have gone the way of all "Westerns" and are at present out-of-print. Eastlake's most recent novel, *Portrait of an Artist with Twenty-six Horses*, is also set in New Mexico and unfortunately may follow the same pattern despite its delightful title—unfortunately, because Eastlake's novels are neither the stereotyped "Westerns," nor are they regional Southwestern novels any more than William Faulkner's novels are "Southern" or regional novels of the South.

Just as Faulkner created his Yoknapatawpha County out of the area surrounding Oxford, Mississippi, William Eastlake is creating a fictional area in the "Checkerboard" region of the Navajo reservation and its adjacent areas in northern New Mexico. His characters live and die in a physical setting that often has dominated the works of lesser writers, turning their expressions into regionalistic descriptions. D. H. Lawrence once received a letter from Leo Stein which described the New Mexico landscape as the most "aesthetically satisfying" he knew, and Lawrence com-

* *New Mexico Quarterly*, 34 (1964), 188–203.

mented in an article for *Survey Graphic* that "To me it was much more than that. It had a splendid silent terror, and a vast far-and-wide magnificence which made it way beyond mere aesthetic appreciation. Never is the light more pure and overweening than there, arching with a royalty almost cruel over the hollow, up-tilted world. For it is curious that the land which had produced modern political democracy at its highest pitch should give one the greatest sense of overweening, terrible proudness and mercilessness; but so beautiful, God! so beautiful!"

It is a dangerous country for novelists. Because of its very magnitude, its terror, its magnificence, its beauty, its fascinating history, and its mingling of cultures, it has a tendency to overpower the artist. He becomes so involved with the "romance" of the country or its history or its people that his resulting work can be thought of only as regional—as "local color"—literature. But this is not true of Eastlake and his novels. Eastlake is a writer who, like Ernest Hemingway of *The Sun Also Rises* and *A Farewell to Arms*, keeps a tight rein on his materials, using physical descriptions to suggest or enlarge ideological content. He *uses*, then, the New Mexico landscape, history, and people not for ornament but for the enhancement of meaning. Reading Eastlake, one is always aware of the desert, the mesa, the mountain, the sky, in all their color and beauty, their proudness and mercilessness, but one is also aware that they may be the symbol of "home," or of the "cradle" or the "coffin" of civilization.

It is not by accident that Faulkner and Hemingway have been mentioned, for Eastlake appears to have been shaped by both writers. His first novel, *Go In Beauty*, shows the Hemingway influence at its strongest. But a word about influences. One should remember that Hemingway himself said in *Green Hills of Africa* that a "classic" can "steal from anything that it is better than. . . ." This is not to suggest that *Go In Beauty* is a "classic" (*The Bronc People*, yes), nor that Eastlake is guilty of theft. It is only that Eastlake has adapted some of the Hemingway and Faulkner techniques to his own purposes and has made them his own.

Go In Beauty is a rather exceptional first novel. It is the story of the Bowmans, Alexander and George, and the sibling rivalry that eventually leads to Alexander's destruction. Alexander, a writer, sins by commission —he runs away with George's wife, Perrete. Having become successful as a writer through his stories of the "Indian Country," he gradually deteriorates, both as a writer and man, until, in quiet desperation, he places himself in a position to be murdered. George, the trader, is as guilty, though his sin is one of omission. Unable to understand, accept, and forgive—partly because of his own guilt following a childhood incident—he tries again and again unsuccessfully to write the letter that would bring Alexander "home." But it is the mystic interrelationship between man's sins and nature that proves most interesting in the novel. Both sins are against the land. The prediction of the Navajo medicine man, Paracelsus, that a "theft" will cause a drouth, and the drouth that results, are central to the novel. Although there are chapters devoted to the satirical treatment of modern society, the mood of Greek tragedy is felt as an undercurrent throughout the novel—a mood which Lawrence had felt, and which Eastlake creates through his treatment of the land and the oracle-like Paracelsus.

Eastlake's second, most ambitious, and most successful novel is *The Bronc People*. From the opening pages, with the description of the Circle Heart herd and the rifle fight between the white owner of the Circle Heart and the Negro owner of the new Circle R over the fencing-in of water, symbolism extends the meaning of the localized incidents into universals of the condition of man. Two Indians watch quietly from the rocks as the men fire at one another, the Negro from his house, the white man "from behind a sandstone concretion, almost round, that had come down from the Eocene cliff that circled around and made all of the firing echo." The shots echo from Eocene cliffs, thus enlarging symbolically this battle into the battles of all men, for *Eocene* figuratively refers to the earliest era and is specifically an epoch in the period when mammals became the dominant animal. The Indians watch passively, for their war already has been lost. They discuss the philosophical aspects of war—of whether anyone ever knows what wars are all about—concluding that, "As long as people are involved they're about something." They question the white man hidden in the rocks below them, wanting to know, in the first place, why he is firing, and second, why he doesn't fire faster. His first answer is that he wants to "get away" with his cattle. His answer to the second question introduces a concept that is reinforced later on a larger scale.

> "You've lost your nerve?" one of the Indians asked.
> "I don't want to hurt anyone down there."
> "Then why are you firing the gun?"
> "So he does not fire at me."
> The two Indians looked at each other.
> "Oh," they said.

Later, it is the reader who thinks "Oh," when two boys ride high into the mountains overlooking Los Alamos, and one suggests a shortcut.

> "Why don't we just go over the top there? It would save time."
> "No, they got her all fenced off. They got a secret city up there."
> "Secret city?"
> "Yeah."
> "To blow up the world?"
> "Yeah. It's before somebody else does it."

Eastlake's technique of the parallel treatment of isolated incidents focuses attention on meaning, and is one main reason for the tightness of structure of the novel.

The Indians decide something about the gun fight and its relationship to man. One says, "I think this was about water. I think it was important to us before the white man came and the same thing is still the same and everything is still the same."

Perhaps no other concept reveals more adequately Eastlake's break with modern "objective naturalists" than his concept of time. It is a break from the "traditional" objective handling of sequential events into a recognition of both the reality of the continuum and also the validity of the subjective or Romantic treatment of the moment as forever—that everything which is, has been and will be, is now. It is a concept of time that Faulkner expressed in the interview published in *The Paris Review* as "my own theory that time is a fluid condition which has no existence except in the momentary avatars of individual people. There is no such thing as *was*—only *is*." It is a Kantian concept of time that recalls transcendentalists Emerson, Thoreau, and Melville. Emerson in *Nature* tells us that if we are capable of seeing the nature of justice and truth, "We become immortal, for we learn that time and space are relations of matter; that, with a perception of truth, or a virtuous will, they have no affinity." In *The Bronc People*, the Indian, My Prayer, goes on to explain, when talking about a flower, "They call everything by a different name but it's the same thing. And they call everything by a different time but it's the same time. Everything repeats. It would be no different if everything in every language and every time was called Cowboy's Delight."

But this concept is most successfully handled through description. For example, when some Indians, with Sant and Alastair, ride down an incline: "The mesa here was eroding away in five giant steps that descended down to the floor of the valley where the abandoned hogan lay. Each of the five steps clearly marked about twenty million years in time. In other words, they had been laid down twenty million years apart, and were so marked by unique coloration and further marked by the different fossil animals found in each. It took the four boys about twenty minutes to descend these one hundred million years but they didn't think that was very good going." Two pages later, they decide to increase the pace. "They went down together and at once, creating a storm, a tornado of ageless dust, a hundred million years in outrage, that followed them all the way down to the level of the Indians." And here, of course, is the continuum of individual action within all time, not discussed in dialogue or stated directly, but implicit in the description of action.

There are other Romantic elements to Eastlake's novels, for example, his use of what Jungian critics might call archetypal symbols to suggest or to explore the mythic consciousness of the human race. Little Sant Bowman, son of the owner of the Circle Heart, is at the rodeo. Traditional to the cowboy, the rodeo is the traditional and symbolic expression of a way of life. Like the Olympic games of ancient Greece, it is the place where only the best compete. Or perhaps it might be likened to the Roman arena before it was corrupted. And certainly it may be compared to the bullfight, traditional and meaningful to the Spaniards. Or, it is as meaningful as the annual hunt in Faulkner's "The Bear." The primitive but religious nature of the rodeo is suggested in a description of one of the events. "What they did with these was to put a clutch of pigs in a pickup truck out at one end of the field, then all the horse-mounted men came hell for leather, dismounted, grabbed a greased pig, remounted, held the flashing object high, like Montezuma's men the golden mantle, like offerings to the gods, the animals flashing and screaming, fighting along the arms, upward to the sun."

As at the bullfight and the Olympic games, there are judges, "pulling on their chins as wise men will." Into this scene comes a hometown boy made good, the professional bronc buster Lemaitre (The Master) to ride a mythical black bronc that is of the literary progeny of Melville's Moby Dick, or of Faulkner's bear, "Old Ben." The mythical character of the animal is carefully delineated.

> No one knew where the horse came from. He had suddenly appeared on the mountain one day, full, enormous, black. All the people and half the dogs from Coyote had climbed up to see him. The mangled, bloodied remains of an ancient high-backed Spanish saddle hung downward around his belly, and a man, quickly killed, went toward him with a rope.
>
> On Spanish fiesta days, when the town was lighted with provoking torches for the feast of San Antonio, the killer was sure to come off the mountain and tear through the streets, scattering the pilgrims and sending the dark-robed people retreating back into the church. Caballo de Muerto? Or He Alone Who Was Free? All the people and half the dogs of Coyote wondered.

One notices in each paragraph the curious and humorous allusion to the dogs. This is not the age of Hawthorne, and unrelieved allegory is hardly acceptable to the modern reader—case in point, Norman Mailer's *Barbary Shore*. Eastlake's writing is a controlled mixture of realistic detail (to the point of being specific about the exact number of shells a Winchester .30-.30 will hold), and of allegorical symbol (the "marvelous," as Hawthorne would have called it)—the whole conditioned by a humorous treatment that makes it all credible and thus acceptable.

This mythical beast is the animal that Lemaitre is to ride. The ride is to be a sacrificial battle which is likened to the crucifixion of Christ. The judge pauses, knowing that the challenge to the professional cowboy is too severe—one rodeo manager has already refused to buy the horse, saying, "Hell, that's not a horse, it's an electric chair." The judge says, " 'Like as not they'll try us for murder, and yet it was they'—he indicated the mob—'asked for it. Demanded it.' " Another judge offers to cancel the event. Lemaitre refuses. The people are waiting for an emotional reaction—a release—from the event. It is up to Lemaitre whether the release will be through the comic or the tragic. But even more important is the horse. Lemaitre decides, "Maybe we got to do what we're expected to do. The horse is ready, expecting me. The people are expecting me. . . . Particularly the horse. To keep the horse waiting— . . . it wouldn't b polite."

Lemaitre rides the horse—with one hand. As the horse breaks out c the chute, the barricade on which Little Sant is standing collapses, an Lemaitre clutches him with one hand, holding him like one of the grease pigs, like the mantle of Montezuma's men. "Together they shot straigh upward into the nearing sun. . . ." The ride was "fixed in Sant's mind a a dream, unclouding till ever. Not till another country, even, or anothe land, ever. Not even in the big death of Little Sant. Never."

As Lemaitre takes Little Sant home to the Circle Heart in Lemaitre Imperial, they study the concept of "not freedom" and release the blac bronc that Lemaitre has mastered and won. When Little Sant arrive home, Millicent Bowman, his mother, asks him where he's been. " 'U there,' Sant said, pointing to the tough sun, the clean distant sky."

Though Millie Bowman studies and practices various religions, sh is, ironically, unable to recognize Little Sant's religious experience. H has been in direct contact with divine principles, both by revelatio through experience and action, and also by contemplation of "nc freedom." Millie passes through stages of Zen, Zoroastriansim, I AM, an various other religions in order to make her own life bearable. For he religion is the opium, or the aspirin, that allows her to forget the traged of life. Not so her husband, Big Sant Bowman. He faces the life he has lec He had returned from the battle at the Circle R with a livid scar on h face from the burns he received when he tried to rescue from the burnin house the man he had shot. The scar is the guilt that man bears from h own actions, the brand of humanity. It is the birthmark of Hawthorne, c the veil in his "The Minister's Black Veil."

Alastair Benjamin is the son of the man Sant killed, the man who wa firing from the house. He was hiding under the bed during the battl When the house burned, he vanished out the back door, was picked up b Indians, lived in an orphanage in Albuquerque, and finally found his wa back to the Circle Heart country. The Bowmans take him as their owi The Indians accept him as another white boy—though black—and Bi Sant Bowman watches him carefully in his attempt to discover h heritage. Little Sant now has someone "to be a cowboy with." They trav together, Little Sant of the Circle Heart, and Alastair of the Circle I Like the conflict between the heart and the intellect in Hawthorne novels and short stories (Could R stand for reason?), the two boys seem t represent the poles of emotion and intellect. Little Sant's question to th rodeo riders is always "Is it fun?" and he is constantly concerned abou *living*—experiencing. Alastair, the intellectual, is fascinated with th books with the burned edges that Big Sant rescued from the burnin house, and one of his main efforts is vocabulary development. Alastai uses the word "presume" so often that Little Sant and even the Indian begin using it. This usage is as forceful and as significant as the scrivene

Bartleby's "I prefer not to," in Melville's famous story. It is not until late in the novel, after Alastair has found out the truth about his father's death and decides to understand and forgive Big Sant, that he can quit presuming long enough to "feel." It is not until then that he is ready to seek his education. Discussing it with Mr. Sanders, the missionary who has been "converted" by the Indians, Little Sant makes the important distinction.

> "Alastair feels so," Sant said.
> "Well, if he feels it, doesn't presume it, I guess he will make it now."
> "I believe he will," Sant said. "I think maybe we can all make it now."

Sant leaves home to find Lemaitre and to become a member of the bronc people. Alastair goes to a university in another area, and finds that he still has a lesson to learn—there is a war going on, a racial war of which he had been unaware in the corner of New Mexico. He journeys toward home, defeated, until he meets with Mr. Sanders and "Blue-eyed" Billy Peersall, the spokesman for the Western spirit. At the age of one-hundred-and-one, he looks on what Robinson Jeffers calls the "thickening center" of corruption—that is, civilization—and says:

> We fought the wrong people. We should have joined the Indians, fought the whites, the Easterners. That's why we come here, mountain men, the plainsmen, to escape all that. And then we joined them to fight the people who were the same, who wanted to live like us—the Indians. I don't know why we did it except we were confused by the color of their skins, the Easterners' skins, their language. Because they were the same color, spoke the same language, we must have been confused into thinking, into forgetting we had come out here to escape them.

This theme—the destruction by civilization of nature and a way of life that was in harmony with nature—is a theme that runs through much of Southwestern and Western literature. Mr. Peersall also reflects the skepticism toward law and order in the civilized community that is traditional with the Westerner. Note, for example, Eugene Manlove Rhodes's treatment of the lawyer Octaviano Baca in *Hit the Line Hard*, or Emerson Hough's character Dan Anderson in *Heart's Desire*, who laments, "The Law has come to Heart's Desire. May God forgive me! Why could we not have stayed content?" Or one might recall that Horace Greeley named the wolf "the prairie lawyer" because it fed on the weak and unfortunate.

But it is not just the Western philosophy that Mr. Peersall espouses. It is deeper than that, and more consistent with the main stream of American literature and thought. Mr. Peersall often sounds like a Western Thoreau. He is a naturalist with a love for, as well as a curiosity about, nature. He is an individualist, and a proponent of moral courage. And in civilization, he sees the loss of freedom for the individual. His action during the Tularosa school dispute is Thoreau-inspired, though active instead of passive. In "Civil Disobedience," Thoreau says, "Even voting *for the right* is *doing* nothing for it. It is only expressing to men feebly your desire that it should prevail." Mr. Peersall seems to have such an attitude when he questions Alastair.

> "All right, supposing you were born free, as some of us were, as some people must be still being born free, what land is there to go to now? What are you going to do now?"
>
> "Vote," Alastair said.
>
> "Yes, that's about it," the old man said. "We lost the wrong war."

Alastair never gets home to the Bowmans. He finds Mr. Peersall dying, and learns his most important lesson—the lesson on moral courage and the responsibility of the individual. Alastair understands and comes to terms with it.

> "You mean I've got to do it alone?"
>
> "Yes."
>
> "But the missionary used to say no man is an island."
>
> "Well, he is."
>
> "You think he just got that from another preacher?"
>
> "Yes."

That "no man is an island" is perhaps true, but in another sense we are all alone. Eastlake, the unmodern—or perhaps the more modern—accepts that condition. The modern tendency has been to merge with the herd, to conform to the "other-directed" society, to be forgotten in the mass. American writers, from the twenties on, have elaborated on that tragic aspect of man's nature—his physical and spiritual (or psychological) isolation from his fellow man. Eastlake's answer is a return to certain important aspects of frontier individualism. Big Sant and Mr. Peersall do not bemoan their nature; they accept their isolation, their individuality, and gain from it both the pride and the humility necessary to face life. Midway through the novel, Alastair stood on a mountain above low-hanging clouds and saw parts of New Mexico sticking through. "Each mesa was an island above the earth and each large island was very sufficient unto itself." But Alastair could not have learned then; he had not yet learned to feel. Now that Alastair can "go it alone," Billy Peersall joins forces with him, but dies as they start out to do battle. Alastair buries him, takes Peersall as his middle name, and returns to the conflict. He has learned, as Eastlake warns the reader, that "As long as there are cowboys there will be alive the legend and the dream, the frontier, the hardihood and the hardness, the independence and the myth, the iron line to fall back on. And as long as there are cows there will be cowboys. So the secret, and the miracle, of America lies in the bull. Save the bull and save the country. Nurture the legend. Remember Big and Little and Millie Sant, the keepers of the bulls. Remember our triumphs and our tragedies and remember our humor, the coin that makes both bearable."

In Eastlake's novels, the triumphs are the momentary, and often illusory, achievements of man; the tragedy is in the land, and in nature—the continuum. Perhaps no other writer has used the New Mexico landscape so artistically and meaningfully to point up the timelessness of the earth on which man lives.

Portrait of an Artist with Twenty-six Horses has generally the same theme as *The Bronc People*, but with a different emphasis. It is the story of two people "coming home"; that is, learning enough about themselves to be able to accept life. The first chapter concerns the homecoming of Twenty-six Horses, really "The Son of the Man with Twenty-six Horses," but the novel then concentrates on the story of Ring Bowman, who lies sinking in quicksand and whose hands busily paddle trying to keep his body from sinking while his mind goes out to the past, both to keep his spirit from sinking and to try to understand the meaning of his life. What he and his trader father, George Bowman, both discover in this longest day of the year is what Hawthorne would have called the truth of the human heart. Or as George Bowman says as he searches for Ring, "Yes. Everyone wants to help, but the only way back is home, and they ran. We spend our lives fleeing as fast from everything the human heart wants, demands. Maybe it's that. We are afraid, in deadly fear of, not each other, but ourselves, and we blame fate, a black horse." And when Ring has been found, his father interprets Twenty-six Horses' painting on the cliff that Ring, himself, has also finally understood. It is "a picture of everyone," the father said, "who is at the mercy of everybody. . . ." Those who fear themselves, of course, are the most merciless.

In this novel, too, one finds a symbolic treatment of the land and the use of a mythical horse, the black horse of fate, Luto. Loosely translated, Luto may mean "fate" or, more precisely, "grief" or "sorrow." He is the horse who comes to Ring, unbranded and ownerless, and who needs no training. He carries Tomas Tomas, the Navajo medicine man, to his funeral, and finally tricks Ring into the quicksand. Luto stands watching Ring sink until a stronger medicine, a snake, strikes the horse. Ring crawls out of the quicksand on the horse, but the horse goes down. Ring, telling his father and Twenty-six Horses about it, says that Luto is dead.

> "No," Twenty-six Horses announced. "Luto's not dead."
>
> "I saw Luto die."
>
> "No, you saw Luto sink in the sand, that's all. Luto will be back, you'll see."

No one can find the snake, but it is a rattler, one of Twenty-six Horses' guardian spirits, that turned Twenty-six Horses and George Bowman from their search up the mountain back to the arroyo. It is a strange contrast to the "magic" that Ring and Twenty-six Horses had manufactured in Chapter Two. They had used blanks and catsup to fool the old medicine man into believing that Ring could kill an Indian and bring him back to life.

Again in this novel, Eastlake uses the New Mexico landscape, not only for setting and for the beauty of the color, but to show its timelessness and to set the mood of the action. The novel opens at dawn, with all the colors of New Mexico coming alive, set against the lively deer and the deathly buzzard.

> With eyes wet and huge the deer watched; the young man watched back. The youth was crouching over a spring as though talking to the ground, the water pluming up bright through his turquoise-ringed hand, then eddying back in the bottomless whorl it had sculptured neat and sharp in the orange rock. The rock retreated to a blue then again to an almost chrome yellow at the foot of the deer. The deer was coy, hesitant and greasewood-camouflaged excepting the eyes that watched, limpid and wild. . . . The deer wheeled and fled noiselessly in the soft looping light, and now all around, above and far beyond where the youth crouched at the spring, the earth was on fire in solstice with calm beauty from a long beginning day; the sky was on fire too and the spring water tossing down the arroyo was ablaze. The long Sangre de Cristo range to the east had not fully caught; soon it would catch, not long after, in maybe half an hour, the world would be all alight. . . . Here, directly here above this sea of sage and straight up in the hard blue New Mexican sky, a huge buzzard hurtled and wheeled toward the planet earth—monstrous and swift.

As has been suggested, there is a continuation of New Mexico as a symbol of time in the Romantic tradition; that element which, Kant maintained, had been invented by man and was partially responsible for man's distortion of reality.

> There was a brooding silence at the mouth of the prehistoric cave on the Portales Mesa, a slow ballooning of hushed time on the Portales, because at this point, now, here, a stasis had arrived on the mesa so that this day, hour, this second did not flow but remained fixed without a continuum in any time or even place. . . .

Or, in the final triumphant chapter, the description of New Mexico establishes the mood; as Ring, George Bowman, and Twenty-six Horses ride out of the dark arroyo, they "gained the wide and endless undulating country gilded in light, all of them in the big sunset." The description concludes: "They flew lightly and all together up a gaudy-thrown profusion of raging color and the sharp high scent of Indian Country until they topped out on the end of a day, on a New Mexican sky infinity of burnished and dying gold."

Portrait of an Artist With Twenty-six Horses is marred by more technical difficulties than either of the earlier novels. It appears to be a loosely constructed collection of episodes, some previously published as short stories, held together by an incident that, in itself, might make another fine short story but that does not provide a satisfactory structure for a novel despite Eastlake's ability to provide transitional materials to blend the stories together. The situation of the sinking man reflecting on his life is obviously rather trite, but, strangely enough, the treatment is not. Nor, on closer examination, does the structure seem so loose. The novel does center around the meaning of the portrait by the young Indian artist named Twenty-six Horses.

On his return home, in the first chapter, Twenty-six Horses had heard the "human" cry of Ring trapped in the quicksand, but he was unable to interpret it. Until the end of the novel, Ring dominates the book (except in the episode of "The Prince," the jazz-trumpet player whose music and self-sacrifice had influenced Twenty-six Horses). But by the end of the novel, Twenty-six Horses has changed from Ring's straight man in a vaudeville act to Ring's savior in a near tragedy. It is the Indian's painting that gives meaning. It is the Indian tradition of basic or primitive meaning that saves Ring. As Twenty-six Horses tells him,

> "You're not the center of the world."
> "I suppose the Indians are."
> "That's nice of you, Ringo. I've always supposed they were too."

One is aware *despite*, or perhaps even because of, some of this novel's deficiencies that, as Herbert Gold has said, Eastlake is an "important writer." One can, for example, overlook the unevenness of tone—say, from the comic-pathetic episode of the Jewish refugees who seek revenge on a former Nazi to the unhappily slapstick characterization of a between-the-breasts gun-toting Texas schoolmarm and wife of a timid atom-bomb worker—and recognize that *Twenty-six Horses* contains some of the most brilliantly and humorously satirical passages of all the Eastlake novels. As Jonathan Swift's most successful passages were those in which man's faults could be exaggerated through the reflecting mirror of the Lilliputians, the Brobdingnagians, and the Houyhnhnms, so too can the foibles of modern man be reflected through the mirror of the Indian.

In *Go In Beauty*, there is the wonderful speech of Paracelsus, who tries to convince his fellow Navajos that the white man is not completely inferior. In *The Bronc People*, there are My Prayer, and President Taft, and The Other Indian. But none of these can match, for example, the mother of Twenty-six Horses, who, when she feels that she is losing her son, buys a restaurant in the village of Coyote and hangs up signs like "REAL LIVE WHITE PEOPLE IN THEIR NATIVE COSTUMES DOING NATIVE WHITE DANCES" and "WE RESERVE THE RIGHT TO REFUSE SERVICE TO EVERYBODY." She explains to her husband that she is only trying to make money.

There is Rabbit Stockings, who, when George Bowman wants him to go along to chase the gun-toting Texas women from the rocks, first refuses, and then—

> "You first, Kit Carson," the Indian said. "You know, Sansi," the Indian said seriously and drawing a careful lungful of smoke, "I think you been away from the white people too long. Living out here alone among these Indians can do things to you."
>
> "I only wanted to find out," the trader said, "whether they saw a young man on a black horse. Me first."
>
> "I'm with you," the Indian said, following, "I've lived out here a long time myself."

The Indian is not the only mirror for satire. There is the vice-president of an oil company who confides his unhappiness with the system to James. He concludes:

> It was good to sound off. It wasn't often you got a chance. It wasn't often you could find someone like an Indian. And it would never get around. No one of his friends would ever suspect for a moment that he was sane.

Or there is Ben Helpnell and his new Montgomery Ward pump.

> The new pump was the latest thing, later even than the piston pump. It worked on the theory that "it is easier to push water than it is to pull it. It is a hermetically sealed, self-contained unit, and without any fuss or bother or expensive plumbers or electricians, you just drop the whole thing in the well." Ben had done that yesterday and since, he had been looking for it.

And there is the Texas twentieth-century woman whose husband

> . . . was a shy, retiring man, embarrassed and self-conscious, a timid, small and self-effacing man who seemed to have finally found his niche assembling the trigger section of the hydrogen bomb at the Sandia subassembly plant in Lubbock. As Doris Bellwether examined the long empty stretches of the Indian Country from her position above the wheel the pistol seemed to give her that little something that her analyst had worked so hard to achieve.

But, as already suggested, although the Indian is not the only mirror, he is the most effective. And he is most effective because Eastlake has broken from the realistic treatment of the Indian. Eastlake's Indians are closer to Faulkner's Ikkemotubbe, Herman Basket and Craw-ford than to Oliver La Farge's Laughing Boy and Red Man. In other words, they are not realistic Indians, although they act and speak more like Indians than the real ones. George Washington Cable, in describing his technique for reproducing "realistic" dialect, said that he did not try to reproduce the exact sounds, but tried to suggest the *quality* of the sounds from the most prominent features of the dialect. It is the same technique of characterization that makes Eastlake's Indians so real. In 1942, Stanley Vestal published an article in *Southwest Review* in which he outlined the outstanding traits of the American Indian. Among these were the almost "Occidental" need for approval, physical hardiness, endurance, loquaciousness and fun-loving affability, the desire for prestige rather than wealth, and the deep-seated sense of honesty. Eastlake has studied his Indians well, and he has taken some of these traits and added others, such as the Indian's distrust of change and his harmonious relationship with nature, to construct Indian characters that reflect the most ridiculous aspects of the twentieth-century Anglo's frantic need for material progress with its resulting destruction of the Anglo's own psychological balance. The important point is, of course, that Eastlake has not been content with describing the Indian as he is, but has used the Indian for an artistic purpose.

In the *New Mexico Quarterly* of February 1935, Dudley Wynn pointed out in "The Southwestern Regional Straddle" that "The Regionalists of the Southwest—the writers, critics, artists, all who use the Spanish and Indian cultures as material for their art or their criticism—can justly be charged with a futile romanticism which grows more futile every day. . . . It is now time for interpretation. Southwestern Regionalism is not, I believe, assuming this task of interpretation."

With a few exceptions, Dr. Wynn's charge is a valid one. Emerson Hough's *Heart's Desire*, for example, is an interpretative novel, and some of Eugene Manlove Rhodes's works border on the interpretative. But literary scholarship and criticism have passed them by. Of contemporary Southwestern writers, only two seem to have been able to break from a description of the land, its people, and its traditions to interpret them in the novel form in a manner that breaks from the restrictions of regionalism. These two are Edward Abbey, in *The Brave Cowboy* and *Fire on the Mountain*, and William Eastlake in all three of his novels. Of the two, William Eastlake is the more complex and the more interesting. There has been no other Southwestern writer, certainly, who has used the Southwestern land, its people, its traditions, and then added the symbolic undertones that lend the depth of universal meaning; who has created a new mythology out of the old; and who has treated all this through a full use of tone that includes the comic, the tragic, and the satirical. It will be a serious loss to American literature if Eastlake's novels are neglected because they happen to be set in the country where there are cowboys and Indians. At a time when most novelists are busily being psychoanalyzed during the long periods between their self-psychoanalyzing novels, there is a need on the American literary scene for a novelist who is capable of interpreting the old frontier and its values for the needs of the new.

Edward Abbey: Western Philosopher

William T. Pilkington*

Will Gatlin and Art Ballantine, characters in Edward Abbey's *Black Sun*, are conversing earnestly.[1] Ballantine, who cannot understand why Gatlin has retired to the splendid isolation of a forest ranger's watch tower, speaks first:

> "What in God's name do you think you're doing here? What do you *really* want to do anyway?"
>
> "Really want to do," Gatlin repeats softly, still gazing out over the forest. Toward the desert. A pause. "Stare at the sun," he says.
>
> "What?"
>
> "Stare it down."
>
> Ballantine sighs. "Will, you're crazy."
>
> "Stare it out," says Gatlin smiling. "Stand on this tower and stare at the sun until it goes . . . black."[2]

In a later conversation, between Gatlin and a Hopi Indian acquaintance, the sun is again a main topic of discussion. "The sun will eat the earth," says the Indian. "No," says Gatlin. "Because we shall eat the sun." "You white men," replies the Indian incredulously. "You'll eat anything."[3] How does one stare the sun black or eat it? And what is accomplished if one manages to do these things? Edward Abbey has set himself the difficult task of posing such riddles and then—partially at least—solving them, a magician's performance that well deserves our amazed attention.

Abbey is, without question, one of the most controversial and challenging of contemporary writers from the American West. Nearly a decade ago, when I was but a naive and callow youth, I published a hasty and ill-considered essay on Abbey and his books. At the time I had only a couple of early novels—*The Brave Cowboy* (1956) and *Fire on the Mountain* (1962)—on which to base a judgment concerning the author's achievement. I did not hesitate, however, to make such a judgment. Though I praised Abbey's talent for constructing fast-paced and exciting

*"Edward Abbey: Western Philosopher, or How to Be a 'Happy Hopi Hippie,' " *WAL*, 9 (1974), 17–31.

narratives, I was sharply critical of what appeared to me to be his philosophical incoherence—an incoherence that seemed inappropriate in the writings of an ex-professor of philosophy (in the early 1950s Abbey taught philosophy at the University of New Mexico). I accused the writer of espousing the rankest and most implausibly romantic variety of anarchism. I advised him, in effect, to grow up and cast off his willfully prolonged adolescence. The last sentence of the piece reads as follows: "Abbey's works are as good as any that have been written by a Southwesterner in recent years, but they still have a way to go before they attain maturity, much less greatness."[4]

I am pleased to report that I now detect evidence in Abbey's most recent books of that late blossoming of maturity that I so brashly demanded long years ago. (I claim no credit, incidentally, for the author's development, since I am certain that all this time he has remained happily ignorant of my stern criticisms, those criticisms having been published in one of the littlest of little mags.) I shall attempt to demonstrate in this paper, in any case, that the controlling subjects and themes of Abbey's books have progressed over the years from a rather simplistic protest in his early fiction against the outrages and encroachments on personal liberty often perpetrated by modern society, to a consideration in his later works of the most complex of philosophical questions. In the course of this progress Abbey, it seems to me, has contributed significantly to that ongoing tradition of Western American literature that Professor Max Westbrook has called Western "sacrality."[5] This contribution, characteristically enough, has been made in the writer's own unique and quirky way.

Edward Abbey recognized a long time ago—long before most of us did—that the social and economic assumptions that have governed Western (that is, Western European and American) civilization for several centuries are rapidly becoming obsolete, unworkable, in many cases cruelly destructive. He saw that the concept of continual and unlimited growth, and the technological advances that necessarily accompany growth, destroy people and things when those people and things refuse to assist in the business of further growth. Such growth, he perceived, is propelled by a crazy and inexorable logic. "There are some," Abbey writes, "who frankly and boldly advocate the eradication of the last remnants of wilderness and the complete subjugation of nature to the requirements of . . . industry. This is a courageous view, admirable in its simplicity and power, and with the weight of all modern history behind it. It is also quite insane."[6]

The destructive insanity of modern American society is heavily underscored in almost all of Abbey's writings. *The Brave Cowboy*, a novel published in 1956, effectively introduces the theme. *The Brave Cowboy* recounts the adventures of a stubborn cowpoke named Jack Burns, who asserts his independence and individuality by casually turning outlaw. Unfortunately Burns's quixotic behavior, which might have been tolerated in the loose law-and-order framework of the nineteenth-century American West, occurs in a context of twentieth-century legal and social restraint (some say repression). Attempting to cross the ridge of a mountain range and escape into Mexico, the cowboy is zestfully pursued by a human houndpack armed with jeeps, helicopters, walkie-talkies, the most efficient modern weaponry. Against incredible odds Burns almost succeeds in eluding the posse—but in crossing a busy highway his horse spooks, and he and the horse are run down and killed by a truck loaded with bathroom fixtures. Most Americans, probably, are familiar with this story, not because they have read the novel, but because *The Brave Cowboy* was made into an exceptional motion picture called *Lonely Are the Brave*, a movie that has been shown on television many times in recent years. The tale is unquestionably exciting and suspenseful, but the circumstance that it was so easily, and excellently, translated into film suggests a considerable simplicity and directness in both book and movie. Movies—those that are commercially successful anyway—seem to require clear-cut dramatic situations and themes that can be quickly grasped by the millions who watch films in theaters and on television. Certainly *The Brave Cowboy* meets that requirement of the commercial movie medium, for its storyline is extremely simple and straightforward. The book's message is right there on the surface; it demands no digging to unearth. The allegory of the novel's ending, which might seem heavy-handed to some, can scarcely be mistaken, even by TV's legendary "lowest common denominator." As Abbey himself recently confessed, *The Brave Cowboy* was written by a "rather simple-minded but very passionate kid,"[7] and the book clearly displays both the strengths and weaknesses of that kid's youthful enthusiasm.

Fire on the Mountain, a novel published in 1962, is a variation on the same theme developed in *The Brave Cowboy*. The story's principal character is John Vogelin, an old-time cowboy, a man whose roots are in the sun, sand, and sagebrush of the southern New Mexico desert. In the twentieth century, however, Vogelin is considered a throwback, a dangerous anachronism. Inevitably he falls victim to the insatiable demands of technological growth and expansion. The government insists that he give up his ancestral home, his ranch, so that the White Sands Missile Range may be enlarged to accommodate bigger and "better" missiles. Vogelin decides to go down fighting, as a desert creature should, scratching and clawing. "If I have to give in," he resolves, "I'm going to give in like an Apache. That's part of the pattern . . . That's the tradition here."[8]

Vogelin, needless to say, is defeated.[9] Following a near shoot-out with a small army of federal agents, he is dispossessed of his ranch and sent off to live with relatives in a nearby town. Sensing his imminent death, however, Vogelin sneaks back to his beloved land, to the ruthless, inhospitable desert which he both loves and respects. The old man dies peacefully in a small cabin on the side of Thieves' Mountain. Vogelin's grandson, accompanied by a close friend, finds the body there and sets the cabin ablaze, using the structure as a primitive crematorium—a Viking funeral, we are told, appropriate for a deceased warrior. Again, as in *The Brave Cowboy*, the message implicit in these events is clear and unmistakable; Abbey hardly needs to spell out his intentions. He has done so nevertheless: *Fire on the Mountain*, the author says, was written "in defense of all the lost people whose homes are destroyed by government for the sake of more and bigger highways, more and bigger dams, more and bigger factories, more and bigger prisons, more and bigger bombing ranges, more and bigger government."[10] Abbey admits that the novel was hurriedly written—in a month's time—and "was always meant quite calmly and frankly for Hollywood . . ."[11] Though no film version of *Fire on the Mountain* has yet been produced, I predict that some day it will make a first-rate movie, for essentially the same reason that *The Brave Cowboy* made such a good motion picture: its dramatic and thematic simplicity.

Both *The Brave Cowboy* and *Fire on the Mountain*, then, spring from the author's simplistic and determinedly unambiguous beliefs concerning the modern world, a world in which society gradually and inescapably nibbles away at the principle of personal liberty. Both novels give voice to a young writer's sense of outrage and desire to register his impassioned protest against the inhuman atrocities often committed by government and the social mechanism. They simplify in order to arouse the reader's emotions, and in this regard they are highly successful; their simplicity, however, is achieved at the expense of depth and solidity. No one, I think, would ever feel it necessary for clarity's sake to give these novels more than one reading.

Abbey's most recent books—*Desert Solitaire* (1968) and *Black Sun* (1971)—are another matter altogether. Though they retain something of the former works' contentious style and hyperbolic tone, and though they expand ideas and themes latent in *The Brave Cowboy* and *Fire on the Mountain*, they seem a conscious departure from the early novels. In these later books, in place of simplicity we find complexity, complexity mainly in the philosophical vision they express. In place of a direct assault on our emotions we find a provocative but tentative exploration of life's ultimate question—the nature of reality and existence. In place of gut-wrenching dramatic action we find situations and authorial commentary that gauge the breadth and depth of human experience. In short *Desert Solitaire* and *Black Sun*, while not totally successful in achieving the things they set out to do, are fascinating and thought-provoking books, and they amply repay all who are willing to give them the close study they deserve.

Desert Solitaire, subtitled "A Season in the Wilderness," is a composite account, in the tradition of Thoreau's *Walden*, of several summers that the author worked as a park ranger in Arches National Monument in southeastern Utah. It is, in some sense, and again in the tradition of Thoreau, a work of fiction. It might even be considered a philosophical novel. In any event, the theme of the work, says Abbey, is "wilderness and freedom . . . We have a moral obligation," he asserts, "to preserve the wild, the original, the untamed. . . . Wilderness is almost the only thing left in America that is *worth* saving . . ."[12] The book rambles through a series of tales and episodes, colorful descriptions of scenery, scientifically precise observations of desert flora and fauna. Although the writer's ruminations are clouded by the specter of technological change and "progress," *Desert Solitaire* is essentially a joyful book, which celebrates the most fundamental gift of life—the ability "to see and touch and hear in the midst of tangible and mysterious things-in-themselves . . ."[13]

The surface account, however, the desert travelog—and even the writer's professed reason for writing the book, his affirmation of the necessity for wilderness and freedom—are only incidental to the real purpose of *Desert Solitaire;* their function is to serve as vehicles for conveying the mind of the author, that mind being the actual landscape that the book explores. Perhaps the book's main theme, certainly one of its root concerns, is the gap (and the possibility of bridging that gap) between reality and an individual's perception of reality. Abbey states the problem forthrightly: the danger "of confusing the thing observed with the mind of the observer, of constructing not a picture of external reality but simply a mirror of the thinker."[14] No writer, apparently, can wholly avoid this hazard, for every linguistic description is an artistic creation, shaped and modified by the artist's perceptions; it is inevitably a distortion of the thing described. In *Desert Solitaire* the desert—the world of sun and rock—is important (to the reader) because it is important to Abbey's thought. The reader participates in the writer's thoughts, but he cannot directly experience the reality that the writer attempts to describe—a "paradox" Abbey toys with throughout the book but never really resolves.

Black Sun, a novel, is Abbey's last published book to date,[15] and it is a very good book, perhaps his best so far. The story's setting, as Thomas J. Lyon has noted, is in our time—"the sundown century: jets overhead, zoo-like obsessions with sex, manic pseudo-philosophy all around."[16] The main character of *Black Sun* is Will Gatlin, a thirty-seven-year-old forest ranger who initiates into sex—and falls in love with—a naive, nineteen-year-old virgin named Sandy MacKenzie. The texture of this relationship, which ends with Sandy's death, is conveyed through dialogue, often very witty and humorous, even brilliant dialogue. The pervading tone of the work, however, is, not lightheartedness or (at the other extreme) despair, but a sense of irrevocable and inconsolable loss. But the sense of loss is Will Gatlin's, and it is not necessarily objectively justified.

Indeed, as in *Desert Solitaire*, the shifting relation between reality and an individual's perception of reality is a major theme of *Black Sun.*[17] Will Gatlin, in the conversation with Art Ballantine quoted above, wants to stare at the sun until it goes black, but the blackness of the sun, of course, would be merely a phenomenon of Gatlin's perception; the sun, in reality, would remain unchanged. Gatlin's perceptions, in any event, are crucial, since the reader must assume those perceptions as his own. It is through Gatlin's consciousness that the events of the story are glimpsed: Gatlin's reflections, his arranging of the sequence in which events are revealed, his possible addition or deletion of events to or from the record—all these facts and possibilities the reader must keep in mind. But Gatlin's character is developed not so much by means of his thoughts as through a dramatic contrast of the ranger's attitudes with those of another character, his friend Ballantine. Will has cut his ties to society, and in Abbey's view he is a free man. Ballantine, a college professor in a large city, is obsessed with sex; he is also frustrated by sex, defeated by sex, cannot see any way of breaking social ties because of sex. Ballantine participates in the meaningless, mechanical exercise of girl-chasing, his actions dictated by his obsession. Gatlin, on the other hand, is free, independent, primitive, solitary, outwardly silent. His freedom allows him to love Sandy MacKenzie in a way that social conventions and civilized hang-ups cannot frustrate.

Sandy, however, is not free. She is engaged to a young man who is the epitome of establishment values: he is an Air Force pilot trainee, a budding technocrat. The symbolism of Sandy's dilemma is painfully obvious. She must choose between her *real* love for Gatlin and the animal passion that he represents, and the *effect* of love that she shares with her official boyfriend, who offers her security and social approval. She cannot decide. She goes into the desert "to think," and the desert devours her. She disappears, and her body is never found; presumably she dies. At novel's end Will Gatlin, uncertain of the future, is preparing to leave his wilderness retreat. He is, as usual, silent, uncommunicative. The reader does not know whether he mutely grieves Sandy's death or stoically accepts that death—perhaps both. For the first time in the book, his thoughts are not recorded. In such an extreme situation thoughts as well as words fail; only emotion remains.

Desert Solitaire and *Black Sun*, as I have said, seem to me to possess a rich complexity that is almost totally absent from *The Brave Cowboy* and *Fire on the Mountain*. The source of this complexity is, for the most part, the philosophy that underlies the two works. In *The Brave Cowboy* and *Fire on the Mountain*, to reiterate, Abbey dramatically illustrates the obsolescence of social, governmental and economic principles around which Western civilization of the past few centuries has been structured. In *Desert Solitaire* and *Black Sun* the writer goes one step further: he attempts to demonstrate the impasse that Western (that is, again, Western European) philosophy, with its emphasis on individualism and rationalism, has reached. In these books he attacks the root system of the Western philosophical tradition: Platonic-Cartesian dualism, which posits mutually exclusive categories of nature and spirit, body and mind, reality and thought (including language). Traditionally, Western philosophers have upheld the importance of spirit, mind, and thought at the expense of nature, body, and reality.

Abbey wants to redress the imbalance, to reassert the primacy—or at least the equal importance—of nature, body, and (most significant of all) concrete, finite reality. "Turning Plato and Hegel on their heads," he says, "I sometimes choose to think . . . that man is a dream, thought an illusion, and only rock is real. Rock and sun."[18] Implicit in that statement is the author's belief that twentieth-century men have lost perspective through over-reliance on the rational intellect; that loss of perspective may well explain humanity's current drift toward disaster, for Abbey warns that modern men have become automatons wandering through a jungle of asphalt and machinery, impervious to the natural world that surrounds them. Like the dinosaur before him, modern man faces extinction because of his arrogant refusal to adapt himself to his environment. In this regard Abbey holds a special fondness for deserts, since he seems to view the desert as a kind of microcosm of the world. The desert imposes a rigid discipline on those who manage to survive in it. Any deviation from that discipline is disastrous; in the desert adaptation to existing conditions must be immediate and complete. To Abbey—and hopefully to many of his readers—the parallels between desert experience and man's present precarious situation on earth are chastening and instructive.

In order to survive, then, according to Abbey, modern man must learn to accept his proper—and limited—role in that finite ecosystem which is our planet. He must abandon his "man-centeredness, anthropocentricity, the opinion that the world exists solely for the sake of man . . ."[19] To do this, he must first of all break down the barrier between past and present, acquire an awareness of the present that incorporates time past. Men must go backward in time in order to learn about themselves, to discover the essence of the human race, an essence that has its source in primeval slime. A scene in *Desert Solitaire* vividly illustrates the necessity for men to retrace their footsteps back to the source. The author sees a pair of gopher snakes performing what appears to be a mating dance. He slithers over the ground on his belly to meet the snakes face to face. "For an instant," Abbey writes, "I am paralyzed by wonder; then stung by fear too ancient and powerful to overcome . . . If I had been as capable of trust as I am susceptible to fear I might have learned something new or some truth so very old we have all forgotten it."[20] The involuntary fear, Abbey suggests, springs from loss of trust in the real world, the world in which snake, spider, and rocks exist. Fear results from man's expulsion from Eden; from his having acquired knowledge of good and evil (useful metaphors for various kinds of knowledge). The snakes seem to possess a primeval awareness that transcends or antedates the concept of good and evil. They exist harmoniously with other natural things and creatures, a state that prelapsarian man enjoyed and that modern man must now attempt to recapture. Modern man, says Abbey, must "cut the bloody cord," must reacquire a "delirious exhilaration of independence, a rebirth backward in time and into primeval liberty, into freedom in the most simple, literal, primitive meaning of the word, the only meaning that really counts."[21]

But a gopher snake, the author finds, has little to teach an individual who has forfeited his instinct for the questionable benefits of rational knowledge, a knowledge that can only be expressed through the medium of language. Language, according to Abbey, has a legitimate function in human society, as a form for communicating ideas, but the writer is thoroughly skeptical of philosophies of reality—perceptions of reality—which are based on linguistic formulations. He makes the point explicitly in *Desert Solitaire:* language, he says, is "a screen of words . . . issuing from the brain like a sort of mental smog that keeps getting between a man and the world, obscuring vision."[22] Through language, he asserts, we

> create a whole world, corresponding to the other world out there. Or we trust that it corresponds. Or perhaps . . . we cease to care, becoming more concerned with the naming than with the things named; the former becomes more real than the latter. And so in the end the world is lost again. No, the world remains—those unique, particular, incorrigibly individual junipers and sandstone monoliths—and it is we who are lost.[23]

The same point is made humorously, though nonetheless seriously, in *Black Sun.* The girl Sandy calls Will Gatlin "an animal," "a hairy beast," "a dirty old man," "a sex maniac," and other similar terms of endearment. Her feelings are positive, joyful, but her reason apparently compels her to express those feelings in a negative way. At one point Will and Sandy are about to perform the sexual act, and Sandy demands a word or phase to define their action. Will offers suggestions, and Sandy comments on their appropriateness. The simplest four-letter word, she decides, is much too blunt. "Sexual intercourse" sounds too clinical, even criminal. "Conjugal relations" she calls ridiculous, likewise "carnal knowledge." "Sexual congress" sounds like a convention; "intimate relations" prompts thoughts of mom and dad. "Make love" seems, in the last analysis, the most satisfactory term. But even it is inadequate, for there *is* no word or phrase that describes the spontaneous sexual surrender they feel and act out.[24]

Is Will and Sandy's difficulty in naming their action a semantic or linguistic problem only, or is it a problem of philosophy? For Abbey, I think, it is a profoundly philosophical problem, one that penetrates to the heart of modern man's spiritual crisis. In Abbey's view, reality must be intuitively felt, instinctively experienced. Most modern men, however, settle for labeling reality rather than actively participating in it, for intellectual exercises rather than authentic experience. The possibility remains, however, that men may yet dispel their spiritual inertia and acquire a fresh, clear perception of the world, a direct access to experience. But they must first accept, Abbey suggests, certain basic assumptions about the nature of life and the universe:

God: Several years ago one version of a popular joke ran as follows: "God is alive and hiding in the Grand Canyon." To Abbey and to other writers from the American West, this joke contains more truth than humorous fiction. Abbey rarely uses the work "God" to describe the "whatever-it-is" that resides in the Grand Canyon, and when he employs the term he usually does so with whimsical intent. There is nonetheless a measure of high seriousness in the author's claim, in *Desert Solitaire,* that he repaired to the desert "to meet God . . . face to face . . ."[25] The necessary qualification is that "God," to Abbey, is an ineffable divine force inherent in the elemental bare-bones reality of nature. "I am not an atheist," says the writer, "but an earthiest."[26] Men could and should learn, he asserts, "to perceive in water, leaves and silence more than sufficient to the absolute and marvelous . . ."[27] It is on that "bedrock of animal faith," he concludes, that he chooses to stand.[28] In dealing with the concept of "God," the problem is once again that of language, for Abbey insists that this sacred force not be named, labeled, or in any way quantified. To call it "God" or "collective unconscious" or " sacrality" is only to succeed in labeling once more. The sacred force can be felt but never tangibly grasped, much less defined. It is simply the unnamable energy that is the source of man's intuitive and instinctual knowledge.

Sex: Most modern men are victims of a dualism (an aspect of the more inclusive mind-body dualism) that compartmentalizes spiritual love and physical love; both kinds of love are required, but they are obtained, it is widely thought, in separate packages. In *Black Sun,* for instance, Art Ballantine seeks (unsuccessfully) spiritual love in marriage, while at the same time he satisfies his biological needs by means of a series of casual couplings. He recognizes no connection between his failure in both marriage and adultery. Abbey seems to believe that sex and love are inseparable—that love begins with sex, has its source in the physical act itself, the animal passions. The story of Will and Sandy in *Black Sun* is a cautionary parable on the subject of sex. Will Gatlin feels and then acts; he has no guilt feelings because he trusts his intuition. Sandy is attracted to this view of sex, but can never really accept it. For one thing she continues to try to define their love through language. She is torn between her intuitive, natural love for Will and her rational, socially acceptable love for her Air Force cadet. The more she thinks about her choice, the more her ability to choose is undermined. In *Desert Solitaire* Abbey notes that "reason is and ought to be, as Spinoza said, the slave of the passions."[29] Unfortunately this is a lesson Sandy never learns, and she pays dearly for her ignorance.

Death: In all of his works Abbey seems to suggest that, if one loves life, one should love *all* of life—including one's awareness of the finiteness of the world and of one's existence in the world. The ultimate personal reminder of that finiteness is, of course, death. Death in the desert—unceremonial, brutal death—is an important subject of Abbey's writing. In *The Brave Cowboy* Jack Burns is run down and killed by a truck, an untimely and heroic death that seems more symbolic than real. A more believable death is that of old man John Vogelin in *Fire on the Mountain*. Vogelin dies of natural causes, aggravated by technological "progress." His intuition tells him he is about to die, and he returns to a line shack on his expropriated ranch where he dies as he had lived—a part of the land. As the shack burns and flames consume his body, a mountain lion—the last lion left alive in the area—screams in the distance, nature's tribute to one of its own.

In *Desert Solitaire* death is a recurring motif. One practical message the book clearly conveys is that all creatures who attempt to survive in the desert—whether rabbits, lizards, or men—must accept the possibility of sudden and unexpected doom. An illustrative episode is Abbey's description of the death of a tourist, an old man who, not knowing how to adapt to an extreme climate, is extinguished by an inexorable cause-effect progression; the tourist's end is simply the inevitable "conclusion to a syllogism . . ."[30] The author comments:

> Given this man's age, the inevitability and suitability of his death, and the essential nature of life on earth, there is in each of us the unspeakable conviction that we are well rid of him. . . . A ruthless, brutal process—but clean and beautiful.[31]

In *Black Sun* Sandy MacKenzie, in an effort to think through her difficult situation, disappears into the desert. She is evidently ill-equipped; like the foolish tourist, she does not possess the knowledge to effect the extreme adaptation that deserts demand. She does not return, and her body is never recovered. But there are many worse fates than death in the desert—the death-in-life, for example, in which Art Ballantine exists—and Sandy's death, though unfortunate because of her youth, is not meaningless. To Gatlin her death is a great personal loss, but he seems never to sink into hopelessness. He senses that Sandy's spirit, in a way, lives on; that in yielding her body to the desert—if only to provide meals for scavengers—she had become part of the cycle of life, death, and rebirth.

The deaths described in Abbey's books occur in heat of sun and fire; the deceased give up their life energy (their "souls") to the desert, to wilderness, to nature. In the cases of John Vogelin and Sandy MacKenzie, this is literally true since their bodies are lost to "civilized" burial; they are simply absorbed back into the earth—no ceremony, no certificates of death, no loss of unity with nature. Death of this kind, Abbey indicates, should be accepted, even welcomed in some instances, as the natural complement of life, the clearing away that allows new life to sprout. The only principle that governs death in the desert (and in the world) is necessity, the balancing of the ecosystem—"a ruthless, brutal process," as the writer says, "but clean and beautiful."

What is Edward Abbey working toward, particularly in *Desert Solitaire* and *Black Sun*, the philosophical substructure of which I have tried to sketch? It seems to me that he is attempting to establish an effective integration of those things that dualism separates: good and evil, life and death, sex and love, experience and language, objective reality and private perceptions. The final chapter of *Desert Solitaire*, entitled "Bedrock and Paradox," provides a clue to the author's intentions. The "bedrock" is, of course, solid reality, that inorganic but very substantial world that endures, remains unchanged in the midst of human flux. "Paradox" the writer defines as "the inconvertible union of contradictory truths."[32] When Abbey dreams, for instance, of "a hard and brutal mysticism in which the naked self merges with a nonhuman world and yet somehow survives still intact, individual, separate,"[33] he conceives such a paradoxical union. "Paradox" is the foundation of Abbey's philosophy, since it is the principle that allows for the integration of opposites, ultimately for the dissolution of dualism.

To this point the author has been only partially successful in his efforts at integration; at the very least, however, he has constructed a provocative platform to support future writing. Meanwhile difficulties remain to be worked out. One difficulty lies in the fact that the writer must establish the integration (for readers anyway) by means of language, a medium he distrusts, even rejects on occasion. Another is the problem of whether or not such an integration can be *consciously* achieved by a exertion of will. In *Black Sun* Will Gatlin wants to eat the sun, to blend his being with nature and attain that instinctual level of awareness that modern man, in Abbey's view, has lost. Gatlin's Hopi Indian friend sees no need to eat the sun—or to stare at it until it goes black. The Indian does not have to rationalize. He knows the truth intuitively: that one cannot conquer or control the sun, one can only coexist with it in the actual world. The task, then—for Will Gatlin, for Edward Abbey, and for Americans generally—is, as Gatlin's Indian friend says, to learn how to be "a happy Hopi hippie."[34]

Notes

1. I am grateful to the Organized Research Committee of Tarleton State University, Stephenville, Texas for two summer grants to support my study of Edward Abbey's work.

2. Edward Abbey, *Black Sun* (New York: Simon and Schuster, 1971), pp. 29–30.

3. Abbey, p. 56.

4. William T. Pilkington, "Edward Abbey: Western Anarchist," *Western Review*, 3 (1966), 62.

5. For a definition of Western "sacrality" see Max Westbrook, "The Practical Spirit: Sacrality and the American West," *WAL*, 3 (1968), 193–205. See also Chapter 2, titled "The Western Esthetic," of Westbrook's book *Walter Van Tilburg Clark* (New York: Twayne, 1969), pp. 39–53.

6. Edward Abbey, *Desert Solitaire: A Season in the Wilderness* (New York: McGraw-Hill, 1968), p. 47.

7. Statement from a foreword, dated 1970, to *The Brave Cowboy: An Old Tale in a New Time*, paperback reprint (New York: Ballantine, 1971), p. xi.

8. Edward Abbey, *Fire on the Mountain* (New York: Dial Press, 1962). p. 167.

9. In *Tularosa*, C. L. Sonnichsen recounts a true-life story that may well have provided inspiration and much of the storyline for *Fire on the Mountain*. According to Sonnichsen's account, in the late 1950s a tough old New Mexico cowman named John Prather resisted, very much in the manner of John Vogelin in the novel, the federal government's attempts to annex his land for expansion of the White Sands Missile Range (though Prather, unlike Vogelin, was able to marshal public opinion and win important concessions from the government). The Prather case ballooned into a local *cause célèbre* and, as Sonnichsen's documentation shows, was extensively reported in El Paso and Albuquerque newspapers. See C. L. Sonnichsen, *Tularosa: Last of the Frontier West* (New York: Devin-Adair, 1960), pp. 285–91.

10. Quote from the dust jacket of *Fire on the Mountain*.

11. Les Standiford, ed., "Desert Places: An Exchange with Edward Abbey," *WHR*, 24 (1970), 397.

12. Standiford, p. 395.

13. Abbey, *Desert Solitaire*, p. 37.

14. Abbey, *Desert Solitaire*, p. 240.

15. This statement ignores two books by Abbey that have appeared since *Black Sun* was published in early 1971: *Slickrock: The Canyon Country of Southeast Utah* (San Francisco: Sierra Club, 1971) and *Cactus Country* (New York: Time-Life Books, 1973). Both volumes are briskly and professionally put together, and both feature excellent photography; both also fall more into the category of coffee-table journalism than of serious literature. [Since this essay was written, Abbey has published three more noteworthy books: a novel, *The Monkey Wrench Gang* (Philadelphia: Lippincott, 1975); and two collections of essays, *The Journey Home* (New York: E. P. Dutton, 1977), and *Abbey's Road* (New York: E. P. Dutton, 1979).]

16. Thomas J. Lyon, rev. of *Black Sun*, *WAL*, 6 (1971), 157.

17. I do not wish to leave the impression that I believe Abbey is unique in his exploration of this theme, though I think he has some original things to say on the subject. A long line of American writers and thinkers—Emerson, Melville, and Whitman in the nineteenth century, Wallace Stevens in the twentieth century, are but a few of the many who might be named—have been concerned with tracing the connections, and disconnections, between the world of concrete objects and the mind's reconstruction of that world. Interestingly the phrase "black sun" occurs at least twice in poems by Stevens. For instance, in "Thunder by the Musician," the poet speaks of a thundercloud that "Rose up, tallest, in the black sun. . . ." See *Collected Poems of Wallace Stevens* (New York: Alfred A. Knopf, 1957), p. 220. Elsewhere in various of Steven's poems the sun appears to be white, purple, blue, green, and red.

18. Abbey, *Desert Solitaire*, p. 194.

19. Abbey, Ibid., p. 244.

20. Abbey, Ibid., pp. 20–21.

21. Abbey, Ibid., p. 155.

22. Abbey, Ibid., p. 184.

23. Abbey, Ibid., p. 257.

24. Abbey, *Black Sun*, pp. 117–18.

25. Abbey, *Desert Solitaire*, p. 6.
26. Abbey, Ibid., p. 184.
27. Abbey, Ibid., p. 177.
28. Abbey, Ibid., p. 268.
29. Abbey, Ibid., p. 265.
30. Abbey, Ibid., p. 83.
31. Abbey, Ibid., p. 214.
32. Abbey, Ibid., p. 99.
33. Abbey, Ibid., p. 6.
34. Abbey, Ibid., p. 54.

More D'Urban: The Texas Novels of Larry McMurtry

Kerry Ahearn*

Recently, I met a young woman who adores the work of Larry McMurtry and who confided that she was first drawn to him when she heard he often wears a sweatshirt inscribed, "I am a regional writer." I don't know if the sweatshirt ever existed, but I am certain that at least figuratively, McMurtry has taken it off. The irony of the "regional writer" pose is no longer tolerable to him, and he has written off Texas. A recent *Atlantic Monthly* essay explains why his fiction subsequent to *Terms of Endearment* (1975) will feature an "international" cast:

> [Novelists] exploit a given region, suck what thematic riches they can from it, and then, if they are able, move on to whatever regions promise yet more riches. I was halfway through my sixth Texas novel when I suddenly began to notice that where place was concerned, I was sucking air.

Just a few years ago, his book of essays, *In a Narrow Grave*, defended Texas as rich ground for the novelist:

> The state is at that stage of metamorphosis when it is most fertile with conflict, when rural and soil traditions are competing most desperately with urban traditions—competing for the allegiance of the young. The city will win, of course, but its victory won't be cheap—the country traditions were very strong. As the cowboys leave the range and learn to accommodate themselves to the suburbs, defeats that are tragic in quality must occur and may be recorded.

What went wrong? McMurtry's five Texas novels, from *Horseman, Pass By* (1961) through *All My Friends Are Going to Be Strangers* (1973), showed a writer eager to tell a good story and willing to experiment. He tried short novels and long (*Moving On* [1970] fell just short of eight hundred pages); he has employed the different points of view, rural and urban locales, male and female protagonists. Such a course implies a writer serious about his craft, and yet differences may hint at McMurtry's uncertainly with how to use Texas experience. The two quotations above signal

**TQ*, 19, no. 3 (1976), 109–29. ©1976 by *Texas Quarterly*. Reprinted by permission of publisher and author.

one difficulty: they imply different approaches to fiction—the first presenting an obviously superficial conception of setting, and the second an obviously deep sympathy for the intricacies of human character and situation. The pair of statements charts a change in McMurtry rather than in the Texas material; he has come more and more to subscribe to that peculiar Eastern parochialism which views that Great Plains only as a place, denying it the complexity of reality. We may take McMurtry at his word: he has become an "exploiter" rather than an explorer of Texas experience. His work shows an increasing absence of psychological depth and artistic refinement (from individual word choice to total vision). *Horseman, Pass By* is superior to the *Hud* Paramount made of it, more alive and more controlled; the film version of *The Last Picture Show* (1966) is a finer piece than the novel because it imposes restraint the book badly needs. That comparison hints at what might be called McMurtry's "decline to success."

The sudden disenchantment with place is not surprising. The writer of serious fiction in the West has always battled the cultural version of the Myth of the Great American Desert. McMurtry's *Atlantic* essay shows him especially vulnerable, since it pictures the novelist as a kind of carpetbagger who uses his repertoire of tricks before a regional backdrop and then moves on when the place will provide no more variety. At the time of his greatest successes, in fact, McMurtry wrote that being a Texas writer was leaving him in a progressively darker humor: "We [Texans] aren't thought of as quaintly vulgar any more. Some may find us *dangerously* vulgar, but the majority just find us boring."

McMurtry's first two novels, *Horseman, Pass by* and *Leaving Cheyenne* (1962), fight this majority view, exploring as they do the people, the rhythms of their lives, and the meaning they derive from life on the Texas plains, which tend to reflect their beholder's mood and emphasize it. Lonnie's first words in the prologue to *Horseman* convey something of this purpose:

> I remember how green the early oat fields were, that year, and how the plains looked in April, after the mesquite leafed out. . . . When I rode out with him on Saturdays, Granddad would sometimes get down from his horse, to show me how the grass was shooting its runners over the droughty ground; and he told me that nature would always work her own cures, if people would be patient, and give her time.

To Hud, the land is something to poke wellholes through, and from that contrast in views comes the tension that moves the novel to its sad end. It also moved McMurtry to subsequent novels. His center is Thalia, a North Central Texas cattle town similar to his childhood home, and though his focus has moved from adolescents to young adults and the scene has shifted to Houston, the plains remain vastly important as memory, escape, even value. His people are either from the plains or they go to them. The landscape moves people, and a consideration of how he explores and exploits its possibilities reveals a good deal about his difficulties and successes, and also about the problems of the contemporary Western writer, for McMurtry, like the best Western writers we have, Wallace Stegner and Wright Morris, attempts to escape the stereotypes of the Wild West myth and to free himself from our persistent frontier fantasies.

That stance is evident even in *Horseman, Pass By*, more than a eulogy to a vanishing, ennobling way of life, and more than a sentimental response to the Texas plains. The prologue hints too at the discouraging emptiness of the scene and the temptations in the distance. While his grandfather Homer sleeps, Lonnie climbs the windmill:

> Sitting there with only the wind and darkness around me, I thought of all the important things I had to think about: my honors, my worries, my ambitions. . . . When it was clear enough I could see the airplane beacons flashing from the airport in Wichita Falls.

The plains setting, McMurtry implies, is important to Western fiction, but should not be presented as a formula influence because in sum it is everything everyone has described it to be, and at any given moment it could reflect a variety of those attributes. Considered in the abstract, McMurtry's attitude is deceptively simple, but because it avoids stereotypes, it allows the physical landscape to become the complex and subtle influence one would expect from the fiction of any region.

Remarkably, the few serious critics to deal with the novel have overlooked or misinterpreted this aspect of McMurtry's independence from traditional approaches. One of the most perceptive essays yet to appear on *Horseman, Pass By*, James K. Folsom's "*Shane* and *Hud:* Two Stories in Search of a Medium," argues that the book reflects a "belief, inherent in primitivism, that man reflects in moral terms the physical nature of his environment," in this case, "an attitude that has been present in Americans' treatment of their epic since the West was first assumed to be the most significant factor in the American experience." The "physical nature" in McMurtry's story he characterizes as "ugliness," implying that Hud's evil personality should be taken as a reflection of the place where he grew up. Such a position ignores the presence of old Homer as a moral touchstone, and Hud's absolute indifference to the land his stepfather loves. Their clearest confrontation on that issue concerns oil leases, which Hud favors: Homer says, "What good's oil to me? I can't ride out every day an' prowl amongst 'em, like I can my cattle. I can't breed 'em or tend 'em or rope 'em or chase 'em or nothin.' I can't feel a smidgen a pride in 'em, cause they ain't none a my doin'." Late in the novel, when Hud kills him, the act symbolizes the supplanting of Homer's traditional yeomanry by the get-rich-quick ethic that disconnects itself from nature's rhythms and depends purely upon exploitation. Homer had pointed with relief at grass roots spreading out to knit the land together;

he knew the oilmen would work the opposite effect ("They ain't gonna come in and grade no roads, so the wind can blow me away").

Folsom correctly identifies ugliness as a basic quality in McMurtry's picture of Texas life, but it comes not as he would have us believe, from the "physical nature of the environment," which is actually neutral, but rather from human habitation. Thalia is ugly, but McMurtry portrays the town with the same restraint he exhibits in presenting the natural world. His most reliable technique is Lonnie's tone: ranch life might be monotonous, but at least it presses people together, directs their energies, and keeps them busy—when Lonnie speaks of Thalia, or other, larger towns, an unappeasable longing changes his voice. Yet Thalia offers nothing beyond the inevitable pool hall and all-night cafe, and two of the novel's finest "town" sequences detail, first, an adolescent night-out where nothing happens (adventure comes from their fantasies; they can't even get a fight started), and second, the final night of the annual rodeo—the biggest day on the social calendar—a mad whirl of drunken fights, banal honky-tonk tunes, and Lonnie's quiet anguish. As he gets closer to town, he leaves farther behind the close and (relatively speaking) satisfying human relationships of the ranch, which only increases his frustration. He looks to the city, to the distant places Homer's cowboy Jesse has been, and when the people he loves on the ranch disappear from his life—Halmea, the proud and understanding Negro cook who leaves after Hud rapes her; Jesse, released when the diseased Bannon herd is destroyed; Homer himself—his first impulse is to cross the great spaces that surround him and search for new people and good times. The reader recognizes, and Folsom has pointed out, that Lonnie views the adult, especially the urban, world with a romantic bias; Hud shakes that attitude just enough to leave Lonnie adrift—although in the final scene he is "tempted to do like Jesse once said: to lean back and let the truck take me as far as it was going," he suspects that such an escape won't bring him the satisfaction he once expected. Yet he knows that what lies behind offers him little. The spacious landscape which in stereotype acts as an oppressive influence, and which in Lonnie's occasional view separates him from life's real enjoyments, is also, ironically, an insulator. Lonnie's acceptance of that possibility leaves him in a true dilemma. The puzzled young man who at the book's end withdraws his savings and heads north, ultimate destination unknown, actually continues an initiation barely begun, and will learn some predictably hard lessons that may dwarf his Thalia-bred discontent. In Hud he has encountered real evil, but he still does not comprehend it fully; he ends his tale in a quiet daze, puzzled that "Hud seemed calm and fairly friendly, and he didn't act depressed at all." The truly pitiable fact is that when we leave him, Lonnie is a seventeen-year-old without a dream. And if the empty landscape becomes an analogue for his condition, it is because we make it so. Others, we know, lived well there.

McMurtry's distinguishing so completely between those living in harmony with the plains' natural rhythms, and the sordid, frantic world of violence, lust, and amorality Hud represents, may constitute overstatement. Homer, in his eighties, has passed the time of such excesses, though he admits to having seen another day: "I used to think [money] was all I was after, but I changed my mind." Lonnie is too young, too restless in the incipience of some of the drives from which the older Hud has made his life style. Yet even if the trio seems to represent the "ages of man" too systematically, they never become predominantly types. Homer, for example, maintains his individuality as a "contrary old bastard" (his own description). McMurtry's sentiment for the days of small ranches is more than balanced by his realism and the alternate focus upon town life.

The relative emphasis between ranch and town, so crucial in his fiction, goes far in explaining radical changes in the tactics of his next two novels, *Leaving Cheyenne* and *The Last Picture Show.* They sit on opposite ends of the Texas spectrum he introduced in *Horseman, Pass By,* the former a ranch novel, the latter a study of Thalia. Both are disappointing, for *Leaving Cheyenne* embodies too much of the sentiment, and *The Last Picture Show* too much of the distaste which, when mixed together in McMurtry's first novel, forced him to greater narrative caution and refinement than either of the following novels can match.

Leaving Cheyenne was born of what McMurtry called his special "interest in situations in which a person loves or is loved by more than one person. . . . I think, humanly, it's a very interesting question, how many people one can love." Depending upon what limitations one puts on that crucial term "love," the question might well be interesting, but the dangers of such exploitation in fiction are manifold. In this case, McMurtry's tendency to make characters represent vectors plagues the narrative. He emphasizes sexual love, and has his patently unselfish heroine Molly Taylor relating with three men; recognizing that his study must explore the psychological implications, he has each of the men represent a distinct "type"—for Eddie Taylor, the man Molly inexplicably marries, sex is a weapon; for Gideon Fry and Johnny McCloud (best friends from boyhood), it expresses affection, but whereas Johnny's free spirit allows him to enjoy it completely, Gid, whom Molly loves most, is bothered throughout his life by guilt. He can never, as she says, go "whole hog in love," so she refuses to marry him. Still, she bears Gid and Johnny each a son while Eddie stays conveniently away and finally dies in an oil-field accident. As though to prove that she is not simply a nymphomaniac or a mental case, McMurtry has her care for a mean and drunken father, and agonize in purest maternal fashion over her sons, both finally killed in World War II.

Even Hollywood's *Lovin' Molly* could not make the situation come alive. Because the ranch setting isolates the group, McMurtry can do little with them except have them go about their chores between couplings, forty years' worth. And because McMurtry shows such uncertainty in his psychological probings, it is impossible to take the novel seriously, though a Texas critic or two has tried. *Leaving Cheyenne* illustrates limitations both in a "just folks" approach to the rural West, and also in McMurtry's skills at writing problematical fiction.

The novel's three sections, first-person narratives by Gid, Molly, and Johnny, have a fatal sameness about them, an empty garrulousness signaling McMurtry's inability to establish the three minds as distinct, interesting, and worthy of our attention. Gid's opening lines capture the essential banality of the rest (one is never quite sure whether one is expected to laugh at the teller or the tale):

> When I woke up, Dad was standing by the bed shaking my foot. I opened my eyes, but he never stopped shaking it. He shook it like it was a fence post and he was testing it to see if it was in the ground solid enough. All my life that's the way he'd wake me up—I hated it like poison. Once I offered to set a glass of water by the bed, so he could pour that over me in the mornings and wake me up, but Dad wouldn't do it. I set the water out for him six or seven times, and he just let it sit and shook my foot anyway. Sometimes, though, if he was thirsty, he'd drink the water first.

Sometimes, too, one of them rises to such a line as "Sometimes you can't get around being lonesome for a while." So severely has McMurtry limited himself in these narrators, who, as far as we know, never read even a newspaper, that any note other than banality rings false, as when the cowboy Johnny, thinking of his dead friend, says, "Gid was off in the Great Perhaps." The absence of "thoughts," the narrow uniformity of experience, vocabulary, and expression (people "tremble like leaves," are "pretty as a picture," etc.) are not implausible, but still boring. Had McMurtry chosen to limit the span of time and narrate the same events from three points of view, the differences in the three individuals' attitudes toward love might have been emphasized into significance. As it is, Molly begins her section when Gid is forty-seven, and Johnny's final section covers events of later decades. I can find nothing about the respective periods that demands to be told by any of the narrators. Gid and Johnny go through life loving the same woman, remaining best of friends, and never, even by implication, revealing why they should be able to escape the savage, possessive impulses of that love. Explanations of a sort have obviously been planted in the story: Gid gets religion suddenly, and Johnny has little interest in marriage. What effect any of that has in real life upon the imperatives of male hormones is a question McMurtry must avoid.

The superficiality of the portraits, and the rather ineffective choice of the extended quotations initiating each new section, imply that *Leaving Cheyenne* was conceived and largely written before *Horseman, Pass By*. Its syrupy beginning, seeking to establish the close relationship between Gid and Johnny, reads like the archetypal First Novel. The rest moves clumsily and fitfully; at times, McMurtry's trio seem like antinarrators. Gid, for example, gives a single paragraph to relate his father's suicide and how he retrieved the body from a nearby pasture; Johnny tells how they raced over to a neighboring farm, grabbed a drowned boy from his mother's arms and brought breath back rolling him over a rain barrel, all in twelve lines. Ironically, words seem cheap to these people, and dramatic emphasis beyond them. Their low-key, long-suffering personalities make reader response equally weak. Where, one keeps asking, is the exploitation of human desire and its behavior? In the end, Molly has loved everyone, good and bad, as though conscious of the reader watching and determined that she can pull off the prodigious feat; now that all but she and Johnny are dead, none of it seems to have mattered much. Everyone has lost, and no one has learned much about love or anything else. The force within Molly and Gid that compels them to think of love in terms of singular possession, summarized in various lectures she gives him over the years, seems to answer the novel's central "question": we prefer to love one above all. Gid's inability to "go whole hog" forces Molly to marry another man simply because "[she] thought Eddie needed a wife the worst." Gid marries an equally unlikely person for an equally implausible reason. Occasionally, one catches sight of the puppet-showman's strings. If, however, the novel is meant as an ironic commentary on the mind-reducing cultural poverty of the North Central Texas plains, it becomes a classic case of human stagnation and boredom conveyed through boring and stagnant fiction. Lonnie Bannon's narrative, infinitely more refined, avoids so many of the misleads and limitations McMurtry forces upon himself here that it is difficult to believe *Leaving Cheyenne* came after it.

In any case, McMurtry clearly saw the slim possibilities remaining to be exploited in his vision of rural Texas, and came for a time to distrust the first-person mode because it reveals more sentiment than he is comfortable with (he has formally repudiated *Horseman, Pass By* as "a slight, confused, and sentimental first novel"). Self-criticism is usually a symptom of health for an artist; a Western novelist must be especially careful of sentimentality, and McMurtry, who relies heavily upon his own life and family for some of the substance and much of the emotion in his first novels, is understandably wary. His next two novels, *The Last Picture Show* and *Moving On*, accordingly depart from the subject and manner of the earlier works, but they illustrate two very important problems for McMurtry: 1) when he leaves the first-person mode, he has great difficulty maintaining coherence, and 2) the distance between sentimentality and cynicism (like love and hate) is not vast.

His ability as a storyteller is brilliantly testified to by *The Last Picture Show*, which focuses upon another parentless boy of seventeen and traces the same themes of sexual awakening, initiation to evil and absurdity, and loss of human companionship that McMurtry dealt with in Lonnie's story. Hollywood made an excellent film by faithfully reproducing the feeling in his opening line: "Sometimes Sonny felt like he was the only human creature in the town," a desolation similar to Lonnie's at the end of his novel. By retaining the full variety of vivid and energetic characters (which it failed to do in *Hud*), Hollywood kept the texture of McMurtry's tale and emphasized serious themes without eliminating their dark comedy.

McMurtry's decision to focus upon the town signals a change in his use of landscape; his desire in *The Last Picture Show* to become a social critic of small-town life leaves physical setting without an important function in his work. Furthermore, his manner of criticism excludes most of Thalia itself from the scene. His preoccupation is sex; we should assume, I take it, that what he presents to us comments metaphorically upon the quality of life in the general community. That physical setting and the town at large enter McMurtry's picture only to offer predictable effects—the land is desolate, isolating, depressing; the town illustrates bigotry and/or stupidity on a large scale—implies a shift in his interest to the purely popular, the exploitation of complex human problems for less-than-complex portraits. My reservations about this change come not from a bias against "popular culture," but from the obvious fact that McMurtry's quality has suffered. What he has written in the past seven or eight years has been too easy; his concern for pleasing the audience has engendered a disappointing carelessness in his work, so much so that I wonder what community of writers he works in, and whether there is anyone to read and seriously criticize him as he writes.

Nothing in McMurtry's sardonic view of Thalia demands the simplistic treatment he gives the town; he made the same point in *Horseman, Pass By*, without the excesses that characterize this novel. His tactic here is to combine the purely popular concern with the sex lives of Thalia's most adventuresome with his serious "invisible man" theme, presented through Sonny Crawford, the victim-hero. In theory, the two might mix, but in *The Last Picture Show* they don't, largely because McMurtry never convinces the reader that he values the "serious" above the "popular"—the latter is just too much fun. Although he displays sporadic sympathy for Sonny and Ruth Popper, the football coach's wife with whom Sonny has a long affair, and to some extent Sam the Lion and his retarded ward Billy, McMurtry confuses the realism of their story with the grotesque buffoonery and sideshow atmosphere of the rest of visible Thalia. The same adolescent qualities that make Sonny an object of his concern—especially the boy's sexual problems—are employed with greatest enthusiasm to make the rest of his friends maniacal masturbators, voyeurs, and sodomites.

The most pervasive and disturbing evidence that McMurtry has little interest in pursuing serious social criticism or psychological complexity is the norm and texture of the narrative itself. Perhaps the "invisible man" theme could have profited from the juxtaposition of sensitive, recognizably human characters and a townscape of frenetically sexed caricatures—the surreal metaphor might have worked. McMurtry expends considerable effort presenting Thalia in terms of stereotypes, but the narrative suggests that he considers the portrait something other than surreal. Through most of the novel, the norm of his language moves about so wildly that the teller often sounds like one of the caricatures (though not in a systematic way; the narrator does not "imitate" the voice of the person being described). Had these modulations been used to emphasize a variety of voices in the town, and to reinforce the themes McMurtry attaches to Sonny's story, the combination would have strengthened the novel.

Before the story has really begun, McMurtry's uncertainties with the omniscient point of view become apparent; the narrator seems to have no sense of direction, as though unsure of what to do with the characters once they have been drawn together. Within a single paragraph, for example, the focus might jump to three or four different consciousnesses. A sentence seemingly dedicated to one character will shift to another for no better reason than mere proximity. Scenes habitually have their development interrupted three or four times by extended "asides" (bits of history, anecdotes to illustrate a personality trait just mentioned, etc.); these diversions, uniformly pursuing the eccentric, have an annoying monotony. The result is a fragmented, jerky narrative; we are, it seems, at the mercy of association, though this lack of shape and flow does not finally justify itself by creating out of its wandering course either a sense of the variety of experience or a Shandian personality. McMurtry may have had such a posture in mind; his use of incidental names such as Mr. Wean (the timid home economics teacher at rival Paducah High), Bobby Sheen (a smooth seducer), Charlene Duggs (who lets Sonny fondle her breasts, but nothing else), Frank Fartley (owner of the bottled-gas works), and Lois and Jacy Farrow (almost all the men in the novel plough one or both) sounds very faintly like Sterne, but also hints at the imaginative level of the general narrative. Whenever McMurtry can exploit that sort of humor, he does so, whether or not he violates impressions previously established. It would seem, for example, that Thalia has some good athletes (so confident is the town that the football team will win the championship that they present Coach Popper with a new shotgun two weeks before the season ends; the next year, Thalia wins every game), but when basketball season arrives, McMurtry shifts the boys into his formula for caricature and includes a long account of Thalia's 121–14 loss at Paducah (a not unusual score)—with all the predictable effects: players knocked out against the walls or hit in the groin by malicious passes; biased officiating which allows the home team to block, tackle, and gouge.

The narrator emerges not as a voice with consistent position or attitude, but as three separate voices. There is the high-toned, to convey humor and condescension:

> The prospect of copulation with a blind heifer excited the younger boys almost to frenzy, but Duane and Sonny, being seniors, gave only tacit approval. . . . Sensible youths, growing up in Thalia, soon learned to make do with what there was, and in the course of their adolescence both boys had frequently had recourse to bovine outlets. At that, they were considered overfastidious by the farm youth of the area . . . .

And the low-toned, to capture the racy rhythms of street talk:

> She was nostalgic for days when the boys necked with her and wanted her desperately and didn't get her. That was better than actually screwing, somehow. When she got to college she could start screwing again, and there it would probably be altogether great. Fraternity boys were gentlemen and would fall right in love with her when she let them screw her.

Most common is a more subdued, ungracious, matter-of-fact style, though it, like the second example above, does not maintain a completely consistent norm. A single scene might employ all three voices describing the same characters: the "copulation" is also referred to as "screwing heifers," and one of the participants is seen "beating his member against a cold aluminum gate." Sonny gets up one night with an erection, "embarrassed by his own tumescence"; a little later he is described as "jacking off." McMurtry undercuts the seriousness of the Sonny–Ruth affair whenever a cute pun can be made: ". . . Sonny was really beginning to get in touch with Ruth . . ." or "The thought of Ruth popped into his mind. . . ." In the middle of a serious analysis of Ruth's suffering after Sonny stops seeing her, the narrator notes: "From time to time she tried playing with herself . . ." The variety of usage may add "color" to the account, but so unsystematically that the final effect is confusion. McMurtry's "social criticism" sounds in the end like cheap cynicism. The "invisible man" theme is something he comes back to periodically, but it never gets the serious treatment it demands. The crucial turn of the book's final scene, where Sonny returns in existential anguish to Ruth, concludes a movement from loneliness to involvement to lonely involvement that McMurtry has been uncertain with throughout. In a novel with the ironic inscription, "Lovingly dedicated to my home town," his creative energies have been directed toward presenting Thalia as a pitiable place where sex is the only available means of personal expression. The wasteland surroundings are somehow responsible, but he cannot capture their essence or explain their influence. Satisfied with merely showing the results, he never challenges himself to make the book out of the material he would like serious readers to think most important to him. The few "normal" people seem lifeless compared to the caricatures they move among; in the end, McMurtry doesn't demonstrate that they interest him as much as do the freaks.

With his first three novels, McMurtry answers the question of what he wishes to do with the Texas plains as raw material for fiction. All three contain the themes of male initiation, loss of loved ones, despair, and, to an increasing degree, sex. To make fiction out of a rural culture requires specific talents of an author, notably a touch for sensitive psychological portraits, for subtleties of growth, and for complexities of human relationships. These talents are, of course, essential to any serious writer, but their absence in rural stories is more obvious because less complex routines and a slower pace rule such scenes. McMurtry has not yet shown those talents. He tends to give more surface detail rather than probing deeper; since his Texas world offers, literally and figuratively, a severely limited amount of surface variation, he has understandably turned to sexual behavior as a major resource—it is the most obvious manifestation of psychology, and readers never tire of it.

McMurtry has also become increasingly influenced by his urban reading audience. His first two novels portray the life of ranch and small town with a clear effort to balance distaste for its limitations with recognition of the value of community, but *The Last Picture Show* seems to me a sudden turning to purest exploitation: he will tell the city people that all their myths about depraved country life are true. In doing so, he has become a popular writer, but I wonder what "truth" he seeks as an artist.

In *Moving On*, he brings his vision to the city and finds a new kind of anguish; it becomes apparent with this, the fourth novel, that though the settings may change, his view of life emphasizes a belief in the illusory nature of personal fulfillment—people do not progress, they move on. Although reviewer Martha Duffy complained that the novel has no "discernible direction," that "his books are constructed like tumbleweed" (presumably she meant that they move as the weed tumbles), McMurtry would surely defend those very qualities in *Moving On*. Consciously picaresque, it stops, not ends. Whether the novel can afford to be merely expansive and episodic is a question we will consider.

The picaresque structure does provide McMurtry with excellent opportunities to combine pictures of the rural and urban West into a single narrative. He makes the movement plausible because the prime mover, *pícaro* Jim Carpenter, is a rich dilettante afflicted with the ailment McMurtry finds endemic to young America: restlessness. First as a Kodak chronicler of the rodeo, then as a graduate student of literature in Houston, Carpenter runs himself and his wife Patsy through a gantlet of striking characters, rich and poor, Wild West and high society. McMurtry has many little stories to tell.

Moving On, an interesting novel because of its variety, finally suffers from an excess of that quality; it (and almost every important character except Patsy) seeks only diversity, and has only that to justify its movement. Patsy creates most of the tension by dragging her feet. At eight hundred pages, the book is about twice the length it should be; its very excesses tell something about McMurtry's problems in unifying his material into coherence, and his tendency to give more little stories instead of probing deeper into essential relationships. *Moving On* disguises that propensity better than *The Last Picture Show* or *Leaving Cheyenne*, because its narrative breaks in half (a term of emphasis, and to some extent sequence), one dealing with the rodeo world, the other with Houston. It reads like two separate but interfused novels. The problem is that they make the same effect, have the same organization, and feature the same cast of character types. Both halves are dominated by predatory males: Sonny Shanks, World Champion Cowboy, and William Duffin, English professor; both predators have a woman "accomplice" to attract Jim and reveal the instability of the Carpenter marriage (Eleanor Guthrie, Shanks's wealthy mistress, and Duffin's wife Lee); the rodeo and Houston sections each feature a sweet but eccentric married couple, the Tatums and the Hortons, respectively, and a true regional clown, Peewee Rankin and Dixie McCormack.

This diversity allows McMurtry to tell some good stories, especially in the early rodeo chapters, when Sonny Shanks dwarfs Jim and becomes a constant sexual threat to Patsy, a source of tension whether or not he is present. A fight scene in a low-life Houston bar, Peewee's favorite off-season hangout, is one of the funniest sequences I've ever read. In fact, those portions of the novel dealing with the rodeo group contain so much more force than the long English Department section, I wish McMurtry had been satisfied with three or four hundred pages and eliminated the Houston academic scene altogether. The graduate-school experience might be material to arouse some imaginations but McMurtry's failure to give it life (and his instinctive touch with the rodeo people) confirms what *The Last Picture Show* and *Leaving Cheyenne* implied about his creative temperament: he is not a novelist of manners; he finds his topics not in a positive, "realistic" vision, but rather from a strong reaction to themes which themselves have vast energy and mythic potential. Thus in Sonny Shanks's hyperglandularity he both exploits and spoofs the stereotype of cowboy virility, and also mocks the earliest literary tradition of the sexless six-gun hero; Peewee Rankin is Shanks's negative image. The rodeo scene, capturing the violence and transience of mythical Wild West cowboy life, is the kind of overstatement McMurtry handles best. When he applies his techniques to academe, the resulting eccentricities reveal nothing of the world they are meant to portray. Perhaps in America there are famous scholars like Duffin who move with their dissatisfied wives from one campus to another, seduction teams who separate students from the group the way Shanks would rope calves from a herd, and perhaps such scholars have developed come-ons like, "You're awfully pretty. Let's go out in the back yard and neck," and perhaps such methods work, but in all, it is not very interesting. When McMurtry published the first twenty-page section of the novel in *The Redneck Review* (1968), he claimed that it was the opening of a thousand-page novel; he came close to achieving his goal more by repetition than through the imperatives of his tale.

The two worlds of *Moving On* are valuable, however, in illustrating why McMurtry should seek "open" situations for his fiction, situations which provide much of their own movement. Rodeo life, for example, sweeps people along with such velocity that characteristic social encounters are short-lived, and he finds a richness there that allows him to leave the rodeo arena outside his narrative (except for the eerie scene where Shanks leaves Patsy calf-roped at midnight). Sport, hard enough to handle in fiction without the complications of cowboy myths, would be superfluous here. Unfortunately, the Houston college scene offers no such movement, and because McMurtry feels more confident with its routines, he spends a good deal of time describing them, though to little effect. Many times, he loses the reader's interest, and on occasion, the reader's confidence as well. Beyond mentioning the names of books and authors, and reporting in detached fashion the subjects of seminars and paper assignments, he seems at a loss. The few instances where he hazards comments upon literature in attempting to illustrate knowledge of it in his characters, he reveals both carelessness and his own limitations. For instance, he wishes to show that Jim and his few graduate-student friends have questionable aptitude for their chosen discipline, and so enlists Patsy as a foil. A voracious reader, she brings common-sense perceptiveness to literature and makes a mockery of the postures and formulaic thinking of the "professional students." Lightly handled, the contrast is effective, but he returns to it too often, and when he gets specific, it suffers. Early in the novel, for example, when he sets out to characterize her as a very bright young lady, she goes to the film version of *Lolita*, a book she has read three times and loves; she enjoys the movie less, and thinks afterward:

> One reason she was annoyed by it was because she had been no nymphet herself, no Lolita, when she was that age. She had been thin . . . and had had no bosom at all . . . The movie left her all the more convinced that as a teenager she had been a complete stick-in-the-mud.

So monumentally ignorant is she of the physical characteristics of nymphetry, its sexual attitudes and age limits, and so completely does this contradict the image McMurtry builds for her, that I suspect the mistake is her creator's. The scene is symptomatic of the absence of psychological clarity that plagues McMurtry's omniscient narratives, especially among the supposedly intelligent characters. He seems more comfortable demeaning his people and exhibiting their faults, and when he must present them seriously, he proceeds with less confidence and success. That more than anything else explains the sluggishness of the Houston sections; McMurtry's intelligent characters can always be identified by their use of language, but he does not seem to have sorted out for himself what qualities make the relationships of highly intelligent people truly distinct.

Thus he seeks to demonstrate that the settled academics and the rodeo followers represent the same banality, and to do so finds the lowest common denominator: sexual behavior, which also illustrates the deterioration of the Carpenter marriage and keeps the book moving. McMurtry might well have taken the advice of the psychiatrist who counsels the Carpenters, "Sex is not that important." All relationships in the novel are defined sexually; every character either has or most obviously does not have a sexual problem. His point is clearly that the people in Houston, like their country counterparts, make physical coupling a refuge, acting out their frustrations, illustrating the emptiness of their lives. Yet the artist cannot become obsessed with what obsesses his characters, and long before the end of this novel he has narrated sex so many times in the same discreet tone that none of the episodes has special impact. For example, at least twenty times McMurtry records that the woman gets up and puts on her bra and panties; the garments appear so often as to imply a fetish. Sex plainly becomes his refuge—he seems unable to reveal his characters' problems any other way (another reason why they lack complex inner lives). The pairing of characters between Houston and rodeo groups was clearly intended to underline the theme of community likeness; it strikes me as the same kind of formulaic approach he has Patsy demolish among the graduate students.

The Carpenters give the novel its unity, and the dissolution of their marriage gives it a feeling of progression, if that term can be applied to the scores of sex-initiated spats they have. As several reviewers have pointed out, McMurtry doesn't know himself why Patsy and Jim fall apart. In the end, when he focuses upon Patsy's trip to save her sister Miri from a mindless black dopehead, he consciously diverts our attention from the marriage issue, the implication being that continuity in life is an illusion, and conclusions artificial. Maybe so. But when McMurtry's eye begins falling predictably upon the wildest Haight-Ashbury grotesquerie (Hell's Angels girls hand-pumping their guys' penises in the park, etc.), the reader who has made his way through nearly eight hundred pages in hope of something more than formula vision suspects he has been had.

Moving On represents an artist out of control, without a vision worthy of the name. Perhaps by some abstruse metaphysical architectonics or regional loyalties one could demonstrate that a book so long should result in a question mark (small at that), yet to hold that it is more than an often attractive but superficially conceived and carelessly written novel is to ignore evidence on every page. For an author who can write so well to commit so many blunders means, I think, that we should question whether he wishes to be regarded as a serious Western novelist or a "pop" writer. In this example of omniscient narrative voice, there is no distinction made between "horse manure" and "horse shit," "genitals" and "balls," "empty his bladder" and "piss," nor between "just became a man" and "became just a man." His people can, at various times, be "thrilled to the core," or "strangely incongruous," go "unawakably to sleep," eat "an enormous unstomachable meal" or a warm "unhandleable" candy bar, and feel "slightly inimical" toward their fellows. Worse still, McMurtry's penchant for repetition infects his style at the most basic level:

> a lecture by a famous lecturer,
> Jim had to teach a class for a friend who taught a class,
> wash the pan of oatmeal before the oatmeal stiffened,
> to wipe up spit-ups,
> sipped sly sips,
> a huge pile of papers and magazines piled . . .
> neither came or even came close to coming,
> he began to drive in his memory all the drives he had driven with Patsy.

His prose, especially in this novel, is full of Whooery, Whichery, and Thatery, padded in a host of careless ways and repeatedly betrays or confuses meaning in ill-considered descriptions such as "She felt as cool and unpassionate as if she had become a virgin again," or "He had never touched Clara, though he had looked up her dress a time or two at boring points in the Chaucer seminar. . . ." This breakdown in language is a further hint that McMurtry, having begun a story heavily dependent upon the complexity of its psychological portraits, finds himself in uncongenial surroundings. A sentence like "Patsy pointed out in the wittiest possible terms" characterizes his difficulty—he is forced to name a wide range of attributes he cannot dramatize. Personalities like Sonny Shanks and the host of other eccentrics live because they derive force from their very mysteriousness; the novel does not depend upon them for anything but immediate effects. Patsy and Jim sometimes come alive as well, but in general they, like Peewee Rankin or Eleanor Guthrie or Lee Duffin, repeat themselves over and over, for a single effect. The novel's last lines seem an abdication.

By the appearance of his fifth novel, *All My Friends Are Going to Be Strangers*, the limits of McMurtry's vision have been established. His eye watches for the eccentric details, especially in material related to social, sexual, or Western myths (the *Library Journal* called it "a very popular sort of corn,"), and his pen puts them down in episodic narratives. In *All My Friends*, he returns to the lode: we find his young novelist, Danny Deck, down and out (spiritually rather than financially) in Houston, San Francisco, Hollywood, and what is left of the Wild West. Once again, McMurtry relies upon personal experience, as in *Horseman, Pass By* and *Leaving Cheyenne*, to provide milieu, movement, and emotional tone. He seems intent upon exploiting this contemporary "Western experience" with the vision but not the stylistic grace Philip Roth has used with middle-class Jewish life; Danny Deck sells his first novel to Hollywood, and leaves for California to write a second—McMurtry knows that, taken together, Texas and California provide a greater variety of craziness than any artist could use.

His biggest problem is lack of a consistent comic touch; he tends to overstate his characterizations, thus denying himself overstatement as tactic of surprise (Danny's beating at the hands of two Texas Rangers being a good example). Because he relies so heavily upon the eccentric to make his fiction move, the extra effort of a really comic scene leaves visible marks of strain, the terminal symptom of comedians. Such is the case in Danny's brief confrontation with a rural gas-station attendant:

> "You oughtn't to sass around and use your goddam profanity with me," he said. Suddenly he hunched over, made a fierce face, and gave the air a hard karate chop.
>
> "See that?" he said. "I just finished a karate class, up in Midland. These hands is lethal weapons. I'd about as soon give a curly-headed little fart like you a chop or two, for practice. Hai! Karate!"
>
> . . . . He looked forty, and foolish. I shook my hair at him and smote the air once or twice, for effect.
>
> "Hai!" I said. "Tire tool!"
>
> "Let me get them windshields for you," the man said.

Having met a host of fools before this one, the reader is unlikely to be doubled over by the "goddam profanity" gambit.

McMurtry apparently believes that large effects can be got from merely overstating the sexual, that the technique carries its own insurance, its sensationalism attracting readers and also serving as an ironic and devastating attack upon our preoccupation with sex. Two of the novel's most important women introduce themselves with the lines, "He wanted me to give him a blow job," and "Hi. . . . Does your wife like cunnilingus?" Danny, of course, has serious sex problems with both his wife and the girl he wants to live with. To make this procession seem inevitable, McMurtry creates in Danny Deck an energetic naïf who meets experience with wide-eyed wonder and narrates it straight. His peculiar combination of initiative and innocence explains the kinds of people he draws to him, but his narrative neither directly nor by implication supplies the coherence of an intelligent mind coming to terms with a theme worth considering. "Moving on" has become a necessity.

Evidence in this novel suggests that McMurtry has not from the beginning changed his ideas about the physical Texas landscape, but only rejected it as a valuable resource as he has drifted away from the realism of his early fiction. Occasionally, his feeling for the land appears, as in the *Moving On* sequences at old Roger Waggoner's ranch, quiet interludes away from Houston and the rodeo. He shows, too, that he can employ such scenes for thematic effect: when Patsy invites her lover Hank Morgan to stay with her at the ranch, its association with Roger's simple and honest life style nicely emphasizes her feelings of dishonesty and self-betrayal. Anyone familiar with McMurtry's earlier fiction will recognize that Danny Deck speaks not only for himself when, returning home after a year's writing by San Francisco Bay (as McMurtry did himself), he says,

> It was the sky that was Texas, the sky that welcomed me back. The land I didn't care for all that much—it was bleak and monotonous and full of ugly little towns. The sky was what I had been missing . . . It had such depth and such spaciousness and such incredible compass, it took so much in and circled with such a tremendous generous space, that it was impossible not to feel more intensely with it above you.

Unfortunately, fiction comes from the ground and the ugly little (and big) towns, and McMurtry's distaste for them and much of their population emerges larger than ever in subsequent scenes, especially Danny's visit to the ranch of his Uncle L, the Hacienda of the Bitter Waters.

Nowhere else in McMurtry's fiction is there wilder grotesquerie or vituperation. Uncle L at ninety-two stands straight and mean as the mockery of all the qualities that made Homer Bannon a hero to his grandson. He punches holes in his land "because he hated the earth and wanted to get in as many licks at it as he could, before he died." There is no mystique about his herds, either ("he kept an assortment of animals he planned to eat"). He raises goats, pigs, buffalo, guinea hens, antelope, and camels, but always wanted an ostrich ranch and a few giraffes. He is a stubborn, crazy anachronism, living in this century but largely oblivious to it, squatting in a camp beside the twenty-eight-room ranch house, driving his car across country as though it were a horse, his attention always directed to the past. Every night he and his friend Lorenzo light a signal fire and sit by it, waiting for Zapata to return ("Uncle L actually kept a sack of gold in the jeep in case Zapata needed money"). The manifold stupidities finally sicken even Danny Deck, and he notes: "The Hacienda of the Bitter Waters wasn't the Old West I liked to believe in—it was the bitter end of something." He had come with such enthusiasm and fond memories; to McMurtry it clearly represents the contrast between the essences and the myths we perpetuate about the West—his narrator admits that Uncle L has achieved self-reliance and a kind of timelessness, but also concludes that he is a "sonofabitch."

The Hacienda section shows considerable imagination in its attempt to dramatize McMurtry's antimythical attitudes, yet I wonder at his insistence on overstatement. What purpose, except distraction, does it serve to have a crazed Mexican ranch hand applying his erections to a posthole, Uncle L's camels, the truck's "gas hole" ("The other vaqueros were outraged at seeing a pickup fucked. To them it was unpardonable license")—anything, it would seem, for a joke?

McMurtry begins with the archetypal odyssey theme, the venture-and-return structure, and in doing so has many of his largest strategies set for him; his concern, then, is in the sequence of events and the development of character. Yet the result has no "intellectual resonance," little psychological complexity (for example, no one ever has the slightest idea what motivates Danny's wife Sally, who quietly disappears into a maternity ward); as Ruth Prigozy noted in *Commonweal*, "Although McMurtry catches just about the whole contemporary scene, he doesn't seem to know what to do with his [material]." In the end, he implies that experience smashes the romantic eagerness Danny Deck brings to it. The last scene, a bit of lowgrade John Barth, where Danny acts out his suicidal urge in the Rio Grande, attempts what is by now almost a cliché in our fiction of despair; somehow, its choppy sentences and talkative tone seem out of place:

> . . . the river flowed down to me. I was so glad. I waded deeper. Such a wonderful thing to flow. I wanted to so badly. It was all I had ever wanted to learn. . . . Jill was gone.

Presumably, Danny does not, at least this time, kill himself; we are, after all, reading his narrative. His symbolic drowning of his second novel and the appearance of this personal tale make the final scene one of release not from life, but into a new awareness of self-limitations. Even personal defeat is worth telling. The Rio Grande experience may be the "death" of a novelist, and its narrative the final statement of a sobered, beaten man. We know from Emma Horton in *Moving On* that his car was found, but that he remains missing; unlike Sonny Crawford, Danny cannot even maintain a superficial affair to keep himself from invisibility. I wish only that McMurtry had found a different world to move him through; his concentration upon the "shocking" and perverse seems to me akin to the sentimentality he criticized in *Horseman, Pass By;* both are sins of excess.

McMurtry must decide whether he wishes to be a serious writer or an exploiter of methods others have used better, notably absurdism and black humor. His last three novels have only pretended at meaning; their organization shows his tendency to dodge the responsibility of developing the serious themes they introduce. Danny Deck, in the agony of composing his second novel, laments that he has weaker capacities for anlaysis of life's raw data than he would like. Reading *In a Narrow Grave*, McMurtry's collected essays on Texas, confirms what his fiction implies: social criticism and analysis of large public trends are not his forte, either. Many of the pieces, especially "Eros in Archer County," "A Handful of Roses," and "A Look at the Lost Frontier," reveal embarrassingly superficial thought along with an overabundance of detail and an absence of synthesis. Thomas Landess, his most perceptive critic, called the collection "disappointing"; his justification relates to McMurtry's uncertain course as a novelist: "The heart is McMurtry's true country, and when he strays far from it he usually winds up in trouble." His fiction has contained very few people he cares deeply about, and even they have received something less than his full creative attention as he continues to pursue his reactions against various myths, delusions, and strange life styles, victimized by the very qualities he speaks against because they distract him from the matter of the heart which he handled so well in his first novel. One thinks of Faulkner's or Reynolds Price's ability to create without idealization or condescension rural characters of sensitivity and enduring dimensions. The common folk in McMurtry's later fiction come alive only to exemplify viciousness or simplemindedness. Since the show must go on, he parades the freaks before us.

One irate Dallas reader wrote to the *Atlantic Monthly* editors, placing the Texas of McMurtry's mind, "about five coon-ass miles southwest of reality," a judgment that would be merely humorous had McMurtry shown he possesses the delicate satirical touch his recent fictional strategies require. McMurtry writes that he is "tired of dealing creatively with the kind of mental and emotive inarticulateness that [he] found in Texas," where "drivers are complete solipsists," where the major university cannot "claim a single first-rate artistic talent, in any art," where "informed conversation is simply too hard to get." In general, his essays illustrate a simplistic, puritanical disillusionment he partially hides beneath the attractive flippancy of his fiction. As though he cannot rid himself of the puritanical ghost of Homer Bannon.

Faulkner reportedly said that in order to create, a writer must hate his region as he does his wife. McMurtry certainly possesses the detachment, but when he pulled off that regional-writer sweatshirt, his rejection was something like divorce. After all, the self-deprecating-regional-writer is a pose whose irony means self-protection, too. McMurtry has in a sense "made it" in Washington, D. C.; he no longer can use the irony, and out of his apparent security have come the overzealous attempts to bury the regional image by, of all things, attacking the region. Perhaps the move East, which McMurtry regards as the essential journey for artists of the plains, will provide him with a new vision. Perhaps it will merely supply a new cast of eccentrics. At any rate, the strange case of Larry McMurtry is still to be resolved.

Bibliography

Folsom, James K. "*Shane* and *Hud*: Two Stories in Search of a Medium." *WHR*, 24 (1970), 359–72.

Landess, Thomas. *Larry McMurtry* (pamphlet). Austin, Tex.: Steck-Vaughn, 1969.

McMurtry, Larry. *All My Friends Are Going to be Strangers*. New York: Simon and Schuster, 1972.

———. *Horseman, Pass By*. New York: Harper, 1961.

———. *In a Narrow Grave: Essays on Texas*. Austin, Tex.: Encino Press, 1968.

———. *The Last Picture Show*. New York: Dial Press, 1966.

———. *Leaving Cheyenne.* New York: Harper & Row, 1963.

———. *Moving On.* New York: Simon and Schuster, 1970.

———. "The Texas Moon, and Elsewhere." *Atlantic Monthly*, March 1975, pp. 29–36.

Rev. of *All My Friends Are Going to be Strangers. Library Journal*, 15 Feb. 1972, p. 699.

The Rise of Minority Western Fiction

Words and Place: A Reading of [N. Scott Momaday's] *House Made of Dawn*

Lawrence J. Evers*

> In order to consider seriously the meaning of language and literature, we must consider first the meanings of the oral tradition.[1]

I

Native American oral traditions are not monolithic, nor are the traditions with which Momaday works in *House Made of Dawn*—Kiowa, Navajo, and Towan Pueblo.[2] Yet there are, he suggests, "common denominators."[3] Two of the most important of these are the native American's relation to the land and his regard for language.

By imagining who and what they are in relation to particular landscapes, cultures and individual members of cultures form a close relation with those landscapes. Following D. H. Lawrence and others, Momaday terms this a "sense of place."[4] A sense of place derives from the perception of a culturally imposed symbolic order on a particular physical topography. A superb delineation of one such symbolic order is offered by Tewa anthropologist Alfonso Ortiz in his study *The Tewa World* from which the following prayer is taken:

> Within and around the earth, within and around the hills, within and around the mountains, your authority returns to you.[5]

The Tewa singer finds in the landscape which surrounds him validation for his own song, and that particular topography becomes a cultural landscape, at once physical and symbolic. Like Ko-sahn, Momaday's grandmother, the native American draws from it "strength enough to hold still against all the forces of chance and disorder."[6]

The manner in which cultural landscapes are created interests Momaday, and the whole of his book *The Way to Rainy Mountain* may be seen as an account of that process.[7] During their migration journey the

* *WAL*, 11 (1977), 297–320.

Kiowa people "dared to imagine and determine who they were. . . . The journey recalled is among other things the revelation of one way in which these traditions are conceived, developed, and interfused in the human mind."[8] The Kiowa journey, like that recounted in emergence narratives of other tribes, may be seen as a movement from chaos to order, from discord to harmony. In this emergence the landscape plays a crucial role, for cultural landscapes are created by the imaginative interaction of societies of men and particular geographies.

In the Navajo emergence narrative, for example, First Man and First Woman accompanied by Coyote and other actors from the animal world journey upward through four underworlds into the present Fifth World.[9] The journey advances in a series of movements from chaos to order, and each movement takes the People toward greater social and symbolic definition. The cloud pillars of the First World defined only by color and direction become in the Fifth World the sacred mountains of the four directions, the most important coordinates in an intricate cultural geography. As with the Tewa and the Kiowa, that cultural landscape symbolizes the Navajo conception of order, the endpoint of their emergence journey. Through the emergence journey, a collective imaginative endeavor, the Navajos determined who and what they were in relation to the land.

The extraordinary interest in geography exhibited in Navajo oral literature then may be seen as an effort to evoke harmony in those narratives by reference to the symbolic landscape of the present world.[10] Significantly, a major test theme in Navajo oral literature requires identification of culturally important geographic features. Consider the Sun's test of the Hero Twins in one of the final episodes in the emergence narrative:

> He asked them to identify various places all over the surface of the earth. He asked, "Where is your home?" The boys knew where their home was. They pointed out Huerfano Mountain and said that was where they lived. The Sun next asked, "What mountain is that in the East?"
>
> "That's *Sis Naajini* (Blanca Peak)," replied the boys.
>
> "What mountain is down here below us?"
>
> "That's *Tsoodzi* (Mount Taylor)," said the boys.
>
> "What mountain is that in the West?"
>
> "That's *Dook'o'oosíid* (San Francisco Peak)."
>
> "Now, what mountain is that over in the north?"
>
> "Those are the *Dibé Nitsaa* (La Plata Mountains)."
>
> Because all the boys' answers were correct, the Sun said goodby to them as they were lowered down to earth at the place called *Tó Sidoh* (Hot Springs).[11]

Through their knowledge of the Navajo cultural landscape the Twins proved who and what they were to the Sun.

The pattern of the emergence narrative—a journey toward order symbolized by a cultural landscape—is repeated in Navajo chantway rituals. A patient requires a chantway ritual when his life is in some way out of order or harmony. In order for that harmony to be restored he must be taken through a ritual re-emergence journey paralleling that of the People. It is important to note the role of the singer and his ritual song here, for without songs there can be no cure or restoration of order.[12] Through the power of the chanter's words the patient's life is brought under ritual control, and he is cured.

We come round, then, to another of the "common denominators" Momaday finds in oral traditions: attitude toward language. Of Kiowa oral tradition Momaday writes: "A word has power in and of itself. It comes from nothing into sound and meaning; it gives origin to all things."[13] It is this concept, remarkably like one text version of the Navajo origin giving "One Word" as the name of the original state of the universe, which forms the center of Tosamah's sermon on St. John's gospel in the novel.[14] But more germane to our discussion of oral tradition generally is the related notion that "by means of words can a man deal with the world on equal terms."[15] It is only through words that a man is able to express his relation to place. Indeed, it is only through shared words or ritual that symbolic landscapes are able to exist. So it is that the Tewa singer, the Navajo chanter, and the Kiowa "man of words" preserve their communities through their story and song. Without them there would be no community. One contemporary Navajo medicine man suggests that loss of ceremonial words will signal the end of the world: "The medicine men who have knowledge in the Blessing Way (*Hozho ji*) will all evidently be lost. The words to the song will vanish from their memory, and they will not know how to begin to sing."[16]

In this context we can better appreciate Abel's dilemma in *House Made of Dawn*. As Momaday suggests: "One of the most tragic things about Abel, as I think of him, is his inability to express himself. He is in some ways a man without a voice. . . . So I think of him as having been removed from oral tradition."[17]

II

House Made of Dawn opens and closes with the formulaic words which enclose all Jemez pueblo tales—*dypaloh* and *qtsedaba*, placing it consciously in that oral tradition.[18] As many oral narratives, the novel is shaped around a movement from discord to harmony and is structurally and thematically cyclic. The prologue is dominated by the race, a central theme in the novel as Momaday has suggested:

> I see [*House Made of Dawn*] as a circle. It ends where it begins and it's informed with a kind of thread that runs through it and holds everything together. The book itself is a race. It focuses upon the race, that's the thing that does hold it all together. But it's a constant repetition of things too.[19]

Parsons tells us that racing is a conspicuous feature of Jemez ceremonialism.[20] The winter race Abel runs in the prologue and at the end of the novel is the first race in the Jemez ceremonial season, an appropriate ceremonial beginning. But the race itself may be seen as a journey, a re-emergence journey analogous to that mentioned in connection with Navajo and Kiowa oral tradition. Indeed, the language echoes a Navajo re-emergence song sung in the Night Chant, from which the title of the book is taken.[21]

These journey and emergence themes begin to unfold in the following scene as Francisco goes in his wagon to meet the bus returning Abel to Walatowa after WW II. The wagon road on which he rides is parallel to the modern highway on which Abel rides. The two roads serve as familiar metaphors for the conflicting paths Abel follows in the novel, and Momaday reinforces the conflict by parallel auditory motifs as well. As the wagon road excites in Francisco memories of his own race "for good hunting and harvests," he sings good sounds of harmony and balance.[22] At the same time the recurrent whine of tires on the highway is constantly in the background until "he heard the sharp wheeze of the brakes as the big bus rolled to a stop in front of the gas pump. . ." (p. 13). The re-emergence theme is suggested in the passage by the presence of the reed trap (p. 10)—recalling the reed of emergence, and the fact that Abel returns "ill" (p. 13).[23] He is drunk, of course, but he is also ill, out of balance, in the manner of a patient in a Navajo chantway.

Abel's geneaology, the nature of his illness, and its relation to the auditory motifs mentioned above are further defined in the seven fragments of memory he experiences as he walks above the Cañon de San Diego in the first dawn following his return. At the same time these fragments establish a context for Abel's two prominent encounters in Part I with Angela Grace S. John and with the albino Juan Reyes Fragua.

Abel's genealogy is complicated. He did not know who his father was. "His father was a Navajo, they said, or a Sia, or an Isleta, an outsider anyway," which made Abel "somehow foreign and strange" (p. 15). The ties Abel does have to Walatowa are through his mother whose father, Francisco—both sacristan and kiva participant—is the illegitimate son of the consumptive priest Fray Nicholas V. (p. 184). Through Francisco, Abel is a direct descendant of the Bahkyush, a group of Towan-speaking pueblos who immigrated to Jemez in the mid-nineteenth century.[24] He is a "direct [descendant] of those men and women who had made that journey along the edge of oblivion" (p. 19), an experience which gave them a "tragic sense." Abel, as his Bahkyush ancestors, is on just such a "journey along the edge of oblivion" in the novel.

Abel's journey in Part I is a journey of return to Walatowa and his illness is most explicitly related to a WW II experience. At the end of his seven memory fragments in the first dawn of his return Abel recalls:

> This—everything in advance of his going—he could remember whole and in detail. It was the recent past, the interventions of days and years without meaning, of awful calm and collision, time always immediate and confused, that he could not put together in his mind (p. 25).

In the confusion of war among soldiers who recognized him only as a "chief" speaking in "Sioux or Algonquin or something" (p. 108), Abel lost both the sense of place which characterized his tribal culture and the very community which supports the sense of place. "He didn't know where he was, and he was alone" (p. 26). Incredibly, he doesn't even recognize the earth: "He reached for something, but he had no notion of what it was; his hand closed upon the earth and the cold, wet leaves" (p. 26).

Mechanical sounds are associated with Abel's disorientation. The "low and incessant" (p. 26) sound of the tank descending upon him reaches back in the novel to the "slow whine of tires" Francisco hears on the highway and looks ahead to the sound of Angela's car intruding on his vision in the first dawn above the valley as it creeps along the same highway toward the Jemez church (p. 27). These are the same mechanical sounds Abel tried "desperately to take into account" as the bus took him away to the war—again on the same highway (p. 25). They are the sounds that reminded him as he left the pueblo to go to war that "the town and the valley and the hills" could no longer center him, that he was now "centered upon himself" (p. 25).

That Angela Grace St. John, the pregnant wife of a Los Angeles physician who comes to Walatowa seeking a cure for her own ailments, will become an obstacle in Abel's re-emergence journey is first suggested by the extensive auditory motifs of Part I. Yet her perceptions of his problems and of the Indian world generally have earned the sympathy of some readers.[25] Perhaps her most seductive perception is that of the significance of the corn dancers at Cochiti Pueblo:

> Their eyes were held upon some vision out of range, something away in the end of distance, some reality that she did not know, or even suspect. What was it that they saw? Probably they saw nothing after all. . . . nothing at all. But then that was the trick, wasn't it? To see nothing at all, . . . nothing in the absolute. To see beyond the landscape, beyond every shape and shadow and color, *that* was to see nothing. That was to be free and finished, complete, spiritual. . . . To say "beyond the mountain," and to mean it, to mean, simply, beyond everything for which the mountain stands of which it signifies the being (pp. 37–38).

As persuasive as Angela's interpretation of the Cochiti dancers may seem, it is finally a denial of the value of the landscape which the novel celebrates. Angela's assumption that the Cochiti dancers possess a kind of Hindu metaphysics which rejects phenomena for noumena is a projection of her own desires to reject the flesh.[26] Her attitude toward the land is of a piece with her attitude toward her own body: "she could think of nothing more vile and obscene than the raw flesh and blood of her body, the raveled veins and the gore upon her bones" (p. 36). We become almost immediately aware of the implications of that denial she craves in the following two scenes: the *corre de gaio* and Abel's second reflection on the Cañon de San Diego.

We view the *corre de gaio* through Angela who again projects feelings about her own existence on the ceremony. For Angela the ceremony like herself is "so empty of meaning . . . and yet so full of appearance" (p. 43). Her final impression of the ceremony is sexual. She senses some "unnatural thing" in it and "an old fascination returned upon her" (p. 43). Later she remarks of the ceremony: "Like this, her body had been left to recover without her when once and for the first time, having wept, she had lain with a man" (p. 45). In the albino's triumph and Abel's failure at the *corre de gaio* she finds sexual pleasure.

The etiological legend of Santiago (St. James) and the rooster is told by Fr. Olguin appropriately enough for his "instinctive demand upon all histories to be fabulous" (p. 68).[27] The legend explains the ceremonial game which follows in the novel. Just as the sacrifice of the rooster by Santiago produced cultivated plants and domesticated animals for the Pueblo people, so too does ritual re-enactment of the sacrifice promote fertility at Walatowa. While ethnographers suggest that the *corre de gaio* is of relatively minor ceremonial importance in Pueblo societies, in the context of the novel the rooster pull affords Abel his first opportunity to re-enter the ceremonial functions of the village.[28] It is, we are told, the first occasion on which he has taken off his uniform. Though the ceremony itself seems efficacious, as rain follows in the novel, Abel is "too rigid" and "too careful" (p. 42) at the game and fails miserably.[29]

Abel's failure at the rooster pull demonstrates his inability to reenter the ceremonial life of the village, as he realizes in his second reflection at dawn, July 28, 1945. The section opens with an explicit statement of the relation of the emergence journey and the landscape: "The canyon is a ladder to the plain" (p. 54), and is followed by a description of the ordered and harmonious existence of life in that landscape. Each form of life has its proper space and function in the landscape, and by nature of that relation is said to have "tenure in the land" (p. 56). Similarly, "man came down the ladder to the plain a long time ago. It was a slow migration . . ." (p. 56). Like the emergence journeys of the Kiowa and the Navajo mentioned earlier, the migration of the people of Walatowa led to an ordered relation to place which they express in their ceremonial life. As Abel walks in this landscape in the dawn he is estranged from the town and the land as well. "His return to the town had been a failure" (pp. 56–7) he realizes because he is no longer attuned to its rhythms. He has no words to express his relation to the place. He is "not dumb," but "inarticulate" (p. 57).

Despite his inarticulateness, the rhythm and words are still there "like memory, in the reach of his hearing" (p. 57). We recall that on July 21, seven days before, "for a moment everything was all right with him" (p. 32). Here however;

> He was alone, and he wanted to make a song out of the colored canyon, the way the women of Torreón made songs upon their looms out of colored yarn, but he had not got the right words together. It would have been a creation song; he would have sung lowly of the first world, of fire and flood, and of the emergence of dawn from the hills (p. 57).

Abel is at this point vaguely conscious of what he needs to be cured. He needs a re-emergence. He needs words, ceremonial words, which express his relation to the cultural landscape in which he stands. He needs to feel with the Tewa singer quoted earlier his authority return to him. But here out of harmony with himself and his community he needs most of all the kind of re-emergence journey offered in a Navajo chantway.

Significantly, the passage closes, as did the dawn walk of July 21, with an emblem of Angela St. John intruding on Abel's vision: "the high white walls of the Benevides house" (p. 58). The house itself is another symbol of Angela's denial of the land or more particularly the landscape of the Cañon de San Diego. [30] In contrast to Francisco and the other native residents of Walatowa who measure space and time by reference to the eastern rim of the canyon, Angela measures hers in relation to this "high, white house":

> She would know the arrangement of her days and hours in the upstairs and down, and they would be for her the proof of her being and having been (p. 53).

His re-entry into the village spoiled, Abel turns not to the ceremonial structure of the pueblo for support but to Angela. And it is the Benevides house, not the land, which provides "the wings and the stage" for their affair (p. 53). Abel's first sexual encounter with Angela is juxtaposed in the novel with Francisco's encounter with the albino witch in his cornfield. Indeed, Angela, who "keened" to the unnatural qualities of the albino during the *corre de gaio*, echoes the auditory symbols of evil mentioned earlier. Just as Nicolas *teah-whau* "screamed" at him (p. 15), and the moan of the wind in the rocks (p. 16) frightened him earlier, as Angela and Abel make love "she wanted to scream" and is later "moaning softly" (p. 62).[31]

Earlier in his life Abel found physical regeneration through a sexual experience with Fat Josie (pp. 93, 106–7). His affair with Angela has just the opposite effect. Lying physically broken on the beach in Part II Abel reflects:

> He had loved his body. It had been hard and quick and beautiful; it had been useful, quickly and surely responsive to his mind and will. . . . His body, like his mind, had turned on him; it was his enemy (p. 93).

The following couplet in the text implicates Angela in this alienation:

> Angela put her white hands to his body.
> Abel put his hands to her white body (p. 94).

Later Abel tells Benally that "she [Angela] was going to help him get a job and go away from the reservation, but then he got himself in trouble" (p. 161). That "trouble" derives in part from Abel's separation from his land.

Auditory symbols follow Abel directly from his affair with Angela to the climactic scene of Part I, the killing of the albino. Just before the murder the albino laughs "a strange, inhuman cry" (p. 77). Like the sound of Nicolas *teah-whau* it is "an old woman's laugh" that issues from a "great, evil mouth" (p. 77). At the very scene of the murder the only sound that breaks the silence is "the moan of the wind in the wires" (p. 77).

That Abel regards the albino as evil, as a witch (*sawah*), is clear enough even without the explicit statements of Father Olguin, Tosamah, and Benally later (pp. 94–5, 136–7). Moreover, it is clear at the time of the murder that Abel regards the albino as a snake. He feels "the scales of the lips and the hot slippery point of the tongue, writhing" (p. 78). But that Abel is "acting entirely within the Indian tradition" when he kills the albino is wrong.[32]

Abel's compulsion to eradicate the albino-snake reveals an attitude toward evil more akin to the Christian attitude of Nicolas V.: "that Serpent which even is the One our most ancient enemy" (p. 50). The murder scene is rife with Christian overtones. The killing takes place beneath a telegraph pole which "leaned upon the black sky" (p. 77); during the act "the white hands still lay upon him as if in benediction" (p. 78); and after the albino's death, "Abel knelt" and noticed "the dark nails of the hand seemed a string of great black beads" (p. 79). Abel appears to kill the albino then as a frustrated response to the White Man and Christianity, but he does so more in accordance with Anglo tradition than Indian tradition. Indeed, he has been trained in the Army to be a killer.

We recall here that the murder takes place squarely in the middle of the fiesta of Porcingula, the patroness of Walatowa, and that a central part of the ceremony on that feast is a ritual confrontation between the Pecos bull and the "black-faced children, who were the invaders" (p. 73). Parsons describes the bull-baiting at Jemez during the fiesta of Porcingula, August 1, 1922, as follows:

> An hour later, "the Pecos bull is out," I am told and hasten to the Middle. There the bull-mask is out playing, with a following of about a dozen males, four or five quite young boys. They are caricaturing Whites, their faces and hands painted white; one wears a false mustache, another a beard of blond hair. "U.S.A." is chalked on the back of their coat or a cross within a circle. . . . They shout and cry out, "What's the matter with you boy?" or more constantly "*Muchacho! Muchacho!*"
>
> . . . . . .
>
> The bull antics are renewed, this time with attempts of his baiters to lassoo. Finally they succeed in dragging him in front of their house, where he breaks

> away again, to be caught again and dragged into the house. From the house a bugler steps out and plays "Wedding Bells" and rag-time tunes for the bull-baiters to dance to in couples, "modern dances," ending up in a tumble. Two by two, in their brown habit and sandalled feet, four of the Franciscan Fathers pass by. It grows dark, the bugler plays "taps" and this burlesque, reaching from the Conquistadores to the Great War, is over for the night.[33]

The very day then that Abel kills the albino the community from which he is estranged could have provided him with a way of ritually confronting the white man. Had his return not been a failure, he might have borne his agony, as Francisco had "twice or three times" (p. 76), by taking the part of the bull. "It was a hard thing," Francisco tells us, "to be the bull, for there was a primitive agony to it, and it was a kind of victim, an object of ridicule and hatred" (p. 75). Hard as that agony was, Abel as Francisco before him might have borne it with the support of his community. Separated from that community, he acts individually against evil and kills the white man.

Momaday forces us to see the murder as more complicated and subtle in motivation despite Benally's sympathetic reflections on the realities of witchery (p. 137), Tosamah's reference to the murder as a legal conundrum (p. 136), and Abel's own statement that the murder was "not a complicated thing" (p. 95). Death has not been a simple thing for Abel to cope with earlier in the novel, as shown by his emotional reactions to the deaths of the doe (pp. 16–7), the rabbit (p. 22), the eagle (pp. 24–5), as well as the deaths of his brother Vidal and his mother. More to the point is the fact that the White Man Abel kills is, in fact, a white Indian, an albino. He is the White Man in the Indian; perhaps even the White Man in Abel himself. When Abel kills the albino, in a real sense he kills a part of himself and his culture which he can no longer recognize and control. That that part should take the shape of a snake in his confused mind is horribly appropriate given the long association of the Devil and the snake in Christian tradition (cf. Fray Nicolas V.) and the subsequent Puritan identification of the American Indians as demonic snakes and witches in so much of early American literature.[34] In orthodox Pueblo belief the snake and the powers with which it is associated are accepted as a necessary part of the cosmic order: "The Hebrew view of the serpent as the embodiment of unmitigated evil is never elaborated among the Pueblos; he is too often an ally for some desired end."[35]

Yet, the whiteness of the albino suggests something more terrible than evil to Abel. As the whiteness of the whale does to Ishmael, it suggests an emptiness in the universe, a total void of meaning. It is an emblem complementary to Angela's philosophizing over the Cochiti dancers. The albino confronts Abel with his own lack of meaning, his own lack of a sense of place.

This reading is reinforced by the poignant final scene in Part I. Francisco stands alone in his corn field demonstrating the very sense of place Abel has lacked on his return. We recall that in this very field Francisco too had confronted evil in the shape of the albino, but that he responded to the confrontation very differently:

> His acknowledgement of the unknown was nothing more than a dull, intrinsic sadness, a vague desire to weep, for evil had long since found him out and knew who he was. He set a blessing upon the corn and took up his hoe. (p. 64)

Because of Abel's act, Francisco is for the first time separated from the Walatowa community. He stands muttering Abel's name as he did in the opening of the chapter, and near him the reed trap—again suggesting the reed of emergence—is empty.

III

Part II of the novel opens with Abel lying broken, physically and spiritually, on the beach in Los Angeles. Like the helpless grunion with whom he shares the beach, he is out of his world. Abel's problem continues to be one of relating to place. As in Part I at Walatowa he fails to establish a sense of place in Los Angeles because of a failure to find community. Not only is he separated from other workers at the factory, but even Tosamah and the Indian men at the Silver Dollar reject Abel. That rejection is a major cause of Abel's second futile and self-destructive confrontation with evil in the person of Martinez, a sadistic Mexican policeman.[36] The pattern of the second confrontation is a repetition of the first. Just as Abel kills the albino at Walatowa after he has failed to find community there, so too he goes after Martinez, also perceived as a snake (*culebra*), after he has failed utterly to find community in Los Angeles. Implication of Anglo society in this failure is again explicit and powerful, as Abel has been sent to Los Angeles by the government on its Relocation Program after serving time in prison for killing the albino.

On the beach Abel "could not see" (p. 92). This poverty of vision, both physical and imaginative, is akin to the inability of one-eyed Father Olguin to "see" and is related to Abel's prison experience: "After a while he could not imagine anything beyond the walls except the yard outside, the lavatory and the dining hall—or even walls, really" (p. 97). Yet it is by the sea that Abel gains the insight required to begin his own re-emergence. For the first time he asks himself "where the trouble had begun, what the trouble was" (p. 97), and though he still cannot answer the question consciously, his mind turns again to the mechanical auditory images noted earlier:

> The bus leaned and creaked; he felt the surge of motion and the violent shudder of the whole machine on the gravel road. The motion and the sound seized him. Then suddenly he was overcome with a desperate loneliness, and he wanted to cry out. He looked toward the fields, but a low rise of the land lay before them (p. 97).

The bus takes Abel out of a context where he has worth and meaning and into a context where "there were enemies all around" (p. 98). From the cultural landscape of the Cañon de San Diego to the beach where "the world was open at his back" (p. 96), Abel's journey has taken him, as his Bahkyush ancestors, to "the edge of oblivion": "He had been long ago at the center, had known where he was, had lost his way, had wandered to the end of the earth, was even now reeling on the edge of a void" (p. 96). On the beach, then, Abel finally realizes that "he had lost his place" (p. 96), a realization accompanied by the comprehension of the social harmony a sense of place requires. Out of his delirium, as if in a dream, his mind returns to the central thread of the novel, the race, and here at last Abel is able to assign meaning to the race as a cultural activity:

> The runners after evil ran as water runs, deep in the channel, in the way of least resistance, no resistance. His skin crawled with excitement; he was overcome with longing and loneliness, for suddenly he saw the crucial sense in their going, of old men in white leggings running after evil in the night. They were whole and indispensable in what they did; everything in creation referred to them. Because of them, perspective, proportion, design in the universe. Meaning because of them. They ran with great dignity and calm, not in hope of anything, but hopelessly; neither in fear nor hatred nor despair of evil, but simply in recognition and with respect. Evil was. Evil was abroad in the night; they must venture out to the confrontation; they must reckon dues and divide the world (p. 96).

We recall that as Abel killed the albino "the terrible strength of the hands was brought to bear only in proportion as Abel *resisted them*" (p. 78, emphasis added). The murder is an expression of Abel's disharmony and imbalance. As Abel here realizes "evil is that which is ritually not under control."[37] In the ceremonial race, not in individual resistance, the runners are able to deal with evil.

Tosamah's description of the emergence journey and the relations of words and place serve as a clue to Abel's cure, but the role he plays in Abel's journey appears as ambiguous and contradictory as his character. He is at once priest and "clown" (p. 165). He exhibits, often on the same page, remarkable insight, buffoonery, and cynicism. He has then all the characteristics of Coyote, the trickster figure in native American mythologies.[38] Alternately wise and foolish, Coyote in native American oral tradition is at once a buffoon and companion of the People on their emergence journey. As Coyote, a member of "an old council of clowns" (p. 55), the Right Reverend John Big Bluff Tosamah speaks with a voice "full of authority and rebuke" (p. 55). As Coyote, "he likes to get under your skin; he'll make a fool out of you if you let him" (p. 165). Note how Momaday describes Tosamah:

> He was shaggy and awful-looking in the thin, naked light; big, lithe as a cat, narrow-eyed, suggesting in the whole of his look and manner both arrogance and agony. He wore black like a cleric; he had the voice of a great dog (p. 85).

The perspective Tosamah offers Abel and the reader in the novel derives not so much from his peyote ceremonies, for which Momaday seems to have drawn heavily on La Barre's *The Peyote Cult*, but rather from the substance of the two sermons he gives.[39] The second sermon, "The Way to Rainy Mountain," which Momaday has used in his book by the same title and several other contexts, addresses the relation of man, land, community, and the word. In it Tosamah describes the emergence of the Kiowa people as "a journey toward the dawn" that "led to a golden age" (p. 118). It was a journey which led the Kiowa to a culture which is inextricably bound to the land of the southern plains. There, much in the manner of Abel looking over the Cañon de San Diego in Part I, he looks out on the landscape at dawn and muses: "your imagination comes to life, and this, you think, is where Creation was begun" (p. 117). By making a re-emergence journey, Tosamah is able to feel a sense of place.

That coherent native relation to the land described so eloquently by Tosamah is counterpointed in the novel not only by Abel's experiences but also by the memories of Milly, the social worker who becomes Abel's lover in Los Angeles. Milly, like Tosamah, is from Oklahoma. There her family too had struggled with the land, but "at last Daddy began to hate the land, began to think of it as some kind of enemy, his own very personal and deadly enemy" (p. 113). Even viewed in the dawn her father's relation to the land was a despairing and hopeless one:

> And every day before dawn he went to the fields without hope, and I watched him, sometimes saw him at sunrise, far away in the empty land, very small on the skyline turning to stone even as he moved up and down the rows. (p. 113)

The contrast with Francisco, who seems most at home in his fields, and with Tosamah, who finds in that very landscape the depth of his existence, is obvious. The passage also recalls Angela's denial of the meaning of the land and Abel's own reflections on "enemies."

In his first sermon in the novel, Tosamah addresses the crucial role of words and the imagination in the re-emergence process. The sermon is a bizarre exegesis of St. John's gospel which compares Indian and Anglo attitudes toward language. As participants in oral traditions, Indians, Tosamah tells us, hold language as sacred. They have a childlike regard for the mysteries of speech. While St. John shared that sensibility, he was also a white man. And the white man obscures the truth by burdening it with words:

> Now, brothers and sisters, old John was a white man, and the white man has his ways. Oh gracious me, he has his ways. He talks about the Word. He talks through it and around it. He builds upon it with syllables, with prefixes and suffixes, and hyphens and accents. He adds and divides and multiplies the Word. And in all this he subtracts the Truth (p. 87).

The white man may indeed, Tosamah tells us, in a theory of verbal overkill that is wholly his own, "perish by the Word" (p. 89).

Words are, of course, a problem for Abel. On the other hand, he lacks the ceremonial words—the words of a Creation song—which properly express his relation to community and place. He is inarticulate. On the other, he is plagued by a surfeit of words from white men. The bureaucratic words of the social worker's forms effectively obscure his real problems. At the murder trial, he thinks: "Word by word by word these men were disposing of him in language, *their* language, and they were making a bad job of it" (p. 95). Again when Benally takes him to the hospital after the beach scene bureaucratic words get in the way. Indeed, Benally perceives Abel's central problem as one of words, as he equates finding community with having appropriate words:

> And they can't help you because you don't know how to talk to them. They have a lot of words, and you know they mean something, but you don't know what, and your own words are no good because they're not the same; they're different, and they're the only words you've got. . . . You think about getting out and going home. You want to think that you belong someplace, I guess (p. 144).

Tosamah perceives a similar dislocating effect of words on Abel, though he relates it to religion. Scorning his inarticulateness and innocence, he sees Abel as caught in "the Jesus scheme" (p. 136). Beyond his sermons, there is a special irony in the fact that Tosamah doesn't understand Abel and his problems, for he is described several times in Part II as a "physician." Though they put Abel's problems in a broader and clearer perspective, Tosamah's words are of little use to Abel.

IV

Part III is told from the point of view of Ben Benally, a relocated Navajo who befriends Abel in Los Angeles. Roommates in Los Angeles, Ben and Abel share many things in their backgrounds. On his one visit to Walatowa, Benally finds the landscape there similar to that in which he grew up. Like Abel he was raised in that landscape without parents by his grandfather. Benally even suggests that he is somehow related to Abel since the Navajos have a clan called Jemez, the name of Abel's pueblo. Moreover, we recall that Abel's father may have been a Navajo, and that Francisco regards the Navajo children who come to Walatowa during the Fiesta of Porcingula as "a harvest, in some intractable sense the regeneration of his own bone and blood" (p. 72). This kinship gives Benally special insight into Abel's problems and strengthens his role as Night Chanter.[40]

Benally's childhood memories of life with his grandfather near Wide Ruins reveal a sense of place very like that Abel groped for on his return to Walatowa:

> And you were little and right there in the center of everything, the sacred mountains, the snow-covered mountains and the hills, the gullies and the flats, the sundown and the night, everything—where you were little, where you were and had to be (p. 143).

Moreover, this sense of place gives him words: ". . . you were out with the sheep and could talk and sing to yourself and the snow was new and deep and beautiful" (p. 142).

In Los Angeles, however, Benally's sense of place is lost in his idealism and naïveté. Return to the reservation seems a pale option to the glitter of Los Angeles. "There would be nothing there, just the empty land and a lot of old people, going noplace and dying off" (p. 145). Like Milly, Benally believes in "Honor, Industry, the Second Chance, the Brotherhood of Man, the American Dream . . ." (p. 99). Theirs is a fifties American Dream of limitless urban possibilities. Benally believes you can have anything you want in Los Angeles and that "you never have to be alone" (p. 164). Yet in the very scene following his reflection on this urban cornucopia, we find Benally excluded even from the community of The Silver Dollar, counting his pennies, unable to buy a second bottle of wine. Idealism obscures Benally's vision, even as Tosamah's cynicism obscures his.

Nevertheless, Benally is the Night Chanter, the singer who helps restore voice and harmony to Abel's life. In the hospital having realized the significance of the runners after evil, Abel asks Benally to sing for him:

> "House made of dawn." I used to tell him about those old ways, the stories and the songs, Beautyway and Night Chant. I sang some of those things, and I told him what they meant, what I thought they were about (p. 133).

The songs from both the Beautyway and the Night Chant are designed to attract good and repel evil. They are both restorative and exorcising expressions of the very balance and design in the universe Abel perceived in the runners after evil. Ben's words from the Night Chant for Abel are particularly appropriate, since the purpose of the Night Chant is to cure patients of insanity and mental imbalance.[41] The structure and diction of the song demonstrate the very harmony it seeks to evoke. Dawn is balanced by evening light, dark cloud and male rain by dark mist and female rain. All things are in balance and control, for in Navajo and Pueblo religion good is control. Further note that a journey metaphor is prominent in the song ("may I walk. . . .") and that the restorative sequence culminates with "restore my voice for me." Restoration of voice is an outward sign of inner harmony. Finally, note that the song begins with a culturally significant geographical reference: *Tségihi*. One of its central messages is that ceremonial words are bound efficaciously to place. No matter how dislocated is Benally or idiosyncratic his understandings of Navajo ceremonialism, the songs he sings over Abel clearly serve a restorative function.

Angela also visits Abel in the hospital and offers him words. She tells Abel the story her son likes "best of all" (p. 169). It is a story about "a young Indian brave," born of a bear and a maiden, who has many adventures and finally saves his people. Benally marvels at the story which reminds him of a similar story from the Mountain Chant told to him by his grandfather.[42] Yet unlike the Navajo legend and the Kiowa bear legend told by Tosamah earlier (pp. 120–1), both etiological legends tied firmly to cultural landscapes, Angela's story is as rootless as a Disney cartoon. Abel seems to realize this, if Benally does not, for he does not respond to Angela. Benally "couldn't tell what he was thinking. He had turned his head away, like maybe the pain was coming back, you know" (p. 170). Abel refuses to play Angela's game a second time.

V

Part IV opens with a description of a grey, ominous winter landscape. Olguin is reflecting on his seven years' service at Walatowa. He claims to have grown "calm with duty and design," to have "come to terms with the town" (p. 174). Yet he remains estranged from the village; it is not his place. He measures his achievement in the language of commerce, noting with his predecessor Nicolas V. what good works "accrued to his account" (p. 174). Like Angela who was offended that Abel "would not buy and sell" (p. 35), Olguin seeks to at least make good the "investment" of his pride.

Whereas Abel looks to Benally's Night Chant for restoration Olguin seeks and claims to find restoration from the journal of Nicolas. In that same journal we recall Nicolas V. himself sought restoration of his Christian God:

> When I cannot speak thy Name, I want Thee most to restore me. Restore me! Thy spirit comes upon me & I am too frail for Thee! [p. 48]

The passage leaves off in a fit of coughing and seems a singularly ineffectual request.

At the same time Abel sits with his dying grandfather. Though Francisco's voice had been strong in the dawn, it now grows weaker and fades as it has on each of the six days since Abel's return to Walatowa. The few words Francisco does speak, in Towa and Spanish, juxtapose in the manner of Parts I and II the memory fragments which Abel seeks to order in his own mind. Francisco is here, as Momaday suggests, "a kind of reflection of Abel."[43] The passage translates:

> Little Abel . . . I'm a little bit of something . . . Mariano . . . cold . . . he gave up . . . very, very cold . . . conquered . . . aye [exclamation of pain], Porcingula . . . how white, little Abel . . . white devil . . . witch . . . witch and the black man . . . yes . . . many black men . . . running, running . . . cold . . . rapidly . . . little Abel, little Vidal . . . What are you doing? What are you doing?

As the seventh dawn comes these words grow into coherent fragments in Francisco's memory and serve as a final statement of the realizations about the relation of place, words, and community Abel has had earlier in the novel.

Each of the fragments is a memory of initiation. In the first Francisco recalls taking Abel and Vidal to the ruins of the old church near the Middle to see "the house of the sun." [44]

> They must learn the whole contour of the black mesa. They must know it as they knew the shape of their hands, always and by heart. . . . They must know the long journey of the sun on the black mesa, how it rode in the seasons and the years, and they must live according to the sun appearing, for only then could they reckon where they were, where all things were in time (p. 177).

This is the sense of place Abel lost in "the intervention of days and years without meaning, of awful calm and collision, time always immediate and confused" (p. 25). As he is instructed to know the shape of the eastern mesa like his own hands, it is appropriate that in the *corre de gaio* the albino should first attack his hands (p. 44), that in the murder scene (and Abel's memory of it) hands should be so prominent (pp. 77–9, 94), and finally that as he lies on the beach after Martinez's brutal beating of his hands, Abel should think of Angela's effect on him in terms of hands (p. 94). The relation of place taught him by Francisco is broken by each, as are his hands. Now through Francisco's memory Abel is re-taught his ordered relation to place and how it is expressed in "the race of the dead" (pp. 185–6). Abel similarly participates in Francisco's memories of his initiation as a runner (in the race against Mariano pp. 187–8), as a dancer (from which he gained the power to heal pp. 186–7), as a man (with Porcingula, "the child of the witch" pp. 184–5), and as a hunter (as he stalks the bear pp. 178–84).

All signs then point to a new beginning for Abel as he rises February 28, the last day of the novel. His own memory healed by Francisco's, for the first time in the novel he correctly performs a ceremonial function as he prepares Francisco for burial and delivers him to Father Olguin. [45] He then joins the ashmarked runners in the dawn. Momaday comments on that race in his essay "The Morality of Indian Hating":

> The first race each year comes in February, and then the dawn is clear and cold, and the runners breathe steam. It is a long race, and it is neither won nor lost. It is an expression of the soul in the ancient terms of sheer physical exertion. To watch those runners is to know that they draw with every step some elementary power which resides at the core of the earth and which, for all our civilized ways, is lost upon us who have lost the art of going in the flow of things. In the tempo of that race there is time to ponder morality and demoralization, hungry wolves and falling stars. And there is time to puzzle over that curious and fortuitous question with which the people of Jemez greet each other.[46]

That very question—"Where are you going?"—must ring in Abel's ears as he begins the race. The time and direction of his journey are once again defined by the relation of the sun to the eastern mesa, "the house made of dawn." Out of the pain and exhaustion of the race, Abel regains his vision: "he could see at last without having to think" (p. 191). That vision is not the nihilistic vision of Angela—"beyond everything for which the mountain stands." Rather, Abel's "last reality" in the race is expressed in the essential unity and harmony of man and the land. He feels the sense of place he was unable to articulate in Part I. Here at last he has a voice, words and a song. In beauty he has begun.

Notes

1. "The Man Made of Words," in *Indian Voices: the First Convocation of American Indian Scholars* (San Francisco: Indian Historian Press, 1970), p. 55.

2. For surveys see Ermine Wheeler-Voegelin, "North American Native Literature," *Encyclopedia of Literature*, Vol II, ed. Joseph T. Shipley, pp. 706–21; Mary Austin, "Aboriginal," in *The Cambridge History of American Literature*, ed. William Peterfield Trent et al. (New York: Macmillan, 1945), pp. 610–34; and more recently Alan Dundes, "North American Indian Folklore Studies," *Journal de la société des Américanistes*, 56 (1967), pp. 53–79.

3. "A Conversation with N. Scott Momaday," *Sun Tracks: An American Indian Literary Magazine*, 2, No. 2 (1976), p. 19.

4. See Momaday's column "A Special Sense of Place," *Viva, Sante Fe New Mexican* (May 7, 1972), p. 2; D. H. Lawrence, *Studies in Classic American Literature* (1923; rpt. New York: Viking, 1964), pp. 1–8; Aldo Leopold, *A Sand County Almanac: With Essays on Conservation from Round River* (1949; rpt. New York: Ballantine, 1970), pp. 238–40; Eudora Welty, "Place in Fiction," *Three Papers on Fiction* (Northampton, Mass.: Metcalf, 1955), pp. 1–15; etc. The Autumn 1975 issue of the *South Dakota Review* is given entirely to a symposium and commentaries on "The Writer's Sense of Place."

5. *The Tewa World: Space, Time, Being, and Becoming in a Pueblo Society* (Chicago: Univ. of Chicago Press, 1969), p. 13.

6. Momaday, "An American Land Ethic," *Sierra Club Bulletin*, 55 (February, 1970), p. 11.

7. *The Way to Rainy Mountain* (1969; New York: Ballantine, 1970). See also Momaday's "A First American Views His Land," *National Geographic*, 150, No. 1 (1976), pp. 13–18.

8. *Rainy Mountain*, p. 2.

9. Ethelou Yazzie, ed., *Navajo History* (Many Farms, Ariz.: Navajo Community College Press, 1971).

10. See Margot Astov, "The Concept of Motion as the Psychological Leit-motif of Navajo Life and Literature," *Journal of American Folklore*, 63 (1950), pp. 45–56; and Gladys A. Reichard, *Navajo Religion: A Study of Symbolism*, 2nd ed. (1950; Princeton: Princeton Univ. Press, 1974), p. 19.

11. *Navajo History*, p. 57.

12. Leland Wyman, *The Windways of the Navajo* (Colorado Springs: The Taylor Museum, 1962), pp. 27–8; and the whole of Reichard's *Prayer: the Compulsive Word* (Seattle: Univ. of Washington Press, 1944).

13. *Rainy Mountain*, p. 42.

14. See P. E. Goddard, "Navajo Texts," *Anthropological Papers of the American Museum of Natural History*, 34 (1933), p. 127.

15. *Rainy Mountain*, p. 42.

16. Curley Mustache, "Philosophy of the Navajos," (Navajo Community College: mimeo, 1974), p. 11. Compare *Navajo Religion*, p. 289.

17. "A Conversation with N. Scott Momaday", p. 19.

18. Walatowa, "Village of the Bear," is the Jemez name for their village. See Frederick Webb Hodge, ed., *Handbook of American Indians*, Part I (1907; rpt. New York: Roland and Littlefield, 1965), p. 630. See Elsie Clews Parsons, *The Pueblo of Jemez* (New Haven: Yale Univ. Press, 1925), p. 136, for the formula; and Dennis Tedlock's discussion of the convention in "Pueblo Literature: Style and Verisimilitude," in Alfonse Ortiz, ed., *New Perspectives on the Pueblos* (Albuquerque: Univ. of New Mexico Press, 1972), pp. 219–42.

19. An Interview with N. Scott Momaday," *Puerto del Sol* 12 (1973), p. 33.

20. Parsons, p. 118.

21. The song first appeared in Washington Matthews *The Night Chant: A Navajo Ceremony*, Memoirs of the American Museum of Natural History, 6 (1902); and in another version in Matthews, "Navajo Myths, Prayers, and Songs," University of California Publications in American Archaeology and Ethnology, 5 (1907), which was posthumously edited by Pliny Earle Goddard.

22. N. Scott Momaday, *House Made of Dawn* (1968; New York: New American Library, 1969), p. 11. Subsequent citations refer to the NAL edition and appear parenthetically in the text.

23. Compare the emergence log in *Rainy Mountain*, p. 1, and the reed in *Navajo History*, p. 9.

24. See Parsons' account of the Pecos migration in *Pueblo of Jemez*, p. 3. Note that one of the five Bahkyula making that journey was named Francisco. The genealogical relations of Abel are further defined in Part I by the journal of Nicolas V., through which the incidence of albinism at Walatowa is also established. See Parsons, pp. 49–50. Again note the name of one albino mentioned there, Juan Reyes Fragua, is also the name of the albino in the novel.

25. Carole Oleson, "The Remembered Earth: Momaday's *House Made of Dawn, SDR*, 11 (1973), 63; H. S. McAllister, "Incarnate Grace and the Paths of Salvation in *House Made of Dawn*," *SDR*, 12 (1975), 115–25.

26. See Mark Porter, "Mysticism of the Land and the Western Novel," *SDR*, 11 (1973), 82. Angela is closely associated with the Roman Church throughout. She shares a brand of piety with Father Olguin and his predecessor Fray Nicolas V. which emphasizes the denial of the flesh. The links between Angela and Olguin appear even closer in an earlier version of parts of the novel where Angela appears with her mother and brother, one Fr. Bothene (Olguin?). See "Three Sketches from *House Made of Dawn*," *SoR*, 2 (1966), 941. Bothene reappears in "Cryptic Tale from the Past," a column in *Viva, Santa Fe New Mexican*, 1 April 1973, p. 7. There Momaday writes of Ellen Bothene, "an elderly matron"; Raoul Bothene "a man of the cloth"; and Angela, "the less said about her the better."

27. San Diego is the patron of Jemez pueblo. Stories of him abound in Mexico and the American Southwest. Compare "The Adventures of San Diego," in Leslie White, *The Acoma Indians*, 47th ARBAE (Washington; G.P.O., 1932), pp. 180–89.

28. See Parsons, p. 95; and Edward Dozier, *The Pueblo Indians of North America* (New York: Holt, Rinehart, and Winston, 1970), p. 199. Parsons observed the *corre de gaio* on July 25, 1922. Note the corresponding day of the month in the novel. Another description of the rooster pull appears in Albert Reagan's novel *Don Diego* (New York: Alice Harriman Company, 1914) which is also set at Jemez.

29. Of the rooster pull at Acoma, Leslie White writes "It is said that rooster blood is 'good for rain,' " *The Acoma Indians*, p. 106.

30. The Benevides name seems to have come to the area with the Franciscan Fray Alonso de Benavides, author of a detailed report on the missionary effort in New Mexico.

Benavides brags that "from the house of one old Indian sorcerer I once took out more than a thousand idols of wood, painted in the fashion of a game of nine pins, and I burned them in the public plaza." Frederick Webb Hodge, George P. Hammond, and Agapito Rey, eds. and trans. *Fray Alonso de Benavides' Revised Memorial of 1634* (Albuquerque: Univ. of New Mexico Press, 1945), p. 46.

31. *Teah-whau* means "people-hair" or "mustache."

32. Marion Willard Hylton, "On a Trail of Pollen: Momaday's *House Made of Dawn*," *Crit*, 14 (1972), 62; Oleson, p. 62.

33. Parsons, pp. 96–7.

34. See Leslie Fiedler, *The Return of the Vanishing American* (New York: Stein and Day, 1968), pp. 116–19; and Roy Harvey Pearce, *Savagism and Civilization: A Study of the Indian Mind and the American Mind*, revised ed. (Baltimore: Johns Hopkins Press, 1965), pp. 13–16.

35. Hamilton A, Tyler, *Pueblo Gods and Myths* (Norman: Univ. of Oklahoma Press, 1964), p. 226. See also the serpent as an integral part in Jemez iconography in Parsons, Plates 3, 5, 7, and elsewhere; and Reagan, pp. 4–5. Of Navajo witchery Kluckhohn writes: "several informants volunteered remarks such as 'witches are needed for rain—just as much as the good side' which would indicate that such malevolent activities are actually necessary to the natural equilibrium." See *Navajo Witchcraft* (1944; rpt. Boston: Beacon, 1967), p. 60.

36. There is slight evidence suggesting that Momaday based Abel's confrontations with evil in part on an actual case history. On Good Friday in 1952 two Acoma Pueblo men, Willie and Gabriel Felipe, killed Nash Garcia, a Mexican state policeman, near Grants, New Mexico. A part of their defense at the subsequent trial was the contention, supported by the psychotherapist George Devereux, that they perceived Garcia as a witch. See *Albuquerque Journal*, February 27, 1953. The killing is the basis for short stories by Simon Ortiz and Leslie Silko printed in Kenneth Rosen, ed., *The Man to Send Rain Clouds* (New York: Viking, 1974).

37. *Navajo Religion*, p. 5; see also Dozier, p. 200.

38. See my note "Further Survivals of the Coyote," *WAL*, 10 (1975), 233–36.

39. Weston La Barre, *The Peyote Cult* (1964; rpt. New York: Schocken, 1969). Compare, for example, La Barre, p. 7, and Tosamah, *House Made of Dawn*, p. 101.

40. Benally may once have framed the whole novel. Note the unmistakable diction which introduces "The Sparrow and the Reed" in "Three Sketches from *House Made of Dawn*," p. 933.

41. *Navajo Religion*, p. 12.

42. The very suggestive system of elder brother/younger brother analogies which runs through the novel—and is implicit here in the legend from the Mountain Chant—is worked out provocatively in relation to Navajo and Pueblo twins legends in Joseph E. DeFlyer's doctoral dissertation *Partition Theory: Patterns and Partitions of Consciousness in Selected Works of American and American Indian Authors* (Nebraska, 1974). See especially p. 231.

43. "An Interview with N. Scott Momaday," p. 34.

44. See Parsons, pp. 59–60, and figure 5.

45. See Parsons, p. 50.

46. *Ramparts* 3 (1964), p. 40.

Extensive/Intensive Dimensionality in [Rudolfo] Anaya's *Bless Me, Ultima*

Daniel Testa*

> To be a man means, for each of us, membership of a class, a society, a country, a continent, and a civilization. For those of us who are earth-bound Europeans, our adventurings into the heart of the New World have a lesson to teach us: that the New World was not ours to destroy, and yet we destroyed it; and that no other will be vouchsafed to us. In grasping these truths we come face to face with ourselves. Let us, at any rate, set them out as they first appeared to us, in that place, and at that moment in time, when our world lost the chance that was still open to it: that of choosing between its missions.[1]

The modern Chicano cultural movement dates from the middle sixties and it was during a few short years that we can sense that a qualitative transformation took place in the struggle for self-determination and liberation. The force of that cultural awakening has given impetus to a surprising quality of literary publication, and whether the works are written in English or Spanish, or in a mixture of the two languages, we can already see the beginnings of the differentiation of literary trends. The historians and scholars who have found it difficult to establish a basis for groupings among Chicanos will be helped in their work by some fairly clear lines of literary development. If *Bless Me, Ultima*[2] is a faithful manifestation of what will become its author's artistic trajectory, Anaya may be that kind of Chicano who does not focus directly and explicitly on the confrontation between his own culture and an oppressive Anglo society. His interest, rather, is more attuned to the differences between the European-Hispanic-Catholic heritage and Indian-mestizo modes of viewing the world. The socio-economic problems or political concerns, although present in his work, do not seem to weigh directly or heavily on Anaya's literary mind, or at least they are submerged and subordinated to other matters. Anaya, unlike many other Chicano writers, draws from an Hispanic-Anglo geographical area that was settled at a much earlier time than most other areas. Perhaps this situation helps to explain why Anaya

* *LALR, 5, no. 10 (1977), 70–78. © 1977 by Latin American Literary Review*. Reprinted by permission of *Latin American Literary Review*.

is more attracted to or is more susceptible to a freer fantasized mode of fiction.

If scholars insist on the need to define the Mexican-American, they should give up the idea that he can be easily abstracted into a concept or treated as though he were a mythic being. What the Chicano is, to a great extent, depends on where he has lived, and for how long, that is, his cultural milieu and his history. Given the special circumstances of the Hispanic-Indian tradition in New Mexico, which is Mr. Anaya's birthplace and the locale of *Bless Me, Ultima*, it is perhaps natural not to find in his work the anguished voices of the urban barrios (as in Alurista) or the troubles and heartbreak of the migrant farm-workers (as in Tomás Rivera). What we do find is a curious mélange of elements: a sensitivity to physical surroundings, an almost primitive preoccupation with the elemental forces of nature, a bold spirit that inquires into the ultimate questions of life and destiny, an impure fantasy that dares to juxtapose sacred matters and impious horseplay, and a sustained desire and capacity to make the self the emotional center of excruciating experiences.

Bless Me, Ultima can be taken first of all as a good action novel, a work in which intense and dramatic happenings make up a considerable part. There are violent fights and deaths. The technique and calculated effects of certain scenes seem deliberately to have been drawn from popular literature and movies that reflect the legendary "wild" west, replete with stock situations and characters. One difference we note is that all, or almost all, the heroes, victims, and villains are members of the Hispanic, Indian, or mestizo communities. Some of the stereotyped elements used in the work are a Longhorn saloon, a poolroom, a bawdy house, a wise old Indian who lives in a cave, settlers and sheepherders, farmers and cowboys. But Anaya also moves beyond that borrowed type of scenario by giving symbolic value to places and objects. Thus, we have the house on the hill that is a place of refuge, the bridge that connects to the larger world, the river that becomes such a dominant presence in the lives of several of the characters, the open prairies, the closed valleys, the unproductive terrain that must be worked inch-by-inch, among others.

Anaya adds to the texture of his narrative by tapping other sources of folklore, legends, mythologies, and cosmologies. He shows great skill in narrative acceleration at certain intervals in the work. These dramatic episodes give the novel a dimension of intensity that is worthy of the dramatist or the short story writer. Such set-pieces vary in content, tone, and dramatic impact. The legend of the Golden Carp is one such substructure that serves as a story in itself and also contributes to the larger purposes of the book. From the *curandera* Ultima, Antonio comes to learn about popular superstitions, magic, the occult, good and evil in a modified Christian or un-Christian context. Perhaps the most dramatic episode of the whole work is the carefully prepared and executed ceremony of the lifting of the curse that had been placed on one of Antonio's uncles. The boy himself is drawn into a secret, shadowy world because of his innocence and blood connection to the victim and it is this unspecified, mysterious participation of the boy that contributes naturally in intensifying the action that slowly unfolds before his eyes and ours. What also adds to the suspenseful procedure that has the primary function of saving a man's life is the spiritual conflict sharply felt by Antonio over the efficacy of Ultima's curative power. "Why didn't they call you sooner?" the boy asks the *curandera*. The answer he already knows:

> The priest at El Puerto did not want the people to place much faith in the powers of la curandera. He wanted the mercy and faith of the church to be the villagers' only guiding light (p. 90).

But still the outcome is not assured: "Would the magic of Ultima be stronger than all the powers of the saints and the Holy Mother Church?" the boy cannot help but wonder. It will take more experiences, more conversations, more questioning, and more growth for Antonio to feel confident about his "new religion," but at this point in the novel, all he has to go on is what he sees before his eyes and what Ultima explains in her typically laconic manner:

> . . . good is always stronger than evil. Always remember that, Antonio. The smallest bit of good can stand against all the powers of evil in the world and it will emerge triumphant (p. 90).

But perhaps the dramatic intensity of this episode, as well as of a second exorcistic ceremony carried out later in the work, is simply due to the presence of occult phenomena, the explanation of which is never given more than a hint.

There are many other examples of narrative intensification, and many of these are normal in the typical novel of any length. What seems to be quite extraordinary, however, is the variety of materials in Anaya's work. He intersperses the legendary, folkloric, stylized, or allegorized material with the detailed descriptions that help to create a density of realistic portrayal. Several violent encounters that end in death work up to a crescendo and create an excitement that contrasts with the beauty and idyllic quality of the surrounding countryside. As with the exorcisms, what dramatizes the action is the gradual and careful preparation of details and the tension generated in the young boy's mind, through which the story is narrated. In this same category of realistic description we should include those set-scenes in which Antonio mixes with a group of boys who become his friends. Human vignettes in dialogue form, the language reflects the youngsters' spontaneity, restlessness, frankness, and sometimes coarse and vulgar behavior. In that series of scenes, the gem is no doubt the Christmas play (pp. 144–151), with its humor and youthful vitality. An impious playfulness is also evident in the communion scene (chapter 17).

The last group of separable compositions, the dreams or visions, are again as different from the realistic scenes as the latter are from the episodes in which the occult plays a part. The ten dreams are indicated in the text in italics and are placed at intervals throughout the novel. The basic function of the sometimes hallucinatory visions is to create and sustain a non-realistic view of reality, and in that sense they contribute to one of the larger themes of the work. In the dreams, there is often a direct relationship to the events that have happened in Antonio's life. An event will enter the dream and will lose the context it had in life and become fused, distorted, and transformed. The boy will dream about his mother's dream for his life, and will dream about his father's dream for himself and his family. He will dream about his brothers as giant spectral figures. The elements of reality and the elements of his fantasy world, legends, stories, etc., appear obsessively and dynamically charged and join to make new combinations that surprise, frighten, and shock. A profusion of motifs crowds the subconscious mind: the Virgin, *la llorona*, the mermaid, the Golden Carp, the brothel, the sense of guilt associated with sexual pleasures, the men who die violently. The dead men appear as three restless, tortured spirits who are driven by three women with whips. Figures in groups of three make their appearance again and again. The crisis of his vocation comes to haunt him, and in one such moment it is Ultima who steps in to point the way to his destiny. In one dream, the conflict between his mother's "earth" tradition and his father's "free spirit" tradition breaks into cataclysm, a cosmic upheaval that threatens to destroy everything until at a given moment Ultima again appears. As she speaks, the storm abates and peace is restored. In the last dream of the work, in the midst of conflict and savagery, Antonio cries out and asks: "Why must I be a witness to so much violence?" A voice answers: "The germ of creation lies in violence" (p. 232).

The visionary mode, with its confusions, chaos, and conflicts, leaves us with a sense of fear and mystery about life and the cosmos. From one point of view, the dreams may be seen as dramatic representations of the conflict between levels of the self, each vying for dominance. Equally important, however, is the wealth of cosmological material that Anaya has brought into the dreams. By using mythic or archetypal constructs, it is evident that Anaya has tapped the deep structures of the collective mind. At any rate, we should note the contrast between the unrestrained flow of the dreams and the other parts of the book, between the condensation and obsessiveness of certain horrorific patterns and the stability and relative security of Antonio's "real" world. The dramatic intensity of the dream experiences is so great that they sometimes seem to have their own esthetic thrust and autonomy. Perhaps their value is precisely that they refuse to be subsumed or incorporated into the outer frame, although they have obvious connections to it.

Bless Me, Ultima may also be seen as a Chicano *bildungsroman*, and in spite of the fact that Antonio, the boy-hero of the story, is only eight years old at the end of the novel, we are convinced that his character has been formed in a radically profound way. The novel is structured ostensibly by the chronological span of about two years, something which might be called the plot time. The action of the work begins when Ultima comes into Antonio's life and ends when she dies, so that it is the ultimate relationship between teacher and pupil that gives internal coherence to the boy's life. As important as that cycle of time may be, what is much more significant is the extensive dimensionality of time given through the intrusion of the past into the present. Through Antonio's parents and the conflict of the two blood lines, the Lunas and the Márez, the beginnings of the Hispanic settlement in New Mexico are kept actively alive:

> . . . his forefathers were men of the sea, the Márez people, they were conquistadores, men whose freedom was unbounded (p. 23)

> Then there was the strange, whispered riddle of the first priest who went to El Puerto. The colony had first settled there under a land grant from the Mexican government, and the man who led the colonization was a priest, and he was a Luna. That is why my mother dreamed of me becoming a priest, because there had not been a Luna priest in the family for many years (p. 27).

This past is kept alive not only by the references to the origins of the Hispanic settlements. There are the changes that took place later in history and as recently as just prior to the time that Antonio's father left his town of Las Pasturas. The changes were met with reluctantly and would be the subject of conversation among the old timers:

> Always the talk turned to life on the llano. The first pioneers there were sheepherders. Then they imported herds of cattle from Mexico and became vaqueros. . . . They were the first cowboys in a wild and desolate land which they took from the Indians. Then the railroad came. The barbed wire came. The songs, the corridos became sad, and the meeting of the people from Texas with my forefathers was full of blood, murder, and tragedy. The people were uprooted. They looked around one day and found themselves closed in. The freedom of land and sky they had known was gone (p. 119).

As others had migrated westward to California, Antonio's father keeps his dreams alive of moving on to those lands also, and in people like him the frustrations of the present make the past all the more meaningful.

It is not only through the parents and their families and friends that the sense of the past enters the boy's consciousness as he gropes towards a solution to the problem of his future. Through Ultima Antonio learns about a different past, which is not remembered precisely as history, but rather as legend and as a timeless, mythic past. " 'Long ago,' she would smile, 'long before you were a dream, long before the train came to Las Pasturas, long before the Lunas came to their valley, before the great Coronado built his bridge—' Then her voice would trail off and my thoughts would be lost in the labyrinth of a time and history I did not know." (p. 37). When Antonio hears the stories of the origins of the Indians, the remoteness and imprecision stand as a contrast to the clearer sense that he has of the Hispanic past. The coming of the Indians was described by one of his friends, Samuel, who was repeating something told a thousand times down through the ages, and if affects Antonio more profoundly because it is no longer simply history but rather fable:

> A long time ago, when the earth was young and only wandering tribes touched the virgin grasslands and drank from the pure streams, a strange people came to this land. They were sent to this valley by their gods. They had wandered lost for many years but never had they given up faith in their gods, and so they were finally rewarded. This fertile valley was to be their home. There were plenty of animals to eat, strange trees that bore sweet fruit, sweet water to drink and for their fields of maíz . . . (p. 73).

This introduction to the fabilized pre-Hispanic and pre-historic past penetrates and quickens a level of the young boy's being that up to then had been dormant. With the legend of the Golden Carp, Antionio feels the beginnings of an internal process that brings his consciousness closer into contact with the physical world surrounding him. In the boy's fertile imagination, the river is suddenly transformed into a potential source of emotion, feeling, and human meaning. "I felt," he says, "I sat on the banks of an undiscovered river whose churning, muddied waters carried many secrets." Entranced by the beauty of the legend, he has the sensation that "the lapping of the water was like the tide of time" on his soul. Towards the end of the novel, when the boy is capable of summarizing what he has learned from the cycle of events revolving around him, he will refer to pre-Hispanic history as that "dark, mystical past, the past of the people who lived here and left their traces in the magic that crops out today" (p. 220).

Bless Me, Ultima gives us the kind of extensive dimensionality that the genre of the novel, after the epic poem, is best equipped to give us. One of the functions of the novel, as a genre, is to exploit the relationship between plot time and historical, fable, or remembered time. As fable time increases in importance and extension, there is undoubtedly more diffuseness or a lessening of tension in the work, but what is lost in compactness and immediacy, is gained in lyricism, subjective tonality, atmosphere, mood, and what might be called a heightened sense of spatialized reality.

In addition to the extensive dimensionality of time, there is, in Anaya's novel, a thematic dimension that runs throughout the whole work. What slowly emerges from the work is a view of the world in which evil plays a strong and constantly threatening role in the lives of people. This view of the world holds that life is a cosmic drama played out through individuals, and although some of the characters including

Ultima suggest that it is essentially humans acting against humans, there persists the overpowering belief that supernatural or superhuman forces are everywhere at work. The actions of people are often interpreted from that perspective. The Christian explanation of things does not seem to predominate, and at times the people need to go beyond that body of beliefs to give a satisfactory answer to events and situations. As the boy grows under the tutelage of the *curandera*, there is a direction in his life that will move him farther and farther away from his Christian teachings. Ultima's influence, which is natural and unimposed, slowly wins out because her way of life blends with the feelings of concreteness and of the closeness of the forces of nature, which Antonio comes to realize is so much a part of him and his world.

There is a third aspect, that of character, which also contributes to the work's extensive dimensionality. Here we find two overall or unified complexities: the first is the boy-hero Antonio, who is the focal point of important relationships; the other is Ultima, around whom gravitates much of the significant action in the work. At one level of characterization, there is clearly visible a separate or individual trajectory in each of the two protagonists. Their separate trajectories owe much of their importance to the factor of age: Ultima, when she comes into the boy's life, is a fully-formed individual; Antonio, on the other hand, is unformed and therefore open to development. It is his receptiveness to Ultima's being and "strange" way of life which is the basis for the unfolding of his character. Thus, we learn about Ultima through the technique of gradual revelation and about Antonio through his participation in the action and through self-analysis. In the latter's case, there is a double perspective since Antonio is both a developing character and a narrating consciousness. But what is of significance is not their individuation so much as their special relationship with each other and the process through which Antonio acquires an unfamiliar way of life. Fascinated by the "new" life view which Ultima embodies, Antonio is drawn into it by a mysterious force and beauty which emanate from her and which affect him from his first encounter with the *curandera*. From the point of view of the two principal characters, the novel is the story of the transference of Ultima's half-revealed truths and beliefs to Antonio. The story ends when Ultima dies and the boy has grasped her way of life sufficiently to promise a future of existential substance and meaning.

As in most novels that are integrated wholes, *Bless Me, Ultima's* overall structure, or what I have called its extensive dimensionality, is based on the primary elements of time, theme, and character. There is, moreover, an inordinate tension in the work which is the result of an uneasy relationship between the overall unifying elements and several of the individual parts. The sub-structures of ritual, legend, myths, dreams, and dramatic vignettes serve not only to enrich and reflect the whole but they often express an intensity that is not aborbed or integrated by the unifying elements of the work.

It is perhaps characteristic of all long works of art that periodic richness of texture and particularity are unavoidable. The pace and rhythm of narrative must vary, just as our lives psychologically have their valleys of slumber and quietness and their soaring heights of crisis and ecstasy. But we sense in Anaya's work that the set pieces contribute to the work in an unusual and purposeful way. We can see how they function if we correlate them to the novel's implicit meaning.

There is, Anaya seems to be saying, a totality of life. But this totality of life is so constituted that it is only knowable through the specially endowed person. In our novel, this person is Ultima, and her name tells us what she symbolizes. But the primitive mind, which is what Ultima possesses, does not know in the same way that the rationally developed or scientific mind knows. Her "knowledge" is more a complicated series of maneuvers or movements to contain and capture the "real," the power in reality. She does not seek to analyze it nor to change it, because that would represent an attitude or rejection of the natural. The *curandera* has learned skillfully to participate in the cosmic drama, and such participation does not lead to superiority or control of natural forces but is based rather on self-imposed limitations that are partly learned through cultural heritage and partly through personal intuition and experience. Ultima's healing practices and devices are intimately related to her natural "philosophy," in which body, mind, and spirit are fused and in which a differentiation between the human and non-human worlds is not clearly established. Thus, there will always be something unexplained, an excess of emotion or intensity, in what she is called upon to do.

Like the *curandera*, Anaya, as novelist, would like to come to terms with the complex reality around him and, with respect to much of his material, has found it useful to adopt similar techniques. The use of legends and myths helps to structure the remote and seemingly unknowable past. But it is with the dreams that we find a profusion of excessively charged "fantasies," in which the personal and the cosmic are interrelated. One pattern which appears throughout the work and particularly in the dream sequences, for example, is the groupings of three. Why has Anaya projected the action of his novel around the three brothers, the three violent deaths, the three evil spirits, etc.? We seem to be in the presence of a form or device that has come into existence solely to structure or "capture" reality. The specific meaning of the pattern "three" is perhaps elusive from a rational or literal point of view, but we cannot help speculate about its symbolic possibilities. We recall that the novel is basically an account of Antonio's psychological, vocational, religious or philosophical, and cultural struggle. It would not be fanciful to suggest that in the various aspects of that struggle we can see the following patterns of psychic content (deep structures of feeling and thought): 1) the Freudian tripartite division of the self, in which there is conflict within the boy's intimate being as he gropes toward maturity; 2) an epistemological conflict among the three primary modes of knowing, that is, the experiential or empirical, the subconscious, and the legendary or mythic; 3) the three cultural traditions (the Indian-mestizo, the Hispanic-Catholic, and the Anglo) which are experienced internally at certain times in Antonio as conflicting systems.

We have speculated with possible meanings of the recurring pattern of three only to suggest the kind of narrative complexity that Anaya has been able to achieve. The author has not only brought into his work a dramatic sense of rhythm and a fascinating variety of narrative sub-structures but, perhaps more significantly, he has created a symbolic discourse which underlies and gives substance to much of the narrative action itself. There is no doubt that Anaya, like his child-protagonist Antonio, has fallen under the spell of the half-real, half-fantasy world which Ultima represents. By venturing into that seemingly distant world of the past, Anaya discovered that a considerable part of that world was buried in his own being. His renewal of a lost heritage brings him closer to his own inner anxieties and enlarges his imaginative powers. By integrating the mytho-poetic content of popular tradition into a modern setting,[3] Anaya has not only begin, with his *Bless Me, Ultima*, to create a sense of existential wholeness for himself but he has also succeeded in projecting into the collective Mexican-American experience an harmonious and coherent cultural base. As creative writer and spokesman for the Hispanic-mestizo minority, who for too long has struggled in the back-waters of American life, Anaya gives every indication of invigorating the cultural growth of his people and of verifying the existence of an inner force and power in their daily lives.

Notes

1. Claude Levi-Strauss, *Tristes Tropiques* (New York: Atheneum, 1970).

2. Rudolfo A. Anaya, *Bless Me, Ultima* (Berkeley, Calif.: Quinto Sol, 1972).

3. William Irwin Thompson states the case well for a "mythopoetic mentality": "Myth is not an early level of human development, but an imaginative description of reality in which the known is related to the unknown through a system of correspondences in which mind and matter, self, society, and cosmos are integrally expressed in an esoteric language of poetry and number which is itself a performance of the reality it seeks to describe." *At the Edge of History* (New York: Harper & Row, 1971), p. 190.

INDEX

Abbey, Edward, 210; critical analysis of Abbey's writings, 211–220
Across Texas (Edward S. Ellis), 44–45
Adams, Andy, x, 29, 112
Adventure, Mystery, and Romance (John G. Cawelti), xiii
All My Friends Are Going to Be Strangers (Larry McMurtry), 223, 237–240
Alurista, 263
The American Western Novel (James K. Folsom), xiv
Anaya, Rudolfo, 262; critical analysis of *Bless Me, Ultima*, 262–270
Angle of Repose (Wallace Stegner), 90–91, 92
Apples of Paradise (Frederick Manfred), 180–181
April (Vardis Fisher), 130–132
Archetypal realism in Western fiction, 75–78
Arfive (A. B. Guthrie), 89, 141, 142, 143, 144, 145–146, 147–148
Austin, Mary, 6

Badger, Joseph E., Jr., 43–44
Barker, Warren, M. D., 9
Barzun, Jacques, 168
Bent's Fort (David Lavender), 94
Beyond the Desert (Eugene Manlove Rhodes), 31
Biddle, Nicholas, 97–98
The Big It and Other Stories (A. B. Guthrie), 149n
The Big Range (Jack Schaefer), 36
The Big Rock Candy Mountain (Wallace Stegner), 4, 12
The Big Sky (A. B. Guthrie), 10–11, 94, 136–139, 143, 144, 145, 146, 187
Black Sun (Edward Abbey), 210, 213, 214–215, 217–218, 219, 220
Blake, Forrester, 5, 14
Bless Me, Ultima (Rudolfo Anaya), 262–270
Boatright, Mody C., 39, 56
Bransford in Arcadia (Eugene Manlove Rhodes), 31
The Brave Bulls (Tom Lea), 38
The Brave Cowboy (Edward Abbey), 210, 211–212, 213, 215, 219
The Brazos Tigers; or, The Minute Men of Fort Belknap (Sam Hall), 50
The Bronc People (William Eastlake), 5, 197, 199–205, 207
Buck Taylor, King of the Cowboys (Prentiss Ingraham), 47–48, 50
Buck Taylor, the Comanche Captive (Prentiss Ingraham), 55n
Buck Taylor, the Saddle King (Prentiss Ingraham), 48–49
Bulow, Ernest L., 158
Bushnell, William, 42–43

Carrington (Michael Straight), 188
Cather, Willa, 5, 83
Cawelti, John G., xiii, 111, 116
Chapman, Arthur, 95
Children of God (Vardis Fisher), 16
The Chokecherry Tree (Frederick Manfred), 131
The City of Trembling Leaves (Walter Van Tilburg Clark), 76, 84, 167–168, 169
Clark, Walter Van Tilburg, 12–13, 38, 76–77, 78, 79–85: critical analysis of Clark's writings, 164–171
The Closed Frontier: Studies in American Literary Tragedy (Harold Simonson), 87
Collected Stories (Jean Stafford), 182
Conquering Horse (Frederick Manfred), 172, 173, 174, 175, 177
Cooper, James Fenimore, xvi, 7, 46
The Covered Wagon (Emerson Hough), 113, 117
The Cowboy Clan in Cuba (Prentiss Ingraham), 49
The Cowboy Clan; or, The Tigress of Texas (Prentiss Ingraham), 48, 49
Cowboy Chris, the Desert Centaur (William G. Patten), 52–53

Cowboy Chris, the Vengence Volunteer (William G. Patten), 53
Crevecoeur, Hector St. John de, 176
Crimson Kate, the Girl Trailer (Prentiss Ingraham), 46, 49

Dale, Edward Everett, 95–96
Dark Bridwell (Vardis Fisher), 17, 132–135
Davis, H. L., 88
The Daybreakers (Louis L'Amour), 155–156
Desert Solitaire (Edward Abbey), 213–214, 215, 216–217, 218, 219, 220
DeVoto, Bernard, x, xii, 30, 96
Dime novel Westerns, 43–54, 57
Dobie, J. Frank, 39
Druid, David, 53

Eastlake, William, 5–6, 197; critical analysis of Eastlake's writings, 198–209
Ellis, Edward S., 44, 46
Etulain, Richard W., xvii

Faust, Frederick Schiller, 27
Fergusson, Harvey, 3, 14, 106, 187
Fiedler, Leslie, xiii, 164
Fire on the Mountain (Edward Abbey), 210, 212–213, 215, 219
First Blood (Jack Schaefer), 37
Fisher, Vardis, 16–17, 188; critical analysis of Fisher's writings, 125–135
Foerster, Norman, ix
Folsom, James K., xiv, 225
Formula in popular Western fiction, 63–71, 111–112, 116–117
French, Warren, 56
From Hopalong to Hud: Thoughts on Western Fiction (C. L. Sonnichsen), xiii–xiv
The Frontier in American Literature (Lucy Lockwood Hazard), ix–x

Garland, Hamlin, 22
Go in Beauty (William Eastlake), 197, 198–199, 207
The Golden Bowl (Frederick Manfred), 179, 180
Goyen, William, 6
Grant of Kingdom (Harvey Fergusson), 187
The Great American West (Emerson Hough), 117n
Grey, Zane, 8, 25
Gurian, Jay, xiv
Guthrie, A. B., xvi, 5, 10–12, 88–89, 94–95, 187; critical analysis of Guthrie's writings, 136–148

Hall, Sam, 50
Harte, Bret, 7, 21, 37–38
Hazard, Lucy Lockwood, ix–x
Heart's Desire (Emerson Hough), 112, 203
Henry, Will, 104
The Hermit of the Colorado Hills (William Bushnell), 42–43
History in Western fiction, 93–106
Hondo (Louis L'Amour), 151–152
Honey in the Horn (H. L. Davis), 88
Homans, Peter, 63–66
Horgan, Paul, 14
Horseman, Pass By (Larry McMurtry), 223, 224–227, 229, 230, 237, 240
Hough, Emerson, 23, 111, 203; critical analysis of Hough's writings, 112–117
House Made of Dawn (N. Scott Momaday), 243, 245–259
Hustler Harry, the Cowboy Sport (William G. Patten), 50–51
Hutchinson, W. H., x

In a Narrow Grave: Essays on Texas (Larry McMurtry), 223, 240
Ingraham, Prentiss, 46–50
In the American Grain (William Carlos Williams), 172, 175–176, 177–178
In Tragic Life (Vardis Fisher), 127
The Iron Mistress (Paul I. Wellman), 40

"Jeremy Rodock" (Jack Schaefer), 36
The Journal of Popular Culture, xii–xiii
Jungian interpretation of Western fiction, 18, 76–77, 85n

Kilrone (Louis L'Amour), 153–154
King of Spades (Frederick Manfred), 172, 173, 174, 177, 178

La Barre, Weston, 254

La Farge, Oliver, 5
L'Amour, Louis, 150; critical analysis of L'Amour's writings, 151–163
Landess, Thomas, 240
The Last Picture Show (Larry McMurtry), 224, 227, 229–233, 234
Laughing Boy (Oliver La Farge), 5
Laughing Leo; or, Spread Eagles Sam's Dandy Pard (Joseph E. Badger, Jr)., 54
Lavender, David, 94–95
The Law of the Land (Emerson Hough), 114
Lawrence, D. H., 77–78, 172–173, 176, 177, 180, 197–198, 243
"The Leader of the People" (John Steinbeck), 87–88
Lea, Tom, 38
Leaving Cheyenne (Larry McMurtry), 224, 227–229, 234, 237
Letters from an American Farmer (Hector St. John de Crevecoeur), 176
Lewis, Alfred Henry, 37, 38
A Literary History of Southern California (Franklin Walker), x
Literary History of the United States, x
The Literature of the Middle Western Frontier (Ralph Leslie Rusk), ix–x
The Log of a Cowboy (Andy Adams), x
The Lonely Men (Louis L'Amour), 156
Loomis, Edward, 5
Lord Grizzly (Frederick Manfred), 16–17, 172, 173, 174, 175, 176, 179

McMurtry, Larry, xvi, 223; critical analysis of McMurtry's writings, 224–241
Manfred, Frederick, 14–15, 131: critical analysis of Manfred's writings, 172–181
The Man from the Broken Hills (Louis L'Amour), 157, 160–161
Mexican-Americans in Western fiction, 26, 262–270
Milton, John R., xiv–xv, 188
Momaday, N. Scott, 243; critical analysis of *House Made of Dawn*, 245–259
Monte Walsh (Jack Schaefer), 5
Morning Red (Frederick Manfred), 180
Morris, Wright, 5, 83
The Mountain Lion (Jean Stafford), 182–186
Moving On (Larry McMurtry), 223, 229, 233–237, 238, 240
My Blood's Country: Studies in Southwestern Literature (William T. Pilkington), xiv

Nash, Roderick, 59
Native Americans in Western fiction, 114–115, 243–259
"The New West and the Old Fiction" (Arthur Chapman), 95
Nobby Nat, the Tenderfoot Detective (William G. Patten), 54
Norris, Frank, 6
North of 36 (Emerson Hough), 117
The Novel of the American West (John R. Milton), xiv
No Villain Need Be (Vardis Fisher), 129

The Octopus (Frank Norris), 6
O Pioneers! (Willa Cather), 83
Ortiz, Alfonso, 243
Overholser, Wayne D., 39
Over on the Dry Side (Louis L'Amour), 160, 161
The Ox-Box Incident (Walter Van Tilburg Clark), 12–13, 84, 165, 169–170, 187, 197

Parson Jim, King of the Cowboys (Frederick Whittaker), 53
Parsons, Elsie Clews, 246, 250–251
Passions Spin the Plot (Vardis Fisher), 127–128
Patten, William G., 50–53
The Peyote Cult (Weston La Barre), 254
Philosophical primitivism in Western fiction, 41–42
Pilkington, William T., xiv
The Pioneers (James Fenimore Cooper), 46
Pomeroy, Earl, 92
Popular Culture Association, xii
Porter, Katherine Anne, xv–xvi
Portrait of an Artist with Twenty-Six Horses (William Eastlake), 5, 197, 205–207

The Prairie (James Fenimore Cooper), 173
The Prairie Ranch; or, The Young Cattle Herders (Joseph E. Badger, Jr.), 43–44
Progressive Era, as background of popular Western fiction, 58, 60n
Psychoanalytic interpretation of the Western novel, 9

Reilly's Luck (Louis L'Amour), 154
The Return of the Vanishing American (Leslie Fiedler), xiii
Rhodes, Eugene Manlove, 30, 31–32, 38
Richter, Conrad, 5, 37
Riders of Judgment (Frederick Manfred), 172, 173, 174–175
The Riders of Lost Creek (Louis L'Amour), 163
Riders of the Purple Sage (Zane Grey), 25
Rivera, Tomás, 263
Rivers West (Louis L'Amour), 157 158, 159
Rusk, Ralph Leslie, ix

Sackett (Louis L'Amour), 155
The Sackett Brand (Louis L'Amour), 155, 159
Sackett's Land (Louis L'Amour), 156–157, 158, 159, 161
Sacrality in Western literature, xv, 78–84, 211
The Sagebrusher (Emerson Hough), 113
Sam Strong, the Cowboy Detective (David Druid), 53
San Francisco's Literary Frontier (Franklin Walker), x
Scarlet Plume (Frederick Manfred), 172, 173, 174, 176–177, 178
Schaefer, Jack, 5, 36, 37, 156
The Sea of Grass (Conrad Richter), 5, 37
Seth Jones (Edward S. Ellis), 46
Shane (Jack Schaefer), 5, 39
Showdown at Yellow Butte (Louis L'Amour), 151
Simonson, Harold, 87
The Six-Gun Mystique (John G. Cawelti), xiii
Smith, Henry Nash, x–xi, xii, 53, 86
Sonnichsen, C. L., xii, xiii, 221n
The Sound of Mountain Water (Wallace Stegner), xiv
Stafford, Jean, 182; critical analysis of *The Mountain Lion*, 182–186
Start with the Sun (Karl Shapiro, James Miller, and Bernice Sloate), 77
Stegner, Wallace, xiv, 4–5, 90–92
Steinbeck, John, 6, 78, 87
Straight, Michael, 188; critical analysis of *A Very Small Remnant*, 188–194
Studies in Classic American Literature (D. H. Lawrence), 77–78, 172

Tale of Valor (Vardis Fisher), 16, 126
Terms of Endearment (Larry McMurtry), 223
The Tewa World (Alfonso Ortiz), 243
These Thousand Hills (A. B. Guthrie), 11, 140–141, 142, 143, 144, 145, 146–147
This Is the Year (Frederick Manfred), 180
"The Tin Star" (John M. Cunningham), 40
Toilers of the Hills (Vardis Fisher), 129–130
The Track of the Cat (Walter Van Tilburg Clark), 12, 13–14, 164, 166–167, 169
Tragedy in Western fiction, 187–194
The Trusty Knaves (Eugene Manlove Rhodes), 31
Tularosa: Last of the Frontier West (C. L. Sonnichsen), 221n

Under the Sweetwater Rim (Louis L'Amour), 154–155
Utah Blaine (Louis L'Amour), 151

A Vaquero in the Brush Country (J. Frank Dobie), 39
A Very Small Remnant (Michael Straight), 188–194
Vestal, Stanley, 208
The Violent Land (Wayne D. Overholser), 39
The Virginian (Owen Wister), 8, 21, 29, 59, 118–124
Virgin Land: The American West as Symbol and Myth (Henry Nash Smith), x–xi, xii, 53, 86

Walker, Franklin, x
The Watchful Gods and Other Stories (Walter Van Tilburg Clark), 166
Waters, Frank, 14
The Way to Rainy Mountain (N. Scott Momaday), 243–244
The Way West (A. B. Guthrie), 11, 37, 39, 136, 139–140, 141–142, 143, 144
We Are Betrayed (Vardis Fisher), 128–129
Wellman, Paul I., 40
Wendell, Barrett, ix
Westbrook, Max, xv, 211
Western American Literature (journal), xi
Western American Writing: Tradition and Promise (Jay Gurian), xiv
Western Literature Association, xi, xiv
Where the Long Grass Blows (Louis L'Amour), 161–162
Whittaker, Frederick, 53
Who Rides with Wyatt (Will Henry), 104
Wild Vulcan, the Lone Rider (William G. Patten), 51–52
Williams, William Carlos, 172, 175, 177
Wister, Owen, 29, 36, 38, 57, 59; critical analysis of *The Virginian*, 118–124
Wolf Song (Harvey Fergusson), 106
Wolf Willow (Wallace Stegner), 4
Women in Western fiction, 25, 30, 49, 177
Wynn, Dudley, 209